Portland Community College

The Truth of the Matter

The Truth of the Matter

Art and Craft in Creative Nonfiction

Dinty W. Moore

Penn State Altoona

PEARSON
Longman

New York San Francisco Boston
London Toronto Sydney Tokyo Singapore Madrid
Mexico City Munich Paris Cape Town Hong Kong Montreal

Managing Editor: Erika Berg
Executive Marketing Manager: Ann Stypuloski
Production Manager: Ellen MacElree
Project Coordination, Text Design,
  and Electronic Page Makeup: Stratford Publishing Services
Cover Design Manager: Wendy Ann Fredericks
Cover Designer: Nancy Sacks
Cover Art: Sabina McGrew/Zefa/Corbis
Senior Manufacturing Buyer: Alfred C. Dorsey

For permission to use copyrighted material, grateful acknowledgment is made to the copyright holders on pages 297–299, which are hereby made part of this copyright page.

Library of Congress Cataloging-in-Publication Data

Moore, Dinty W.,
    The truth of the matter : art and craft in creative nonfiction /
Dinty W. Moore—1st ed.
        p.   cm.
    Includes bibliographical references.
    ISBN 0-321-27761-9
    1. English language—Rhetoric—Study and teaching.   2. Reportage
literature—Authorship—Study and teaching.   3. Prose literature—Authorship—
Study and teaching.   4. Creative writing (Higher education)   5. Prose literature—
Authorship.   6. Creative writing. I. Title.

PE1404.M6635 2006
808'.042071—dc22   2005034708

Please visit us at http://www.ablongman.com

ISBN 0-321-27761-9

For
Renita Marie Romasco
and Maria Raphaella Romasco Moore

Contents

Preface   xi
About the Author   xv

PART I
About Creative Nonfiction

Chapter One: True Stories, Innovative Forms   3
   Basic Forms of Creative Nonfiction   4
   The Art of Narrative   4
   The Narrative Craft   5
   The Truth of the Matter   6
   Curiosity and Passion: The Indispensable Tools   6

Chapter Two: What Makes Nonfiction Creative?   8
   A Way of Seeing   9
   More than "Just the Facts"   11
   Creative Nonfiction versus Standard Journalism: An Illustration   12
   Honesty, Memory, and the Stranger in the Room   14
   Writing Prompts: What Is Creative Nonfiction?   17

PART II
Building Blocks of Creative Nonfiction

Chapter Three: Building Blocks of Creative Nonfiction: Detail and Description   21
   Detail and Description   22
   Specific and Particular   24
      "Injection," Jane Armstrong   24
   Revising for Detail and Description   26
   Writing Prompts: Detail and Description   28

Chapter Four: Building Blocks of Creative Nonfiction: Characterization and Scene   29
   Characterization through Dialogue   29
      "A Dramatic Dogalog," Art Homer   32
   Characterization through Action   34
      "Drink It," Patricia Ann McNair   35

Scene: Letting the Facts Speak for Themselves   38
Revising for Scene   39
Writing Prompts: Characterization through Dialogue   40
Writing Prompts: Characterization through Action   41

**Chapter Five: Building Blocks of Creative Nonfiction: Distinctive Voice
and Intimate Point of View**   42
Distinctive Voice   43
    "Pop Art," Brian Doyle   43
Intimate Point of View   46
    "Sunday," Henry Louis Gates   49
Revising for Voice and Point of View   51
Writing Prompts: Distinctive Voice and Intimate
Point of View   52

Chapter Six: Building Blocks of Creative Nonfiction: Discovery   54
What You "Make of It"   55
    "Solstice," Richard Terrill   55
    "Tino & Papi," Norma Elia Cantú   58
Discovery and Details   60
Revising for Discovery   60
Writing Prompts: Discovery   62

PART III

From Building Blocks to Complete Essay

Chapter Seven: The Memoir Essay   65
Examining the Memoir Essay   66
    "Genesis," Bret Lott   66
    "Thumb-Sucking Girl," Sonja Livingston   68
Writing Your Own Memoir Essay   69
But "Who Cares?"   70
Writing Prompts: Memoir   72

Chapter Eight: The Literary Journalism Essay   74
Examining the Literary Journalism Essay   76
    "Hope," Brian Doyle   76
    From "Where Worlds Collide," Pico Iyer   78
Writing Your Own Literary Journalism Essay   80
Writing Prompts: Literary Journalism   82

Chapter Nine: The Personal Essay   84
    Examining the Personal Essay   85
        "The Meadow," James Galvin   85
        "In Bed," Joan Didion   86
    Writing Your Own Personal Essay   90
    Writing Prompts: Personal Essay   91

Chapter Ten: Revision and Narrative Structure   93
    On Serious Revision   94
    Revision and Narrative Structure   94
    Braiding   95
    Collage   96
    Frame   97
    Other Strategies   97
    Writing Prompts: Narrative Structure   99

PART IV
The Anthology

The Brief Essay   103
    Drummond, Laurie Lynn   "Alive"   103
    Jakiela, Lori   "You'll Love the Way We Fly"   105
    Martin, Lee   "Dumber Than"   107
    Tall, Deborah   "The Stories Tell the Land"   109

The Conventional Length Essay   111
    Baldwin, James   "Notes of a Native Son"   111
    Beard, Jo Ann   "Out There"   127
    Cofer, Judith Ortiz   "Silent Dancing"   132
    Dillard, Annie   "Living Like Weasels"   140
    Earley, Tony   "Somehow Form a Family"   143
    Gerard, Philip   "What They Don't Tell You About
        Hurricanes"   151
    Grealy, Lucy   "Mirrorings"   157
    Gutkind, Lee   "Difficult Decisions"   167
    Hemley, Robin   "Reading History to My Mother"   174
    Hoagland, Edward   "The Courage of Turtles"   184
    Iyer, Pico   "Where Worlds Collide"   189
    Kincaid, Jamaica   "Biography of a Dress"   200
    Lott, Bret   "Brothers"   207
    McPhee, John   "The Search for Marvin Gardens"   211

Nye, Naomi Shihab   "Three Pokes of a Thistle"   220
Sanders, Scott Russell   "Buckeye"   224
Sedaris, David   "The Drama Bug"   229
Selzer, Richard   "The Knife"   236
Shields, David   "42 Tattoos"   243
Tan, Amy   "Mother Tongue"   252
Williams, Terry Tempest "The Clan of One-Breasted
                             Women"   257

Essays on the Craft of Creative Nonfiction   263
Dillard, Annie   "Seeing"   263
Kidder, Tracy   "Making the Truth Believable"   276
Lott, Bret   "Toward a Definition of Creative
                             Nonfiction"   279
Schwartz, Mimi   "Memoir? Fiction?
                             Where's the Line?"   286

Notes on the Authors   293

Credits   297

Index   301

Preface

One of the key challenges we face as writing teachers is helping our students to recognize that successful creative nonfiction is the result of both artistry *and* craftsmanship. Students—particularly those new to this genre—seldom realize either the level of difficulty or the significant rewards inherent in writing for a broad audience of literate readers. Writing well is certainly hard work, but it is work well worth doing.

To aid both beginning writers and those new to creative nonfiction, *The Truth of the Matter: Art and Craft in Creative Nonfiction* examines the building blocks of nonfiction prose one by one, first through a discussion of *how* and *why* these techniques work, and then by illustrating each of these techniques with clear examples. Along the way, student writers encounter numerous prompts and opportunities for practice and are exposed to outstanding essays chosen from both classic and contemporary nonfiction. The underlying philosophy behind *The Truth of the Matter* is that writers at all levels can improve their craft through intelligent analysis of successful writing and through regular practice.

Key Features of the Book

A Step-by-Step Approach

Creative nonfiction is not simply about "knowing" a good story. The creativity of the form comes from how the story is presented to the reader—the unique ways in which an individual writer makes use of the basic building blocks of literary narrative. *The Truth of the Matter* presents these building blocks in a clear sequence, easily understood by beginning writers. Following a general introduction to the creative nonfiction genre, individual chapters are devoted to detail and description, characterization and scene, distinctive voice, intimate point of view, and the various ways in which writers discover the significance or universality of their work. Later chapters illustrate the limitless ways in which these building blocks can be combined to create compelling memoirs, literary journalism, or personal essays.

Essays Integrated Directly into the Text

Rather than referring to classic or contemporary essays and assuming the student is already familiar with the works and the writers, *The Truth of the Matter* integrates nonfiction from Henry Louis Gates, Brian Doyle, Norma Elia Cantú, Pico Iyer, Joan Didion, and others directly into individual chapters as illustrations of form and the basic building blocks of narrative. In most cases, other authors and works cited as examples are found in the anthology.

A Focused Anthology

The Anthology focuses on essays—both brief and conventional length—that are accessible to the beginning nonfiction writer while at the same time expanding the writer's understanding of the form and possible narrative strategies. A diversity of forms and voices are presented, including works by Annie Dillard, Jamaica Kincaid, David Sedaris, Amy Tan, Lucy Grealy, and Richard Selzer. The Anthology also includes a helpful selection of craft essays, such as Mimi Schwartz's "Memoir? Fiction? Where's the Line?" and Tracy Kidder's "Making the Truth Believable."

Constructive Writing Prompts

Each chapter concludes with a series of writing prompts and constructive activities aimed at making students comfortable with putting their own words down on the page. These writing prompts offer realistic and attainable targets, allowing students to feel confident and successful as beginning writers. The prompts and activities also provide each student with a ready storehouse of ideas and raw material for the essays they will be asked to write. Those instructors who utilize journaling in their classrooms will find that the prompts correlate well with journaling activities.

Ways to Use this Book

There are varied ways in which an instructor might use *The Truth of Matter: Art and Craft in Creative Nonfiction.*

Part One: About Creative Nonfiction is designed to introduce the genre and engage students in a discussion about how literary nonfiction differs from the conventional five-paragraph essay or other standard nonfiction forms. Students are introduced to the importance of curiosity and passion in choosing and pursuing their subjects, and essential questions about truth and memory are shown to be not merely problems, but also opportunities.

Students might then be asked to work chronologically through the craft chapters in **Part Two: Building Blocks of Creative Nonfiction,** trying their hand at the various techniques before attempting the drafting of a complete essay. **Part Three: From Building Blocks to Complete Essay** is designed to help students deepen their understanding and refine their approach.

As an alternative, instructors might guide their students directly from **Part One** to writing their own nonfiction essays, layering the various techniques into classroom discussion as issues arise in the students' work. Some instructors might wish students to flex their writing muscles with shorter essays (and make their early, inevitable fumbles) before attempting a more conventional-length essay. Those instructors who opt to assign the conventional-length essay early on in the semester may utilize the brief essays as excellent examples of craft and efficiency.

No matter which approach an instructor chooses, *The Truth of Matter* strives to be clear, encouraging, and adaptable, allowing a variety of tactics and assignments, and reflecting a diversity of pedagogical aims and methodologies.

Acknowledgments

My sincerest thanks to colleagues Ken Womack, Todd Davis, Kate Latterell, and Stuart Selber for their continued encouragement, to Jerry Zolten for his generosity and friendship, and to John Hunger who helped launch this project with both advice and *paella* in Madrid.

My gratitude goes out as well to the many excellent teachers and writers who offered guidance during the course of this project, including Philip Gerard, Natalia Rachel Singer, Bret Lott, Brenda Miller, and Mike Steinberg. Likewise, my students over the years at Penn State Altoona, at the Mid-Atlantic Creative Nonfiction Summer Writers' Conference, and in the University of New Orleans' Low-Residency MFA Program have taught me as much as I've taught them. Moreover, they have helped immeasurably in keeping my mind nimble and my enthusiasm alive.

I am greatly indebted to the following teachers who offered detailed, thorough reviews at various points during the writing and editing process: James Baumlin, Southwest Missouri State University; Simone Billings, Santa Clara University; Becky Bradway, Illinois State University; Christine Delea, Eastern Kentucky University; Faulkner Fox, Duke University; Jeff Gundy, Bluffton College; Elisabeth Rose Gruner, University of Richmond; Trish Houston, Ohio State University; Fern Kupfer, Iowa State University; Gretchen Legler, University of Maine–Farmington; Patrick Madden, Brigham Young University; Desirae Matherly, The Ohio University; Alyce L. Miller, Indiana University; Kevin Oderman, West Virginia University; John Parbst, Suffolk County Community College; Michael Raymond, Stetson University; Lisa Roney, University of Central Florida; Jim Sanderson, Lamar University;

Jane Satterfield, Loyola College in Maryland; Michelle Tokarczyk, Goucher College; and Alison Umminger, State University of West Georgia.

Finally, I would like to thank my editor, Erika Berg, for her patience and insight, and I would most especially like to thank Lee Gutkind, friend and mentor, who many years ago pushed a reluctant young student firmly onto the creative nonfiction path.

—Dinty W. Moore, Penn State Altoona

About the Author

Dinty W. Moore is the author of *The Accidental Buddhist: Mindfulness, Enlightenment and Sitting Still; Toothpick Men;* and *The Emperor's Virtual Clothes*. And he is the editor of BREVITY, an online journal of brief creative nonfiction essays. He has published essays and stories in *The Southern Review, The Georgia Review, Harper's, The New York Times Sunday Magazine, Utne Reader, Crazyhorse,* and *Arts & Letters*. Moore teaches writing at Penn State Altoona.

Photo by Maria Romasco-Moore

PART I

About Creative Nonfiction

CHAPTER ONE

True Stories, Innovative Forms

CHAPTER TWO

What Makes Nonfiction Creative?

Chapter One

True Stories, Innovative Forms

"It still comes as a shock to realize that I don't write about what I know: I write in order to find out what I know."

—PATRICIA HAMPL

"Sometimes a person needs a story more than food to stay alive."

—BARRY LOPEZ

*H*uman beings are born loving a good story. From the beginning of language (and cave drawing) to the present world of cable television and Internet blogs, stories and storytelling have played a basic role in human life and connection. Every culture, every period in human history, includes some form of shared narrative.

The literary genre known as creative nonfiction focuses on this human desire to tell—and be told—compelling stories. The term *nonfiction* means that real people, actual events, genuine places, and the author's authentic thoughts and observations are being described. The word *creative* relates to the method of storytelling—a careful and skillful application of literary techniques.

The "story" in creative nonfiction is not always a conventional narrative, however. While a work of creative nonfiction might be the account of a significant moment in the writer's life or a profile of an interesting place or person, it might also be the account of an author's meandering intellectual journey.

Often, creative nonfiction writers will employ narrative tools associated with fiction—dialogue, scene, characterization, and plot. The form also encourages the use of poetic techniques such as simile and metaphor, image, or lyric voice.

Creative nonfiction, though, is a genre all its own, an expanding and exciting form of literary writing. This book, *The Truth of the Matter*, is designed to help you understand and practice the basic techniques of this challenging form. The examples, exercises, and suggestions found in the following chapters will help you discover new ways of relating true stories with flexibility, artistry, and energy.

Basic Forms of Creative Nonfiction

Throughout this book, we will closely examine the three most prevalent categories of creative nonfiction:

1. Memoir
2. Literary journalism
3. Personal essay

Memoir is focused on a writer's own life, often providing a thoughtful look back at significant moments and events. Literary journalism, on the other hand, usually focuses outward, on an event, location, or person the author finds worthy of careful examination. The personal essay is the oldest of these categories, predating the term *creative nonfiction* by many centuries, and the most difficult to classify. The personal essay is flexible and adaptable, following the distinctive path of an author's emotions and ideas.

Strict categories can never achieve a perfect fit in any art form, of course, and this certainly holds true for creative nonfiction. Though this book will focus on the three most common types of nonfiction, contemporary authors often combine elements of each of these into their writing, using what is needed, when it is needed, to bring to life whatever complex story they have in mind.

The Art of Narrative

Remember that creative nonfiction is not simply about "knowing" a good story or having lived one. The creativity of the form is in how the story is told. Author Vivian Gornick puts it this way: "What happened to the writer is not what matters; what matters is the larger sense that the writer is able to *make* of what happened."

In other words, creative nonfiction offers much more than "just the facts." Creative nonfiction is a style of *literary* writing, an art form that starts with language and an individual point of view, and then discovers its unique shape through trial and error. To succeed in creative nonfiction, you must be open to new ideas and fresh approaches.

The narrative elements emphasized in this book are designed to make clear the infinite ways in which a story can be told. The techniques can also help with one of the key challenges often facing a beginning writer: the temptation to fall back on familiar and predictable patterns of composition.

Like many students first encountering creative nonfiction, you may have been taught in the past that every essay follows the same form:

1. Introduction
2. Topic paragraph
3. Another topic paragraph
4. Third topic paragraph
5. Final paragraph that reveals the "theme" or main point of the story

Though this "five-paragraph" form can be useful in certain contexts, it is too rigid to allow for much creativity on the part of a writer. Creative nonfiction is about adaptability and discovery, not generic outlines, and if you are new to this genre, you may occasionally have to remind yourself *not* to insert bulky introductions and conclusions into the essays you write and *not* to add topic sentences and other summary statements into each paragraph.

Old habits can be difficult to break, but breaking them is well worth the effort if you want to be a stronger writer.

The Narrative Craft

Storytelling is an art, but there are elements of craft that will strengthen the hand of any serious writer. All writing—whether fiction, nonfiction, poetry, or even technical writing—employs a series of skills and techniques, and these can be learned, polished, and continuously sharpened.

It would be folly to sit down at a piano with no training and expect to play a complex adagio, much less compose one. Nor would it be reasonable to expect yourself to paint an intricate nature scene involving sky, water, forest, reflection, and shadow if you possess only a beginner's idea of how paint transfers from the brush to the canvas.

Writing works this way as well. The beginning chapters of *The Truth of the Matter* illustrate the techniques of detail and description, characterization through dialogue and action, scene, point of view, voice, and discovery with examples and exercises. These techniques often make the difference between a flat story that is merely summarized and a rich, evocative narrative that grabs the reader's attention and refuses to let go.

If these techniques are new to you, spend some time trying them out in your own writing. Practice may not make you the perfect writer, but it will always make you better.

The Truth of the Matter

Though creative nonfiction writers employ considerable imagination in shaping the form of what is being written, in choosing the right words and sharpest metaphors, and in deciding which elements of a story best reveal the significance of a situation, the facts presented by the writer are not imaginary or invented. They are true.

Of course, since much of what is classified as creative nonfiction falls under the memoir category—past events examined through a present lens—questions as to whether absolute accuracy is even possible are inevitable. How can we be sure we are remembering correctly? How can a writer employ dialogue in a memoir if there are no notes, tapes, or records? Did this event happen in April or May, and was it Cousin Kate or Cousin Lucy who fell off the dock?

Even in literary journalism, when we write about current events, and do take notes, the question of a writer's subjective observation comes into play. Scientists have proven that oftentimes two witnesses will see an event differently, and frequently our immediate recall is flawed and inaccurate.

The subtle issue of how reliable we can be when writing creative nonfiction will always serve as a source of energy and debate in the genre, and for that reason you will find a longer discussion of truth and accuracy in Chapter Two, "What Makes Nonfiction Creative?" and in the essay "Memoir? Fiction? Where's the Line?" found in the Anthology.

For now, however, remember that *nonfiction* means the material on the page is not simply imagined, as the events and details in a novel or short story might be, and that the creativity in creative nonfiction primarily refers to the author's artistic choices: language, structure, point of view.

Curiosity and Passion: The Indispensable Tools

Part I of *The Truth of the Matter* introduces the subject of creative nonfiction, makes a distinction between creative nonfiction and traditional journalism, and provides a brief history. Part II is focused on the basic building blocks of nonfiction writing, those tools and techniques that every writer should understand and have readily available. Part III illustrates how these individual techniques combine to form complete memoir, literary journalism, and personal essays.

Along the way, you will read selections from the rich literary tradition of nonfiction writing, a form that attempts to stir a reader's intellect and emotions in much the same way that a fine novel or short story might, or in the way that a piece of music burrows into your soul.

The early chapters of this book focus on the brief essay (fewer than 750 words), a genre of nonfiction expanding in popularity and one that provides an excellent way to closely examine the elements of clear and forceful writing. Your instructor might ask that you write your own brief essays, or you might instead be encouraged to apply what you have learned to longer works. The lessons are applicable whether you are writing in the longer or shorter form, and the Anthology section offers a number of conventional-length essays to serve as models.

Though the purpose of this book is to introduce you to new techniques, innovative forms, and fresh ways of approaching your writing, understand that you could read each page ten times over, even memorize portions of a chapter, and still be only a small way toward where you want to be. The best way to improve your writing is to write. Trial and error, the making of mistakes, and painstaking revision are where the most powerful lessons are learned.

In later chapters, especially in the writing prompts, this book will offer suggestions for where you might find the subject matter for your own creative nonfiction. For now, however, remember these two words: *curiosity* and *passion*.

Curiosity and passion are invaluable if you want to grow as a writer and push your writing to where it doesn't just sit on the page waiting to be read, but seems somehow to literally jump off the page, *demanding* that the reader sit up and pay attention.

Chapter Two

What Makes Nonfiction Creative?

"All truths are easy to understand once they are discovered; the point is to discover them."

—GALILEO GALILEI

To better understand what distinguishes the genre of creative nonfiction from other fact-based modes of writing, it is useful to consider long-standing practices in journalism. Perhaps you have heard the expression "Just the facts, ma'am." Traditional newspaper reporters are expected to adhere to this dictum, providing objective facts, with no shading.

Objectivity means that when you read a front-page account in your local newspaper about a tax hike to fund a new water treatment plant, you should see no indication in that news story of which way the individual reporter leans on the issue. You should not be able to discern whether the author of the story is for the tax hike and the new treatment facility, or against the tax hike and in favor of the status quo. The story should be "bias neutral," with just the pertinent information: what was debated at last night's town council meeting, who spoke, what was decided, and when will the next meeting be held. Though feature writing typically offers a reporter more latitude in structure and style, the author's views and personality are still not considered part of the story.

In the early 1960s and 1970s, however, magazine writers such as Tom Wolfe, Gay Talese, Lillian Ross, and Joan Didion, among others, began to champion a mode of nonfiction writing that ignored these longstanding journalistic norms. Instead, these writers embraced writing that told in-depth, dramatic *true* stories in narrative form, with the author's own ideas and assumptions obvious on the page. It was no longer considered necessary to conceal the personality of the writer; the author's individuality and point of view were an essential part of the tale.

A Way of Seeing

Along with the elements that are fundamental to all good writing—careful word choice, proper mechanics, efficient structure—much of the interest and creativity in creative nonfiction comes from how an author sees the subject at hand.

Gay Talese, for instance, in his magazine essay "Frank Sinatra Has a Cold," describes his subject this way:

> When Frank Sinatra drives to the studio, he seems to dance out of the car across the sidewalk into the front door; then, snapping his fingers, he is standing in front of the orchestra in an intimate, airtight room, and soon he is dominating every man, every instrument, every sound wave.

Talese offers the reader a careful description of what he saw, but also of what he *felt* when observing the celebrated singer and entertainer. Talese did not limit himself to the mere facts at hand: Sinatra left his car, walked into the studio, stood before the musicians. Instead, even in this brief excerpt, we are able to see the awe that Frank Sinatra inspired in Talese and so many others. Simply by adding his own point of view and subjective observations, Talese transformed simple information into creative nonfiction.

For another example, consider these three sentences from Joan Didion's classic essay "In the Islands":

> We spend, my husband and I, and the baby, a restorative week in paradise. We are each the other's model of consideration, tact, restraint at the very edge of the precipice. He refrains from noticing when I am staring at nothing, and in turn I refrain from dwelling at length upon a newspaper story about a couple who apparently threw their infant and themselves into the boiling crater of a live volcano in Maui.

Didion is giving us the facts—how she and her husband behaved during their unhappy, week-long Hawaii vacation—but also considerable insight into her strained marriage. The author's young family sits "at the edge of the precipice," and she feels free to tell us so. Didion employs ironic humor, as well; had she been telling us this story personally, the word *paradise* would likely have been delivered with sarcasm, and the macabre detail about the volcanic suicide might have come with a hidden wink. Notice how much information you receive—most of it about the state of the uneasy relationship and the mood of the narrator—in so few words.

Hunter S. Thompson, the unconventional *Rolling Stone* magazine journalist, took subjective writing to an even greater extreme. Certainly, no effort toward objectivity exists in this passage about a hitchhiker that Thompson and his lawyer picked up in the Nevada desert, excerpted from the psychedelic-inspired book *Fear and Loathing in Las Vegas:*

> How long before one of us starts raving and jabbering at this boy? What will he think then? This same lonely desert was the last known home of the Manson family. Will he make that grim connection when my attorney starts screaming about bats and huge manta rays coming down on the car? If so—hell, we'll just have to cut his head off and bury him somewhere. Because it goes without saying that we can't turn him loose.

There remains legitimate debate as to whether Thompson's writing should even be classified as nonfiction. Given his persona as a gun-toting, amphetamine-popping, vodka-swilling renegade stumbling into whatever story he came to cover—glitzy Las Vegas, the 1972 Nixon-McGovern presidential campaign, the Kentucky Derby—it is not surprising that his version of events can vary widely from what others saw as the truth. But however you categorize his highly individualistic and peculiar style of writing, Thompson was an important personality in expanding the parameters of contemporary nonfiction writing.

These are just a few examples, and it is important to note that while the writers mentioned above helped spur a new movement, they certainly did not invent the idea of using personal reflection and distinctive voice in nonfiction.

The history of nonfiction strengthened by an individual's "creative" sensibility can be traced as far back as the first century AD when Seneca, a Roman statesman, and Plutarch, a Greek biographer, wrote personal reflections on matters of philosophy. The word *essay* itself derives from the work of a sixteenth-century author, Michel de Montaigne. In French, the word *essais* means "to try" or "to attempt." This might serve as another good definition of the form, since what writers of creative nonfiction do is "try out ideas" or "attempt new ways of looking at the truth." More recently, Henry David Thoreau left his distinct mark on American literature with his nonfiction account of the world he found along Walden Pond. His book *Walden*—a blend of personal essay, memoir, and nature writing—demonstrates the simple power of honest, individual observation.

To better understand the art of the personal essay, consider this passage from Richard Selzer's "The Knife":

> A stillness settles in my heart and is carried to my hand. It is the quietude of resolve layered over fear. And it is this resolve that lowers us, my knife and me, deeper and deeper into the person beneath. It

is an entry into the body that is nothing like a caress; still, it is among the gentlest of acts.

Selzer, a surgeon, goes well beyond describing the act of medical incision in his essay. At various points, he considers whether a surgeon is a priest, a poet, or more like "a traveler in a dangerous country"; reminisces about a boyhood at the side of his physician father; examines the surgical procedure from the point of view of the patient; and considers the history of knives. He comes at his subject from a multitude of angles, in a struggle to understand the feelings he has accumulated over a lifetime of surgical practice. Selzer's complete essay can be found in the Anthology.

Over the past few decades, interest in creative nonfiction has shaped new approaches to science writing, travel writing, nature writing, writing about spirituality, sports reporting, and many other types of nonfiction. Two of these forms, nature writing and travel writing, are examined on the *Truth of the Matter* website (www.dintywmoore.com/truth), along with writing prompts and example essays.

In some circles, the genre we call creative nonfiction goes under different names: narrative nonfiction, literary narrative, the literature of fact. Whatever the label, though, success in this genre always results from careful observation, or "seeing," combined with strong writing and literary techniques.

More than "Just the Facts"

Essentially, creative nonfiction writers still act as reporters: they chronicle noteworthy people, places, and events. In creative nonfiction, however, *noteworthy* does not refer solely to celebrities like Frank Sinatra or to breaking news. The rituals played out at the author's own family dinner table or the ancient sycamore tree in the park across the street from where the author lives might be just as important a subject. In the realm of the personal essay, the writer's reflections, ideas, and literary explorations are equally of note.

A subject becomes noteworthy, in other words, because the author takes close notice, and then finds a way to transmit his or her own fascination with the subject to the curious reader. Moreover, a writer of creative nonfiction is *not* asked to be invisible. Along with observing the particular subject matter you have chosen for your essay, and observing it with fresh eyes, you should observe your own thoughts and reactions and, where appropriate or illuminating, include them in your writing. In fact, voice and point of view are fundamental to what is creative in creative nonfiction.

Writers of creative nonfiction do *not* give us "Just the facts, ma'am." Such a straightforward, bare-bones approach might be useful for someone skimming the front page of the local newspaper (or for the detectives on the old TV show *Dragnet*, where the phrase first was heard), but people read this more literary and artistic genre expecting more. Readers who enjoy works of creative nonfiction love a good story and all that a good story involves, and that often includes some or all of the following:

- Careful detail and description
- Characterization through dialogue
- Characterization through action
- Distinctive voice and intimate point of view
- Discovery

To a certain extent, these building blocks of creative nonfiction resemble the ways in which fiction writers incorporate scene, story, style, and character into novels and short stories, though with study and practice you will notice subtle differences in how these elements work when writing nonfiction. Writers of creative nonfiction also make regular use of language tools associated most often with poetry: image, metaphor, and meticulous word choice.

In the end, masterful nonfiction writers such as Judith Ortiz Cofer, Scott Russell Sanders, Terry Tempest Williams, and Richard Selzer want readers to experience their nonfiction just as they might experience a fine poem or short story. The ideas becomes so compelling, the world on the page so real, the language so beautiful, that the reader for a moment forgets that mere black symbols printed onto white paper are creating the effect. The pages turn almost automatically.

This type of writing requires painstaking effort—creating a full scene with clearly delineated characters and fully described action takes far more time and energy than simply summarizing basic facts and a chronology—but when it works, the effort is worth every extra moment spent.

Creative Nonfiction versus Standard Journalism: An Illustration

Perhaps the very best way to define creative nonfiction is by comparison. Consider these paragraphs, from reporter Steve Ritea of the New Orleans *Times-Picayune* newspaper:

> BATON ROUGE—The Baton Rouge serial killer gathered information about his three female victims before attacking them and might even have known them casually, according to a profile released Tuesday by law enforcement officials.
>
> The killer may "come across to some women as a 'nice guy' who might have tried to get a little too close to them too soon, but otherwise is a non-threatening person," the profile says. It adds, however, that "this veneer of harmlessness is his shield of protection from suspicion."

The killer is thought to be a man, 25 to 35 years old, "physically strong and capable of lifting 155 to 175 pounds," with a "shoe size of approximately 10 to 11," based on crime scene information.

This is a clear, straightforward account of the new information provided by law enforcement authorities in Louisiana. We learn the latest police theory on this brutal killer, an idea of how he might come across to his potential victims, and some general information on his physical characteristics. We learn also that the police are taking this matter very seriously, and the investigation is continuing.

Now consider a quite different example, excerpted from Laurie Drummond's essay, "Alive":

There is a serial killer at work in Baton Rouge, and so, as I drive into the city on this rainy mid-August afternoon to visit family, I move from simply alert to hyper alert. In addition to the three murdered women, there have been four attempted abductions in the past two weeks; the last woman fought her attacker off with a machete. Yesterday, a line of women snaked out the door of a police supply store, waiting to purchase pepper spray. The store sold out by noon.

For once, I am not in the minority. Alert is a natural state for me, and the quick transition to hyper alert is easy. I worked as a police officer in this city in the 1980's. I know, intimately, what one human being can do to another. And I've seen crime scene pictures of the serial killer's first victim, examined the evidence, learned details withheld from the press.

I stop at City Newstand to pick up a newspaper. A nice-looking man—bald, early thirties, dark shirt—in a green Chevy Blazer is backing out of the space across from mine. His car stops, and I feel his gaze as I retrieve my wallet, open the car door. Our eyes meet, and he smiles. I keep my face blank and walk briskly into the store. *Creep,* I think. And then I'm ashamed. I've worked hard since I left police work to cultivate tolerance and gentleness, to not live suspicious 24-7.

I grab my newspaper and glance at magazines in the rack beside me. When I look up, the bald man is in the store. He smiles again. My throat constricts. *Don't be a silly panicked female,* I chide, *it's just coincidence.* He leaves as I pay for my newspaper and hovers outside, head down as though he's reading, but his eyes are on me.

And I know, deep in my gut knowing, old habit knowing, that this isn't coincidence. This man is stalking me. That's when the minuscule tremble in my knee kicks in, the tremble I haven't felt since I wore a uniform. If I were still a cop, this wouldn't make my knee tremble. But I am simply a civilian. A female civilian.

I track right, pretend to study a magazine. Five minutes later, when an older gentleman leaves the store, I am right on his heels, walking tough to my car. The bald man paces me step by step to his own car four spaces down.

My hands tremble, my mouth is dry, and I hate, with every screaming fiber of my being, that I gave up all guns two years ago.[1]

The point here is not that the reporter for the New Orleans newspaper has done a poor job. In fact, he has done his job quite well and precisely as he should. Readers turned to the *Times-Picayune* front page that morning for the essential details—the facts they would need to know. The question in their minds was, What is new, since yesterday?

But the differences between these two stories, essentially on the same subject, are abundantly clear. The newspaper story sits flat on the page, conveying information but no emotion. The personal essay by Drummond has life, energy, and the ability to draw the reader strongly into the story. She conveys for us the story behind the story—while police continue to hunt for this brutal killer, women in Baton Rouge are on guard, uneasy, and understandably suspicious of every male stranger they see. It is a tense, unhappy time. And the author herself is worried.

If you need the news—what happened overnight, how the facts have developed since the last time you picked up the newspaper—you know where to turn. But if you are looking for deeper, human stories, and the individual voice of a particular author, you understand that in most cases you will need to look elsewhere. If that second sort of story is what you crave, then you are the audience for creative nonfiction.

Honesty, Memory, and the Stranger in the Room

When you label your writing "nonfiction," you are asking for the reader's trust. *This is the truth,* you are saying. *This is real.* It doesn't matter if you are writing a memoir, offering a journalistic account of a recent event, or presenting your honest thoughts and reflections in a personal essay, readers cannot fully hear what you are saying if they doubt your words.

Trust, however, must be earned. For the average reader, a reader who has never met you and knows you only as an author's name at the top of the page, you are very much like a stranger who just walked into the room.

Think about this situation as it exists in real life for a moment. What do you do when a stranger enters your social arena, maybe a friend of a friend who shows up at a late-night gathering, or someone who sits down next to you at lunch because the tables are crowded? If the person begins to talk, to tell

---

[1] Laurie Drummond's full essay can be read in the Anthology.

you a story, your natural reaction is to listen, and at the same time to size that person up. Do I like this person? Is his story interesting? Do I trust him?

Though what happens in a piece of writing differs from what happens in the situations described above, the two are not *that* different. With each paragraph you write, the reader sizes up your personality on the page. What details do you decide to stress, what details do you summarize quickly, and what details do you omit? Are you letting the reader reach a conclusion, or forcing the reader to a certain place? Do you sound too sure of yourself ? Too unsure? Are you funny, somber, conflicted, irreverent, or stiff?

Soon enough, the reader begins to ask, Do I trust this voice?[2]

Often, the best way to anticipate this question, and to win a reader's confidence, is quite simple: just tell the truth. William Shakespeare suggested, "This above all, to thine own self be true. And it must follow, as the night the day, Thou canst not then be false to any man."

This suggestion—the best way to gain trust is by being honest—may seem flippant or simplistic, but it is not meant to be so. In the end *you* are the only person who can ensure total accuracy in your writing. Nonfiction depends on a pact between writer and reader, and no court of creative nonfiction exists to enforce that pact. You must be your own vigilant judge.

Of course, there are complications even to this simple rule of thumb. You can easily enough remove a bald-faced lie from your work. If you have never visited Niagara Falls in the winter and witnessed cascading ice flows, don't tell the reader that you have. If you didn't have a younger brother who ate glue and wore a tinfoil hat, don't pretend that such a brother existed just because it makes a better story. Save these imaginary moments for fiction, if that is what you want to write. But sometimes the truth is not so clear-cut, especially when dealing with memory and individual perception. What about events that happened in years past, when you weren't taking notes and didn't have the foresight to hide a tape recorder in your pocket?

Authors of memoir are almost always required to utilize "remembered" dialogue and details, yet scientific studies show that memory is never as

---

[2] If you are writing for a class, your teacher and classmates often *do* know you and sometimes know various facts about you. They certainly know your approximate age, whether you are male or female, and how you like to dress. But it is worthwhile to remember that the goal of writing is to create work that exists *by itself* on the page. If one of your essays was to be published in a magazine, you could not go door to door to every subscriber and say, "Here, see, I am about twenty-four years old, and I look like this. And I forgot to mention that I live in Arizona, where it is very hot. And I am the oldest of seven brothers and sisters." If these facts and details are important for the reader to understand, or if they add depth and texture to the story you are telling, it is imperative that you find a way to work them into the essay you are writing. Don't assume the reader knows you or anything about your life. In the best of circumstances, your words will be widely read, by strangers across the country, or across the globe. Though this may seem a distant goal, begin writing *now* with this goal in mind.

reliable as we would like to think. Certain details slip away over time, while others become polished in our minds until they shine a bit brighter than the reality. If you have ever been involved in a discussion with family members about some funny episode in the past—the time your cousin Jimmy tumbled off his bike while showing a trick to his new girlfriend, maybe—you well know how each person's version can be slightly different, or far different, and how funny stories seem to just get better and more exaggerated over time.

Each author of creative nonfiction struggles with this problem of memory and accuracy, and there are no hard-and-fast rules. Readers understand this, and for the most part simply expect that you are doing your best to remember accurately (and that perhaps, when possible, you checked with others who were there to see what you might have missed). Though you may not remember your mother's exact words to you as you walked into the orthodontist's office in eighth grade, chances are pretty good that you remember your mother's usual speech patterns, the expressions she tended to use, and the general idea of what she was trying to tell you. If you combine these elements to portray an honest representation of that conversation, most writers and readers would agree that you have played fairly with memory, even if your version is not a "court transcript."

A helpful way to approach the question of memory in creative nonfiction is to occasionally investigate your own motives. Are you remembering something a certain way in order to make yourself look more like the hero of the situation, or in order to cast your lazy brother-in-law in an even more unpleasant light? If so, you are being dishonest. Moreover, you will probably find that the less straightforward, more complex truth, where you are not "all good" and your brother-in-law is not "all bad," makes for a richer, more interesting story.

If, however, you can look yourself in the mirror (and your reader in the eye) and say, "This is my honest memory, and though my recollection certainly isn't perfect, I've done my absolute best to get it right," you've done your job, even if in the end the color of your sister's dress was yellow not blue on that summer day twelve years in the past.

"But creative nonfiction can never really be true," you may be thinking. "By the very nature of writing, we choose which facts to include and which to leave out. We shape the story to our own ends."

Of course, and this shaping hand of the author, the writer's point of view and perspective, is one of the defining characteristics that separates creative nonfiction from "just the facts" journalism.

Questions of what constitutes truth in nonfiction go beyond just memoir. Even if the nonfiction account you are writing concerns an event which occurred only two days before, and you took painstaking notes, the fact remains that we human beings can observe events right before our eyes and still overlook key details. Moreover, once we decide to write our account of the event, we are making the decision where to "point the camera," what moments to stress and which to pass over because they are unimportant.

The fact that creative nonfiction offers one author's view of the story is a strength of the genre, not a weakness or a disadvantage. In shaping the story, finding the proper starting point and ending point, and choosing which moments or ideas are important for you to emphasize, you are invariably presenting one version of the truth—*your* version. Make your version as honest, and interesting, as you possibly can.

WRITING PROMPTS: What Is Creative Nonfiction?

1. Read Mimi Schwartz's essay "Memoir? Fiction? Where's the Line?" in the Anthology. Schwartz chronicles numerous instances in which authors write about events in their past even though they know their memories are likely clouded by time. She also offers several examples of how these writers "tip off" the reader that the version on the page is a precise accounting of what the author *remembers*, rather than a chronicle of exact historic detail. Do you agree with Schwartz, that the "emotional truth of memory" can be called upon in nonfiction just as readily as verifiable details from a family photo album? Do you agree that if you honestly "remember it, it's true"? Write a brief personal essay in which you discuss *your* views on this matter, but instead of relying merely on abstract ideas and opinion, choose a particular remembered moment from your past to illustrate where you think the lines between memory and fiction might best be drawn.

2. Consider the sorts of stories that often appear in your local newspaper's regional news section: town council votes to extend water and sewer lines; local bridal boutique declares bankruptcy; police chief vows to crack down on area skateboarders. If creative nonfiction is in part "a way of seeing," where might you find a different view of the standard story? Instead of the town council meeting, do you see the family that has subsisted on bottled water for two years because the water lines don't reach an extra sixty feet? Do you see the plight of the bride to be who suddenly doesn't have a wedding dress? Or how about the skateboarder who wants to be congratulated for staying drug free, not hounded off the street? Take the front page of *your* newspaper, make a list of the local and area stories you find there, and—either in a group or

individually—brainstorm a list of other stories you might tell. Is there a more "particular" angle? Does your personal perspective enter into the story at some point and allow for more than "just the facts"? Keep this list you generate; it may come in handy as you respond to writing prompts in later chapters.

3. Creative nonfiction doesn't just come out of the news, of course. It comes out of your world, your passions, and your concerns. Think of ten things you care about deeply: the environment, children in poverty, Alzheimer's research (because your grandfather is a victim), hip-hop music, Saturday afternoon football games. Make your own list of ten important subjects, and then narrow the larger subject down to *specific* subjects you might write about. The environment? How about that bird sanctuary out on Township Line Road that might be torn down to make room for a megastore? Or the changes you've seen in water quality at the spot where your Uncle Jack first took you fishing? Hip-hop music? Is someone in your area starting up a mini-recording label in his basement? Football games? What is it like to be the food service worker who puts mustard on two thousand hot dogs every Saturday afternoon? Don't just wonder about it—talk to the mustard spreader, spend an afternoon hanging out behind the counter, spread some mustard yourself. Transform your list of ten things into a longer list of possible story ideas. Don't worry for now about whether these ideas would take a great amount of research, or might require special permission or access. Just write down a master list of possible stories related to your ideas and passions. Keep the list. You may use it later.

PART II

~~~~~

Building Blocks of Creative Nonfiction

CHAPTER THREE

Building Blocks of Creative Nonfiction:
Detail and Description

CHAPTER FOUR

Building Blocks of Creative Nonfiction:
Characterization and Scene

CHAPTER FIVE

Building Blocks of Creative
Nonfiction: Distinctive Voice and
Intimate Point of View

CHAPTER SIX

Building Blocks of Creative Nonfiction:
Discovery

Chapter Three

Building Blocks of Creative Nonfiction: Detail and Description

> *"Good description begins with observation. The most common things can yield startling surprises when we give our attention to them."*
> —REBECCA McCLANAHAN

Many beginning writers while away their time waiting for a "great idea" or profound inspiration, but experienced writers know that ideas and inspiration can only take you so far. Countless times what seems like a brilliant idea results in nothing more than good intentions, because the writer doesn't know what to do next.

If you have a good idea, by all means write it down, but be aware that a great idea does not make writing come alive on the page. Writing comes to life through careful application of craft and artistry, and an understanding of how words combine to form vivid impressions in the reader's mind.

The following three techniques form the core of many strong narratives, and are fundamental elements of most creative nonfiction:

1. Use of detail and description
2. Characterization through dialogue
3. Characterization through action

In Chapters Three and Four, we will discuss these techniques individually and illustrate how other authors have used these basic building blocks to construct powerful creative nonfiction.

Detail and Description

The quote from essayist and poet Rebecca McClanahan at the beginning of this chapter reminds us that description begins with observation. If you are exploring a subject in which an event or activity is currently unfolding—perhaps a piece of literary journalism about a young woman riding for the first time with the local volunteer fire company—you will need to spend time carefully observing and learning the names and uses of unfamiliar gear and firefighting equipment. There is also the human element to observe—how the young woman acts (does her nervousness show?), how the more experienced volunteers react around her, the silent body language, the ritual of the firehouse, the long hours when very little happens.

Ideally, you will obtain permission to ride along when an alarm sounds, and though it may be "a great idea" to witness firsthand the young woman's heroics in saving three lives during her very first firefighting experience, chances are that such a dramatic rescue will not occur. The first call may in fact be a false alarm, or a small kitchen fire extinguished before the fire trucks even arrive. But remember, that's *also* part of the story.

You may also find that the informal game of Texas Hold 'Em poker that starts up in the firehouse after the pumper truck is washed and the boots lined up against the wall provides a truer glimpse into this young woman's experience; perhaps the card game is actually more interesting than the first, uneventful alarm. Often, you won't know what is useful to your writing until the second or third draft, so the best writers record every detail, even those that don't initially seem dramatic or important. In the words of Rebecca McClanahan, "The most common things can yield startling surprises when we give our attention to them."

But what if you are writing memoir?

Memory can be observed too, and the best writers take the time to observe memory closely. We all have a surface memory—those facts we can recall with only a second's thought—but often the best details are found only after the hard work of really sifting through memory, making the concerted effort to bring recollections to light. The good news, however, is that with each recalled detail more details seem to pop up from the deeper pools of your memory bank. Or to put it another way: The more you remember, the more you remember after that.

Remembering that no matter what the family holiday, your Aunt Calista always seemed to waltz in just five minutes before dinner was served, might help you remember that your elderly aunt quite often would show up in a knee-length raincoat, no matter what the weather. The detail of the coat might remind you that there was always an argument—Aunt Calista didn't want her coat hung in the hallway closet because she needed easy access to her pack of cigarettes, but your grandmother wanted the coat put away, so the house would look nice for the holiday. Remembering the cigarettes might help you to remember the rasp in Aunt Calista's voice. She smoked unfiltered Pall Mall cigarettes, and even though she always retreated to the front porch to smoke them, somehow the smell still seemed to pervade the house. Now you remember how your grandfather always complained, "Calista, if I had wanted to smell smoke instead of my food, I would have bought my own stinking cigarettes."

Despite new scientific understanding, memory is in many ways still mysterious. It often seems at first as if you don't remember much at all about past events, but the more you fish around in the lake of memory, the greater number of interesting facts and creatures you will find living somewhere beneath the surface. Like real fishing, however, it takes time and patience. When trying to recall a specific event or period on your life, you would do well to augment memory by asking questions of others who were there—your parents, your siblings, your childhood friends. The small details they remember often act as catalysts to free up memories you've overlooked or locked away.

No matter what you are writing, once you have thoroughly observed the details, it becomes your job to fully describe them on the page. Beginning writers often overlook the need for careful description, because the scene being described is already so vivid in the author's mind. The simple words "my living room" or "my grandfather" are clear to you, certainly; you have known these people and places all of your life. Just thinking the words "my family living room" reminds you of the carpet, the sofa, the picture behind the sofa, the light coming through the window, the small collection of dusty knick-knacks on the shelf.

But your reader is *not* you, or your family; rather, the reader is a stranger, with a living room and a grandfather of his or her own. Your goal should be to enable that reader to picture *your* grandfather, *your* living room.

To do this, you will need to focus on concrete detail—something that can be tied to our five basic senses—smell, touch, taste, hearing, and sight. In almost all cases, the more specific the detail, the stronger the image formed in a reader's mind. For instance, "A man walked into the room . . ." conveys certain information, but not much. "A short, round gentleman in a brown wool suit strode into the room, his arms filled with flowers" conveys quite a bit more.

Or compare these two sentences:

"My family had a big dinner."

"Aunt Grace swept out of her kitchen with trays of turkey, baked ham, whipped potatoes, plates of green beans and almonds, sweet potato and marshmallow casserole, fruit salad, green salad, sweet and sour pickle wedges, black olives, sourdough rolls, and so many desserts that we feared her antique dining room table would buckle under the heavy load."

Which of the two forms a more vivid picture in your mind?

If you are working primarily in the mode of the personal essay—an inner journey, in which the writer explores particular ideas and emotions—detail is important still. What you as a writer need to closely observe in this instance are your own thoughts, beliefs, and experiences. The surface may be familiar and fairly common, but when you dig down to explore what is most unique about your view of the world, you discover the raw material of an excellent essay.

Specific and Particular

Beyond the basic need to make the picture whole for the reader, description is also important because the meaning of a piece, the significance, is often found in the specific and particular details.

Here, for instance, is a brief essay by Jane Armstrong, offering the reader a window into the reality of living with multiple sclerosis:

INJECTION

Jane Armstrong

You are given a name for the dizziness and stumbling, the electrical parade marching up and down your spinal cord, the flashing lights behind your eyes. MS. You say the initials, but not the words. It's the best you can do.

There's nothing for it, you're told. Wait and see. Try to rest. Avoid stress.

At night, you lie awake and scowl in the darkness while your husband sleeps beside you. You're in it alone.

There's help, you're told. Something new. We don't know how it works, but we're sure it does. You can inject yourself. You're very lucky.

And you are lucky, of course. But it's a shabby sort of luck that finds you alone, sitting on the edge of the bathtub, loaded syringe poised above your prepped thigh. Your hand shakes; your breath quickens. You feel lightheaded and drop the syringe, spilling $250 dollars worth of recombinant DNA onto the bathroom rug,

"I'll give you the shots," your husband says and you laugh. He fears thermometers and blood pressure cuffs.

He goes slowly, afraid of hurting you. He has yet to attain the quick, dart-like thrust recommended in the patient information booklet. His needles tug your flesh, lance your bones. "Did it hurt?" he'll say.

And you'll say no.

He'll put a Band-Aid over the bruise and the blood. He'll install you on the sofa with pillows and blankets and sit at your feet while you wait for the fever and chills and nausea. He'll kiss your forehead, your cheeks, your mouth. He says he'll kiss you no matter how weakened or muddled or crippled or blind. No matter what, he'll kiss you every time.

You rub the place still stinging on your arm.

You're in it alone. Except when you're not.

Armstrong's brief essay would most likely be classified as memoir, since the writer is observing her own life. We also learn a little about her disease, so this essay contains elements of literary journalism. The voice of the personal essayist is likewise present—Armstrong is thinking out loud about her sickness and is commenting throughout on her "shabby sort of luck." Chapters Seven, Eight, and Nine will look more specifically at the differences between these nonfiction categories, but perhaps you can already begin to see how they will often overlap.

Notice that Armstrong chose to tell this story—a true story—in the second person. Instead of "There's help, I'm told . . . I can inject myself. I am very lucky," Armstrong writes, "There's help, you're told . . . You can inject yourself. You're very lucky." Using "you" instead of "I" or "she" is a point-of-view decision, a stylistic choice. We examine point of view more closely in a later chapter, but take a moment now to consider why *you* think Armstrong may have chosen this option.

In the end, the careful details are what make Armstrong's very brief essay more than just a run-of-the-mill passing commentary on the difficulty of living with a chronic illness. If all the author of this essay had told us was that "being sick is really lousy," we may have felt some sympathy, but certainly no interest. The idea that being sick "feels lousy" is nothing that every reader doesn't already know.

Armstrong, however, takes the time and effort to describe the particulars of her disease—"the electrical parade marching up and down your spinal cord, the flashing lights behind your eyes"—and she puts us right there as she attempts the experimental treatment—"alone, sitting on the edge of the bathtub, loaded syringe poised above your prepped thigh. Your hand shakes; your breath quickens. You feel lightheaded and drop the syringe, spilling $250 dollars worth of recombinant DNA onto the bathroom rug."

She paints a complex picture, even in this briefest of essays, and allows us to *see*, without being told or lectured, the specific challenges and difficulties that she faces as an MS sufferer. Moreover, we see her feelings toward her husband, the man who "has yet to attain the quick, dart-like thrust recommended in the patient information booklet," and through the seemingly smallest of details we come to understand just how important his efforts are to her. When he asks "Did it hurt?" and she answers "No" (when we, the readers, know better), we feel her compassion and sympathy toward *him*. He is trying, after all. And his stumbling efforts remind her that she is not, after all, alone.

The details reveal all of this. Armstrong doesn't need to explain the "moral" or the "point" of her essay, because she has already shown us, through simple, careful description.

Another essay that makes excellent use of description is "Buckeye," by Scott Russell Sanders, found in the Anthology. Notice how thoroughly Sanders describes the buckeyes in the opening paragraph: "Once the size of plums, the brown seeds are shriveled now, hollow, hard as pebbles, yet they still gleam from the polish of his hands."

Or study his description of the whitetail deer he counted near his family's rural Ohio home: "One June evening, while mist rose from the ponds, we counted three hundred and eleven, our family record. We found the deer in herds, in bunches, in amorous pairs. We came upon lone bucks, their antlers lifted against the sky like bare branches of dogwood. If you were quiet, if your hands were empty, if you moved slowly, you could leave the car and steal to within a few paces of grazing deer, close enough to see the delicate lips, the twitching nostrils, the glossy, fathomless eyes."

Imagine the effect on the reader if all Sanders had written was, "There sure were a lot of deer out there." His full and careful description reveals the beauty of the moment, allowing readers to see and experience for themselves what Sanders saw and felt as a child.

The second half of the quote that heads this chapter tells us: "The most common things can yield startling surprises when we give our attention to them." Certainly, Sanders' description of the buckeyes his father kept in his pocket show the truth of those words. In fact, Sanders' entire essay rests on the most common of things, yet he manages to cover so much territory.

Armstrong and Sanders use description remarkably well. In fact, every essay reproduced in this book uses meticulous, careful description. Description is a basic building block of nonfiction writing, the foundation of the narrative art.

Revising for Detail and Description

Once you have completed the draft of an essay—either a conventional-length essay or a brief essay such as "Injection"—the real work of writing has only just begun. Your first draft may seem like a mess, riddled with grammatical errors, confusing sentences, and sloppy word choices, or it may be relatively "correct" and well-ordered. Either way, don't make the mistake of imagining that this first effort is your best effort.

The author of the sloppy first draft—with incomplete ideas and slapdash sentences—would gain little by setting the essay aside and muttering, "Oh well, I guess I'm a lousy writer." Instead of giving in to frustration, that author would do better to take the rough draft and start a careful, step-by-step revision. Excellent sentences are often formed from chaotic, clumsy beginnings. Incomplete ideas are sometimes outstanding ideas just waiting to be completed. Many accomplished writers will tell you that some of their most successful writing started as a messy first attempt.

Similarly, the author of the second example—an initial draft that seems correct, clear, and free of error—would be making a mistake to imagine "that's good enough, my job is done." Revision is the most important part of writing, the place where discoveries are made and ideas are polished, where the good becomes very good and the very good becomes excellent. Even a good first effort deserves attention and improvement.

Yes, revision can be hard work, and there may be a voice in the author's head suggesting "wow, you've nailed it, let's take a break now," but excellent writing is a process of discovery. The more that you examine your sentences, making them clearer for the reader *and* yourself, the more you will discover about your subject, and the better your writing will become.

"I often have to write a hundred pages or more before there's a paragraph that's alive," the novelist Philip Roth once told an interviewer. Michael Crichton admits that the need for painstaking revision is "one of the hardest things to accept, especially after the seventh rewrite hasn't quite done it."

Yet, the possibility of revision is also one of the great advantages of being a writer. Unlike surgery or stone carving, with writing you don't need to do the job perfectly the first time. You can shape and refine your thoughts and ideas until they are just as you want them, and you can seem smarter and wiser because of this.

A particularly effective way to approach revision, especially in an early draft, is to ensure that you have enough detail in your essay. Perhaps you are writing about an experience when you were in third grade. Read your draft aloud to yourself (or a friend, if you trust that friend to give you an honest reaction). Does the essay allow the reader (or listener) to see the third-grade classroom? The reader doesn't need every detail, but a few specifics will allow the reader to form a concrete mental image. You want the reader to picture *your* third-grade classroom, not the classroom they attended, or some generic classroom.

Remember that your readers didn't know you at age eight, and didn't know your teacher or classmates. Have you given them a handful of specific details so that they can picture a particular teacher or child? What time of year did this event occur? Did the time of year determine what was found on the classroom walls? Your reader, remember, has no idea if you lived in New York City or on an isolated farm in rural Nebraska. Are there details in your essay that make this clear?

While certain details are often crucial for the reader to know—if you wore a brace on your leg that year, and the brace was part of why the other kids didn't want you on their volleyball team, by all means share that fact with the reader early on—other details are important primarily so that a full picture is formed in the reader's mind. That mental picture helps to hold the reader's interest and helps to make your creative nonfiction believable and real.

WRITING PROMPTS: Detail and Description

1. In this chapter, the sentence "My family had a big dinner" is compared to the detail-filled sentence "Aunt Grace swept out of her kitchen with trays of turkey, baked ham, whipped potatoes, plates of green beans and almonds, sweet potato and marshmallow casserole, fruit salad, green salad, sweet and sour pickle wedges, black olives, sourdough rolls, and so many desserts that we feared her antique dining room table would buckle under the heavy load." Take a similar distinctive memory from your own life and try to paint a full picture. Did your cousin Myra always wear crazy outfits? Show us. Did your brother drive like a maniac? Show us. Did you make a fool of yourself on the first day of soccer practice? Show us, in four or five specific and particular detail-laden sentences.

2. "The most common things can yield startling surprises when we give our attention to them," poet and essayist Rebecca McClanahan suggests. Find an object from your childhood—like the buckeyes in Scott Russell Sanders' essay or the dress in Jamaica Kincaid's "Biography of a Dress" (in the Anthology)—and examine that object closely, from many angles. If possible, find that object and examine it firsthand. But even if that is not feasible, examine this object in your memory. Don't just describe this common thing; think about what it did, where it went, how people used this object. Contemplate what it meant to you, and to other people. Give some thought as to why you still remember it, all of these years later. Then write about it, looking for the startling surprises in common things.

Chapter Four

Building Blocks of Creative Nonfiction: Characterization and Scene

"Sometimes a person needs a story more than food to stay alive."
—BARRY LOPEZ

Careful description is important in nonfiction, but the need for strong detail is certainly not limited to holiday foods, herds of whitetail deer, and third-grade classroom walls. In fact, what will undoubtedly interest the reader most in the creative nonfiction you write will be the people involved. Human beings are inevitably curious about themselves, about others, and about the choices we make and the actions we take.

Unlike in fiction writing, in nonfiction the people you describe are real—they are alive or have lived. It will be helpful to your writing, however, to remember that these people are also characters, because they function as characters once you decide to add them to your essay. These people must be brought fully to life on the page or the writing will fall flat. Even in the personal essay, which is less like a conventional story, there is need for characterization: the reader must know the character of the author, the person who is reflecting on the page.

How do we get to know people in real life? Usually by their words and actions. This is true as well in creative nonfiction.

Characterization through Dialogue

Not every essay in this book, nor every exceptional work of creative nonfiction that you read, will include dialogue, but most will, especially in the categories of memoir and literary journalism. Dialogue is especially effective if the story you are telling involves people, because so much of what makes a person distinctive is the words that he or she uses, and the ways in which particular words are used.

Dialogue can be one of the most challenging techniques for a beginning writer, or for any writer. The cadences and nuances of human speech are complex, peculiar, and often difficult to capture accurately on the page. So why do writers bother, if capturing accurate patterns of speech is so consistently hard? Let's begin by discussing some of the reasons.

You certainly have heard by now how rapidly Hollywood studios abandoned the silent movie once the technology became available to add actual human voices. Silent films were replaced by "talkies" and the film industry grew to such popularity that imagining a world where talking films did not exist is hard to do nowadays. Why did film viewers so readily embrace the change? There is good reason, and it applies to writing as well.

It is a simple truth that human beings are fascinated by the way people speak, by what they say and how they say it. If you want evidence, listen to casual conversations at the local coffee shop:

"What exactly did she tell you?"
"She said what?"
"How did he talk himself out of that?"

People are naturally fascinated by the words of other people, and even if they can't be there, they want somehow to "hear it for themselves."

Carefully chosen dialogue provides two advantages in any essay. First, dialogue lends texture to the narrative, an alternative to the author's voice, and an easy way to change the pacing and flow. But the second advantage, and the one of most importance to the writer of *non*fiction, is that dialogue allows the readers to judge on their own, using their own standards and beliefs, what the characters are saying and what they really mean. "The truth is rarely pure and never simple," playwright Oscar Wilde once observed. Intelligent readers enjoy teasing out the complicated truth of what people say and the manner in which they say it.

This book uses the term *dialogue* rather than the journalistic term *quotes*, by the way, because too often writers have been trained to think of quotes as something boring, a bureaucrat's carefully worded but obscure explanation in a newspaper article about zoning regulations, or a politician's clever effort to form an answer that pleases everyone and offends nobody.

Instead, think of the words within quotation marks in your essay as an element that moves the story forward, reveals character, and adds flavor to your writing. Just as the real people you are writing about become characters once you commit them to the page, the real words they have spoken function as dialogue, by revealing who the people are in your writing, by advancing plot, and by adding detail. But unlike fictional dialogue, *you can't just make it up.*

To the best of your ability, and as honestly as you can, you have to give us the exact words, as they were spoken, how they were spoken, and when they were spoken.

How you manage to utilize dialogue honestly and well depends on what you are writing. If you are writing a direct observation piece, you have a few choices:

- Take along a tape recorder.
- Take careful notes as the event occurs.
- As soon as the event is finished, hurry off to a quiet place and transcribe what you just heard as accurately as you can, before it is all forgotten.

Notebooks and tape recorders work just fine for many stories that fall under the literary journalism heading. Where they don't, however, you will find that your memory is better than you think. The truth is, the more you use your memory, the better it gets.

As a rule of thumb, it is usually best to *not* use dialogue when great amounts of information need to be imparted. Long stretches of dialogue full of complicated facts and details tend to score very high on the boring index. Dialogue is a break in the story, a chance for the reader to take a breath, and also a chance to see our characters as real people (not as lecturers).

But what if you are writing about events that occurred ten or twenty years ago? This issue troubles many writers, beginning and experienced. In memoir—writing about events in our own lives long past—you have no choice but to rely on memory, and as we have discussed in earlier chapters, everyone knows that memory can be inexact.

Certainly you are not able to re-create with complete accuracy long passages of dialogue from when you were five years old. Chances are pretty good that you didn't have the foresight to run a tape recorder on the evening that your parents sat you down to explain that your little sister was going to the hospital for heart surgery. Though in some cases we have diaries and journals that remind us of how we felt, few of us record conversations in our diaries.

So can memoir have dialogue?

Well, it must, for all of the reasons stated previously:

- Dialogue helps to make the people in your creative nonfiction seem "real."
- The reader is interested to hear *how* your parents broke the news.
- The reader wants to experience the flavor of the speech, what was said, and (often of most importance) what was left unsaid.

Sometimes, when an event in our life was very crucial, highly dramatic, we *do* recall with startling clarity, even decades later, but not always. And not all memoir revolves around tragedy and startling moments. Sometimes, you want to re-create a simple conversation you had with your grandmother on a breezy autumn afternoon on the back porch, a conversation that was not particularly momentous.

In these instances, remember, you must simply do your best, as honestly as you can. The first rule is, Don't fake it. Don't put words that you know are entirely fictional into your grandmother's mouth simply to make her seem more warm and generous than she actually was, or to make her seem even more disagreeable. Your obligation to the reader is to capture this woman's speech as accurately as possible. The reader will understand that you are not perfect in your recollection.

Some writers, however, choose to openly acknowledge a lack of perfect recall with a phrase such as this:

"These events are distant, but what I'm recording here is the truth of what remains in my memory."

It is perfectly fine to admit to failures of memory within the writing itself. The reader usually appreciates such honesty.

Still, if you spend time sorting through your memory bank, if you really try to go back into time and into your thoughts and feelings, you will likely find that you *can* remember the way your grandmother *often* spoke—her inflections, some of her favorite expressions, the way she lifted her cup of tea and glanced up toward her bedroom window whenever she referred to your late grandfather. The more you try to remember, the more you will find remaining in your memory. You can offer the reader an accurate summary of what you know was spoken about that afternoon, and a few snippets of how she spoke, to bring her character to life.

For an example of dialogue used effectively, read this essay:

A DRAMATIC DOGALOG

Art Homer

I'm standing outside the supermarket with Hooch, waiting for my wife to pick up a couple of things, when up walks about the fourth elderly woman in a row to say "What a pretty dog."

Thanks, I say. "He thinks so."

"What kind . . ." she begins, then corrects herself. "I mean what do you call this brand of dog?"

"He's a Golden Retriever."

"I like dogs . . ."

"I can see that," I say.

". . . but I'm a widow," she continues, ignoring my impertinence, "and my husband always said—we always lived on the corner of 55th up here. Well, people don't pay attention to the stop signs. They just go like I don't know. It's bad enough when they run over the squirrels, but then the Humane Society has to come out and scrape up a dog, or maybe not so much a cat. Oh, if it were my dog I'd just feel so guilty."

"Well, they do take a lot of looking after." I scratch Hooch on the head. He's pulling a little on the leash, trying as he does to get downwind of the stranger the better to evaluate her. She has a broken blood vessel near the corner of her mouth which is pretty well covered up with makeup, except in the creases. It looks like a spider has hidden in her face.

"He isn't vicious is he?"

I try to sound reassuring. "No, he likes people, but he's a male, so with dogs he gets a little . . ."

"Because my husband was at work," she says as if I've interrupted again, "and he'd get wrapped around the stake and I'd be afraid to go out there and untangle him. *Rowr! Rowr!* Leaping at the chain. Hardly move, poor thing!"

"What kind of dog?" I ask.

"A school teacher, and he didn't get home for two hours. I was too afraid. It was a big dog I tell you, and vicious, not like Lassie on TV."

"A Collie, then," I say, feeling a bit more on solid ground.

"Yes, but black and brown, but the people come by with all kinds. Big and little, I don't know all the brands."

"Yes, well they have to be walked so they don't get bored and run away."

"I would like to have a dog, but are they little when you get them or do they come this size?"

"Well, dogs are animals . . ." I babble. "I mean, they start out . . ." I stop and try again. "We got Hooch here from the pound—so he was grown. We haven't had him since he was a puppy."

"I see. He's a beautiful dog—a beautiful, beautiful dog."

She went into the store. Hooch gave me a puzzled look, sighed, and lay down. "Good dog," I said. "Good dog."

Homer uses dialogue extensively to re-create the character of the elderly woman. As a result of this dialogue, he doesn't need to tell us that the woman is distracted or a very poor listener. We can "hear it with our own ears." He doesn't have to tell us that she is mainly holding a conversation with herself, a conversation focused on the worries that are floating around in her head. We see that clearly.

The author might have given us the necessary information in a summary statement: "She was very self-involved." We tend to believe the scene and believe our own conclusions far more, however, when the full detail is given. The woman seems real because she is right there, on the page, being herself.

Compare Homer's brief essay to a possible sentence that simply reads, "I met this goofy old woman who knew nothing about dogs." That sentence captures the facts, but none of the flavor.

The trick to using dialogue well in nonfiction is often selection.

As a first step, writers should attempt to hear the dialogue that takes place all around them. Just as seeing "with fresh eyes" is important when writing description, hearing with fresh ears is crucial to capturing human speech. Notice that unlike the cautious quotes offered up by candidates for city council, or the lectures delivered from careful notes by your history professor, everyday speech is marked by some surprising characteristics:

- In everyday conversation, people often don't speak in complete sentences.
- People don't always make sense. They contradict and interrupt themselves, and often wander off the topic. Though it is permissible to edit out some of the "ums" and "ahs" that often punctuate human speech, "cleaning up" the meandering way that we talk is usually a mistake. Don't force the human beings in your creative nonfiction to sound like robots.
- People often employ a range of responses to avoid answering when asked a direct question. They might answer a different question, or ask a question in return. "Why do you want to know?" or "Where were *you* last night?"

Take some time to really listen and make your own list of peculiarities in human speech. The imprecise and irregular ways in which we talk to one another almost always makes for a fascinating subject. At the end of this chapter, the writing prompts offer more ideas on how you can capture complex dialogue.

Characterization through Action

Certainly our words reveal who we are and why we act in certain ways. Listen closely, and often you can detect a confusion of purpose, or even hidden motivations, just underneath what a person has said. At other times, the formality of speech or the relaxed attitude tell us something about the person speaking. But certainly you have heard the old proverb "actions speak louder than words," and often they do. Nonverbal ways of communicating are basic to human nature and an essential component of how we form our opinions of others.

Imagine what transpires when someone new enters your arena—a new face in your circle of friends, your sister's new boyfriend, or your divorced uncle's new date at a family dinner. You may form an instantaneous impression, based on clothing, hairstyle, physical characteristics, even a "gut reaction," but if you are like most people, what you do next is watch and wait. "Let's see how they act," you may think to yourself. "Give it a little while and we'll see what sort of person they really are."

This basic human instinct to form conclusions based on what you see "with your own eyes" functions no differently in writing. When a reader encounters a new character on the page—and this is true whether this character is fictional or a real person captured in nonfiction—the reader (probably without consciously thinking about it) reacts in pretty much the same way. "Let's see how this person acts. Then I'll make up my mind what kind of person she is."

For example, consider what conclusions you can draw about the grade school counselor in the following brief essay:

DRINK IT

Patricia Ann McNair

"Coffee?" Mrs. Coates asked. A peculiar, grown-up question. I said yes, the grown-up thing to do, and she poured the dark liquid into a paper cup marked with squiggly lines and set the cup in front of me. I was in sixth grade. I wrapped my hands around the cup like I'd seen women do who sit alone at the Tip Top, staring out the window, waiting. The cup was cold.

The counselor reached for one of my hands. "This is hard to say," she began. I'd been called down to her office over the intercom, pulled out of base 6 drills in Advanced Math. Mrs. Coates' eyes were moist. I looked at the oily film that swirled the surface of my coffee. Mrs. Coates cleared her throat. "Your brother Allen tried to jump out a window today." I knew the words made up a complete sentence, I recognized a subject and a predicate. Why, then, didn't it make sense?

"What?"

"He was being teased in class." My brother was a senior in high school, less than a month from graduation. "I suppose he got fed up, so he went to the window and threatened to jump." Mrs. Coates sniffled. My own nose began to run. "He's at Lutheran General now."

Five South, I thought. A mythical floor of the hospital where kids went when their parents learned they were doing drugs, when they ODed. When they attempted suicide. There'd be whisperings in the school hallways sometimes about a classmate—a popular cool kid: *You hear about Sam? Five South, man.* And it was like a badge of honor, like the stirrings of a legend. But my brother, high-strung and bespectacled, the target of teasing and jokes, was not popular. He was not cool. Allen was, however—then, and many, many times since—suicidal.

"Your mom will be here soon to get you." Mrs. Coates handed me a tissue. "Shall I wait with you?" I shook my head.

Alone in the office, I took a swallow of the cold coffee. It tasted like rusted metal, nearly impossible to keep down. One time when I was six or seven, I'd been painting with one of those long, skinny tins of watercolors. I filled a drinking glass with water to clean my brush. The color of the water became increasingly brown, and when I stirred it up, it developed a frothy head like root beer. Allen loved root beer, and—to be funny, I thought—I told him that's what this was. "Drink it," I said. He took a big swig, and, as soon as he tasted it, spit it out. He looked at me through his glasses, the effect of my betrayal in his eyes.

While I waited for my mother in the counselor's office, I remembered that look. I lifted the foul cup of oily cold coffee. "Drink it," I said. And I did.

The first bit of action that most readers notice is that this woman, Mrs. Coates, is offering a sixth-grader a cup of coffee. That is certainly peculiar behavior, and you might interpret it either of two ways:

1. Mrs. Coates is a particularly unprofessional school counselor.
2. She is set off-balance by the moment, not used to delivering messages such as "Your brother Allen tried to jump out a window today," and in her nervousness, she is acting awkwardly and inappropriately.

If you read on, you will see that the woman eventually reaches for one of the young narrator's hands in an effort to console her and offers the child a tissue. The adult provides basic information about the brother's suicide attempt and his current condition. Her eyes are moist and she is having difficulty speaking.

At this point, evidence may be building up toward conclusion number two. Mrs. Coates is trying, even if her efforts fall somewhat short.

But then she asks, "Shall I wait with you?" When the narrator, only eleven years old, shakes her head, the school counselor leaves the room. Would you expect a woman in that position to leave a sixth-grader alone after delivering such disturbing news?

You can form your own conclusion as to whether Mrs. Coates was doing her job well, though that is just texture and background to the essay, not the center of McNair's narrative. Less important than what conclusion you reach is that you are *given* the opportunity to decide for yourself. McNair doesn't tell us what she thinks, or instruct us on what we should think, about her sixth-grade counselor. Instead, she gives us the actions so that we might reach our own conclusion. Because the conclusion is one that we reach on our own, we tend to believe that conclusion much more firmly.

That's the point: to let the reader decide. Your job as writer is to provide the details which make that possible.

The essay also reveals much about the young McNair. The child accepts the cup of cold coffee because it seems the "grown-up thing" to do. She mimics the women she has seen at the Tip Top diner, "staring out the window, waiting." What conclusions can you form about the youthful narrator from these actions? What is she feeling inside?

Does the brief dialogue, or the fact that there is so little dialogue, reinforce the opinions you form about the child and the adult in this essay?

It is, by the way, worth mentioning again that McNair likely does not have a "court transcript" memory of the exact words that were spoken that day. Instead, she is doing her best in this essay to capture the emotion in the room, the woman's nervous manner, and her own reactions to the counselor's words. A sophisticated reader understands that McNair is not working from detailed notes—in the way that we would expect of the White House reporter for the *Washington Post*—but the reader also trusts that McNair is attempting to give us the truth, and has thought hard about what really happened that day. *Here is what it was like,* she is saying to her reader. *Here is my best effort to recreate that experience, so you can experience it as well.*

In the end, McNair's brief memoir hinges on two moments: the flashback sentences, where we learn about a time the author tricked her brother into drinking dirty watercolor water, and the final moment, when she lifts "the foul cup of oily cold coffee" to her mouth and drinks it. The essay is about feelings of betrayal, about guilt, and about the inability of a sixth-grader to fully understand such horrendous family events as her brother's mental illness and suicidal tendencies.

But notice how none of this has to be explained. The details, the dialogue, and mainly the action hold the meaning.

One more aspect of excellent writing that McNair demonstrates in this essay has to do with rounded, rather than flat, characters. A flat character is all one way: the totally despicable villain or the completely helpless victim. Think of a one-dimensional cardboard cutout.

Mrs. Coates, though only a secondary character in a very brief scene within a short essay, is rounded, given more than one side. She *does* try to help the child, even if awkwardly. She *is* saying nice things. But like many of us, at times she probably didn't do her job so well, and this seems to be one of them.

Real human beings are not all bad and not all good. Even your heroes probably have annoying characteristics or selfish moments on difficult days. Conversely, those people who do things poorly, or act badly, almost always wish to be better at what they do, or more acceptable in society, but are unable to meet their own expectations for complex reasons. Fiction writers know this, and this aspect of human behavior is worth remembering in nonfiction as well.

Moreover, a character with depth and "roundness" is simply more interesting for the reader to encounter. A complex character gives the interested reader more to chew on and ponder.

(Remember that we are calling the real people you write about "characters," even though they are *not* fictionalized. Approaching the people in your nonfiction as characters reminds you that your job, as author, is to bring them fully onto the page: how they look, how they act, their reactions to other people and events, the ways in which they move through a scene.)

This basic advice about rounded character applies to the dangers of stereotypes as well. Whenever you hear a writer characterize someone as "a slut" or "white trash," you would do well to become very skeptical. If you have a good "crap detector," it should beep loudly. Labels such as these are offensive, intolerant, and usually applied with malice. Even a so-called positive stereotype—"she was born in Korea, and thus she is obviously very good at math"—should give you pause.

Blanket stereotypes can be destructive in society and human relationships, but this is also a writing issue. As long as you think of your characters as destined to act a certain way simply because they come from a particular background or family situation, you will lack the ability to see the depths of a character or to truly understand someone's world other than your own. The writer's job is to attempt a comprehensive and nuanced understanding of every character—the ones you like, the ones you don't like, and especially those you think that you can never really understand. To do this well, you must throw all of your prejudices and preconceptions aside. An open mind is a writer's greatest strength, if that writer is after truth rather than mere cliché.

Scene: Letting the Facts Speak for Themselves

In each of the brief essays in this chapter, description, dialogue, and action combine to create a complete scene. In Jane Armstrong's "Injection," the basic scene is the author sitting alone on the edge of the bathtub, shaking as she tries to inject herself with an experimental treatment for multiple sclerosis. Eventually her husband enters, and offers help. In Art Homer's "A Dramatic Dogalog," the author is waiting outside a supermarket with his dog Hooch, when an elderly woman approaches him, full of questions and opinions. And of course, in Patricia McNair's "Drink It," the scene we have is the few minutes in the school counselor's office, when the young narrator receives bad news about her brother.

What is a scene? A scene is the opposite of a still photograph. In a scene, detail, sensory information, and actions (including dialogue) combine to re-create a sense of movement. A scene is when real people in actual space take concrete actions for a set period of time.

In addition to a description of setting, and the names of the people in the room, a good scene often includes the actions ("she lifted the flower vase and moved it to the bedside table"), important facial expressions ("he winced when she mentioned his mother"), and often some sense of change ("she seemed to sink into her chair the longer they spoke").

Describing how you feel about your childhood backyard is not a scene. Giving us a static description of your childhood backyard—"there was a sliding board over by the fence, and a stack of firewood by the garage"—is not a scene. But showing us a few moments one Tuesday afternoon when you and your little sister played with GI Joes and Barbie dolls in the dirt patch worn away by the swing set, letting us hear the dialogue, and ending when the skies open and the rain begins to pour, is a scene.

Another way to think of scene is to imagine a shooting script for a Hollywood film. Though the form is different, a good prose scene is cinematic, and if you were to hand that scene to a filmmaker, she would know where to place the actors, how to cast those actors, what the set should look like, what lines the actors would speak, and perhaps other details such as lighting, costuming, and ambient sound.

Revising for Scene

Writing a scene, remembering what happened in what order and determining how to construct phrases, sentences, details in such a way that it all becomes clear in a reader's mind, is *much more work* than summarizing the action. It is far easier to simply give the readers a shorthand version of events and inform them what conclusion you want them to reach. Often it takes multiple drafts before you get to a clear first draft of a scene, a draft in which the moments come alive, and the action is easy to follow.

All of this hard work is worth it, however. Why? Because if you take the trouble to write the full scene, the reader really sees what occurs, and if the reader sees what occurs with his or her own eyes, it becomes real. And your reader is convinced.

A great way to revise for scene and detail, especially if you are writing memoir or literary journalism, is to utilize Lee Gutkind's yellow pen test. Take your first draft, or whichever draft you are working to revise, and read through it with a yellow highlighting pen in your hand. (Any color will do, of course.) Each time you read a sentence or paragraph of summary—"my parents got divorced when I was in fifth grade and I was miserable because I had to change schools"—leave that section unhighlighted. Whenever you run across a scene, however, a portion of your draft in which there is action, when the reader is given a moment-to-moment description of an event as if it were happening right then, color that entire section with your highlighter. You might try this same exercise with an essay like Sanders' "Buckeyes" or McNair's "Drink It."

If your essay is showing more highlighted sections than unhighlighted sections, you are on the right track. Many writers will aim for a 70–30 percent mix, though lively writing is never simply a mathematical equation. Usually, however, far more unhighlighted sections (summary and exposition, "telling" the reader) and too few highlighted sections ("showing the reader") can serve as a warning. Your job of detail and description, bringing the scene to life, is not yet finished.

WRITING PROMPTS: Characterization through Dialogue

1. Spend time in the campus snack bar, at a coffee shop, or anywhere that people congregate and have conversations (close enough that you can overhear). Listen closely, and either take notes or—if you wish to be more discreet—remember well and then jot down some notes immediately afterward. Later, write a one-page scene in which you illustrate as accurately as possible what was said, how the people looked and acted as they were saying it, and how the conversation wandered from point to point. Don't worry now if your scene or the conversation you recount has any great meaning or significance—just try to capture the intricacies and unusual logic of normal human conversations. (Remember, human beings seldom speak in complete sentences. Hardly ever.)

2. Find a quiet place where you will not be distracted. Turn off the TV and the Internet, and ask your roommate to leave you alone for a while. Now attempt to think back to when you were five, or six, or somewhere around that early age. Take notes on a conversation entirely from your memory. Attempt, as best as possible, to remember how your best friend would snort when she laughed, or the way your Mom would twist the ring on her finger when she was worried. Try to capture the cadence of that person's speech. Don't worry if you are 100 percent accurate in what you recollect, but instead see how much you *can* remember. Notice how much of memory begins to flow off the pen when you really, really try to remember back. Take fifteen minutes with no other distractions to write down as much as you can—the words, the actions, the facial expressions, where it all took place.

WRITING PROMPTS: Characterization through Action

1. Phillip Lopate, an award-winning personal essayist, tells us that in creating characters of ourselves, "a good place to start is your quirks. These are the idiosyncrasies, stubborn tics, antisocial mannerisms, and so on that set you apart from the majority of your fellowmen." Lopate also warns against "coming across . . . as absolutely average. Who wants to read about that bland creature, the regular Joe?" Letting the reader know that you are willing to laugh at your own foibles, or at least look honestly at your own human limitations, is more interesting, certainly, but also creates a sense of trust. If she is honest about herself, maybe she is honest about others, the reader thinks. So be honest about yourself. Write a nonfiction scene in which we see what sets you apart, makes you other than the regular Joe or Jane. Shine a light on your idiosyncrasies, stubborn tics, or antisocial mannerisms. Make yourself into a character by showing that you are less than perfect. We all are.

2. Blanket stereotypes show shallowness of thought, and in that regard they are bad writing. Determining where you harbor an unexamined prejudice, however, is often an opportunity to tackle a highly worthwhile subject. Pick someone who doesn't live the way you think she should live: someone who doesn't keep her house clean, raises her children all wrong, can't hold a job, or somehow makes a mess of her life day in and day out. If that description, or some part of it, does not capture one of the unfathomable characters in your life, pick one that does—the friend who again and again sabotages relationships, the stoned slacker who wastes his considerable potential, or the unimaginative older sibling who always follows the rules and plays it safe. Then remember—no one wakes up in the morning and thinks, "I'm planning to make dumb choices today." This person is likely trying to do well, even if she fails in your eyes. If you can make an honest attempt to understand the pressures that make such a person take actions which on the surface seem inexplicable or wrong, then you'll be able to write about that person. And that person is perhaps *exactly* the person you should be writing about.

Chapter Five

Building Blocks of Creative Nonfiction: Distinctive Voice and Intimate Point of View

"Not only is your story worth telling, but it can be told in words so painstakingly eloquent that it becomes a song."

—GLORIA NAYLOR

Of course, as important as it is to understand the power of detail, description, dialogue, and a fully rendered scene, if successful writing consisted of nothing more than capturing the action precisely as it unfolded, writers would be automatons, and all writing would sound alike. It would be a dull world, indeed.

Put another way, what if movies were created by simply setting a single camera onto a tripod left in a stationary location? That technique would rule out the very important roles of the cinematographer and the film editor, and would make for extremely static films.

Successful creative nonfiction has a cinematographer and film editor as well, but in both cases this person is the author. You, as writer, decide not just what goes into a scene, but how it will look, how it will sound, and the various camera angles. To extend the metaphor even further, good writing also has a musical director—the writer, again—but instead of picking a soundtrack of songs, the creative nonfiction "musical director" chooses which words are used, the structure and rhythms of the sentences, and whether and where to employ metaphors and other evocative language.

Of course, in writing we don't use these filmmaking terms. We use the terms *voice* and *point of view*.

Distinctive Voice

An author's voice consists of many things, including word choice, sentence structure and rhythm, metaphor and imagery, sometimes a regional flavor or dialect, perhaps humor or irony, and always the personality of the writer. Voice is what distinguishes creative nonfiction from an encyclopedia entry: unlike the latter, in creative nonfiction we *want* to feel the writer behind the words, to know that a living human being with a distinct personality is shaping what we read.

Author Philip Gerard, whose work appears in the Anthology, believes that readers seek "the sense not only that you are hearing a story, but that *somebody is telling you* that story—somebody distinctive, somebody you could pick out of a crowd, somebody whose voice you'll listen for and recognize the next time your hear it."

Certain modes of writing—much of business and technical writing for instance—strive to eliminate a sense of individual voice from the page. Creative nonfiction is just the opposite.

Notice, for instance, the word choices, sentence rhythms, use of repetition, and other stylistic moves made by Brian Doyle as he writes from a father's point of view in this essay:

Pop Art

Brian Doyle

In nine years I have been graced with three children and here is what I have learned about them. They are engines of incalculable joy and agonizing despair. They are comedy machines. Their language is their own and the order of their new halting words has never been heard before in the whole history of the world. They are headlong and hilarious. Their hearts are enormous and sensitive beyond calculation by man or machine. Their pride is vast. They are cruel, and move in herds and gaggles and mobs, and woe unto the silent one, the one who looks funny, the one who speaks awkwardly, the fat one, for she will be shouldered aside, he will never get the ball, she will never be asked to jump rope, he will not be invited to the pool party, she will weep with confusion and rage, he will lash out with sharp small fists. Yet they are endlessly kind, kind by nature, and among them there is often an artless democracy, a linking of arms against the vast puzzle of the long people. They search for rules and rank, for what is allowed and what is forbidden, and poke the rules to see which bends and which is steel, for they wish to know their place in the world, where they might walk, what they may wear, which shows are allowed, how far they can go, who they are. They rise early in excitement and return reluctantly to barracks at night for fear of missing a shred of the daily circus. They eat nothing to speak of but grow at stunning rates that produce mostly leg. They are absorbed by dogs and toast. Mud and jelly accrue to them. They are at war with wasps. They eat no green things. Once they learn sarcasm they use it with abandon, slashing here and there without control and wreaking havoc. When they weep they weep utterly from the marrows of their lonely bones. They will not speak of death but when it comes, a dark hooded hawk on the fence, they face it without fear. They are new creatures hourly, and what you think you know of them is already lost in the river. Their hearts are dense books no one can read. They speak many languages of the body. To them you are a stone who has always been and will always be. When they are ill they shrivel. To father them is not a brief noun but an endless verb that exhausts, enrages, edifies, elevates, educates; I am a thinner and grayer man than I was; and closer to joy. They frighten me, for they will make a new world on the bowed back of the one I love; but they delight me, for to have loved them is to have tasted the furious love the Maker has for what He made, and fathers still, and always will.

Doyle, you may have noticed, borrows liberally from that portion of the writer's toolbox often associated with poetry. For instance, how many "h" words can be found in these three sentences?

Their language is their own and the order of their new halting words has never been heard before in the whole history of the world. They are headlong and hilarious. Their hearts are enormous and sensitive beyond calculation by man or machine.

In addition to alliteration, Doyle also makes effective use of repetition. Notice the number of sentences in the essay which begin with the word "they." This use of the same sentence opening, if unplanned, might seem like an error—beginning writers, when writing memoir, often begin every sentence with "I"—but Doyle has taken care to vary the pattern at regular intervals, and his writing is tight, free of superfluous phrases and clauses. When he breaks a rule—"don't start too many sentences the same way"—he breaks it knowingly, for a reason.

Doyle uses metaphor as well, as in "They will not speak of death but when it comes, a dark hooded hawk on the fence, they face it without fear."

Notice, too, how Doyle follows up a string of very brief sentences with a lengthy and complex sentence full of clauses: "They are cruel, and move in herds and gaggles and mobs, and woe unto the silent one, the one who looks funny, the one who speaks awkwardly, the fat one, for she will be shouldered aside, he will never get the ball, she will never be asked to jump rope, he will not be invited to the pool party, she will weep with confusion and rage, he will lash out with sharp small fists."

Reading Doyle's essay aloud is an excellent way to get a feel for the rhythms of the piece, the "camera angles" chosen by the cinematographer/writer, and the cuts made by the metaphorical film editor. Reading aloud, both your own writing and the writing of authors that you admire, is always a good idea. Like a musician, a writer who aspires to a distinctive prose style does well to develop an ear for sound.

Jamaica Kincaid is another author with a highly distinctive voice and a clear sense of storytelling. Consider her essay "Biography of a Dress," found in the Anthology. Throughout her memoir piece, Kincaid makes use of parenthetical asides or clarifications, some of them reflecting what she didn't know as a child but has since learned, others adding background or new information.

In the following passage, for instance, Kincaid challenges the reader to keep track of intertwining narratives—what she knew then and knows now, what her mother may or may not have understood—even as she carries forward the action of the story, having her ears pierced:

> One day, at dusk (I would not have called it that then), I was taken to someone's house (a woman from Dominica, a woman who was as dark as my mother was fair, and yet they were so similar that I am sure now as I was then that they shared the same tongue), and two thorns that had been heated in a fire were pierced through my earlobes. I do not now know (and could not have known then) if the pain I experienced resembled in any way the pain my mother experienced while giving birth to me or even if my mother, in having my ears bored in that way, at that time, meant to express hostility or aggression toward me (but without meaning to and without knowing that it was possible to mean to).

This is a complex and somewhat risky strategy that Kincaid employs. But notice that Kincaid, like Brian Doyle in the example earlier, is very careful to keep the narrative moving forward, to provide the reader with fresh insight and interesting imagery at every turn, so that we do not become bogged down by her parenthetical interruptions. In fact, the interruptions become part and parcel of the very rhythm of the piece, and come to represent the adult author's struggle to understand.

Voice does not always employ such tour de force moves, of course, as those used by Doyle and Kincaid. Often, an author's voice is quieter, more subtle. Remember the voice of Patricia McNair in her essay "Drink It"? Part of the power of that brief memoir is the simplicity and starkness of the language. Or consider Bret Lott's essay "Brothers" in the Anthology. Lott, a best-selling novelist as well as a nonfiction writer, simply "gives us the scene" to illuminate the story of his brother and of his two sons. Lott, however, is no less careful in his word choice, diction, and sentence rhythms. He is constantly aware of how each new bit of information and visual image will advance the picture in his reader's mind.

A beginning writer hoping to establish his or her own distinctive voice would do well to read as much good writing as possible, often reading out loud. Make your language as rich, flexible, and varied as you can, always learning new words and trying for fresh imagery or metaphor. Make it a point to experiment with different ways of arranging words, sentences, and information. If the experiment doesn't work, you can always hit the "undo" key, but you will have learned something.

Remember also, however, that a writer can't fake a distinctive voice. The minute a writer tries too hard to overlay some clever technique or idiomatic language on the work, it usually sounds false, forced, or phony. You don't *need* to fake it or push it; you only need to find it. Your voice is already there. Your voice is how you talk to your friends, how you talk to yourself, how you learned to talk from your parents and aunts and uncles and neighbors.

Voice is also determined by what you are passionate about—if you care deeply about your subject, your passion invariably comes through in the writing. Can you tell how Brian Doyle feels about his children by the words he has chosen to describe them? Is it clear how Jamaica Kincaid feels about her mother and the poverty of her youth?

Voice can change as well. A writer's voice may evolve over time, so that the work of that writer at age twenty seems very different from work the writer produced much later in life. Or a writer may acquire a range of voices, picking and choosing with each new piece of writing the voice that works best.

To understand voice, and to acquire a consistent mastery of voice in your own writing, the first step is to cultivate your sensitivity to language. Listen to the voices around you, make note of odd or interesting colloquial phrases that pass your way, listen hard for slight differences in speech found in people from different parts of the state or region where you live, or for the subtle differences between your Italian American grandparents and your Irish American grandparents, even though all four of them were born in the same Ohio town. The music of language is all around us, but too often we just don't stop to listen.

Intimate Point of View

Point of view and voice overlap in key ways, especially when point of view is used to refer to an author's intimate perspective on the world. Before we discuss intimate perspective, however, it is important to introduce some technical aspects of point of view.

Traditionally, prose writers talk about three points of view, common to both fiction and nonfiction:

In first-person point of view, the story is narrated by an "I" voice, as in the sentence "I walked to the store, and my little brother followed." In fiction, this first-person "I" is *not* the author, but instead an imagined character on the page. In nonfiction, it is fair to assume that the "I" represents the author.

Second person is trickier. This point of view uses "you" rather than a first-person pronoun or character name to indicate the person at the center of the story. The example shown above for first person—"I went to the store, and my brother followed"—might appear in second person as "You walk to the store, but your brother is right behind, tugging at your shirt, begging for a piece of candy." Second person is used rarely, and should always be applied carefully. Glance again, for instance, at Jane Armstrong's essay "Injection," where "You are given a name for the dizziness and stumbling, the electrical parade marching up and down your spinal cord, the flashing lights behind your eyes." Armstrong, of course, is putting "you" in *her* place. The essay is about the author's experience with illness, but the use of second person creates a direct connection and immediacy for the reader.

Third-person point of view uses a character name rather than "you" or "I," and is encountered most often in literary journalism. For instance, if you were writing a profile of someone in your neighborhood, your essay might begin: "Noah Davis crossed the street, heading to Womack's Corner Store, his little brother Nathan tagging close behind." Third-person point of view often requires meticulous research, since you are presenting the perspective of someone other than yourself. In the book *Praying for Sheetrock*, for instance, Melissa Faye Greene shows us the world of McIntosh County, Georgia, through the eyes of various residents. One passage begins, "Shivering in the dark, the teenaged Thurnell Alston rode in the bed of an old pickup truck in January 1955 between his father and a dozen other McIntosh black men. This was to be his first real experience of work." Greene is able to do this only because she interviewed her subject at great length. She can tell us that Alston was shivering, that it was his first experience of work, and later even what he was thinking, because she asked him (many years later) and he told her. More information on research methods in creative nonfiction can be found on the textbook website, www.dintywmoore.com/truth.

Even in third person, by the way, the voice of the author is present, though sometimes the sense of the author is quite subtle. The literary journalist Tracy Kidder often does not refer to himself at all in his writing. Still, we sense his shaping presence in the work because he has chosen which details to emphasize and which scenes to bring fully to life.

Two other terms to remember are *omniscient* and *limited*.

Omniscient literally means "all-knowing." In fiction the omniscient point of view is one in which the author (and thus the reader) is privy at any moment to the inner thoughts of each character (not just the main character or protagonist). Most fiction, however, is written from a limited point of view, meaning we are restricted to the thoughts, observations, and ruminations of one character. The author (and reader) cannot suddenly jump "into the head" of a minor character to clear up some confusion or to add a plot point. Though limited point of view is—as the name clearly suggests—limiting, it allows the reader to experience the world of the fictional narrative through a specific and unique perspective, and this is one of the pleasures of good fiction.

In nonfiction, where we rely on the author's own sensibility and perception, the point of view on the page is the author's point of view, and in almost all cases point of view is "limited" to that one perspective. The exception would be in works of literary journalism such as *Praying for Sheetrock*, mentioned above, in which numerous points of view are represented, in different portions of the book, based on research and interviews.

Now, however, let's return to the idea of *intimate* point of view.

As important as first-person/third-person, limited/omniscient distinctions can be, it would be a shame if your understanding stopped with basic technical matters. Instead, the real power of point of view has to do with intimacy.

Intimate point of view allows readers to experience the world (or whatever portion of the world is being considered in a given piece of writing) through the eyes and ears of a thoughtful author. This art of directed perspective removes readers (temporarily at least) from the constraints of their own lives so that they might see a wider, or different, view of things.

A good dictionary will offer up many definitions for the word *intimate,* but in this instance the meaning "to enter deeply or closely into a matter" is most relevant. Any piece of writing that offers only a surface view of the subject is going to come up short. Whether writing about the self or a subject outside of the self, the author has first to see and consider every aspect, beyond first impressions and easy generalizations, and then share those close observations with the reader.

Intimate point of view shows you not only what Joan Didion, for instance, sees in her world and finds most important, but how she thinks about each detail, and how these details affect the choices made in her life.

Have you heard the expression "you had to be there"? Well, intimate point of view, done carefully, allows you to be there, residing in the author's world, seeing through the author's eyes, smelling what the author smelled on a Sunday morning, feeling the unique moment through the one-of-a-kind perspective of another person.

Look at "Sunday," and notice how the author invites you both to see his world and to see how the outside world looked while sitting in his seat (when he was a boy):

Sunday

Henry Louis Gates

White people couldn't cook; everybody knew that. Which made it a puzzle why such an important part of the civil rights movement had to do with integrating restaurants and lunch counters. The food wasn't any good anyway. Principle of the thing, Daddy's buddy Mr. Ozzie Washington would assert. They don't know nothin' about seasoning, my Aunt Marguerite would say. I like my food seasoned, she'd add.

If there is a key to unlocking the culinary secrets of the Coleman family, it is that a slab of fatback or a cupful of bacon drippings or a couple of ham hocks and a long simmering time are absolutely essential to a well-cooked vegetable. Cook it till it's *done*, Mama would say. Cook it till it's dead, we'd learn to say much later. When I first tasted a steamed vegetable, I thought it was raw. The Colemans were serious about their cooking and their eating. There was none of this eating on the run; meals lasted for hours; with lots of good conversation thrown in. The happiest I ever saw my aunts and uncles in the Coleman family was when they'd slowly eat their savory meals, washing everything down with several glasses of iced tea. Especially at the Family Reunion, or on Christmas Day up at Big Mom's house. "Eating good"—with plenty of fat and cholesterol—was held to be essential to proper health and peace of mind.

There were plenty of Colemans: nine brothers—known as "the boys"—and four sisters, the youngest of whom had died when she was a day or two old. (There's enough niggers in your mother's family, Daddy would remark, to cast a Tarzan movie.)

Sunday in Piedmont was everybody's favorite day, because you could eat yourself silly, starting just after church. Mama didn't go to church on Sundays, except to read out her obituaries. She'd cook while we were at Sunday school. Rarely did the menu vary: fried chicken, mashed potatoes, baked corn (corn pudding), green beans and potatoes (with lots of onions and bacon drippings and a hunk of ham), gravy, rolls, and a salad of iceberg lettuce, fresh tomatoes (grown in Uncle Jim's garden), a sliced boiled egg, scallions, and Wishbone's Italian dressing. We'd eat Mama's Sunday dinners in the middle of the day and keep nibbling for the rest of the afternoon and evening. White people just can't cook good, Aunt Marguerite used to say; that's why they need to hire us.

From a technical standpoint, this brief essay is written in the first-person point of view. At times, though, Gates seems to be writing from the first-person *plural* point of view, with sentences such as "We'd eat Mama's Sunday dinners in the middle of the day and keep nibbling for the rest of the afternoon and evening." Though it may occasionally seem that Gates is employing an omniscient perspective—he tells us what everyone in his family loves about Sunday dinners—the point of view is in fact limited. Those thoughts and observations he projects onto others in his family— "Sunday in Piedmont was everybody's favorite day"—are really just his thoughts. He assumes, as families often do, that everyone agrees.

Notice that Gates makes two important moves in his opening paragraph. The first line, simple and direct—"White people couldn't cook; everybody knew that"—clues us in that this essay will look at both race and food, and suggests that the author may be nonwhite. That is a lot of information conveyed, in just seven simple words. But Gates actually accomplishes even more with that brief sentence. Gates is welcoming the reader into his *intimate* point of view with the phrase "everybody knew that." If you *do* agree with Gates' assertion, or are willing to accept it for the brief time that you are reading, then you become part of the "everybody" in Gates' world.

Immediately after his opening sentence, Gates notes how it puzzled him that white restaurants were integrated in his youth, since "The food wasn't any good anyway." Gates is nudging the reader in the ribs and winking, stylistically at least. He is aware that his readership will include readers of all races, both rich and poor, some inclined to agree with his ideas about "white people" and cooking and some not inclined to agree at all. A little humor goes a long way toward putting everyone at ease.

But this essay is not *really* an argument about culinary accomplishment, and Gates is not trying to convince anyone as to who should win the best cooking prize. Gates' essay is instead a window into his childhood, and into the ways in which food and the Sunday afternoon rituals cemented the bonds of the Coleman family.

In establishing his voice, note that Gates sprinkles (like oregano, perhaps) a bit of dialect into the essay, "They don't know nothin' about seasoning, my Aunt Marguerite would say." He also uses a device that your grade school writing teacher would most likely have circled in red and marked as incorrect—the incomplete sentence. "Especially at the Family Reunion, or on Christmas Day up at Big Mom's house." Gates is an accomplished writer, so he certainly didn't drop this fragment into his essay because he doesn't know better. Why do you suppose he felt the incomplete sentence served his purpose at that point?

Much of the intimacy here is in the family secrets Gates chooses to share, and the generous description of the table laden with food: "fried chicken, mashed potatoes, baked corn (corn pudding), green beans and potatoes (with lots of onions and bacon drippings and a hunk of ham), gravy, rolls, and a salad of iceberg lettuce, fresh tomatoes (grown in Uncle Jim's garden), a sliced boiled egg, scallions, and Wishbone's Italian dressing." Instead of a weak line like "you can't imagine how much food there was," Gates puts us right at the table.

Additionally, look at the sentence Gates inserts in parentheses: "(There's enough niggers in your mother's family, Daddy would remark, to cast a Tarzan movie.)" Gates uses the "N word," a word most of us have been taught to avoid, and uses it in a humorous context.

Like every decision that a careful author makes, Gates surely weighed in his mind the effect of that joke, and that word, in that part of the essay. Does the father's use of the word allow us to see and understand something we might not have understood if we grew up in a very different family? Did it catch you off guard and make you think?

Gates is a noted author, African American scholar, and chair of Harvard University's African American studies program. If he were writing a scholarly essay, Gates would have used a very different voice. For this memoir essay, however, Gates avoided academic diction and professorial tone. "Big" words were not necessary, would have detracted from the sense of being with that small boy at the dinner table, and might only have added confusion.

Amy Tan, whose essay "Mother Tongue" is reproduced in the Anthology, writes about race and family as well. She shares intimate details of her Chinese-born mother's speech patterns and of her own embarrassment. "It has always bothered me that I can think of no way to describe it other than 'broken,'" she says of her mother's use of English words and syntax, "as if it were damaged and needed to be fixed, as if it lacked a certain wholeness or soundness."

Tan can tell us how difficult it is to negotiate two languages, to live with a parent who is only sometimes understood by others, to switch between two very separate linguistic worlds, but the power of the essay comes in the intimate details she chooses to share: the call to the stockbroker when Tan was fifteen, the trip to the doctor to find the lost CAT scan. We see the difficulties (and occasional humor) through Tan's point of view and can imagine ourselves in her spot.

For another example of intimate point of view, read Philip Gerard's "What They Don't Tell You About Hurricanes" in the Anthology. Gerard acknowledges the clichés we so often hear on the Weather Channel, but then shows us up close the sorts of details only a hurricane survivor would be able to relate: the penny-sized, suction-footed tree frogs that appear out of nowhere, the way that ice and air conditioning can seem miraculous when power is restored after a lengthy outage, the painful loss of a dream.

Revising for Voice and Point of View

The first step in revising for voice and point of view is to read what you have written already. Attempt, however, to read your work in progress as if you were not the author. Try to approach your text as if you were someone encountering these words for the first time.

Who is writing this? Do you get a sense of the person behind the pen (or keyboard)? Is the person funny or somber, passionate or lackadaisical? Do the word choices reflect the humor or seriousness of the subject at hand? If memoir, are we seeing this remembered world through the eyes of the child or through the more discerning eyes of an adult? Is the author letting you in on intimate, specific details that only someone who had been there, or who had observed closely, could share?

These questions are always worth asking, and often lead the way to stronger writing in later drafts.

Remember, though, achieving distinctive voice does not mean that you must sound intellectual or eccentric, or that you should riddle your pages with flowery words. It is not necessary for the writer's presence to leap off the page with every sentence. At times, in fact, a restrained voice is best, allowing the power of the story to take center stage.

Often, it is best to heed the wise advice of novelist and essayist Kurt Vonnegut:

> Find a subject you care about and which you in your heart feel others should care about. It is this genuine caring, not your games with language, which will be the most compelling and seductive element of your style.

WRITING PROMPTS: Distinctive Voice and Intimate
Point of View

1. After reading Philip Gerard's "What They Don't Tell You About Hurricanes," draft your own brief essay, entitled "What They Don't Tell You About _____." Avoid the truisms and clichés that everyone has already heard about your topic in favor of the intimate knowledge that comes from firsthand experience. This essay does *not* have to be about weather, of course. It could be "What They Don't Tell You About Childhood Asthma" or "What They Don't Tell You About Ice Fishing" or even a humorous "What They Don't Tell You About Babysitting Three-Year-Old Twins." Try to capture details that may surprise or give the reader a deeper understanding, and let the reader see from an "intimate" point of view.

2. Your family, like Henry Gates' family, most likely also had holiday dinners, but the food at your table was different from the food at

the Coleman table, because of either ethnicity, regional tastes, family idiosyncrasy, or unexplained tradition. Don't worry what the particulars mean for the moment, or if they have any meaning at all; just make an exhaustive list of all the distinct details in your childhood holiday meals, including not just the food, but the table setting, the people, the conversation. Is there an essay here? How can voice and point of view help you to capture not just the facts, but the flavor of your family?

3. Joan Didion has offered the opinion that even basic grammar and usage choices are part of the point-of-view equation. "To shift the structure of a sentence," she tells us, "alters the meaning of that sentence, as definitely and inflexibly as the position of a camera alters the meaning of the object photographed." Take an essay you are working on now, and change the sentence structure of a particular paragraph in as many different ways as you can devise: by breaking it up into short, abrupt sentences, or by combining three or more sentences into one very long sentence, or by altering the order of the words and independent clauses, or by adding parenthetical statements (like Jamaica Kincaid). Use alliteration. Play around with sentence structure in bold and unconventional ways, even if you think the result may be confusing. (You can always put it back.) When you are done playing, write a short analysis of how the meaning in your paragraph, or the emotional effect, or the rhythms of the words, or the sense of "the author" who is speaking, changed with each alteration.

Chapter Six

Building Blocks of Creative Nonfiction: Discovery

"I write personal essays to find out what I didn't know I knew."
—SYDNEY LEA

"I write to find out what I'm thinking, what I'm looking at, what I see, and what it means."

—JOAN DIDION

One reason that literary writing poses such a continuing challenge is that so many important elements of artistry and craft are involved. Writers are often compared to jugglers, because a serious author must endeavor to keep numerous balls in the air: concise writing, careful description, characterization, voice, point of view, and so on. Drop one of those balls, even briefly, and the reader will take notice.

Writers, of course, don't want readers distracted by dropped balls, inconsistent details, or awkward sentences, because the moment a reader becomes distracted, that reader is no longer fully caught up in the story or carefully listening to what the writer has to say. That is why successful writers pore over their work, draft after draft, until the writing seems perfect.[1]

But what is the purpose of all these balls circling in the air? Writers work hard to be clear and interesting because they want to communicate. They

---

[1] There is good news, however, within the juggling metaphor. A juggler has just one chance to perform perfectly, and that chance comes before a live audience. But if *you* as writer drop a ball, you can revise that sentence or paragraph until the act is perfect once again. Writers, like jugglers, must work very hard, but we have the considerable advantage of making *our* mistakes behind closed doors.

hope that the details and description, the characterization, the voice and intimate point of view in their memoir, literary journalism, or personal essay will ultimately achieve meaning or significance.

What You "Make of It"

Remember essayist Vivian Gornick's advice: "What happened to the writer is not what matters; what matters is the larger sense that the writer is able to *make* of what happened." Yet what you "make of it" can be one of the trickiest and most challenging aspects of creative nonfiction.

Even finding a precise name for this aspect of writing can be difficult. You have likely heard "theme" or "deeper meaning" used to describe a writer's ultimate conclusion, but these terms imply some deep "moral" to the story, or that the writer has set out to teach a lesson. Dropping some lesson to be learned into the last few sentences of an essay can often, however, result in a deadly thud. Interesting creative nonfiction becomes a sermon or a Sunday school parable.

Sometimes the term *universality* is used, but this word seems to deny the existence of unique experience or reflection. Often, your experience *will* resonate with other readers, because in the end human beings are very much alike and do share common feelings, but we are not alike in all ways. Moreover, our most idiosyncratic and peculiar reactions to events sometimes make far better reading than those stock outcomes we've all come to expect—when our high school classmate died unexpectedly, we were shocked and saddened.

For those reasons, we will use the term *discovery* to indicate the deeper subject or ideas that underlie a work of creative nonfiction. As the observations of Sydney Lea and Joan Didion at the head of this chapter indicate, the "significance" of a piece of nonfiction, why the story or ideas fascinate the author and why that writer wants to share them with readers, is often discovered only during the act of writing, in piecing together sentences and paragraphs.

"Writing is an act of faith, and nothing else," E. B. White once suggested. What he meant, perhaps, is that writing is exploration, and the success of your writing can often be measured by how open your mind is to discovery and how far you are willing to explore.

Rather than continuing to discuss discovery in the abstract, however, let's look at a specific example. Read this essay about an aging parent and see if you can identify the simple ways in which the author discovers and conveys his "deeper" ideas:

SOLSTICE

Richard Terrill

"Life used to be fun," my mother says a few days before her eighty-ninth birthday. "Now it's shit."

It's hard to argue with her. Her memory is such that she asks me questions and by the time I answer, she's forgotten what she's asked. Our conversations take on an Abbot and Costello circularity. Suddenly disagreeable, she starts every sentence with "but." She no longer remembers my father, and calls me by my brother's name.

"You just have to get out of bed and start your routine." I tell her. It's a lame proposition, I know.

"Why?" she asks.

Her contradictions, out of character for the person she used to be, are now the most rational feature of her discourse.

"I just want to be somewhere where I can help someone," she says.

She will never help anyone again, not even herself.

"I'm trying to be *a person*."

I walk her down to the lunchroom of the nursing home and sit with her next to her roommate "What's-Her-Name." Six months older than my mother, roommate Mabel has a broken knee that will now never heal, and a mind as cloudless as a mid-June day.

"When we got the farm, I cleared sixty acres of rocks," Mabel tells me. "*Sixty acres*. . . . But I loved it."

"This?" Mabel adds. "It's a hell of a life. But as long as I have my wits about me, I'll get by." I'm thinking that Mabel needs someone to point to who's got it worse than she does. Maybe we all need that.

After lunch I leave my mom and drive for the woods. I've forgotten my fishing gear back in the city, but on Audie Lake I paddle my kayak on a day that's a poster for Wisconsin in early summer. Wild irises are in bloom wherever sun hits the shoreline. Water lilies. The lake with many bays and inlets I can explore. There are no cottages; there is no development to mar the shore. There are two skiffs fishing, some kids laughing at a campsite out of view, a mother bald eagle tending her nest on a dead tree, wary of my little boat. Otherwise, only me. I drink two cans of beer in the sun and get delightfully toasted. I'm happy to forget who I am, one week before solstice, that mid point. It will be the longest day, but the hottest weather comes in July.

I load my kayak atop my car for the drive home. There in the sand of the parking lot is a painted turtle, just more than the size of my hand. She doesn't move, though I could touch her with my paddle. Could kill her. Except I love turtles, love all creatures of the lake and its shore.

What is she doing here, seeing me, yet not moving away? Is she lazy, like me, avoiding something, enjoying something else? No, she's laying eggs. On this one day when something in the water or the air or herself tells her it's time.

She makes a kicking motion to cover the hole she's dug, then ambles off, her shell pieces of a puzzle, black lined by orange, flash of orange from her underside. A yellow line along each cheek. Her legs ancient skin, sinuous. She can smell the lake and knows which way to go.

She's crawling through a parking lot, so I step behind her to quicken her pace. I follow her all the way back to the water, which she crawls into the way someone tired might crawl into bed. She is beautiful to me. There is no way those eggs will ever hatch, ever bring forth life.

Heading out of the woods and on my way home too, six more times I stop my car, hurry turtles out of the sand, in the middle of the gravel road, before they're run over by some driver who doesn't care.

Terrill's essay conveys his story through careful detail, in the precise description of his mother's failing mind and of her tenuous connection to the realities of everyday life. Later in the essay, he is equally careful and exact in describing the lake and the female painted turtle. Nowhere does Terrill tell us why he is relating these two events which occurred on the same early summer day, or what he hopes we will take away from his essay. His meaning, what he has discovered, becomes clear through the details he chooses to share.

For instance, of the turtle (a mother), he says "I could touch her with my paddle. Could kill her." This is a jarring moment in the essay, and a brief switch in tone, but certainly not a haphazard one. Notice that Terrill relies on a sentence fragment here, setting this odd revelation apart from the sentences on either side. He wants it to be noticed.

Why? Unless we interview the author and ask him directly, as readers we can only speculate. Perhaps the moment suggests that the writer may be angry at his mother. Watching a parent go downhill in this manner is always difficult, and though the author certainly loves his mother, the truth is that we can love someone and be angry at them at the same time. Or perhaps he is worried ahead to a day when he may be asked to "pull the plug" on life support, as his mother's condition inevitably worsens. These are speculations, not certainties, as to why the author inserted this moment in this way, but Terrill has given us the clues to work with.

Understand, too, that the author himself may not be 100 percent positive why he added that detail ("Could kill her") and why in revision he decided to leave that detail in the essay. He may not even be entirely certain why he chose to talk about his mother's deterioration and his afternoon trip to the lake in the same essay. This is the essence of discovery. Like Didion, Terrill likely writes to find out what he's thinking, what he's looking at, and what it means. What Terrill *does* know, however, is that when he puts these two subjects—the visit to his mother, and his encounter with the painted turtle—one against the other, something interesting occurs. So he embarks on White's "act of faith," and attempts to discover the truth.

If you are dead set on understanding what Terrill "means" by this essay, or what he feels that he has discovered, an important clue may be in the title. The day Terrill so carefully describes for us occurred one week before summer solstice. Solstice has long symbolized a turning point in the lives of human beings: the seasons change, and people stop to take stock of themselves. Terrill might, in fact, have titled his work "Turning Point"—his mother is clearly at a turning point in her life, and the author may have reached his own turning point by the end of the essay. He is helping along every turtle he sees stranded on the gravel road, "before they're run over by some driver who doesn't care." A reader can easily see the possible connections between Terrill's actions with the turtles and his need to take responsibility for an aging parent. Beyond that, Terrill is perhaps reminding us of the healing power of the natural world, and of how our connection to simple things—a Wisconsin lake in early summer—sometimes allows for clearer perspective.

One of the greatest challenges for a beginning writer is learning to put experience under the creative nonfiction microscope in order to see what is really there, all the while remaining open to the small, unexpected revelation. Terrill's brief essay serves as a good example. He isn't making a major point about politics or national health care, lecturing us, or trying to describe "the meaning of life." He is simply showing the reader, so that we might understand a bit more now than we did before, the conflicting feelings an adult often experiences when faced with an elderly parent who doesn't even remember his name. What he has discovered in his essay, and what he is sharing with us, is not the most flattering portrait possible. It is not, "Look at me, I'm the perfect son, and I always do the right thing." Instead, Terrill shares his honest struggles. Is it possible to love someone deeply and still be filled with irritation and impatience? Of course.

Here is another example of discovery, by the Mexican American author Norma Elia Cantú:

Tino & Papi
Norma Elia Cantú

I. Tino

In the photo, he stands to the side with his hand out as if pointing a gun or a rifle. Everyone else, sisters, cousins, friends, neighbors crowd around me; the piñata in the shape of a birthday cake sways in the wind above our heads. Everyone's there: aunts, uncles, cousins, the neighbors, my madrina, everyone, even Mamagrande Lupita from Monterrey. I'm holding the stick decorated with red, blue, yellow tissue paper that we will use to break the piñata. And at age nine he holds out the imaginary gun, like a soldier. Only ten years later, 1968, he is a soldier, and it's not a game. And we are gathered again: tias, dos, cousins, comadres, neighbors, everyone, even Mamagrande Lupita from Monterrey, and Papi's cousin Ricardo who's escorted the body home. We have all gathered around a flag-draped coffin. Tino's come home from Vietnam. My brother. The sound of the trumpet caresses our hearts and Mami's gentle sobbing sways in the cool wind of March.

II. Papi

On the wall, the image of the Virgen de San Juan, a pale rose background, grayish black outline, shines like silver in the dark. Bueli lights candles when Tino is so sick el Doctor del Valle, the doctor across the river in Nuevo Laredo, fears he will die. He's only three. The illness has taken over. But Papi cries in front of another image of our Lady. It's a calendar from Cristo Rey Church with the image of Nuestra Senora del Perpetuo Socorro. He prays, he weeps, hits the wall with his fists, like he would hit the mesquite tree in the backyard with his head sixteen years later like a wounded animal, mourning, in pain, that morning when Tino's death came to our door. But the child Tino survives the illness; the injections, the medication, the prayers, the remedios—something works, and Papi frames the calendar image in gold leaf, builds the image a repisita—a shelf for candles. In 1968, in his pain, tears running down his face, he'll talk to the image, "For this, you spared my son," he'll take the image down from its place on the wall, cannot bear to see it, to be reminded. On the wall, a rectangle of nothing, the color of the wallpaper Mami had hung for Tio Moy's last visit three years ago, like new-lines of green fern leaves on dusty beige. The votive candle on the tiny shelf is left burning to an empty space.

Cantú, you may have noticed, makes some interesting choices here. First, she tells this whole story—a highly complex tale of family, childhood sickness, religion, and war—in just two paragraphs. The second interesting choice is that she moves forward and backward in time, rather than holding to chronological order. She opens with the photo of her brother at age nine, and then moves quickly forward to 1968, when her brother has returned in a casket from Vietnam. In the second section, Cantu goes backward in time again, to when her brother was three and seriously ill, and then returns again to 1968, a time when her grieving father removes the picture of the Virgen de San Juan.

Quite simply, this is the story of a young brother who died at war, but there is clearly much to be discovered here, threads relating to hope, prayer, family, and loss of faith. Every detail—the boy at nine holding his hand out "as if pointing a gun," the "new-lines of green fern leaves" on the wallpaper (echoing the jungles of Vietnam), the extended family, "even Mamagrande Lupita from

Monterrey," gathered first for a festive birthday and then for a premature funeral—points to the central irony of prayers answered when Tino was three but denied when he was nineteen, yet Cantú never lectures or explains.

Cantú doesn't tell us what we should think. Perhaps there is nothing to think about such a horrible turn of events. She allows us, instead, to feel some of her pain and confusion, and the horrible anguish of her father. She allows us to discover the significance for ourselves.

Discovery and Details

Another way of looking at discovery is to notice how the essays we have examined thus far have two subjects: the subject closest at hand and an underlying subject.

Richard Terrill's "Solstice" is an account of the author's visit to his mother's nursing home and later to a lake, but the underlying subject is aging, grief, and responsibility. Though "Tino & Papi" is about a brother's funeral, Cantu raises a deeper issue that has bothered human beings for centuries: Why do terrible things happen, even to families that worship, pray, and believe? In Chapter Four, the essay "Drink It" is simply the recollection of a day when the author received disturbing news, but it is also a story about regret and guilt.

Note, however, that the underlying story, or discovery, in each of these essays is found in the details related by the author, not in explanatory sentences or ending summaries. Terrill doesn't have to tell us what his essay means or why it seems significant to him; a careful reader can find plenty to think about in the descriptions of his mother, her words, and his own reactions. Cantu doesn't have to raise difficult issues of faith and doubt because these issues are embedded in the action, especially when the father takes down the Virgen de San Juan calendar.

This concept of showing the reader rather than lecturing or explaining is central to all of creative nonfiction. When readers see for themselves what has happened, or follow for themselves the circuitous path of the author's thinking and emotions, they have all the information they need to draw their own conclusions. Those conclusions will inevitably ring far truer than "packaged" homilies.

It is human nature to think "I'll believe it when I see it," and therefore it is the creative nonfiction writer's job to let readers see and experience. Moreover, the process of reading carefully crafted details and forming one's own opinion is far more interesting to the reader than a lecture or explanation.

Revising for Discovery

This idea of discovery in creative nonfiction is perhaps the greatest challenge for a beginning writer. Whether working on memoir, a journalistic account of a recent event, or the exploration of thoughts and feelings in a personal essay, it is not uncommon for any writer to wonder "what's interesting about this and why would a reader care?" The truth is, sometimes you often don't know at the beginning. That is why E. B. White calls writing "an act of faith."

Another reason discovery can be difficult is that discovery takes time. There simply is no reliable shortcut.

The first method for dealing with these challenges is to acknowledge them: understand that you might begin writing simply because an incident or idea is stuck in your head somehow, though you will have no clear idea of the underlying story or where it might take you after two or three drafts. Understand too that your understanding of what you have discovered may not be immediate. It likely will not happen as soon as you would like.

Let's say, however, that you have done two or three drafts of an essay and still feel that nothing is clear and little has been discovered. Distance and perspective are two ways to work on discovery problems in revision.

Distance means stepping away and letting your early draft simmer on a back burner. Countless authors will tell you from experience that setting the work aside briefly to do something else, perhaps strolling around the neighborhood or vacuuming the rug, or even taking a day or two to work on another project, gives a fresh perspective upon returning. Sometimes you need to take your eyes away from the page a while in order to see what is really there.

The other way to gain perspective is to show the work to someone you trust, but you must trust that this person will be honest, not blindly supportive. (A friend who says "this is great" no matter what you write is no friend at all, at least where revision and improvement is concerned.) Ask your friend or outside reader, "What does this mean to you? What does it seem like I am trying to say?" If you take this step, by all means don't be defensive, don't argue, and don't explain what you *meant* to say. Your job at this point of the revision process is to just listen. The fresh eyes of the reader may help you to discover something in the work that you hadn't seen.

Once you feel that you can define the underlying story or discovery of your essay—"This is about my worry as a child that I would never live up to the legacy of my dead cousin," or "This is about the conflict between my strict religious upbringing and an urge to go out and experience the world"— pull out the yellow highlighter you used to define scenes in Chapter Four and highlight the various moments, details, and interactions that shed light on the underlying emotions or questions. Do each of your scenes and most of your details directly or obliquely relate to the essay's discovered center?

This is where the cutting begins. You may find a section of your essay that no longer belongs, despite being clearly written and well described. Setting aside a piece of an essay that you have been working on for weeks because the essay has grown to be about something else is always difficult, sometimes heartbreaking. But successful writers will tell you that this is an integral part of the discipline and process. You may also discover at this point that a scene or detail is missing. Now is the time to add it in.

Earlier in this chapter, it was suggested that a deadly thud could often be heard when a writer dropped a lesson or moral into the last few sentences of an essay. If you find that you are explaining too much, or are trying too hard to drive home your point, one revision strategy is to merely take that explanation out. Use your Delete key wisely. Perhaps the explanation is not needed, because the details, description, scenes, and other elements of your essay already contain all that the reader needs.

Excellent writing is a process of trial and error, addition and subtraction, making your best attempt and then refining the result. Expecting a complete and brilliant work of prose to appear at your fingertips the first time you sit down to write is only setting yourself up for frustration and failure. Like any activity worth doing, successful writing demands hard work, repeated over time.

WRITING PROMPTS: Discovery

1. Write a brief essay entitled "The One Minute I Regret the Most." Focusing on such a brief period of time—the exact moment when you made a decision or took an action that you later regretted, or when something unfortunate happened to you that was out of your control—is an excellent exercise in forcing description, detail, and dialogue. You have only sixty seconds to work with, so you might as well describe it all. Moreover, you may very well find that the entire story—as well as the underlying discovery—is fully encapsulated in just that brief moment of time.

2. In the essays by Terrill and Cantu, essentially two separate incidents are described. The "meaning" or significance is not found in one—Terrill's visit to the nursing home/Cantu's brother recovering from a grave childhood illness—or in the other—the turtle at the lake/the brother's death in Vietnam. Rather, these essays have depth because the two parts are more interesting when set one against the other. The reader discovers what is most interesting about these essays when considering the incidents side by side. What two events in your life, separated by thirteen years or just an afternoon's drive, might take on meaning when placed together in this way? Make a list of three or four pairs, and then choose one. Mimic Terrill or Cantu, if you wish, or find your own unique form and voice, but write the essay, sticking to the details and leaving all explanation on the cutting room floor.

PART III

~~~~

From Building Blocks to Complete Essay

CHAPTER SEVEN

The Memoir Essay

CHAPTER EIGHT

The Literary Journalism Essay

CHAPTER NINE

The Personal Essay

CHAPTER TEN

Revision and Narrative Structure

Chapter Seven

The Memoir Essay

"I think the purpose of the memoir, the same as the purpose of the novel or any other writing, is to enlighten. It is to bring light where there is darkness."

—SUSAN CHEEVER

"Writing is a struggle against silence."

—CARLOS FUENTES

As you might guess from the word itself, memoir has its roots in memory. Often, that memory may relate to childhood, with an adult writer looking back at her early life to consider how certain youthful experiences shaped and molded the person that she has become. All memoirs are not about childhood, however. Memoirs have been written about a person's years away at college, about marriage, about childbirth and child rearing, and even about retirement. Memoir can relate to any period of someone's life, as long as the writing derives energy and interest from an exploration of past events.

William Zinser describes memoir this way: "Unlike autobiography, which moves in a dutiful line from birth to fame, memoir narrows the lens, focusing on a time in the writer's life that was unusually vivid, such as childhood or adolescence, or that was framed by war or travel or public service or some other special circumstance."

Though memoir takes as its subject the life of the author, Zinser is making clear that successful memoir is almost always driven by an event or circumstance outside the norm, an "unusually vivid" episode. This circumstance needn't be extreme or newsworthy, but it has to have caught the writer's imagination, shifted the writer's world in some way, and that shift is what the writer takes the time to carefully illuminate and examine.

Memoir has become increasingly popular for readers and writers over the past few decades. A strongly written account of some episode in another person's life allows us, as readers, to see ourselves, to weigh the choices *we* have made, to wonder how *we* might have acted, and to consider the endless variety of human experience.

Examining the Memoir Essay

Though memoir will occasionally focus on life-changing or tragic events—battling a disease, seeking refuge from war or famine, a violent childhood—even a simple moment spent at a common task might be a fruitful subject. What matters is that the writer sees some significance in the moment, and can communicate that significance to a reader.

Look at this memoir essay by Bret Lott, an award-winning author of novels and works of nonfiction:

GENESIS

Bret Lott

I am sitting in the sanctuary, a few rows from the front, to my left my mom and dad, my little brother Timmy in Mom's lap and sleeping, to my right my older brother Brad. Brad and I have just received these thin blue books, every kid in the service passed a brand new copy by men in gray or black suits standing at either end of the pews, stacks of these books in hand.

The blue paper cover is bordered with green grapevines, tendrils working up and down either side with bunches of grapes here and there; at the top and bottom of the cover those tendrils meet sheaves of wheat in the same green ink.

The pastor says it is the book of *somms,* and I wonder what that is, look at the words in black ink centered a little high on the cover. I sound out the words to myself, The Book of, and stop.

P-S-A-L-M-S. How does that, I wonder, spell out *Somms?*

But even if I don't understand, this is the first Bible—or piece of it—I have ever gotten, and I don't want to lose this book. I want to keep it.

So I take one of the nubby pencils from the back of the pew in front of me, nestled in its tiny wooden hole beside the wooden shelf where attendance forms are kept, and beside the larger holes where the tiny glass cups are placed once we've emptied them of grape juice.

And I begin, for the first time in my life, to write my name by myself.

I start at the upper left hand corner, just below the border, but the first word trails off, falls toward that centered title in black as though that title is a magnet, the letters I make iron filings. They fall that way because there are no lines for me to balance them upon, as

I am able to do with the paper given me by my kindergarten teacher, Mrs. Pasley.

I finish that first word, feel in my hand the cramp of so much strenuous, focused work, and hold the book away from me, look at it while the pastor rolls on.

There is no place for the second word, I see, the last letter of my first name too near the first of the title.

This is a problem. I know the second word must follow the first on the same line, a little space needed between them. Mrs. Pasley would not approve. This is a problem.

But there is space above my name due to its falling away, a wedge of blue field that might, if I am careful enough, be able to hold that second word, and I write, work out the riddle of letters without lines, letters that will line up to mark this book as mine, and mine only.

Then I am finished, and here is my name. Me.

The first time I have ever written my name myself, alone.

Later, on the way home, my older brother Brad will look at the book, say, "Lott Bret. Who's that?" and laugh at my ill-spaced effort. Later still I will write my name again on the cover, this time with a blue pen and holding the book upside down. The words will be a little more jaunty, full of themselves and the confidence of a kid who knows how to write his name, no problem at all. Beneath this second round, though, will be the lone letter B, a practice swing at making that capital letter as good as I can make it.

Later, I will be baptized into the church at age fourteen, a ritual it seems to me is the right thing to do.

Later still, in college, I will be born again, as Christ instructed Nicodemus.

And later even still, I will have written entire books of my own, created lives out of the whole cloth of the imagination. I will have created, and created in my name.

But on this Sunday, the pastor still rolling on, these two words themselves are enough.

Only a kid's scrawl. My own small imitation of God.

Lott confines his memoir to a brief span of time—the few minutes it takes him, at age five, to scrawl his name on the cover of his new psalm book, and the short moment on the way home when his older brother Brad makes fun of his childish effort. These are scenes, with carefully chosen dialogue and description. Notice that the essay begins with Lott and his family already in church, already in the pew, just as the new books are handed out. Lott doesn't waste any time filling in background—what we need to know becomes clear enough as the story unfolds.

Notice too that Lott writes almost entirely from the kindergarten-aged child's point of view. We see what the five-year-old saw, and thus those matters that confused Lott as a child are simply presented as confusing—"P-S-A-L-M-S. How does that, I wonder, spell out *Somms*?"

Only in the few closing lines does the adult Bret Lott enter the picture and pull back to give the reader a fuller view of what this memory means to him. The last seven sentences cover a lot of ground—Lott's religious faith, the connection he feels between his work as a writer and the biblical story of creation, and how all of this may tie back to that small moment in kindergarten when he first wrote his name on a cover.

Had Lott lectured us about his beliefs, or insisted that we agree with his views, this would have been a very different essay. Instead, his process of discovery allows us to see for ourselves how religion connects with his creative urge. Whether you find your views similar to his or quite different, he gives us plenty to think about when we are done reading.

Perhaps you too have strongly held religious beliefs, or perhaps you have intense feelings about where religion has failed. Whichever is the case, creative nonfiction challenges you to find, as Lott has found here, a moment or two that bring the picture to life and represent the truth of your experience.

Here is a very different essay. Author Sonja Livingston attempts a portrait of herself, and her world as a child of poverty and shame, in only 255 words:

THUMB-SUCKING GIRL

Sonja Livingston

Look at me.

At me, over here.

Look and shake your head. At my uneven bangs, these broken-down shoes, my momma, all us kids, and all our belongings shoved into just one car. Whisper and sigh all you want because I have something better than good clothes and a permanent address. I've got my thumb. My right thumb to be precise—and the soft pink underside of its arch. Forget that the nail on that thumb grows smooth and flat as the inside of a seashell on account of all that sucking. Forget that my mother has tried everything (except hot pepper and mustard on my thumb like my cousin Judith suggests, because my mother—though determined to rid me of my disgusting habit—thinks pepper and mustard too cruel for a child). Forget that I once deprived myself of the luxury of my thumb for a whole month just to show I could. Forget that my teeth have begun to split down the front, that the space will stretch wide eventually, will ruin my permanent teeth according to my mother. Forget all that and understand that the plug of it in my mouth is what brings me sleep and until you've plopped a thumb into your mouth and sucked on it while using the index finger of that same hand to cradle the line of bone under your eye, to rub up and down the fleshy valley of your nose—until you have done such a thing, you know nothing of comfort.

Perhaps your first reaction to this essay is negative—"I don't want to hear about that!" Such a reaction is understandable. Livingston asks the reader to consider a number of subjects which people often find unpleasant or disturbing—thumb sucking, childhood poverty, our habit of shaking our heads in disapproval at "the way some people live" instead of trying to help.

Livingston is aware that these issues may upset readers, and her choices about voice and point of view seem to address our discomfort. Notice how Livingston addresses the reader directly—"Look at me"—from the very first sentence. She remains in the child's perspective throughout, inviting us to see through the eyes of a child why sucking a thumb may be worth all of the negative feedback and parental warnings.

Livingston seems to be saying "don't be so quick to judge," but rather than offering up a lecture, she uses detail and description in order to put us in the child's shoes. Livingston (writing as an adult) doesn't expect you, the reader, to agree that a soft pink thumb is "something better than good clothes and a permanent address," but perhaps you can see why she, as a young child, might have thought so, and why she resented the stares of disapproval.

Writing Your Own Memoir Essay

Your first step in writing a memoir essay is to review possible ideas. If you completed writing prompts at the end of previous chapters, now would be a good time to look back at the material generated by those prompts. Consider also the questions posed in the prompts at that end of this chapter. Sometimes an idea fails to pan out as well as a writer first expects, so having a few different ideas to consider is good practice.

If you are truly ambitious, try writing a quick rough draft of three different ideas, and see which one looks most interesting after that step. Work on the one that raises the most questions.

But no matter what your idea or which moment of your past life you choose to explore, keep these suggestions in mind:

- Choose a brief period of time. If you try to cover many months or years of your life in your essay, all you will likely produce is summary. The goal is sharp detail and careful description.
- Consider point of view. Are you at your current age, looking back at an event, considering it from hindsight? Or are you letting the reader see some situation from the perspective of yourself at that earlier age? Try it both ways.

- Remember that the reader has no idea who you are and has no preconceived picture of your friends or family. How can you use dialogue and action to bring the "characters" alive in your true story? What specific traits best differentiate your grandmother or grandfather from everyone else's grandparents?
- Author Patricia Hampl has said, "Memoir isn't for reminiscence; it's for exploration." What she means is that the narrative urge should spring from the writer's desire to better understand his or her world, not merely to explain it or recall what it was like. Writing memoir is a journey of discovery.

Beginning writers should remember that simply because an event happened it is not necessarily suitable material for a memoir meant to be shared with a general readership. Let's say you took a vacation to Disney World and had a fantastic time. That fantastic time, moreover, is loaded with resonance for you and your immediate family or the friends who traveled with you. Recalling that vacation can be fun, certainly, but these mere memories are not fodder for a successful memoir unless you can find some aspect of the event or time that will be of interest to a reader who did *not* share the experience.

Is there some greater reason for recounting your happy memory? Is there some part of that experience that you still don't understand, or some aspect that troubles you and continues to be a source of contemplation? As much fun as a trip to Disney World can be, the Orlando theme park is a very artificial environment, with synthetic trees, animatronic jungle creatures, and simulated thrills. Do you see people around you spending more and more of their time enjoying artificial or virtual activities, instead of spending time with friends and family?

Or let's say, for another example, you recently traveled to Central America for the first time. Does some feature of that trip—the cultural differences you observed, your own feelings of being "on the outside" in a culture where everyone else seemed comfortable and at home—raise some interesting issues? Do you suddenly see how disorienting and perhaps at times even frightening it must be for a foreigner visiting your nation?

In other words, the impulse "you should have been there, it was really great" doesn't usually result in interesting writing—not interesting to the reader at least, and keeping your reader awake, alert, and engaged is your goal in all forms of creative nonfiction.

But "Who Cares?"

The idea that just because it happened doesn't make it interesting to others seems to beg the question, "Why would anyone care?" Why do readers care about Henry Louis Gates' childhood, Richard Terrill's aging mother, or

Norma Elia Cantu's brother Tino? Why would they care about you, your family, or your experience?

Part of the answer, of course, is curiosity. Any dedicated reader brings along a healthy interest in other people and other lives. Whenever a story is vividly told, that story is a distinct pleasure to read and experience.

But the other reason people care relates to what the writer has made of the experience and how the author's discovery often rings true for a wide readership. Scott Russell Sanders, author of the essay "Buckeye," has written beautifully about how his own personal moments become fodder for literary memoir. "I assume the public does not give a hoot about my private life," he tells us. "If I write of hiking up a mountain with my one-year-old boy riding like a papoose on my back, and of what he babbled to me while we gazed down from the summit onto the scudding clouds, it is not because I am deluded into believing that my baby, like the offspring of Prince Charles, matters to the great world. It is because I know the great world produces babies of its own and watches them change cloudfast before its doting eyes . . . I choose to write about my experience not because it is mine, but because it seems to me a door through which others might pass."

Even David Sedaris, a humorist who writes tongue in cheek about the most absurd situations, touches basic human experience with his work. Take a look at "The Drama Bug" in the Anthology. Most likely, none of us has ever felt compelled to speak lines such as "Perchance, fair lady, thou dost think me unduly vexed by the sorrowful state of thine quarters" when encountering our mother vacuuming the living room carpet. But despite what appears to be obvious exaggeration,[1] Sedaris is examining a situation common to many: when we become very interested, even obsessed, with some new subject (in Sedaris's case, Shakespearean drama), it is common human behavior to want everyone around us to share our enthusiasm and honor our new interest.

Essayist Michel de Montaigne once said, "Every man has within himself the entire human condition." We all know grief, fear, longing, fairness, and unfairness. We all worry about losing someone dear to us. We crave attention, from everyone, or from certain people. We love our families, yet sometimes those families greatly disappoint us. All of us who hold deep religious

---

[1] Sedaris raises an interesting test to the limits of creative nonfiction in most of his writing. Though he is writing memoir based on actual life experiences, he often seems to skirt the edges of honesty and accuracy in order to increase the humor. The same might be said of earlier humorists, such as James Thurber or Robert Benchley, who drew on their own lives for material. There is, of course, no Supreme Court of Creative Nonfiction to rule on whether Sedaris's hilarious essays are really nonfiction or whether his work belongs in another category entirely. There is no doubt, however, that Sedaris is very, very funny.

beliefs also know that moments come along when those beliefs are hard to maintain. These basic human worries and emotions will always resonate when brought clearly to life on the page.

WRITING PROMPTS: Memoir

1. Henry Louis Gates wrote vividly about family meals in his essay "Sunday." Home and family is more than just food, however. Take the time to list the differences in your childhood home, as compared to the homes of everyone up and down the block (or country road). Go room to room in your memory (or actually visit, if you can) and make note of each distinctive detail: the pictures on the wall, the clothes in the front closet, the sports gear on the back porch, the medications in the medicine cabinet, the comforters on the beds, the boxes in the basement (and the contents of those boxes), the music in your parents' album or CD collection, your sister's posters, the hair products, the family photos, the junk in the garage, the knickknacks on the dining room shelf. These all seem so normal to you, because they were part of your life, but attempt to see them through the eyes of a reader, and imagine what might seem peculiar or fascinating. What sets your family apart, and where is the hidden story?

2. Curiosity is one of the best impulses from which to begin any form of writing, and that certainly includes memoir. Make a list of six to ten events or circumstances in your own life, or the lives of those very close to you, that still provoke your curiosity. Why did your high school soccer coach seem to ignore you, even though you were trying so hard to do well? Why did your Uncle Ted divorce his wife after only one year of marriage, when to the outside world everything seemed fine? Why did your former good friend suddenly make a choice in lifestyle or acquaintances that you thought was clearly ill-advised, perhaps even dangerous? These are just examples, of course. Mine your own life for the events and circumstances that still raise questions in your mind. Once you have the list (and this list should be private—don't share it with others—and don't hold back because you think someone else will be looking), pick one of the questions on the list that you are willing to explore. Don't try to answer it right away, or "solve" it. Just write down as much as you can remember—facts, details, conversations, descriptions of the people and places involved. Ask questions on

the page that you think cannot be answered. Feel free to speculate as to what others might have been thinking, or why they acted the way that they did (and label it as speculation, since this is nonfiction). Consider possible reasons, even if they seem at first unlikely. Write some sentences examining where *you* may have misunderstood, acted badly in some small or large way, or contributed to the problem. Once you have done all of this, and taken some time really thinking it over, look at your notes. This may be the essay you need to write.

3. Livingston speaks directly to the reader: "Look at me. At me, over here. Look and shake your head." This is something she can say as an adult, in her essay, but that she couldn't say as a young child. What is it that you couldn't say as a child? What is it that people didn't understand about you or your family, because they couldn't see your world or understand the circumstances? Can you write about it now? Can you help the reader to see from the child's point of view?

Chapter Eight

The Literary Journalism Essay

"People say, 'Your books read like novels' . . . well the techniques of storytelling don't belong exclusively to fiction."
—TRACY KIDDER

Literary journalism is the creative nonfiction genre that comes closest to traditional newspaper or magazine reporting. Instead of centering directly on the author's life experiences, as memoir primarily does, literary journalism focuses on some person, event, place, or idea outside of the writer's direct life experience.

An author writing literary journalism may be exploring aspects of nature or geography, like John McPhee in his books *Coming into the Country* and *The Survival of the Bark Canoe*, or may be examining social history, as Melissa Faye Greene does in *Praying for Sheetrock*, an account of the difficult movement toward racial integration in parts of rural Georgia. In some cases, literary journalism centers on another individual, in the form of a profile, like Gay Talese's essay "Frank Sinatra Has a Cold." In other cases, literary journalism might center on an idea. Pico Iyer, for instance, whose journey into the unseen corners of the Los Angeles airport is excerpted later in this chapter, has spent a lifetime chronicling the changing definitions of *home* and *nationality* in our increasingly global culture.

Though memoir and personal essay are often both enhanced by research, literary journalism depends on it. The basic building blocks, such as detail and description, scene, voice, and discovery, all still apply. Point of view, however, is sometimes handled differently.

In memoir and personal essay, the point of view is almost always that of the author. Literary journalism can be written from the first-person perspective as well, but in some cases point of view in literary journalism is not primarily the author's perspective.

Writers like Tracy Kidder have spent weeks, months, and years living with the subjects of their nonfiction accounts, observing them closely, asking them about their inner thoughts, studying their every action and reaction, so that they could write accurately from the point of view of another person. Kidder's essay on writing, "Making the Truth Believable," found in the Anthology, offers more insight on his process.

Lee Gutkind's essay "Difficult Decisions," which appears in the Anthology, uses both the author's point of view *and* occasionally that of his subject. The essay begins clearly in Gutkind's point of view as observer, but also provides sections that allow the reader access to the veterinarian's inner perspective.

Consider this passage:

> Sometimes the veterinarian, shivering violently in the freezing night air, drained of all energy and spirit, will begin to envision the unmentionable but tempting notion of failure—of giving up—and the alluring rewards such a decision might bring: warmth, food, coffee, sleep.
>
> But even in triumph, when the calf is finally pulled out, she will often experience a momentary and panicky feeling of failure. Calves in difficult births frequently look dead when they are first born. Their eyes are glassy; their tongues bloated.

Gutkind is attempting to portray what Dr. Wendy Freeman faces during a long, cold night on her job, especially when the calf delivery is not going well. Moreover, he wants us to *feel* some of the emotions and confusion that the vet might herself be feeling out there in the field, surrounded by mud, pouring rain, and the worried farmer.

How does he know these things, since Gutkind is not a veterinarian? The answer is simple: he asked.

Literary journalists don't just stand back in the corners. They engage the subject, in whatever ways are possible. That is why literary journalism is sometimes called immersion journalism: a writer in this genre works hard to become immersed in the subject at hand. Whether you are writing about a person, a particular place, the world of veterinary medicine, or the effects of Ritalin on schoolchildren, the key to successful literary journalism starts with close and detailed observation.

What you can't find out by simply watching—what the subject is thinking, for instance, or the mental steps he goes through before making a particular decision—can be learned through the interview, or sometimes by trying an activity yourself. If you are writing about the fellow who makes two hundred pizzas each night, ask if you can help. Feel the weight of the dough and try tossing it in the air. If you are writing about the world of whitewater rafting, you should probably get into a raft.

By all means, spend the time it takes to look at your subject closely. The nonfiction writer is faced with the task of recognizing and recording the significant detail that is often missed by those who just pay a cursory glance.

The writing invariably falls flat and is uninteresting when the writer only captures the stereotype or paints the conventional portrait that many observers have discovered and recorded before. Readers are not interested in a quick impression—they can do that for themselves. They are looking for depth and complexity.

Examining the Literary Journalism Essay

Look at the following essay by Brian Doyle. (You may remember another Doyle essay, "Pop Art," from Chapter Five.) Doyle chooses as his subject one woman and her challenging life, and though his essay spans many years, he keeps the focus very tight—what she told him.

HOPE

Brian Doyle

I met a woman named Hope recently. She is seventy-nine years old. She was born on Fourth Street in San Francisco. Her mother was a nurse. Her father sold flowers. When she was an infant her father was crushed by a train. When she was seven her brother drowned. When she was seventeen she and her mother and brother and sister were evicted from their house by the state of California and sent to live in a horse stall at a racetrack with other men and women and children of Japanese ancestry.

My brother slept in the front of the stall, she says, and my mother and sister and I slept in the rear of the stall. It was raining on the night we arrived there. We were given Army mattress covers and told to go to the barn and fill them with hay. We were there six months. Then we were sent to Camp Topaz in Utah. It was in the high desert. The barracks was made of wood and tar-paper. In the winter it was very cold and in the summer the dust came through the windows and doors and walls.

In the camp I went to high school and became engaged to a boy named Hiroshi. He was Japanese. His family was sent back to Japan on prisoner exchange. I went with them. We were two months at sea. We slept on the deck. We washed our hair in the rain when the rain came every afternoon. We went around Africa. The captain of the ship told us one day that Japan was losing the war and there wasn't enough food in Japan and he would let us off the ship before we got to Japan if we wanted to get off. All the young people on the ship had a meeting and we decided to get off the ship in Singapore or Manila. I got off in Singapore. All the ones who got off in Manila were killed. Where I was the bombs fell all around. When the war ended all I had was the clothes on my back. All the women were scared of rape so they cut their hair real short like a man.

I went on to Japan. First time I ever set foot there. It was very cold and we sewed coats and pants from blankets. I left Hiroshi because he treated me badly. I found a job with the United States Eighth Army. That's how I met my husband. His name was Art. He had red hair. He was Scottish, English, Irish, and Cherokee was in there too. All the other American soldiers worked very hard but he seemed to spend all his time fooling around and teasing the girls. One day the promotion list came out and I took his name off. He didn't get the promotion. When he found out he came storming into the office and lit me up and down and I heard words I never heard before. Two weeks later he came to apologize and he brought me silk stockings. A month later he invited me to the theater with him. We went to see the Mikado. That was our first date.

After a while he asked me to get married. I said no: I had to go home and find out what happened to my family. So he said okay, fine, and he went home to Oklahoma. I saved my money and a year later I went home, and when my ship came into San Francisco there was Art waiting for me at the wharf. He asked me to get married again and I said no again. Then he went to my family and asked my brother if he could marry me and my brother said no. I went to work at a hospital and lived in a rooming house, and Art was working for the railroad and living in a rooming house. He kept asking me to get married and I kept saying no but finally one day I said yes. We got married in the morning at city hall and moved in together that afternoon and I was so excited I got sick and that was our honeymoon, me sick in our new apartment and Art taking care of me.

Hope folds her hands in her lap and smiles. She tells me about their two sons, one named for Davy Crockett, and about the house they built in the California mountains, and how her husband lost his voice at the end of his life, which was a great blow to the both of them, for he loved to tease her and she loved to hear him, and how when she was a little girl she loved to run barefoot in the city, and how in summer she and her sister and brothers would sing on the roof of their building at night, huddled and hungry and happy, a long time ago but not very long ago at all.

Notice how Doyle launches into this piece using a simple and direct voice— "I met a woman named Hope recently"—and notice too the subtle shift in point of view in the second paragraph. Doyle made a conscious decision to let the woman tell her own story, so he dispenses with "she says" or "she told me" for most of the essay. Only at the end does he shift back: "Hope folds her hands in her lap and smiles. She tells me about their two sons. . . ."

You may notice too that Doyle chooses not to put quotation marks around Hope's dialogue. Why do you suppose he made this choice? Does it create confusion, as you might expect, or does Doyle find a way to make it clear to the reader who is speaking?

The essay unfolds so simply that it might be easy to imagine that Doyle merely turned on his tape recorder when the woman began her story and later just transcribed her words directly onto the page. Read the essay over more than once, however, and you can see that Doyle spent a lot of time talking with his subject, perhaps putting her at ease, certainly asking questions to elicit more information. He decided to leave these parts out, however, in order to let the woman's voice speak for itself.

Where is the discovery in Doyle's story of Hope? His subject may at first glance seem to be just a particular interesting woman, and the essay works on that level certainly, but the subject is also the hardship, fear, and persecution facing those displaced by war. The subject, too, is hope, with a small *h*—how this woman eventually found happiness and peace in her life. Doyle or another writer may have tackled these subjects—hardship and hope—by providing the reader with multiple examples, interpretation, and authorial opinion. But in this case, Doyle decided that one woman's story told it all, clearly and succinctly.

Here is an excerpt from Pico Iyer's longer essay "Where Worlds Collide." This essay is also a portrait, but instead of portraying an individual person, Iyer attempts to portray the Los Angeles International Airport's International Terminal, in all of its intense complexity.

From "Where Worlds Collide"

Pico Iyer

LAX is, in fact, a surprisingly shabby and hollowed-out kind of place, certainly not adorned with the amenities one might expect of the world's strongest and richest power. When you come out into the Arrivals area in the International Terminal, you will find exactly one tiny snack bar, which serves nine items; of them, five are identified as Cheese Dog, Chili Dog, Chili Cheese Dog, Nachos with Cheese, and Chili Cheese Nachos. There is a large panel on the wall offering rental-car services and hotels, and the newly deplaned American dreamer can choose between the Cadillac Hotel, the Banana Bungalow (which offers a Basketball Court, "Free Toast," "Free Bed Sheets," and "Free Movies and Parties"), and the Back-packer's Paradise (with "Free Afternoon Tea and Crumpets" and "Free Evening Party Including Food and Champagne").

Around one in the terminal is a swirl of priests rattling cans, Iranians in suits brandishing pictures of torture victims, and Japanese girls in Goofy hats. "I'm looking for something called

Clearasil," a distinguished-looking Indian man diffidently tells a cashier. "Clearasil?" shouts the girl. "For your face?"

Upstairs, in the Terrace Restaurant, passengers are gulping down "Dutch Chocolate" and "Japanese Coffee" while students translate back and forth between English and American, explaining that "soliciting" loses something of its cachet when you go across the Atlantic. A fat man is nuzzling the neck of his outrageously pretty Filipina companion, and a few Brits are staring doubtfully at the sign that assures them that seafood is "cheerfully served at your table!" Only in America, they are doubtless thinking. A man goes from table to table, plunking down on each one a key chain attached to a globe. As soon as an unsuspecting customer picks one up, touched by the largesse of the New World and convinced now that there is such a thing as a free lunch in America, the man appears again, flashes a sign that says "I Am a Deaf," and requests a dollar for the gift.

At a bank of phones, a saffron-robed monk gingerly inserts a credit card, while schoolkids page Jesse Jackson at the nearest "white courtesy telephone." One notable feature of the modern airport is that it is wired, with a vengeance: even in a tiny, two-urinal men's room, I found two telephones on offer; LAX bars rent out cellular phones; and in the Arrivals area, as you come out into the land of plenty, you face a bank of forty-six phones of every kind, with screens and buttons and translations, from which newcomers are calling direct to Bangalore or Baghdad. Airports are places for connections of all kinds and *loci classici*, perhaps, for a world ruled by IDD and MCI, DOS and JAL.

Yet for all these grounding reminders of the world outside, everywhere I went in the airport I felt myself in an odd kind of twilight zone of consciousness, that weightless limbo of a world in which people are between lives and between selves, almost sleepwalking, not really sure of who or where they are. Lightheaded from the trips they've taken, ears popping and eyes about to do so, under a potent foreign influence, people are at the far edge of themselves in airports, ready to break down or through. You see strangers pouring out their life stories to strangers here, or making new life stories with other strangers. Everything is at once intensified and slightly unreal.

Iyer's full essay can be found in the Anthology section, but notice how much detail and description is packed into even this brief excerpt. Iyer uses an onslaught of absurd, disconcerting, or silly particulars—Cheese Dog, Chili Dog, Chili Cheese Dog, Nachos with Cheese, and Chili Cheese Nachos; Japanese girls in Goofy hats; a saffron-robed monk with a credit card—to re-create how overwhelming the experience of entering LAX must be for foreign travelers arriving for the first time.

Given the rapidity with which Iyer's essay moves, you might think he has failed to provide action or characterization. But this excerpt, in fact, illustrates how even a single sentence can function as a scene: "A fat man is nuzzling the neck of his outrageously pretty Filipina companion . . . a few Brits are staring doubtfully at the sign that assures them that seafood is 'cheerfully served at your table!' . . . A man goes from table to table, plunking down on each one a key chain attached to a globe."

Though we are seeing from his point of view—the details Iyer himself catalogued—he stays mostly out of the piece, placing the readers themselves directly into the swarming confusion.

Writing Your Own Literary Journalism Essay

A first suggestion is to consider limiting your subject. If you try to fit too many things into your essay, you run the risk of not adequately bringing any one thing to life. Specific and particular detail and description remain important.

You would also do well to remember that creative nonfiction most often centers on the story, so it is not enough to just list a sequence of facts, as an encyclopedia entry might. You need to find the action that reveals the subject, a way of adding movement to your piece.

Most often, centering your essay on a person creates this movement and makes the human element come alive. For example, rather than trying to capture the entire world of deer hunting, a complex subject that could fill the pages of a book, you might focus instead on a fifteen-year-old girl going hunting for the first time, and even further, focus on the first twenty minutes she spends settling into her deer stand. You will find that there is no need to summarize the entire day or the two weeks building up to that day. Those first twenty minutes in the cold woods give you plenty of opportunity to show the excitement, expectation, and preparation that goes into such an outing.

Or if you are interested in what goes on backstage at a theatrical production, focus perhaps on the person whose job it is to set each prop at the correct location before each show, and also how this person tracks down the props at the end of the night and puts them away, taking care that nothing is missing. Focus on one particular performance. This one person's story on this one night encapsulates all of the careful detail and work that goes into staging a play, backstage work that the audience never sees.

There is *no* subject that is not suitable for a literary journalism essay. Almost any aspect of our world becomes interesting once you study it closely enough.

Brian Doyle suggests that stories are everywhere, happening all around you: "A cat kills a bird on our lawn and my children conduct a funeral service and I find them praying not for the soul of the bird but for the death of the cat. There is a story. A friend referees a basketball game between two teams of deaf players. There is a story. In a small seaside town where I once lived a goose was arrested at the corner of Summer Street and Winter Street. There is a story. I attend a basketball game with two blind friends who can tell who is winning by the sound of the sneakers. There is a story."

Pico Iyer spent an entire week at the LAX International Terminal, attempting to capture the energy of the place and people. To shape his hours upon hours of experience and observation into a coherent essay certainly took weeks more. An airport terminal is a place most all of us visit but few of us really stop to examine. Consider an essay about some other location many people visit but few scrutinize closely. The dry cleaner. The fruit market. The local recycling center. Your subject doesn't have to be a place, however: look closely at an event (hanging the holiday lights downtown) or a person (a relative who once played minor league baseball). You might even attempt humor: Who is that person dressed in the fish costume trying to wave folks into the new seafood restaurant out by the mall?

When you've chosen a subject, or narrowed down your list to a few lively possibilities, here are some suggestions to keep in mind:

- Do your research. This means reading up on your subject beforehand and asking pertinent questions, but also watching and taking notes. All of this takes time, so plan ahead.
- Your observations, and the eventual writing that occurs, may end up being flattering or critical, supportive or dismissive, or a bit of both, but while you are doing your research, your eyes should be wide open and your attitude flexible. You are trying to see what is really there, which may be very different from what you expected beforehand.
- When you start writing, consider narrowing the essay to a brief period of time. If you follow a mail carrier for six hours one morning, look for the representative moment, the one house where something interesting happens. That will mean "throwing away" a lot of your notes, but that, too, is part of the process. Know what to include and what to cut in order to maintain focus and offer the reader sharp detail and careful description.
- Though there is no prohibition against using "I" in your literary journalism essay, use it sparingly. Your observations and reactions may indeed become part of what you have to tell, but ideally you will not become the center. Instead of telling us about your reactions, show us what you saw or heard. Let the reader have the reaction.

More information on research methods in creative nonfiction can be found on the textbook website, www.dintywmoore.com/truth.

And finally, don't assume that just because you walk past something every day, or that because you have known someone all of your life, that there is not an interesting essay to be uncovered. Don't presuppose that your hometown is "so boring" that you could never write about it. These common places and people may seem uninteresting to you, but only because you have settled into a lackluster point of view. Strap on a fresh pair of eyes and go have another look.

Maybe the people in your small town spend day after day just sitting and staring at the steel plant that shut down twenty years ago. Well, that's your story.

WRITING PROMPTS: Literary Journalism

1. Curiosity was listed as a good starting place for memoir, and it is not a bad place to start a literary journalism essay either. Focusing not on the self, but on the world around you, think about what makes you stop and wonder. Do you drive by a small church with an exotic, unfamiliar name every day on the way to class and speculate as to what goes on inside? Do you have a neighbor who spends hours on her ham radio (or some other hobby), and you can't for the life of you understand the appeal? Maybe you've donated blood, but have you ever considered what it must be like to be a Red Cross nurse who draws blood all day? Does the nurse dream of needles in her sleep? Can she discuss the differences in veins the way some people compare their favorite sports teams? Why are all of the streets in your town named after trees, yet they don't seem to have many trees on them? Serious or silly, world-shattering or just quirky—it doesn't matter. For the next week, travel with a notebook in your pocket and make a list of possible topics for a literary journalism exploration.

2. Many people live day in and day out in towns (Warrior's Mark, Parachute) or neighborhoods (Dutch Hill, Hell's Kitchen) with interesting, evocative names, yet never spend the time it might take to learn where the name originated. Think about where you live now and where you have lived in the past, or small towns or neighborhoods that border your current location. Pick one with an interesting name, a name that might harbor a story, and begin some research. Your research might begin at the library, checking local history books. (The reference librarian can help you find the right source.) It may involve a trip to the chamber of commerce or a talk with a member of the local historical society. It

might also involve interviewing people on the street to get their opinions about where the name originated. Remember, even incorrect answers and wild speculation can be interesting. Add your own thoughts about the name and how it may or may not fit today.

Chapter Nine

The Personal Essay

"I write as a witness to what I have seen. I write as a witness to what I imagine."

—TERRY TEMPEST WILLIAMS

The personal essay is the creative nonfiction form with the longest history and is perhaps the most flexible of the forms. The author of a personal essay will often experiment, looking at a question from numerous perspectives, trying out a range of ideas, and occasionally thinking out loud on the page. For this reason a personal essay may at times seem to wander, but it is always a journey with a purpose, and the author serves as idiosyncratic tour guide.

"An essay," Scott Russell Sanders tells us, "is the closest thing we have, on paper, to a record of the individual mind at work and play." Phillip Lopate, a master of the genre and editor of *The Art of the Personal Essay*, explains that the finest essays "surprise me and take me through a mental adventure." This "mental adventure," the idea that the author heads off into the forest of ideas without a clear map or even destination in mind, reflects the root of *essais*, the trial run.

Though an author of a personal essay is often in search of the truth, remember that essays should not be lectures, diatribes, or sermons by someone convinced of their own infallibility; the best essays are true explorations. Some of the most engaging essays, in fact, are those in which the author readily acknowledges not being entirely sure of the right answer, though finding the questions a source of continuing fascination.

Henry David Thoreau is a prime example of this sort of writer. On the surface, Thoreau's *Walden* is about a wooden shack along a pond somewhere in Massachusetts, but the book actually offers us Thoreau's thoughtful meditations on a variety of complex ideas—the appeal of wilderness, our role in the natural world, and the hazards of encroaching technology.

In other words, a writer with some fresh ideas about culture or about spirituality or perhaps about human behavior (always an interesting subject), tests those ideas out on the reader, looking at them one from one angle, challenging them from another, holding them up to different lights. The personal essay might contain bits of memoir (an anecdote from the author's past included to illustrate a point) or literary journalism (research and observation). Always, the personal essay contains discovery.

Examining the Personal Essay

At the heading of this chapter, Terry Tempest Williams tells us "I write as a witness to what I have seen. I write as a witness to what I imagine." Earlier in the book, you encountered Carlos Fuentes' suggestion, "Writing is a struggle against silence." Both authors are making the same point: we write about our most heartfelt concerns, often matters difficult to speak about, and always about matters that are intriguing to us.

This certainly does not mean, however, that we are limited to confession. The personal essay might be spiritual, political, ecological, focused on economic issues, on technological issues, or on the world of television, movies, and other popular media, but the essay should always be motivated by the author's genuine interest in wrestling with complex questions.

Consider the following essay, found in James Galvin's book of the same title. Galvin begins with a meditation on snow and its many properties, but ultimately reflects on an even larger subject: the relationship of human beings to the land.

THE MEADOW
James Galvin

According to scientists who study avalanches for a living, snow has the widest range of physical properties of any known substance. What's amazing is that the Eskimo language doesn't have *more* words for it. Powder snow, corn snow, sugar snow, windpack. Neve, slab, spring powder, spit, and fluff. Thawing and freezing it changes with every degree of temperature, every passing second. Goose down, ball bearings, broken styrofoam.

Then there are the properties of snow that are not physical, or not exactly physical: its lethal whims, its harmlessness, its delicacy, its power, its relentlessness, its flirtatious disregard, its sublime beauty.

Harmless enough, the season's first flakes arrive in the stubble of the mown field, in the spiked branches of pines. They vanish in the morning sun as though they never meant anything by it. And what do they mean in mid-winter when the hard-packed drifts settle in, oppressing the foreseeable future? A little wind and spindrift makes them smolder.

All winter the drifts come and go. They have a sense of direction, but they aren't going anywhere. The flakes come straight down or sideways, fast or slow; sometimes they don't fall but swirl and hover and take off like swallows. The meadow fills, and drifts make bridges over the fences. Everybody waits.

The fences break under the weight of so much beauty. Who does the meadow belong to now? For half the year it belongs to the snow, not a thing you can do with it, and by April no one thinks it's pretty anymore, though it is.

Lyle said, "If you want to know who really owns your land, don't pay the taxes for a while. Then if you want to know who owns it even more, just look out the window in a blizzard. That's the landlord's face looking in, snooping."

Ray, who didn't own any land and never had, outside the lot his doublewide was on in Laramie, thought of snow as a beautiful way to die.

For those readers more accustomed to academic essay writing—a clearly developed overall thesis with individual topic sentences ordering each paragraph—Galvin's essay may seem formless and peculiar. It certainly does not follow a straight line. The literary essay, however, like the literary poem, is not ruled or constricted by conventional logic. The personal essay might follow the logic of image, the logic of emotion, or trace a logic based on words and language.

Galvin's essay does follow a sort of logic, however. You might trace it this way: He was thinking about snow, and then he began to think about how people are often trapped when heavy snow covers the meadow, and that reminded him of something his friend Lyle once told him, that a blizzard is "the landlord's face looking in," and then he was reminded of Ray, another friend, who once suggested that snow would be "a beautiful way to die."

Galvin takes some unexpected turns, but he knows where he is headed (or more likely, he discovered his direction as he revised). His essay is a perfect example of what Lopate meant when he said an essay should be a "text that would surprise me and take me through a mental adventure."

Another excellent example of the flexibility inherent in the personal essay is Joan Didion's examination of migraines, an essay that contains the personal, the scientific, and the historical:

In Bed

Joan Didion

Three, four, sometimes five times a month, I spend the day in bed with a migraine headache, insensible to the world around me. Almost every day of every month, between these attacks, I feel the sudden irrational irritation and the flush of blood into the cerebral arteries which tell me that migraine is on its way, and I take certain drugs to avert its arrival. If I did not take the drugs, I would be able to function perhaps one day in four. The physiological error called migraine is, in brief, central to the given of my life. When I was 15, 16, even 25, I used to think that I could rid myself of this error by simply denying it, character over chemistry. "Do you have headaches sometimes? frequently? never?" the application forms would demand. "Check one." Wary of the trap, wanting whatever it was that the successful circumnavigation of that particular form could bring (a job, a scholarship, the respect of mankind and the grace of God), I would check one. "Sometimes," I would lie. That in fact I spent one or two days a week almost unconscious with pain seemed a shameful secret, evidence not merely of some chemical inferiority but of all my bad attitudes, unpleasant tempers, wrongthink.

For I had no brain tumor, no eyestrain, no high blood pressure, nothing wrong with me at all: I simply had migraine headaches, and migraine headaches were, as everyone who did not have them knew, imaginary. I fought migraine then, ignored the warnings it sent, went to school and later to work in spite of it, sat through lectures in Middle English and presentations to advertisers with involuntary tears running down the right side of my face, threw up in washrooms, stumbled home by instinct, emptied ice trays onto my bed and tried to freeze the pain in my right temple, wished only for a neurosurgeon who would do a lobotomy on house call, and cursed my imagination.

It was a long time before I began thinking mechanistically enough to accept migraine for what it was: something with which I would be living, the way some people live with diabetes. Migraine is something more than the fancy of a neurotic imagination. It is an essentially hereditary complex of symptoms, the most frequently noted but by no means the most unpleasant of which is a vascular headache of blinding severity, suffered by a surprising number of women, a fair number of men (Thomas Jefferson had migraine, and so did Ulysses S. Grant, the day he accepted Lee's surrender), and by some unfortunate children as young as two years old. (I had my first when I was eight. It came on during a fire drill at the Columbia School in Colorado Springs, Colorado. I was taken first home and then to the infirmary at Peterson Field, where my father was stationed. The Air Corps doctor prescribed an enema.) Almost anything can trigger a specific attack of migraine: stress, allergy, fatigue, an abrupt change in barometric pressure, a contretemps over a parking ticket. A flashing light. A fire drill. One inherits, of course, only the predisposition. In other words I spent yesterday in bed with a headache not merely because of my bad attitudes, unpleasant tempers and wrongthink, but because both my grandmothers had migraine, my father has migraine and my mother has migraine.

No one knows precisely what it is that is inherited. The chemistry of migraine, however, seems to have some connection with the nerve hormone named serotonin, which is naturally present in the brain. The amount of serotonin in the blood falls sharply at the onset of migraine, and one migraine drug, methysergide, or Sansert, seems to have some effect on serotonin. Methysergide is a derivative of lysergic acid (in fact Sandoz Pharmaceuticals first synthesized LSD-25 while looking for a migraine cure), and its use is hemmed about with so many contraindications and side effects that most doctors prescribe it only in the most incapacitating cases. Methysergide, when it is prescribed, is taken daily, as a preventive; another preventive which works for some people is old-fashioned ergotamine tartrate, which helps to constrict the swelling blood vessels during the "aura," the period which in most cases precedes the actual headache.

Once an attack is under way, however, no drug touches it. Migraine gives some people mild hallucinations, temporarily blinds others, shows up not only as a headache but as a gastrointestinal disturbance, a painful sensitivity to all sensory stimuli, an abrupt overpowering fatigue, a strokelike aphasia, and a crippling inability to make even the most routine connections. When I am in a migraine aura (for some people the aura lasts fifteen minutes, for others several hours), I will drive through red lights, lose the house keys, spill whatever I am holding, lose the ability to focus my eyes or frame coherent sentences, and generally give the appearance of being on drugs, or drunk. The actual headache, when it comes, brings with it chills, sweating, nausea, a debility that seems to stretch the very limits of endurance. That no one dies of migraine seems, to someone deep into an attack, an ambiguous blessing.

My husband also has migraine, which is unfortunate for him but fortunate for me: perhaps nothing so tends to prolong an attack as the accusing eye of someone who has never had a headache. "Why not take a couple of aspirin," the unafflicted will say from the doorway, or "I'd have a headache, too, spending a beautiful day like this inside with all the shades drawn." All of us who have migraine suffer not only from the attacks themselves but from this common conviction that we are perversely refusing to cure ourselves by taking a couple of aspirin, that we are making ourselves sick, that we "bring it on ourselves." And in the most immediate sense, the sense of why we have a headache this Tuesday and not last Thursday, of course we often do. There certainly is what doctors call a "migraine personality," and that personality tends to be ambitious, inward, intolerant of error, rather rigidly organized, perfectionist. "You don't look like a migraine personality," a doctor once said to me. "Your hair's messy. But I suppose you're a compulsive housekeeper." Actually my house is kept even more negligently than my hair, but the doctor was right nonetheless: perfectionism can also take the form of spending most of a week writing and rewriting and not writing a single paragraph.

But not all perfectionists have migraine, and not all migrainous people have migraine personalities. We do not escape heredity. I have tried in most of the available ways to escape my own migrainous heredity (at one point I learned to give myself two daily injections of histamine with a hypodermic needle, even though the needle so frightened me that I had to close my eyes when I did it), but I still have migraine. And I have learned now to live with it, learned when to expect it, how to outwit it, even how to regard it, when it does come, as more friend than lodger. We have reached a certain understanding, my migraine and I. It never comes when I am in real trouble. Tell me that my house is burned down, my husband has left me, that there is gunfighting in the streets and panic in the banks, and I will not respond by getting a headache. It comes instead when I am fighting not an open but a guerrilla war with my own life, during weeks of small household confusions, lost laundry, unhappy help, canceled appointments, on days when the telephone rings too much and I get no work done and the wind is coming up. On days like that my friend comes uninvited.

And once it comes, now that I am wise in its ways, I no longer fight it. I lie down and let it happen. At first every small apprehension is magnified, every anxiety a pounding terror. Then the pain comes, and I concentrate only on that. Right there is the usefulness of migraine, there in that imposed yoga, the concentration on the pain. For when the pain recedes, ten or twelve hours later, everything goes with it, all the hidden resentments, all the vain anxieties. The migraine has acted as a circuit breaker, and the fuses have emerged intact. There is a pleasant convalescent euphoria. I open the windows and feel the air, eat gratefully, sleep well. I notice the particular nature of a flower in a glass on the stair landing. I count my blessings.

Didion begins her essay in a fairly straightforward manner, with the immediate facts. "Three, four, sometimes five times a month, I spend the day in bed with a migraine headache, insensible to the world around me." A few sentences further into the essay, she offers background—that she has suffered the headaches since age eight, that they were once thought "imaginary"—and she shares the latest ideas on what triggers a migraine. She also offers a brief look into the chemistry of the brain, and the drugs that sometimes help.

Notice, though, that Didion is not writing a textbook or medical treatise; the personal essay form allows her to give intimate details from her own life, and to follow side roads and digressions if she finds them interesting (and imagines the reader might as well): Grant was suffering from a migraine when he accepted Lee's surrender; a particular migraine drug is related to LSD.

Eventually, Didion illustrates how she has come to accept her affliction and all of the considerable pain that comes along with it. She personifies her own migraine in this sentence: "And I have learned now to live with it, learned when to expect it, how to outwit it, even how to regard it, when it does come, as more friend than lodger."

She ends the essay by returning to the deeply personal. After the migraine has receded, she tells us, "There is a pleasant convalescent euphoria. I open the windows and feel the air, eat gratefully, sleep well. . . . I count my blessings." Her ending is lyric,[1] almost a poem, though presented in prose form, using conventional sentences.

The personal essay has room for all of these modes of expression and forms of information—factual, lyric, journalistic, odd bits of trivia, personal experience. The author's challenge is finding the way to arrange them into a coherent whole.

Writing Your Own Personal Essay

There is perhaps *no* subject that could not be tackled successfully in a personal essay, except of course a subject that the author finds uninteresting. From persuasive to lyrical, humorous to solemn, straightforward to highly experimental, brief to long, the personal essay has adapted itself to every shape imaginable.

There are no hard-and-fast rules, but there are certainly guidelines a beginning writer would do well to consider. Once you have arrived at a subject you want to write on, consider these:

- Once again, narrowing your focus is usually a prudent first step. This does not mean that you can't tackle the largest of subjects, just that you may need to find a part of the subject that represent the whole.

---

[1] A related form of the personal essay is the lyric essay. The editors of the *Seneca Review* define the lyric essay as a "poetic essay" or "essayistic poem" which focuses on "artfulness over the conveying of information." The lyric essay (see for instance Deborah Tall's "The Stories Tell the Land" in the Anthology) often forgoes straightforward narrative for an exploration of language, or explores imagery rather than reason and logic. The lyric essay offers a writer even more freedoms than the considerable freedom already available in the personal essay genre. As always, however, don't worry too much about where one form ends and another begins. Focus, instead, on finding your passions and writing about them with freshness and energy.

Richard Selzer, for instance, in his essay "The Knife," tackles the vital issues of life and death, but keeps his essay focused by concentrating on the instrument most essential to his work as a surgeon.

- Don't begin with one idea and simply try to convince us. "An essay needs conflict, just as a short story does," Lopate warns. "Without conflict, your essay will drift into static mode, repeating your initial observation in a self-satisfied way." Keep an open mind.
- Voice is more important than ever in the personal essay. An encyclopedia entry will offer the facts, and many books are available that collate and summarize the opinions of experts. The personal essay is *personal;* what is your take on this subject, how do you feel, and how do the details and description you have added reveal your individual point of view? It is not necessary that your essay sound like Galvin's essay or Didion's essay. In fact, it shouldn't sound like anyone but you.

Revealing the true you on the page, becoming the person behind the personal essay, can be difficult for some writers. Honesty about one's self or one's views takes a certain amount of courage, and serious essayists cannot shy away from topics that might embarrass the reader or that might be personally embarrassing to themselves. Are you an imperfect human being, given to the occasional petty thought or unbecoming behavior? Welcome to the club. Have you made a few big mistakes? Most people have. Readers are not interested in hearing from writers who believe they are better than others or immune to error.

Most important when writing a personal essay is to be open to discovery. Some of the finest essays develop when a writer decides to tackle a subject that seems at first "too hard to write about." It will take time—and multiple drafts—to find your direction, but subjects that initially seem exceptionally difficult are often those that bear the most fruit.

WRITING PROMPTS: Personal Essay

1. Near the end of her essay "In Bed," Joan Didion writes: "We have reached a certain understanding, my migraine and I." Is there some part of you that some may think of as a disability, handicap, affliction, or flaw, but one with which you have now reached "a certain understanding"? Have you come to accept something about yourself that doesn't put you neatly into the (artificial and unrealistic) category of "perfect, beautiful, healthy, emotionally well-adjusted, successful, and destined for the top one percent"? Everyone has problems, and the most successful people move on despite them.

Imitate Didion and write a personal essay examining your own "migraine," and why this affliction or problem is sometimes okay.

2. Novelist Roxanna Robinson has said, "I write about the things that trouble me. I write about the things that disturb me, that won't let me alone, the things that are eating slowly into my brain at 3:00 in the morning, the things that unbalance my world." Take a large question that you find disturbing and unanswerable—Why do people hurt one another in the name of love? Why are religions that preach peace used as justifications for war? Why are children often mean to other children?—and explore it on the page. Don't force an answer to your question or attempt to nail down a logical explanation. Instead, consider various explanations, look for interesting theories, hold the question upside down and shake it. Examine a specific example of human behavior related to the question, from your own history or world history. Find some theories other people have put forward, especially those you think may be wrong. Try to make your discussion of this unanswerable question more interesting than any precise, watertight explanation would ever be.

Chapter Ten

Revision and Narrative Structure

"Stories move in circles. They don't go in straight lines. So it helps if you listen in circles. There are stories inside stories and stories between stories, and finding your way through them is as easy and hard as finding your way home."

— NAOMI NEWMAN, TRAVELING JEWISH THEATRE

The importance of revision in creative nonfiction has been discussed at various points along the way in this book, but it is worth ending on the subject as well. A willingness to revise, to "re-vision" the words and ideas you have placed on the page, is what sets many successful writers apart from those who never find the time or energy to produce polished, quality work.

Remember that the term *essay* derives from the French word *essais*, meaning to attempt or try out. Author E. B. White's assertion that writing is "an act of faith" holds especially true for the essay, and perhaps translates into multiple acts of faith. First, you must trust that your initial ideas and impressions, often sketchy or unsure, will coalesce into something coherent and complete. Second, the writer must trust that the words and sentences chosen to convey these ideas will interest and make sense to the reader. Eventually, if you become serious about your writing, you must trust that you will find an audience, that your work will be published.

Before ideas become whole and sentences take ideal shape, however, most writers face a point when they need to step back, literally or figuratively, and stare at the page for a moment. This is where the difficult questions are asked: What is working? What isn't making sense? Where in this essay am I bringing my ideas, memories, or observations clearly to life? Where am I relying on dull sentences and half-finished summary?

This is a very important moment in the process of writing, and one when many writers make critical breakthroughs in their work. But the writer must be open to honest assessment and significant change.

On Serious Revision

To make serious use of the revision process, you must let go of the natural urge to preserve the sentences you have already written, especially those you might have labored over for a long time. You should be open to the possibility that large chunks of your current draft were just trial runs. They may need to be replaced, or perhaps your essay will be stronger simply by taking them out and letting what remains stand by itself.

One way to think about the difference between minor revision and serious revision is to imagine that you are remodeling a living room. Simply proofreading your second or third draft and fixing a few awkward sentences is similar to remodeling a room by dusting the end tables and rearranging the pillows on the sofa. Not much of a change occurs with that effort.

The true act of revision comes when a writer is willing to move each piece of furniture out onto the front lawn, roll up the area rugs, and take the pictures down from the wall. Then, on a case by case basis, the writer can decide which furniture returns to the room, and where it will be situated. Sometimes a favorite table has to be left out on the curb for recycling, because it just doesn't fit anymore. Maybe some new furniture is purchased (a new scene is written). Perhaps the walls are painted a new color (voice or point of view shifts.)

In some cases, *all* of the furniture is returned, but not necessarily to the same location. What is important is that nothing goes back inside the metaphorical living room until and unless the writer makes the conscious choice that it belongs.

This may seem like hard work, and indeed it is, but it is always well worth the effort. Writing is an act of detection, an attempt to determine what the writer thinks and feels, so it only makes sense that the author's idea of what an essay should say and do will be more certain after two, three, or four drafts.

Revision and Narrative Structure

Often, when undertaking serious and comprehensive revision, a writer will make discoveries about narrative structure, the sequence and manner in which the story is told or the series of ideas are presented. The word *creative* in the term creative nonfiction has quite a bit to do with these structural decisions.

For instance, a simple memoir about an incident in fifth grade—the first time you felt betrayed by a friend, perhaps—might be told any number of ways. You might structure the narrative:

- In a straightforward chronological order, beginning at the beginning and ending at the end
- In chronological order but with a flash-forward near the conclusion, allowing the adult voice of the narrator to enter into the narrative (see Bret Lott's "Genesis" in Chapter Seven for an example)
- In a way that allows the incident from fifth grade to be contrasted with another incident, from another time in your life, so that the two events might draw meaning from the comparison. (Norma Elia Cantú's "Tino & Papi" in Chapter Six works in this manner.)

Though filmmaking and prose writing are markedly different forms of constructing narrative, practitioners of one art form can still learn from studying the other. Think of films that you have seen and enjoyed recently. Though some take you on a direct journey through time, many of the best films use time shifts and other narrative devices to increase interest, depth, and suspense. "A story should have a beginning, a middle, and an end," filmmaker Jean Luc Godard once said, "but not necessarily in that order."

The straight chronological approach is not wrong, in essay writing or filmmaking, but it might be if no other options have been considered. Along with revising for detail and description, characterization, voice, point of view, and discovery, a writer should ask at some point, "Is this the best structure? Why did I start here and end there? Is there a fresher, more interesting way of presenting this material?"

To that end, look at some of the innovative forms used by other writers and consider whether a similar structure might strengthen or enliven an essay you are currently drafting.

Braiding

One of the more interesting approaches to any form of storytelling has always been to combine two narrative lines in order to show where they intersect, how one speaks to the other, and how both take on greater significance through comparison.

Often, a writer will braid two (or three, or more) strands of the narrative together. The narrative strands might be different stories, or one might be the basic story while another strand brings in outside research or other information that puts the main story into context. In a personal essay, contrasting viewpoints or ideas may be braided.

Look, for instance, at the essay "Silent Dancing" by Judith Ortiz Cofer, found in the Anthology. Notice how Cofer intersperses short sections describing a home movie from her childhood with longer memories of the family's move from Puerto Rico to New Jersey. Eventually, Cofer weaves in the narrative voice of a relative, part of her recurring dream, amplifying the many questions she has about her past. The "dream" voice serves as a sort of soundtrack for the silent 8mm movie.

What would Cofer's memoir essay look like if she had just one of these elements? What would be lost? Thinking about the choices made by accomplished authors is always useful for aspiring or beginning writers.

Cofer's essay is an excellent model of the flexibility inherent in creative nonfiction. Given that much of what we learn from the italicized dream section near the end appears to be fabricated, you might be tempted to call her work partly fictionalized. But in fact, Cofer makes it clear that the italicized voice comes out of her dreams, so she is not misleading or presenting fiction as fact. She is giving us an accurate nonfiction account of the workings of her imagination.

Another excellent example of braiding is Robin Hemley's essay "Reading History to My Mother" (also found in the Anthology). Hemley's essay begins with the sentence "Everything's mixed up in those boxes, the past and the present." The author then uses the boxes his mother has packed (in order to move to an apartment building for senior citizens) as an occasion to probe various moments of his unique family history.

Hemley's mother once attended a writer's colony with the poets William Carlos Williams and Theodore Roethke, so this becomes part of the story, but Hemley also manages to work in Moe Howard of the Three Stooges, a relative by marriage. His braid has multiple strands, and strands within strands, but just when it seems the essay is going off course, Hemley returns to the boxes, or to the act of packing and unpacking, or to a photo or newsletter found in one of the boxes, to remind us of where his story begins and ends.

Compare what Hemley is able to achieve in this longer essay to what Richard Terrill accomplished in his much shorter essay "Solstice" (Chapter Six). The essays are quite different in form and structure, but both deal with an adult son facing the challenge of caring for an elderly mother.

Collage

A collage is an assortment of objects or photos. In grade school, you probably made collages out of various pictures and letters cut from magazines. These collages were meant to express feelings about yourself or some other subject suggested by the teacher.

In creative nonfiction, a collage is still made up of various pieces, or images, but the scraps are cut from the writer's memory and research rather than from old magazines. Still, the various parts all combine to form the whole.

Examine Naomi Shihab Nye's essay "Three Pokes of a Thistle." Notice how Nye combines three pictures cut from the magazine of her life—her shame over a random accident involving a taxi and a mailbox, differences between her Palestinian American family and the family of her friend Marcia, and her first bra—to form a collage. What does the larger picture represent? How does this relate to her choice of title?

Another interesting example of collage is David Shields's "42 Tattoos." Shields's essay is not memoir-based, but derives entirely from research he has done on the art of body modification—specifically tattooing—in cultures ranging from ancient Egypt to the contemporary world of NBA basketball and Tupac Shakur. Note how the author alternates longer and shorter entries, and how he draws a comparison between tattoos on a person's body and words on the page. Shields has devised a unique narrative structure to fit his essay, and a unique essay to fit the uncommon narrative structure.

Frame

James Baldwin begins the title essay of his collection, *Notes of a Native Son*, with these words: "On the 29th of July, in 1943, my father died. . . . A few hours after my father's funeral, while he lay in state in the undertaker's chapel, a race riot broke out in Harlem. On the morning of the 3rd of August, we drove my father to the graveyard through a wilderness of smashed plate glass."

The essay—part personal essay, part memoir—goes on to examine not just Baldwin's life and his father's legacy, but wider issues related to his racial background and "the weight of white people in the world." Only after significant personal history and reflection does Baldwin return, at the end, to the story of his father's funeral. Like a set of parentheses, or a picture frame, the funeral story holds everything firmly in place.

Similarly, Lucy Grealy, in her essay "Mirrorings," fits a complex and painful tale of childhood cancer, disfigurement, and reconstructive surgery within the frame of a year she lived in Scotland and avoided mirrors. Of course, her relationship to mirrors serves not only as a convenient frame for the longer story but as a metaphor as well.

Other Strategies

Braid, collage, frame, and chronological order are common ways to structure creative nonfiction, but they are by no means the only methods. Often, a unique structure will suggest itself, perhaps as a metaphor for your ideas and explorations, or simply because the particular, innovative structure seems to fit.

Authors of creative nonfiction have adapted poetic forms such as *sestina* or *abcedarium*, have imagined themselves into television shows, and have written essays in the form of recipes, quizzes, instruction booklets, and psychiatric hospital intake notes.

Philip Gerard was faced with the challenge of capturing his experience when Hurricane Fran slammed directly into his hometown of Wilmington, North Carolina. He knew his readers were familiar with hurricanes from television news, but Gerard wanted to relate the intimate detail, what it was really like to experience this awesome force of nature and its aftermath. Gerard struggled through multiple drafts of his essay (and a few rejections from magazines) before realizing that it was more than a personal story; that he wanted to capture the point of view of "a whole community of people" who had suffered.

His unique narrative structure for "What They Don't Tell You about Hurricanes," found in the Anthology involves an implied question—What don't they tell you?—as well as repetition—whether, when, how hard, how long, and variations on the title—and shifts between first and second person. Note the small details that make you feel as if you had experienced this event right alongside Gerard and his neighbors.

Norma Elia Cantú's brief essay "Tino & Papi" is uniquely structured as well. Contrasting two events separated by many years is not uncommon, but Cantú moves quickly forward and backward in time to tell her family story, and the essay gains interest because of this.

The key to finding the ideal structure for your essay is to remain flexible, to be open to experimentation and revision. In order to complete a first draft, you must begin one particular way, but keep in mind that your initial structural choice is not carved into granite. Revise and reconsider at every point, and eventually you will find the structure that works best for your essay.

In the quotation at the beginning of this chapter, playwright and theatrical director Naomi Newman promises: "There are stories inside stories and stories between stories, and finding your way through them is as easy and hard as finding your way home." The complete quotation ends this way: "And part of the finding is the getting lost. And when you're lost, you start to look around and to listen."

Don't be afraid to get lost, to take chances, to cover new ground in your essays. This is often where the most enduring discoveries are made. Writing creative nonfiction *is* an act of faith, and if you allow it to be, it is also a challenging and invigorating mental adventure.

WRITING PROMPTS: Narrative Structure

1. Take the scissors to an essay you have been writing—either literally or by using the cut and paste function on your word processor. Separate your latest draft into distinct sections—paragraphs or groups of paragraphs—and then reassemble the sections as if they were puzzle pieces. Try to come up with numerous arrangements, and consider how each new sequencing might influence how the reader encounters your ideas and information. Notice too how each different ordering of the material suggests new material that might be added. If it is a brief essay, pick two very different approaches, and write them both.

2. As an alternative to the exercise above, members of a class could separate into groups and experiment with rearranging essays written by others. What changes? What new questions come to mind?

3. Look at David Shields's innovatively structured "42 Tattoos." Choose a subject you can research in order to write short and longer sections like Shields has done. Can you collage these found items together to form a coherent whole?

4. Look once more at Norma Elia Cantu's "Tino & Papi" (Chapter Six). Can you think of two events in your own life, separated by many years, that take on greater significance when presented side by side in the manner Cantu has done? Study "Tino & Papi" for the narrative choices made by the author, and then mimic those choices, using your material and your life as the raw material.

PART IV

~~~~~

The Anthology

The Brief Essay

Drummond, Laurie Lynn	"Alive"
Jakiela, Lori	"You'll Love the Way We Fly"
Martin, Lee	"Dumber Than"
Tall, Deborah	"The Stories Tell the Land"

The Conventional Length Essay

Baldwin, James	"Notes of a Native Son"
Beard, Jo Ann	"Out There"
Cofer, Judith Ortiz	"Silent Dancing"
Dillard, Annie	"Living Like Weasels"
Earley, Tony	"Somehow Form a Family"
Gerard, Philip	"What They Don't Tell You About Hurricanes"
Grealy, Lucy	"Mirrorings"
Gutkind, Lee	"Difficult Decisions"
Hemley, Robin	"Reading History to My Mother"
Hoagland, Edward	"The Courage of Turtles"
Iyer, Pico	"Where Worlds Collide"
Kincaid, Jamaica	"Biography of a Dress"
Lott, Bret	"Brothers"
McPhee, John	"The Search for Marvin Gardens"
Nye, Naomi Shihab	"Three Pokes of a Thistle"
Sanders, Scott Russell	"Buckeye"
Sedaris, David	"The Drama Bug"
Selzer, Richard	"The Knife"
Shields, David	"42 Tattoos"
Tan, Amy	"Mother Tongue"
Williams, Terry Tempest	"The Clan of One-Breasted Women"

Essays on the Craft of Creative Nonfiction

Dillard, Annie	"Seeing"
Kidder, Tracy	"Making the Truth Believable"
Lott, Bret	"Toward a Definition of Creative Nonfiction"
Schwartz, Mimi	"Memoir? Fiction? Where's the Line?"

The Brief Essay

Alive

Laurie Lynn Drummond

There is a serial killer at work in Baton Rouge, and so, as I drive into the city on this rainy mid-August afternoon to visit family, I move from simply alert to hyper alert. In addition to the three murdered women, there have been four attempted abductions in the past two weeks; the last woman fought her attacker off with a machete. Yesterday, a line of women snaked out the door of a police supply store, waiting to purchase pepper spray. The store sold out by noon.

For once, I am not in the minority. Alert is a natural state for me, and the quick transition to hyper alert is easy. I worked as a police officer in this city in the 1980's. I know, intimately, what one human being can do to another. And I've seen crime scene pictures of the serial killer's first victim, examined the evidence, learned details withheld from the press

I stop at City Newstand to pick up a newspaper. A nice-looking man—bald, early thirties, dark shirt—in a green Chevy Blazer is backing out of the space across from mine. His car stops, and I feel his gaze as I retrieve my wallet, open the car door. Our eyes meet, and he smiles. I keep my face blank and walk briskly into the store. *Creep,* I think. And then I'm ashamed. I've worked hard since I left police work to cultivate tolerance and gentleness, to not live suspicious 24-7.

I grab my newspaper and glance at magazines in the rack beside me. When I look up, the bald man is in the store. He smiles again. My throat constricts. *Don't be a silly panicked female,* I chide, *it's just coincidence.* He leaves as I pay for my newspaper and hovers outside, head down as though he's reading, but his eyes are on me.

And I know, deep in my gut knowing, old habit knowing, that this isn't coincidence. This man is stalking me. That's when the minuscule tremble in my knee kicks in, the tremble I haven't felt since I wore a uniform. If I were still a cop, this wouldn't make my knee tremble. But I am simply a civilian. A female civilian.

I track right, pretend to study a magazine. Five minutes later, when an older gentleman leaves the store, I am right on his heels, walking tough to my car. The bald man paces me step by step to his own car four spaces down.

My hands tremble, my mouth is dry, and I hate, with every screaming fiber of my being, that I gave up all guns two years ago.

I wait for the bald man to leave first. He drives to the far exit, turns right. I expel a deep breath and turn left at the nearest exit, stop at the traffic light. When I look in my rearview mirror, he is behind me. Fear flutters frantic against the walls of my body.

I reach for a pen and piece of paper, jot down a detailed description of him, his car, curse Louisiana for not requiring front bumper license plates.

He follows me through five intersections. Resolve tightens in my gut. *Okay, buddy*, I think, *you've picked the wrong woman.* I will stop at a convenience store, call my friend Ike, a homicide detective. I'll get the whole damn department out here.

We approach the interstate, and he suddenly veers up the entrance ramp. And he is gone.

For the next two days, I'm well beyond hyper alert. I hate being this way and cut my visit short. Tension dissipates as Baton Rouge disappears in my rearview mirror. I turn on the radio, roll down the window, smile.

Thirty minutes later I am crossing the Atchafalaya Swamp, headed toward my home in Texas. When the Whiskey Bay exit sign appears, every particle in my body constricts. This is where the third victim was found, naked, with her throat cut.

And that's when I finally get, really get, what I have always known. Alertness, tolerance, compassion, suspicion: none of it matters. I am vulnerable simply because I'm alive.

You'll Love the Way We Fly
Lori Jakiela

I'm in the galley making coffee. I try to look busy, not in the mood to talk or help. This is the fourth leg of a six-leg day, and already I'm tired. I immerse myself in counting and recounting stacks of styrofoam cups, tightening the handles on metal coffee pots, scrubbing the steel galley counter until I can see my face, distorted and greenish in the plane's fluorescent light, eyes flecked with dried mascara.

I hear him coming before I can see him, the rustle of his nylon bag brushing against seat backs, the heads of other passengers. He is old, thin. He plops the bag on the floor of the emergency exit row, right across from where I'm standing. I'm engrossed now in stocking Cokes into the beverage cart. I watch him from behind the galley wall, a talent all flight attendants learn, covert ways to size people up.

His hair is gray and saliva has settled into the corners of his mouth. He holds a filthy handkerchief to his nose. He is coughing, a deep-lunged cough, the kind that fades into a feathery wheeze then begins again, a terrifying, endless loop. A pack of Marlboros is tucked into his left sock.

I am afraid to go near him, afraid of what I might catch. When you make your living on an airplane, there are things you become afraid of, like germs and crashes and how cold the ocean is off LaGuardia in winter.

"They're not supposed to let them on like this," says my friend, who's working with me. They're not supposed to let them on drunk, either, but this is how it is. This is what I think, but I don't say anything.

The man coughs, then follows with his wet-rattled breaths. I think—this is serious, maybe not contagious, but serious. I call to him from the galley. "Sir, would you like water?"

He wheezes, coughs, shakes his head. I look at my friend, who's busy alphabetizing magazines and stacking pillows in the overhead bins.

"Excuse me, sir?," I say. "Can I get you something?"

He coughs, points. Coffee.

"Cream and sugar?" He nods and so I bring him what he wants, along with some water.

"Thank you," he says, and grabs hold of my hand. I feel myself pull back. His hand is damp and cold, the fingers are all bone. "Thank you, I"— He coughs again, and I don't get the rest, so I have to lean closer—"really appreciate."

Later he tries to give me a tip. Two quarters wrapped in a wet dollar and held together with a rubber band. I say "no, no," but he presses it into my palm, gasps "You take it for taking care. I appreciate."

The effort of breathing has made him sound foreign. He's American, I'm sure, a New Yorker, though disease has taken the hardness out of his eyes. They are brown and damp, the whites yellowing like old paper. Still, he thinks small kindnesses are things you have to pay for.

I haven't really been kind. I've just done my job, against what I wanted, despite my own disgust. I am paid to smile, to talk to strangers about the latest issue of *People* magazine, to bring coffee and water, to make people comfortable.

I take the money.

"What is it you say?" he's asking, but I don't understand. "What is it you say on T.V.?"

"You'll love the way we fly," my friend sing-songs from the galley.

The man nods gravely, repeats it.

I laugh now. I don't know what else to do. He's dying, I'm sure.

Emphysema or lung cancer, probably, like my father.

The flight is only an hour, D.C. to New York. When the man gets up to leave, I keep my head down, eyes focused on my hand, checking off items on a list. What we need: tea bags, stir sticks, Band-Aids, first aid cream, two bags peanuts. I try not to think, but I can't help it.

Who will be there in the airport to meet him? What is his home like? Who brings him coffee the way he likes it? Who is not afraid to touch him?

Dumber Than

Lee Martin

A box of rocks. That boy—oh, you know the one. Dropped his cat from that second-story sleeping porch just to see if it was true, what they said about cats always landing on their feet. Bawled when that tabby hit and bounced, lay dead on the cement walk.

Dumber than dirt.

One day in school, the teacher asked him to name the capitol of Illinois. "*I*," he said, and don't think that one didn't get around—how those kids howled until the windows shook, how even the teacher couldn't stop herself from laughing.

Dumber than a post.

E.T.—that's what folks started calling him. This was way before the movie about the cutesy extra-terrestrial. *E.T.*—for "elapsed time." Whatever went in one ear shot out the other like a laser beam, nothing to stop it. He wasn't all there. He was on a fast road to somewhere no one could see. Wherever it was, when he was dropping that cat, or answering that teacher's question, he was zipping ahead. He was already gone.

Once at Halloween, I caught him soaping the windshield of my '73 Plymouth Duster. It was broad daylight, for Pete's sake, and the car was right there along the street where anyone could see him. He didn't care. He was this big, goofy kid with a bar of Lifebuoy. In a few years, he'd shed his baby fat and become a muscle man. I grabbed him by the arm, asked him what the hell he thought he was doing. He couldn't stop laughing—amused, I like to think, by his own stupidity and how pissed off he could make me. He laughed until he was crying and spitting and his nose was running, and that just pissed me off more. I dragged him into the house, clamped onto him while I used my free hand to rustle up a rag and a pail and fill it with water. "You're hurting my arm," he kept saying. "Hurting my arm." But he couldn't stop laughing. He laughed like an idiot even when I dragged him back outside and told him to by-God clean that soap off that windshield. It was the most joyous sound. He laughed like the Judgment had come and any minute he'd lift up to Heaven.

How was I to know, when I grabbed him by his arm, that one day when he was a grown man, he'd take a golf-club—a five iron—and beat his wife until she was dead? I ask you. Seriously now. How could any of us have known that he'd kill women across three states—at least that's what he told the law. Then, when they asked him for the particulars—how many women, where, what had he done with the bodies—he wouldn't talk. Just dummied up. Wouldn't say a goddamn word.

That's when we got all righteous. Don't act like it's not true. Dumber than a bagful of hammers, we said. Now that's one thing we always knew for sure.

~~~~~~

The Stories Tell the Land
Deborah Tall

ell these stories when you shouldn't and the bees will come and sting your lips, your tongue will swell and fill your mouth, snakes will crawl into your bed while you sleep and choke you . . .

Certain stories weren't told by the Seneca Indians during the summer months because they could offend the "little people," the magical helpers of fruits and vegetables. Tale-telling was so powerful it could unbalance the seasons—creatures might become entranced, wander dazed through forests and forget to go to their winter homes. "To listen to stories made the birds forget to fly to the south lands when winter came," Seneca scholar Arthur Parker explained, "it made the animals neglect to store up winter provisions. . . ." Even plants would cross a threshold to hear a story. "All the world stops when a good story is told."

The story of deer: black silhouettes on warning signs, shot up for practice, for kicks, preseason; drunks in pickups (stay out of the woods now); viewing stands in the crotches of trees; a stiffened carcass mauled by dogs. Deer won't go near human hair—if you want to protect young plants, drape them with your hair. A woman who lost hers to chemotherapy told me this. How do you meet a deer?

The story of deer: when deer come near the house, they are like ambassadors from another realm, willing, for a moment, to flirt at the border. A listening pause. She holds. I stare, rigid lest I spook her. She is just outside my study window. But the span between us is an abyss neither of us can cross. It allows only our gaze, our alert meeting, a summit between two sovereigns with everything to negotiate, conducted in silence. I stress the need for compromise. But she is the first to turn, give up, leave, while I strain for the final white whip of her tail and am left empty-handed.

The story of poetry: thinking the conversation with the deer matters. Not simply, romantically, reading her as a sign, an outward sign of inward grace. Not superstitiously in the old magical way requiring divination, action. But a world to be attended to, silenced by, and recorded—even if I risk misreading her and myself. For this is the all, the only, the unavoidable *is*. It will assert itself despite us, inevitable as weather.

The story of weather: one spring, so cold and interminably wet that the dogwood never bloomed and the peonies disappeared before they could flower. Fierce storms—wind that would be gale force at sea, Seneca Lake slamming and moaning. The trees crying, a kind of keening, low and constant, unintelligible. The trees look to me like banished women, heads forlornly hung, arms sweeping toward earth in the whoosh of each wind blast. What are they grieving?

Story of the earth: my daughter wants to know if the earth is alive. I tell her yes. She wants to know why. I start talking about Gaia, the Iroquois notion of *orenda*, about the old myths in which women were turned into birds and trees, but she interrupts, says, "I know. It's alive because it moves without electricity."

Story of the earth according to a Dakota: "Everything as it moves, now and then, here and there, makes stops. The bird as it flies stops in one place to make its nest, and in another to rest in its flight. A man when he goes forth stops when he wills. So the god has stopped. The sun, which is so bright and beautiful, is one place where he has stopped. The moon, the stars, the winds, he has been with. The trees, the animals, are all where he has stopped, and the Indian thinks of these places and sends his prayers there . . ."

Stop and tell a story. The stories tell the land.

The Conventional Length Essay

Notes of a Native Son
James Baldwin

On the 29th of July, in 1943, my father died. On the same day, a few hours later, his last child was born. Over a month before this, while all our energies were concentrated in waiting for these events, there had been, in Detroit, one of the bloodiest race riots of the century. A few hours after my father's funeral, while he lay in state in the undertaker's chapel, a race riot broke out in Harlem. On the morning of the 3rd of August, we drove my father to the graveyard through a wilderness of smashed plate glass.

The day of my father's funeral had also been my nineteenth birthday. As we drove him to the graveyard, the spoils of injustice, anarchy, discontent, and hatred were all around us. It seemed to me that God himself had devised, to mark my father's end, the most sustained and brutally dissonant of codas. And it seemed to me, too, that the violence which rose all about us as my father left the world had been devised as a corrective for the pride of his eldest son. I had declined to believe in that apocalypse which had been central to my father's vision; very well, life seemed to be saying, here is something that will certainly pass for an apocalypse until the real thing comes along. I had inclined to be contemptuous of my father for the conditions of his life, for the conditions of our lives. When his life had ended I began to wonder about that life and also, in a new way, to be apprehensive about my own.

I had not known my father very well. We had got on badly, partly because we shared, in our different fashions, the vice of stubborn pride. When he was dead I realized that I had hardly ever spoken to him. When he had been dead a long time I began to wish I had. It seems to be typical of life in America, where opportunities, real and fancied, are thicker than anywhere else on the globe, that the second generation has no time to talk to the first. No one, including my father, seems to have known exactly how old he was, but his mother had been born during slavery. He was of the first generation of free men. He, along with thousands of other Negroes, came North after 1919 and I was part of that generation which had never seen the landscape of what Negroes sometimes call the Old Country.

He had been born in New Orleans and had been a quite young man there during the time that Louis Armstrong, a boy, was running errands for the dives and honky-tonks of what was always presented to me as one of the most wicked of cities—to this day, whenever I think of New Orleans, I also helplessly think of Sodom and Gomorrah. My father never mentioned Louis Armstrong, except to forbid us to play his records; but there was a picture of him on our wall for a long time. One of my father's strong-willed female relatives had placed it there and forbade my father to take it down. He never did, but he eventually maneuvered her out of the house and when, some years later, she was in trouble and near death, he refused to do anything to help her.

He was, I think, very handsome. I gather this from photographs and from my own memories of him, dressed in his Sunday best and on his way to preach a sermon somewhere, when I was little. Handsome, proud, and ingrown, "like a toe-nail," somebody said. But he looked to me, as I grew older, like pictures I had seen of African tribal chieftains: he really should have been naked, with war-paint on and barbaric mementos, standing among spears. He could be chilling in the pulpit and indescribably cruel in his personal life and he was certainly the most bitter man I have ever met; yet it must be said that there was something else in him, buried in him, which lent him his tremendous power and, even, a rather crushing charm. It had something to do with his blackness, I think—he was very black—with his blackness and his beauty, and with the fact that he knew that he was black but did not know that he was beautiful. He claimed to be proud of his blackness but it had also been the cause of much humiliation and it had fixed bleak boundaries to his life. He was not a young man when we were growing up and he had already suffered many kinds of ruin; in his outrageously demanding and protective way he loved his children, who were black like him and menaced, like him; and all these things sometimes showed in his face when he tried, never to my knowledge with any success, to establish contact with any of us. When he took one of his children on his knee to play, the child always became fretful and began to cry; when he tried to help one of us with our homework the absolutely unabating tension which emanated from him caused our minds and our tongues to become paralyzed, so that he, scarcely knowing why, flew into a rage and the child, not knowing why, was punished. If it ever entered his head to bring a surprise home for his children, it was, almost unfailingly, the wrong surprise and even the big watermelons he often brought home on his back in the summertime led to the most appalling scenes. I do not remember, in all those years, that one of his children was ever glad to see him come home. From what I was able to gather of his early life, it seemed that this inability to establish contact with other people had always marked him and had been one of the things which had driven him out of New Orleans. There was something in him, therefore, groping and tentative, which was never expressed and which was buried with him. One saw it most clearly when he was facing new people and hoping to impress them. But he never did, not for long. We went from church to smaller and more improbable church, he found himself in less and less demand as a minister, and by the time he died none of his friends had come to see him for a long time. He had lived and died in an intolerable bitterness of spirit and it frightened me, as we drove him to the graveyard through those unquiet, ruined streets, to see how powerful and overflowing this bitterness could be and to realize that this bitterness now was mine.

When he died I had been away from home for a little over a year. In that year I had had time to become aware of the meaning of all my father's bitter warnings, had discovered the secret of his proudly pursed lips and rigid carriage: I had discovered the weight of white people in the world. I saw that this had been for my ancestors and now would be for me an awful thing to live with and that the bitterness which had helped to kill my father could also kill me.

He had been ill a long time—in the mind, as we now realized, reliving instances of his fantastic intransigence in the new light of his affliction and endeavoring to feel a sorrow for him which never, quite, came true. We had not known that he was being eaten up by paranoia, and the discovery that his cruelty, to our bodies and our minds, had been one of the symptoms of his illness was not, then, enough to enable us to forgive him. The younger children felt, quite simply, relief that he would not be coming home anymore. My mother's observation that it was he, after all, who had kept them alive all these years meant nothing because the problems of keeping children alive are not real for children. The older children felt, with my father gone, that they could invite their friends to the house without fear that their friends would be insulted or, as had sometimes happened with me, being told that their friends were in league with the devil and intended to rob our family of everything we owned. (I didn't fail to wonder, and it made me hate him, what on earth we owned that anybody else would want.)

His illness was beyond all hope of healing before anyone realized that he was ill. He had always been so strange and had lived, like a prophet, in such unimaginably close communion with the Lord that his long silences which were punctuated by moans and hallelujahs and snatches of old songs while he sat at the living-room window never seemed odd to us. It was not until he refused to eat because, he said, his family was trying to poison him that my mother was forced to accept as a fact what had, until then, been only an unwilling suspicion. When he was committed, it was discovered that he had tuberculosis and, as it turned out, the disease of his mind allowed the disease of his body to destroy him. For the doctors could not force him to eat, either, and, though he was fed intravenously, it was clear from the beginning that there was no hope for him.

In my mind's eye I could see him, sitting at the window, locked up in his terrors; hating and fearing every living soul including his children who had betrayed him, too, by reaching towards the world which had despised him. There were nine of us. I began to wonder what it could have felt like for such a man to have had nine children whom he could barely feed. He used to make little jokes about our poverty, which never, of course, seemed very funny to us; they could not have seemed very funny to him, either, or else our all too feeble response to them would never have caused such rages. He spent great energy and achieved, to our chagrin, no small amount of success in keeping us away from the people who surrounded us, people who had all-night rent parties to which we listened when we should have been sleeping, people who cursed and drank and flashed razor blades on Lenox Avenue. He could not understand why, if they had so much energy to spare, they could not use it to make their lives better. He treated almost everybody on our block with a most uncharitable asperity and neither they, nor, of course, their children were slow to reciprocate.

The only white people who came to our house were welfare workers and bill collectors. It was almost always my mother who dealt with them, for my father's temper, which was at the mercy of his pride, was never to be trusted. It was clear that he felt their very presence in his home to be a violation: this was conveyed by his carriage, almost ludicrously stiff, and by his voice, harsh and vindictively polite. When I was around nine or ten I wrote a play which was directed by a young, white schoolteacher, a woman, who then took an interest in me, and gave me books to read and, in order to corroborate my theatrical bent, decided to take me to see what she somewhat tactlessly referred to as "real" plays. Theater-going was forbidden in our house, but, with the really cruel intuitiveness of a child, I suspected that the color of this woman's skin would carry the day for me. When, at school, she suggested taking me to the theater, I did not, as I might have done if she had been a Negro, find a way of discouraging her, but agreed that she should pick me up at my house one evening. I then, very cleverly, left all the rest to my mother, who suggested to my father, as I knew she would, that it would not be very nice to let such a kind woman make the trip for nothing. Also, since it was a school-teacher, I imagine that my mother countered the idea of sin with the idea of "education," which word, even with my father, carried a kind of bitter weight.

Before the teacher came my father took me aside to ask *why* she was coming, what *interest* she could possibly have in our house, in a boy like me. I said I didn't know but I, too, suggested that it had something to do with education. And I understood that my father was waiting for me to say something—I didn't quite know what; perhaps that I wanted his protection against this teacher and her "education." I said none of these things and the teacher came and we went out. It was clear, during the brief interview in our living room, that my father was agreeing very much against his will and that he would have refused permission if he had dared. The fact that he did not dare caused me to despise him: I had no way of knowing that he was facing in that living room a wholly unprecedented and frightening situation.

Later, when my father had been laid off from his job, this woman became very important to us. She was really a very sweet and generous woman and went to a great deal of trouble to be of help to us, particularly during one awful winter. My mother called her by the highest name she knew: she said she was a "christian." My father could scarcely disagree but during the four or five years of our relatively close association he never trusted her and was always trying to surprise in her open, Midwestern face the genuine, cunningly hidden, and hideous motivation. In later years, particularly when it began to be clear that this "education" of mine was going to lead me to perdition, he became more explicit and warned me that my white friends in high school were not really my friends and that I would see, when I was older, how white people would do anything to keep a Negro down. Some of them could be nice, he admitted, but none of them were to be trusted and most of them were not even nice. The best thing was to have as little to do with them as possible. I did not feel this way and I was certain, in my innocence, that I never would.

But the year which preceded my father's death had made a great change in my life. I had been living in New Jersey, working in defense plants, working and living among southerners, white and black. I knew about the south, of course, and about how southerners treated Negroes and how they expected them to behave, but it had never entered my mind that anyone would look at me and expect *me* to behave that way. I learned in New Jersey that to be a Negro meant, precisely, that one was never looked at but was simply at the mercy of the reflexes the color of one's skin caused in other people. I acted in New Jersey as I had always acted, that is as though I thought a great deal of myself—I had to *act* that way—with results that were, simply, unbelievable. I had scarcely arrived before I had earned the enmity, which was extraordinarily ingenious, of all my superiors and nearly all my co-workers. In the beginning, to make matters worse, I simply did not know what was happening. I did not know what I had done, and I shortly began to wonder what *anyone* could possibly do, to bring about such unanimous, active, and unbearably vocal hostility. I knew about jim-crow but I had never experienced it. I went to the same self-service restaurant three times and stood with all the Princeton boys before the counter, waiting for a hamburger and coffee; it was always an extraordinarily long time before anything was set before me; but it was not until the fourth visit that I learned that, in fact, nothing had ever been set before me: I had simply picked something up. Negroes were not served there, I was told, and they had been waiting for me to realize that I was always the only Negro present. Once I was told this, I determined to go there all the time. But now they were ready for me and, though some dreadful scenes were subsequently enacted in that restaurant, I never ate there again.

It was the same story all over New Jersey, in bars, bowling alleys, diners, places to live. I was always being forced to leave, silently, or with mutual imprecations. I very shortly became notorious and children giggled behind me when I passed and their elders whispered or shouted—they really believed that I was mad. And it did begin to work on my mind, of course; I began to be afraid to go anywhere and to compensate for this I went places to which I really should not have gone and where, God knows, I had no desire to be. My reputation in town naturally enhanced my reputation at work and my working day became one long series of acrobatics designed to keep me out of trouble. I cannot say that these acrobatics succeeded. It began to seem that the machinery of the organization I worked for was turning over, day and night, with but one aim: to eject me. I was fired once, and contrived, with the aid of a friend from New York, to get back on the payroll; was fired again, and bounced back again. It took a while to fire me for the third time, but the third time took. There were no loopholes anywhere. There was not even any way of getting back inside the gates.

That year in New Jersey lives in my mind as though it were the year during which, having an unsuspected predilection for it, I first contracted some dread, chronic disease, the unfailing symptom of which is a kind of blind fever, a pounding in the skull and fire in the bowels. Once this disease is contracted, one can never be really carefree again, for the fever, without an instant's warning, can recur at any moment. It can wreck more important things than race relations. There is not a Negro alive who does not have this rage in his blood—one has the choice, merely, of living with it consciously or surrendering to it. As for me, this fever has recurred in me, and does, and will until the day I die.

My last night in New Jersey, a white friend from New York took me to the nearest big town, Trenton, to go to the movies and have a few drinks. As it turned out, he also saved me from, at the very least, a violent whipping. Almost every detail of that night stands out very clearly in my memory. I even remember the name of the movie we saw because its title impressed me as being so patly ironical. It was a movie about the German occupation of France, starring Maureen O'Hara and Charles Laughton and called *This Land Is Mine.* I remember the name of the diner we walked into when the movie ended: It was the "American Diner." When we walked in the counterman asked what we wanted and I remember answering with the casual sharpness which had become my habit: "We want a hamburger and a cup of coffee, what do you think we want?" I do not know why, after a year of such rebuffs, I so completely failed to anticipate his answer, which was, of course, "We don't serve Negroes here." This reply failed to discompose me, at least for the moment. I made some sardonic comment about the name of the diner and we walked out into the streets.

This was the time of what was called the "brown-out," when the lights in all American cities were very dim. When we re-entered the streets something happened to me which had the force of an optical illusion, or a nightmare. The streets were very crowded and I was facing north. People were moving in every direction but it seemed to me, in that instant, that all of the people I could see, and many more than that, were moving toward me, against me, and that everyone was white. I remember how their faces gleamed. And I felt, like a physical sensation, a *click* at the nape of my neck as though some interior string connecting my head to my body had been cut. I began to walk. I heard my friend call after me, but I ignored him. Heaven only knows what was going on in his mind, but he had the good sense not to touch me—I don't know what would have happened if he had—and to keep me in sight. I don't know what was going on in my mind, either; I certainly had no conscious plan. I wanted to do something to crush these white faces, which were crushing me. I walked for perhaps a block or two until I came to an enormous, glittering, and fashionable restaurant in which I knew not even the intercession of the Virgin would cause me to be served. I pushed through the doors and took the first vacant seat I saw, at a table for two, and waited.

I do not know how long I waited and I rather wonder, until today, what I could possibly have looked like. Whatever I looked like, I frightened the waitress who shortly appeared, and the moment she appeared all of my fury flowed towards her. I hated her for her white face, and for her great, astounded, frightened eyes. I felt that if she found a black man so frightening I would make her fright worthwhile.

She did not ask me what I wanted, but repeated, as though she had learned it somewhere, "We don't serve Negroes here." She did not say it with the blunt, derisive hostility to which I had grown so accustomed, but, rather, with a note of apology in her voice, and fear. This made me colder and more murderous than ever. I felt I had to do something with my hands. I wanted her to come close enough for me to get her neck between my hands.

So I pretended not to have understood her, hoping to draw her closer. And she did step a very short step closer, with her pencil poised incongruously over her pad, and repeated the formula: ". . . don't serve Negroes here."

Somehow, with the repetition of that phrase, which was already ringing in my head like a thousand bells of a nightmare, I realized that she would never come any closer and that I would have to strike from a distance. There was nothing on the table but an ordinary water-mug half full of water, and I picked this up and hurled it with all my strength at her. She ducked and it missed her and shattered against the mirror behind the bar. And, with that sound, my frozen blood abruptly thawed, I returned from wherever I had been, I *saw*, for the first time, the restaurant, the people with their mouths open, already, as it seemed to me, rising as one man, and I realized what I had done, and where I was, and I was frightened. I rose and began running for the door. A round, potbellied man grabbed me by the nape of the neck just as I reached the doors and began to beat me about the face. I kicked him and got loose and ran into the streets. My friend whispered, *"Run!"* and I ran.

My friend stayed outside the restaurant long enough to misdirect my pursuers and the police, who arrived, he told me, at once. I do not know what I said to him when he came to my room that night. I could not have said much. I felt, in the oddest, most awful way, that I had somehow betrayed him. I lived it over and over and over again, the way one relives an automobile accident after it has happened and one finds oneself alone and safe. I could not get over two facts, both equally difficult for the imagination to grasp, and one was that I could have been murdered. But the other was that I had been ready to commit murder. I saw nothing very clearly but I did see this: that my life, my *real* life, was in danger, and not from anything other people might do but from the hatred I carried in my own heart.

II

I had returned home around the second week in June—in great haste because it seemed that my father's death and my mother's confinement were both but a matter of hours. In the case of my mother, it soon became clear that she had simply made a miscalculation. This had always been her tendency and I don't believe that a single one of us arrived in the world, or has since arrived anywhere else, on time. But none of us dawdled so intolerably about the business of being born as did my baby sister. We sometimes amused ourselves, during those endless, stifling weeks, by picturing the baby sitting within in the safe, warm dark, bitterly regretting the necessity of becoming a part of our chaos and stubbornly putting it off as long as possible. I understood her perfectly and congratulated her on showing such good sense so soon. Death, however, sat as purposefully at my father's bedside as life stirred within my mother's womb and it was harder to understand why he so lingered in that long shadow. It seemed that he had bent, and for a long time, too, all of his energies towards dying. Now death was ready for him but my father held back.

All of Harlem, indeed, seemed to be infected by waiting. I had never before known it to be so violently still. Racial tensions throughout this country were exacerbated during the early years of the war, partly because the labor market brought together hundreds of thousands of ill-prepared people and partly because Negro soldiers, regardless of where they were born, received their military training in the south. What happened in defense plants and army camps had repercussions, naturally, in every Negro ghetto. The situation in Harlem had grown bad enough for clergymen, policemen, educators, politicians, and social workers to assert in one breath that there was no "crime wave" and to offer, in the very next breath, suggestions as to how to combat it. These suggestions always seemed to involve playgrounds, despite the fact that racial skirmishes were occurring in the playgrounds, too. Playground or not, crime wave or not, the Harlem police force had been augmented in March, and the unrest grew—perhaps, in fact, partly as a result of the ghetto's instinctive hatred of policemen. Perhaps the most revealing news item, out of the steady parade of reports of muggings, stabbings, shootings, assaults, gang wars, and accusations of police brutality, is the item concerning six Negro girls who set upon a white girl in the subway because, as they all too accurately put it, she was stepping on their toes. Indeed she was, all over the nation.

I had never before been so aware of policemen, on foot, on horseback, on corners, everywhere, always two by two. Nor had I ever been so aware of small knots of people. They were on stoops and on corners and in doorways, and what was striking about them, I think, was that they did not seem to be talking. Never, when I passed these groups, did the usual sound of a curse or a laugh ring out and neither did there seem to be any hum of gossip. There was certainly, on the other hand, occurring between them communication extraordinarily intense. Another thing that was striking was the unexpected diversity of the people who made up these groups. Usually, for example, one would see a group of sharpies standing on the street corner, jiving the passing chicks; or a group of older men, usually, for some reason, in the vicinity of a barber shop, discussing baseball scores, or the numbers, or making rather chilling observations about women they had known. Women, in a general way, tended to be seen less often together—unless they were church women, or very young girls, or prostitutes met together for an unprofessional instant. But that summer I saw the strangest combinations: large, respectable, churchly matrons standing on the stoops or the corners with their hair tied up, together with a girl in sleazy satin whose face bore the marks of gin and the razor, or heavy-set, abrupt, no-nonsense older men, in company with the most disreputable and fanatical "race" men, or these same "race" men with the sharpies, or these sharpies with the churchly women. Seventh Day Adventists and Methodists and Spiritualists seemed to be hobnobbing with Holyrollers and they were all, alike, entangled with the most flagrant disbe-lievers; something heavy in their stance seemed to indicate that they had all, incredibly, seen a common vision, and on each face there seemed to be the same strange, bitter shadow.

The churchly women and the matter-of-fact, no-nonsense men had children in the Army. The sleazy girls they talked to had lovers there, the sharpies and the "race" men had friends and brothers there. It would have demanded an unquestioning patriotism, happily as uncommon in this country as it is undesirable, for these people not to have been disturbed by the bitter letters they received, by the newspaper stories they read, not to have been enraged by the posters, then to be found all over New York, which described the Japanese as "yellowbellied Japs." It was only the "race" men, to be sure, who spoke ceaselessly of being revenged—how this vengeance was to be exacted was not clear—for the indignities and dangers suffered by Negro boys in uniform; but everybody felt a directionless, hopeless bitterness, as well as that panic which can scarcely be suppressed when one knows that a human being one loves is beyond one's reach, and in danger. This helplessness and this gnawing uneasiness does something, at length, to even the toughest mind. Perhaps the best way to sum all this up is to say that the people I knew felt, mainly, a peculiar kind of relief when they knew that their boys were being shipped out of the south, to do battle overseas. It was, perhaps, like feeling that the most dangerous part of a dangerous journey had been passed and that now, even if death should come, it would come with honor and without the complicity of their countrymen. Such a death would be, in short, a fact with which one could hope to live.

It was on the 28th of July, which I believe was a Wednesday, that I visited my father for the first time during his illness and for the last time in his life. The moment I saw him I knew why I had put off this visit so long. I had told my mother that I did not want to see him because I hated him. But this was not true. It was only that I *had* hated him and I wanted to hold on to this hatred. I did not want to look on him as a ruin: it was not a ruin I had hated. I imagine that one of the reasons people cling to their hates so stubbornly is because they sense, once hate is gone, that they will be forced to deal with pain.

We traveled out to him, his older sister and myself, to what seemed to be the very end of a very Long Island. It was hot and dusty and we wrangled, my aunt and I, all the way out, over the fact that I had recently begun to smoke and, as she said, to give myself airs. But I knew that she wrangled with me because she could not bear to face the fact of her brother's dying. Neither could I endure the reality of her despair, her unstated bafflement as to what had happened to her brother's life, and her own. So we wrangled and I smoked and from time to time she fell into a heavy reverie. Covertly, I watched her face, which was the face of an old woman; it had fallen in, the eyes were sunken and lightless; soon she would be dying, too.

In my childhood—it had not been so long ago—I had thought her beautiful. She had been quick-witted and quick-moving and very generous with all the children and each of her visits had been an event. At one time one of my brothers and myself had thought of running away to live with her. Now she could no longer produce out of her handbag some unexpected and yet familiar delight. She made me feel pity and revulsion and fear. It was awful to realize that she no longer caused me to feel affection. The closer we came to the hospital the more querulous she became and at the same time, naturally, grew more dependent on me. Between pity and guilt and fear I began to feel that there was another me trapped in my skull like a jack-in-the-box who might escape my control at any moment and fill the air with screaming.

She began to cry the moment we entered the room and she saw him lying there, all shriveled and still, like a little black monkey. The great, gleaming apparatus which fed him and would have compelled him to be still even if he had been able to move brought to mind, not beneficence, but torture; the tubes entering his arm made me think of pictures I had seen when a child, of Gulliver, tied down by the pygmies on that island. My aunt wept and wept, there was a whistling sound in my father's throat; nothing was said; he could not speak. I wanted to take his hand, to say something. But I do not know what I could have said, even if he could have heard me. He was not really in that room with us, he had at last really embarked on his journey; and though my aunt told me that he said he was going to meet Jesus, I did not hear anything except that whistling in his throat. The doctor came back and we left, into that unbearable train again, and home. In the morning came the telegram saying that he was dead. Then the house was suddenly full of relatives, friends, hysteria, and confusion and I quickly left my mother and the children to the care of those impressive women, who, in Negro communities at least, automatically appear at times of bereavement armed with lotions, proverbs, and patience, and an ability to cook. I went downtown. By the time I returned, later the same day, my mother had been carried to the hospital and the baby had been born.

III

For my father's funeral I had nothing black to wear and this posed a nagging problem all day long. It was one of those problems, simple, or impossible of solution, to which the mind insanely clings in order to avoid the mind's real trouble. I spent most of that day at the downtown apartment of a girl I knew, celebrating my birthday with whiskey and wondering what to wear that night. When planning a birthday celebration one naturally does not expect that it will be up against competition from a funeral and this girl had anticipated taking me out that night, for a big dinner and a night club afterwards. Sometime during the course of that long day we decided that we would go out anyway, when my father's funeral service was over. I imagine *I* decided it, since, as the funeral hour approached, it became clearer and clearer to me that I would not know what to do with myself when it was over. The girl, stifling her very lively concern as to the possible effects of the whiskey on one of my father's chief mourners, concentrated on being conciliatory and practically helpful. She found a black shirt for me somewhere and ironed it and, dressed in the darkest pants and jacket I owned, and slightly drunk, I made my way to my father's funeral.

The chapel was full, but not packed, and very quiet. There were, mainly, my father's relatives, and his children, and here and there I saw faces I had not seen since childhood, the faces of my father's one-time friends. They were very dark and solemn now, seeming somehow to suggest that they had known all along that something like this would happen. Chief among the mourners was my aunt, who had quarreled with my father all his life; by which I do not mean to suggest that her mourning was insincere or that she had not loved him. I suppose that she was one of the few people in the world who had, and their incessant quarreling proved precisely the strength of the tie that bound them. The only other person in the world, as far as I knew, whose relationship to my father rivaled my aunt's in depth was my mother, who was not there.

It seemed to me, of course, that it was a very long funeral. But it was, if anything, a rather shorter funeral than most, nor, since there were no overwhelming, uncontrollable expressions of grief, could it be called—if I dare to use the word—successful. The minister who preached my father's funeral sermon was one of the few my father had still been seeing as he neared his end. He presented to us in his sermon a man whom none of us had ever seen—a man thoughtful, patient, and forbearing, a Christian inspiration to all who knew him, and a model for his children. And no doubt the children, in their disturbed and guilty state, were almost ready to believe this; he had been remote enough to be anything and, anyway, the shock of the incontrovertible, that it was really our father lying up there in that casket, prepared the mind for anything. His sister moaned and this grief-stricken moaning was taken as corroboration. The other faces held a dark, non-committal thoughtfulness. This was not the man they had known, but they had scarcely expected to be confronted with *him*; this was, in a sense deeper than questions of fact, the man they had not known, and the man they had not known may have been the real one. The real man, whoever he had been, had suffered and now he was dead: this was all that was sure and all that mattered now. Every man in the chapel hoped that when his hour came he, too, would be eulogized, which is to say forgiven, and that all of his lapses, greeds, errors, and strayings from the truth would be invested with coherence and looked upon with charity. This was perhaps the last thing human beings could give each other and it was what they demanded, after all, of the Lord. Only the Lord saw the midnight tears, only He was present when one of His children, moaning and wringing hands, paced up and down the room. When one slapped one's child in anger the recoil in the heart reverberated through heaven and became part of the pain of the universe. And when the children were hungry and sullen and distrustful and one watched them, daily, growing wilder, and further away, and running headlong into danger, it was the Lord who knew what the charged heart endured as the strap was laid to the backside; the Lord alone who knew what one *would* have said if one had had, like the Lord, the gift of the living word. It was the Lord who knew of the impossibility every parent in that room faced: how to prepare the child for the day when the child would be despised and how to *create* in the child—by what means?—a stronger antidote to this poison than one had found for oneself. The avenues, side streets, bars, billiard halls, hospitals, police stations, and even the playgrounds of Harlem—not to mention the houses of correction, the jails, and the morgue—testified to the potency of the poison while remaining silent as to the efficacy of whatever antidote, irresistibly raising the question of whether or not such an antidote existed; raising, which was worse, the question of whether or not an antidote was desirable; perhaps poison should be fought with poison. With these several schisms in the mind and with more terrors in the heart than could be named, it was better not to judge the man who had gone down under an impossible burden. It was better to remember: *Thou knowest this man's fall; but thou knowest not his wrassling.*

While the preacher talked and I watched the children—years of changing their diapers, scrubbing them, slapping them, taking them to school, and scolding them had had the perhaps inevitable result of making me love them, though I am not sure I knew this then—my mind was busily breaking out with a rash of disconnected impressions. Snatches of popular songs, indecent jokes, bits of books I had read, movie sequences, faces, voices, political issues—I thought I was going mad; all these impressions suspended, as it were, in the solution of the faint nausea produced in me by the heat and liquor. For a moment I had the impression that my alcoholic breath, inefficiently disguised with chewing gum, filled the entire chapel. Then someone began singing one of my father's favorite songs and, abruptly, I was with him, sitting on his knee, in the hot, enormous, crowded church which was the first church we attended. It was the Abyssinia Baptist Church on 138th Street. We had not gone there long. With this image, a host of others came. I had forgotten, in the rage of my growing up, how proud my father had been of me when I was little. Apparently, I had had a voice and my father had liked to show me off before the members of the church. I had forgotten what he had looked like when he was pleased but now I remembered that he had always been grinning with pleasure when my solos ended. I even remembered certain expressions on his face when he teased my mother—had he loved her? I would never know. And when had it all begun to change? For now it seemed that he had not always been cruel. I remembered being taken for a haircut and scraping my knee on the footrest of the barber's chair and I remembered my father's face as he soothed my crying and applied the stinging iodine. Then I remembered our fights, fights which had been of the worst possible kind because my technique had been silence.

I remembered the one time in all our life together when we had really spoken to each other.

It was on a Sunday and it must have been shortly before I left home. We were walking, just the two of us, in our usual silence, to or from church. I was in high school and had been doing a lot of writing and I was, at about this time, the editor of the high school magazine. But I had also been a Young Minister and had been preaching from the pulpit. Lately, I had been taking fewer engagements and preached as rarely as possible. It was said in the church, quite truthfully, that I was "cooling off."

My father asked me abruptly, "You'd rather write than preach, wouldn't you?"

I was astonished at his question—because it was a real question. I answered, "Yes."

That was all we said. It was awful to remember that that was all we had *ever* said.

The casket now was opened and the mourners were being led up the aisle to look for the last time on the deceased. The assumption was that the family was too overcome with grief to be allowed to make this journey alone and I watched while my aunt was led to the casket and, muffled in black, and shaking, led back to her seat. I disapproved of forcing the children to look on their dead father, considering that the shock of his death, or, more truthfully, the shock of death as a reality, was already a little more than a child could bear, but my judgment in this matter had been overruled and there they were, bewildered and frightened and very small, being led, one by one, to the casket. But there is also something very gallant about children at such moments. It has something to do with their silence and gravity and with the fact that one cannot help them. Their legs, somehow, seem *exposed*, so that it is at once incredible and terribly clear that their legs are all they have to hold them up.

I had not wanted to go to the casket myself and I certainly had not wished to be led there, but there was no way of avoiding either of these forms. One of the deacons led me up and I looked on my father's face. I cannot say that it looked like him at all. His blackness had been equivocated by powder and there was no suggestion in that casket of what his power had or could have been. He was simply an old man dead, and it was hard to believe that he had ever given anyone either joy or pain. Yet, his life filled that room. Further up the avenue his wife was holding his newborn child. Life and death so close together, and love and hatred, and right and wrong, said something to me which I did not want to hear concerning man, concerning the life of man.

After the funeral, while I was downtown desperately celebrating my birthday, a Negro soldier, in the lobby of the Hotel Braddock, got into a fight with a white policeman over a Negro girl. Negro girls, white policemen, in or out of uniform, and Negro males—in or out of uniform—were part of the furniture of the lobby of the Hotel Braddock and this was certainly not the first time such an incident had occurred. It was destined, however, to receive an unprecedented publicity, for the fight between the policeman and the soldier ended with the shooting of the soldier. Rumor, flowing immediately to the streets outside, stated that the soldier had been shot in the back, an instantaneous and revealing invention, and that the soldier had died protecting a Negro woman. The facts were somewhat different—for example, the soldier had not been shot in the back, and was not dead, and the girl seems to have been as dubious a symbol of womanhood as her white counterpart in Georgia usually is, but no one was interested in the facts. They preferred the invention because this invention expressed and corroborated their hates and fears so perfectly. It is just as well to remember that people are always doing this. Perhaps many of those legends, including Christianity, to which the world clings began their conquest of the world with just some such concerted surrender to distortion. The effect, in Harlem, of this particular legend was like the effect of a lit match in a tin of gasoline. The mob gathered before the doors of the Hotel Braddock simply began to swell and to spread in every direction, and Harlem exploded.

The mob did not cross the ghetto lines. It would have been easy, for example, to have gone over Morningside Park on the west side or to have crossed the Grand Central railroad tracks at 125th Street on the east side, to wreak havoc in white neighborhoods. The mob seems to have been mainly interested in something more potent and real than the white face, that is, in white power, and the principal damage done during the riot of the summer of 1943 was to white business establishments in Harlem. It might have been a far bloodier story, of course, if, at the hour the riot began, these establishments had still been open. From the Hotel Braddock the mob fanned out, east and west along 125th Street, and for the entire length of Lenox, Seventh, and Eighth avenues. Along each of these avenues, and along each major side street—116th, 125th, 135th, and so on—bars, stores, pawnshops, restaurants, even little luncheonettes had been smashed open and entered and looted—looted, it might be added, with more haste than efficiency. The shelves really looked as though a bomb had struck them. Cans of beans and soup and dog food, along with toilet paper, corn flakes, sardines, and milk tumbled every which way, and abandoned cash registers and cases of beer leaned crazily out of the splintered windows and were strewn along the avenues. Sheets, blankets, and clothing of every description formed a kind of path, as though people had dropped them while running. I truly had not realized that Harlem *had* so many stores until I saw them all smashed open; the first time the word *wealth* ever entered my mind in relation to Harlem was when I saw it scattered in the streets. But one's first, incongruous impression of plenty was countered immediately by an impression of waste. None of this was doing anybody any good. It would have been better to have left the plate glass as it had been and the goods lying in the stores.

It would have been better, but it would also have been intolerable, for Harlem had needed something to smash. To smash something is the ghetto's chronic need. Most of the time it is the members of the ghetto who smash each other, and themselves. But as long as the ghetto walls are standing there will always come a moment when these outlets do not work. That summer, for example, it was not enough to get into a fight on Lenox Avenue, or curse out one's cronies in the barber shops. If ever, indeed, the violence which fills Harlem's churches, pool halls, and bars erupts outward in a more direct fashion, Harlem and its citizens are likely to vanish in an apocalyptic flood. That this is not likely to happen is due to a great many reasons, most hidden and powerful among them the Negro's real relation to the white American. This relation prohibits, simply, anything as uncomplicated and satisfactory as pure hatred. In order really to hate white people, one has to blot so much out of the mind—and the heart—that this hatred itself becomes an exhausting and self-destructive pose. But this does not mean, on the other hand, that love comes easily: the white world is too powerful, too complacent, too ready with gratuitous humiliation, and, above all, too ignorant and too innocent for that. One is absolutely forced to make perpetual qualifications and one's own reactions are always canceling each other out. It is this, really, which has driven so many people mad, both white and black. One is always in the position of having to decide between amputation and gangrene. Amputation is swift but time may prove that the amputation was not necessary—or one may delay the amputation too long. Gangrene is slow, but it is impossible to be sure that one is reading one's symptoms right. The idea of going through life as a cripple is more than one can bear, and equally unbearable is the risk of swelling up slowly, in agony, with poison. And the trouble, finally, is that the risks are real even if the choices do not exist.

"But as for me and my house," my father had said, "we will serve the Lord." I wondered, as we drove him to his resting place, what this line had meant for him. I had heard him preach it many times. I had preached it once myself, proudly giving it an interpretation different from my father's. Now the whole thing came back to me, as though my father and I were on our way to Sunday school and I were memorizing the golden text: *And if it seem evil unto you to serve the Lord, choose you this day whom you will serve; whether the gods which your fathers served that were on the other side of the flood, or the gods of the Amorites, in whose land ye dwell: but as for me and my house, we will serve the Lord.* I suspected in these familiar lines a meaning which had never been there for me before. All of my father's texts and songs, which I had decided were meaningless, were arranged before me at his death like empty bottles, waiting to hold the meaning which life would give them for me. This was his legacy: nothing is ever escaped. That bleakly memorable morning I hated the unbelievable streets and the Negroes and whites who had, equally, made them that way. But I knew that it was folly, as my father would have said, this bitterness was folly. It was necessary to hold on to the things that mattered. The dead man mattered, the new life mattered; blackness and whiteness did not matter; to believe that they did was to acquiesce in one's own destruction. Hatred, which could destroy so much, never failed to destroy the man who hated and this was an immutable law.

It began to seem that one would have to hold in the mind forever two ideas which seemed to be in opposition. The first idea was acceptance, the acceptance, totally without rancor, of life as it is, and men as they are: in the light of this idea, it goes without saying that injustice is a commonplace. But this did not mean that one could be complacent, for the second idea was of equal power: that one must never, in one's own life, accept these injustices as commonplace but must fight them with all one's strength. This fight begins, however, in the heart and it now had been laid to my charge to keep my own heart free of hatred and despair. This intimation made my heart heavy and, now that my father was irrecoverable, I wished that he had been beside me so that I could have searched his face for the answers which only the future would give me now.

Out There

Jo Ann Beard

It isn't even eight A.M. and I'm hot. My rear end is welded to the seat just like it was yesterday. I'm fifty miles from the motel and about a thousand and a half from home, in a little white Mazda with 140,000 miles on it and no rust. I'm all alone in Alabama, with only a cooler and a tape deck for company. It's already in the high 80s. Yesterday, coming up from the keys through Florida, I had a day-long anxiety attack that I decided last night was really heat prostration. I was a cinder with a brain; I was actually whimpering. I kept thinking I saw alligators at the edge of the highway.

There were about four hundred exploded armadillos, too, but I got used to them. They were real, and real dead. The alligators weren't real or dead, but they may have been after me. I'm running away from home.

I bolted four weeks ago, leaving my husband to tend the dogs and tool around town on his bicycle. He doesn't love me anymore, it's both trite and true. He does love himself, though. He's begun wearing cologne and staring into the mirror for long minutes, trying out smiles. He's become a politician. After thirteen years he came to realize that the more successful he got, the less he loved me. That's how he put it, late one night. He won that screaming match. He said, gently and sadly, "I feel sort of embarrassed of you."

I said, "Of what? The way I look? The way I act?"

And he said, softly, "Everything, sort of."

And it was true. Well, I decided to take a trip to Florida. I sat on my haunches in Key West for four weeks, writing and seething and striking up conversations with strangers. I had my thirty-fifth birthday there, weeping into a basket of shrimp. I drank beer and had long involved dreams about cigarettes, I wrote nearly fifty pages on my novel. It's in my trunk at this very moment, dead and decomposing. Boy, do I need a cup of coffee.

There's not much happening this early in the morning. The highway looks interminable again. So far, no alligators. I have a box of seashells in my back seat and I reach back and get a fluted one, pale gray with a pearly interior, to put on the dashboard. I can do everything while I'm driving. At the end of this trip I will have driven 3,999 miles all alone, me and the windshield, me and the radio, me and the creepy alligators. Don't ask me why I didn't get that last mile in, driving around the block a few times or getting a tiny bit lost once. I didn't though, and there you have it. Four thousand sounds like a lot more than 3,999 does; I feel sort of embarrassed for myself.

My window is broken, the crank fell off in Tallahassee on the way down. In order to roll it up or down I have to put the crank back on and turn it slowly and carefully, using one hand to push up the glass. So, mostly I leave it down. I baked like a biscuit yesterday, my left arm is so brown it looks like a branch. Today I'm wearing a long-sleeved white shirt to protect myself. I compromised on wearing long sleeves by going naked underneath it. It's actually cooler this way, compared to yesterday when I drove in my swimming suit top with my hair stuck up like a fountain on top of my head. Plus, I'm having a nervous breakdown. I've got that wild-eyed look.

A little four-lane blacktop running through the Alabama countryside, that's what I'm on. It's pretty, too, better than Florida, which was billboards and condos built on old dump sites. This is like driving between rolling emerald carpets. You can't see the two lanes going in the opposite direction because there's a screen of trees. I'm starting to get in a good mood again. The best was Georgia, coming down. Willow trees and red dirt and snakes stretched out alongside the road. I kept thinking, That looks like a *rope,* and then it would be a huge snake. A few miles later I would think, That looks like a *snake,* and it would be some snarl of something dropped off a truck.

Little convenience store, stuck out in the middle of nothing, a stain on the carpet. I'm gassing it up, getting some coffee. My white shirt is gaping open and I have nothing on underneath it, but who cares, I'll never see these people again. What do I care what Alabama thinks about me. This is a new and unusual attitude for me. I'm practicing being snotty, in anticipation of being dumped by my husband when I get back to Iowa.

I swagger from the gas pump to the store, I don't even care if my boobs are roaming around inside my shirt, if my hair is a freaky snarl, if I look defiant and uppity. There's nothing to be embarrassed of. I bring my coffee cup along and fill it at the counter. Various men, oldish and grungy, sit at tables eating eggs with wadded-up toast. They stare at me carefully while they chew. I ignore them and pay the woman at the counter. She's smoking a cigarette so I envy her.

"Great day, huh?" I ask her. She counts out my change.

"It is, honey," she says. She reaches for her cigarette and takes a puff, blows it up above my head. "Wish I wudn't in *here.*"

"Well, it's getting hotter by the minute," I tell her. I've adopted an accent in just four weeks, an intermittent drawl that makes me think I'm not who everyone thinks I am.

"Y'all think this's hot?" she says idly. "*This* ain't hot."

When I leave, the men are still staring at me in a sullen way. I get in, rearrange all my junk so I have everything handy that I need, choose a Neil Young tape and pop it in the deck, fasten the belt, and then move back out on the highway. Back to the emerald carpet and the road home. Iowa is creeping toward me like a panther.

All I do is sing when I drive. Sing and drink: coffee, Coke, water, juice, coffee. And think. I sing and drink and think. On the way down I would sing, drink, think, and weep uncontrollably, but I'm past that now. Now I suffer bouts of free-floating hostility, which is much better. I plan to use it when I get home.

A car swings up alongside me so I pause in my singing until it goes past. People who sing in their cars always cheer me up, but I'd rather not be caught doing it. On the road, we're all singing, picking our noses, embarrassing ourselves wildly; it gets tiresome. I pause and hum, but the car sticks alongside me so I glance over. It's a guy. He grins and makes a lewd gesture with his mouth. I don't even want to say what it is, it's that disgusting. Tongue darting in and out, quickly. A python testing its food.

I hate this kind of thing. Who do they think they are, these men? I've had my fill of it. I give him the finger, slowly and deliberately. He picked the wrong day to mess with me, I think to myself. I take a sip of coffee.

He's still there.

I glance over briefly and he's making the gesture with his tongue again. I can't believe this. He's from the convenience store, I realize. He has on a fishing hat with lures stuck in it. I saw him back there, but I can't remember if he was sitting with the other men or by himself. He's big, overweight, and dirty, wearing a thin unbuttoned shirt and the terrible fishing hat. His passenger-side window is down. He begins screaming at me.

He followed me from that convenience store. The road is endless, in front there is nothing, no cars, no anything, behind is the same. Just road and grass and trees. The other two lanes are still invisible behind their screen of trees. I'm all alone out here. With him. He's screaming and screaming at me, reaching out his right arm like he's throttling me. I speed up. He speeds up, too, next to me. We're only a few feet apart, my window won't roll up.

He's got slobber on his face and there's no one in either direction. I slam on my brakes and for an instant he's ahead of me, I can breathe, then he slams on his brakes and we're next to each other again. I can't even repeat what he's screaming at me. He's telling me, amid the hot wind and poor Neil Young, what he wants to do to me. He wants to kill me. He's screaming and screaming, I can't look over.

I stare straight ahead through the windshield, hands at ten and two. The front end of his car is moving into my lane. He's saying he'll cut me with a knife, how he'll do it, all that. I can't listen. The front end of his Impala is about four inches from my white Mazda, my little car. This is really my husband's car, my beloved's. My Volkswagen died a lingering death a few months ago. There is no husband, there is no Volkswagen, there is nothing. There isn't even a Jo Ann right now. Whatever I am is sitting here clenched, hands on the wheel, I've stopped being her, now I'm something else. I'm absolutely terrified. He won't stop screaming it, over and over, what he's going to do.

I refuse to give him an inch. I will not move one inch over. If I do he'll have me off the road in an instant. I will not move. I speed up, he speeds up, I slow down, he slows down, I can see him out of the corner of my eye, driving with one hand, reaching like he's grabbing me with the other. "You whore," he screams at me. "I'll *kill* you, I'll *kill* you, I'll *kill* you . . ."

He'll kill me.

If I give him an inch, he'll shove me off the road and get his hands on me, then the end will begin in some unimaginable, unspeakable style that will be all his. I'll be an actor in his drama. We're going too fast, I've got the pedal pressed up to 80 and it's wobbling, his old Impala can probably go 140 on a straightaway like this. There will be blood, he won't want me to die quickly.

I will not lose control. I will ride it out. I cannot let him push me over onto the gravel. His car noses less than two inches from mine; I'm getting rattled. My God, he can almost reach me through his window, he's moved over in his seat, driving just with the left hand, the right is grabbing the hot air. I move over to the edge of my seat, toward the center of the car, carefully, without swerving.

In the rearview mirror a speck appears. Don't look, watch your front end. I glance up again; it's a truck. He can't get me. It's a trucker. Without looking at him I jerk my thumb backward to show him. He screams and screams and screams. He's not leaving. Suddenly a road appears on the right, a dirty and rutted thing leading off into the trees. He hits the brakes, drops behind, and takes it. In my rearview mirror I see that the license plate on the front of his car is buried in dried mud. That road is where he was hoping to push me. He wanted to push my car off the highway and get me on that road. He was hoping to kill me. He was hoping to do what maniacs, furious men, do to women alongside roads, in woods. I can't stop pressing too hard on the gas pedal. I'm at 85 now, and my leg is shaking uncontrollably, coffee is spilled all over the passenger seat, the atlas is wet, Neil Young is still howling on the tape deck. By force of will, I slow down to 65, eject the tape, and wait for the truck to overtake me. When it does, when it comes up alongside me. I don't look over at all, I keep my eyes straight ahead. As it moves in front of me I speed up enough to stay two car lengths behind it. It says *England* on the back, ornate red letters outlined in black. England.

That guy chased me on purpose, he *hated* me, with more passion than anyone has ever felt for me. Ever. Out there are all those decomposing bodies, all those disappeared daughters, discovered by joggers and hunters, their bodies long abandoned, the memory of final desperate moments lingering on the leaves, the trees, the mindless stumps and mushrooms. Images taped to tollbooth windows, faces pressed into the dirt alongside a path somewhere.

I want out of Alabama, I want to be in England. The air is still a blast furnace. I want to roll my window up, but I'd have to stop and get the crank out and lift it by hand. I'm too scared. He's out there still, waiting behind the screen of trees. I have to follow England until I'm out of Alabama. Green car, old Impala, unreadable license plate, lots of rust. Seat covers made out of that spongy stuff, something standing on the dashboard, a coffee cup or a sad

Jesus. The fishing hat with a sweat ring around it right above the brim. Lures with feathers and barbs. I've never been so close to so much hatred in my whole life. *He wanted to kill me.* Think of England, with its white cows and broken-toothed farmers and dark green pastures. Think of the Beatles. I'm hugging the truck so closely now I'm almost under it. Me, of all people, he wanted to kill. Me. Everywhere I go I'm finding out new things about myself. Each way I turn, there it is. It's Jo Ann he wanted to kill.

By noon I want to kill him. I took a right somewhere and got onto the interstate, had the nerve to pee in a rest area, adrenaline running like an engine inside me, my keys threaded through my fingers in case anyone tried anything. I didn't do anything to earn it, I realize. His anger. I didn't do anything. Unless you count giving him the finger, which I don't. *He* earned that.

As it turned out, my husband couldn't bring himself to leave me when I got back to Iowa, so I waited awhile, and watched, then disentangled myself. History: We each got ten photo albums and six trays of slides. We took a lot of pictures in thirteen years. In the early years he looks stoned and contented, distant; in the later years he looks straight and slightly worried. In that last year he only appears by chance, near the edges, a blur of suffering, almost out of frame.

Just before we split, when we were driving somewhere, I told him about the guy in the green car. "Wow," he said. Then he turned up the radio, checked his image in the rearview mirror, and smiled sincerely at the passing landscape.

Silent Dancing

Judith Ortiz Cofer

We have a home movie of this party. Several times my mother and I have watched it together, and I have asked questions about the silent revelers coming in and out of focus. It is grainy and of short duration, but it's a great visual aid to my memory of life at that time. And it is in color—the only complete scene in color I can recall from those years.

We lived in Puerto Rico until my brother was born in 1954. Soon after, because of economic pressures on our growing family, my father joined the United States Navy. He was assigned to duty on a ship in Brooklyn Yard—a place of cement and steel that was to be his home base in the States until his retirement more than twenty years later. He left the Island first, alone, going to New York City and tracking down his uncle who lived with his family across the Hudson River in Paterson, New Jersey. There my father found a tiny apartment in a huge tenement that had once housed Jewish families but was just being taken over and transformed by Puerto Ricans, overflowing from New York City. In 1955 he sent for us. My mother was only twenty years old, I was not quite three, and my brother was a toddler when we arrived at *El Building*, as the place had been christened by its newest residents.

My memories of life in Paterson during those first few years are all in shades of gray. Maybe I was too young to absorb vivid colors and details, or to discriminate between the slate blue of the winter sky and the darker hues of the snow-bearing clouds, but that single color washes over the whole period. The building we lived in was gray, as were the streets, filled with slush the first few months of my life there. The coat my father had bought for me was similar in color and too big; it sat heavily on my thin frame.

I do remember the way the heater pipes banged and rattled, startling all of us out of sleep until we got so used to the sound that we automatically shut it out or raised our voices above the racket. The hiss from the valve punctuated my sleep (which has always been fitful) like a nonhuman presence in the room—a dragon sleeping at the entrance of my childhood. But the pipes were also a connection to all the other lives being lived around us. Having come from a house designed for a single family back in Puerto Rico—my mother's extended-family home—it was curious to know that strangers lived under our floor and above our heads, and that the heater pipe went through everyone's apartments. (My first spanking in Paterson came as a result of playing tunes on the pipes in my room to see if there would be an answer.)

My mother was as new to this concept of beehive life as I was, but she had been given strict orders by my father to keep the doors locked, the noise down, ourselves to ourselves.

It seems that Father had learned some painful lessons about prejudice while searching for an apartment in Paterson. Not until years later did I hear how much resistance he had encountered with landlords who were panicking at the influx of Latinos into a neighborhood that had been Jewish for a couple of generations. It made no difference that it was the American phenomenon of ethnic turnover which was changing the urban core of Paterson, and that the human flood could not be held back with an accusing finger.

"You Cuban?" one man had asked my father, pointing at his name tag on the Navy uniform—even though my father had the fair skin and light-brown hair of his northern Spanish background, and the name Ortiz is as common in Puerto Rico as Johnson is in the United States.

"No," my father had answered, looking past the finger into his adversary's angry eyes. "I'm Puerto Rican."

"Same shit." And the door closed.

My father could have passed as European, but we couldn't. My brother and I both have our mother's black hair and olive skin, and so we lived in El Building and visited our great-uncle and his fair children on the next block. It was their private joke that they were the German branch of the family. Not many years later that area too would be mainly Puerto Rican. It was as if the heart of the city map were being gradually colored brown—*café con leche*[1] brown. Our color.

The movie opens with a sweep of the living room. It is "typical" immigrant Puerto Rican decor for the time: the sofa and chairs are square and hard-looking, upholstered in bright colors (blue and yellow in this instance), and covered with the transparent plastic that furniture salesmen then were so adept at convincing women to buy. The linoleum on the floor is light blue; if it had been subjected to spike heels (as it was in most places), there were dime-sized indentations all over it that cannot be seen in this movie. The room is full of people dressed up: dark suits for the men, red dresses for the women. When I have asked my mother why most of the women are in red that night, she has shrugged, "I don't remember. Just a coincidence." She doesn't have my obsession for assigning symbolism to everything.

The three women in red sitting on the couch are my mother, my eighteen-year-old cousin, and her brother's girlfriend. The novia *is just up from the Island, which is apparent in her body language. She sits up formally, her dress pulled over her knees. She is a pretty girl, but her posture makes her look insecure, lost in her full-skirted dress, which she has carefully tucked around her to make room for my gorgeous cousin, her future sister-in-law.*

---

[1] *café con leche:* Coffee with cream. In Puerto Rico it is sometimes prepared with boiled milk.—COFER'S NOTE.

My cousin has grown up in Paterson and is in her last year of high school. She doesn't have a trace of what Puerto Ricans call la mancha *(literally, the stain: the mark of the new immigrant—something about the posture, the voice, or the humble demeanor that makes it obvious to everyone the person has just arrived on the mainland). My cousin is wearing a tight, sequined, cocktail dress. Her brown hair has been lightened with peroxide around the bangs, and she is holding a cigarette expertly between her fingers, bringing it up to her mouth in a sensuous arc of her arm as she talks animatedly. My mother, who has come up to sit between the two women, both only a few years younger than herself, is somewhere between the poles they represent in our culture.*

It became my father's obsession to get out of the barrio, and thus we were never permitted to form bonds with the place or with the people who lived there. Yet El Building was a comfort to my mother, who never got over yearning for *la isla.* She felt surrounded by her language: The walls were thin, and voices speaking and arguing in Spanish could be heard all day. *Salsas* blasted out of radios, turned on early in the morning and left on for company. Women seemed to cook rice and beans perpetually—the strong aroma of boiling red kidney beans permeated the hallways.

Though Father preferred that we do our grocery shopping at the super-market when he came home on weekend leaves, my mother insisted that she could cook only with products whose labels she could read. Consequently, during the week I accompanied her and my little brother to *La Bodega*—a hole-in-the-wall grocery store across the street from El Building. There we squeezed down three narrow aisles jammed with various products. Goya's and Libby's—those were the trademarks that were trusted by *her mamá,* so my mother bought many cans of Goya beans, soups, and condiments, as well as little cans of Libby's fruit juices for us. And she also bought Colgate tooth-paste and Palmolive soap. (The final *e* is pronounced in both these products in Spanish, so for many years I believed that they were manufactured on the Island. I remember my surprise at first hearing a commercial on television in which Colgate rhymed with "ate.") We always lingered at La Bodega, for it was there that Mother breathed best, taking in the familiar aromas of the foods she knew from Mamá's kitchen. It was also there that she got to speak to the other women of El Building without violating outright Father's dictates against fraternizing with our neighbors.

Yet Father did his best to make our "assimilation" painless. I can still see him carrying a real Christmas tree up several flights of stairs to our apartment, leaving a trail of aromatic pine. He carried it formally, as if it were a flag in a parade. We were the only ones in El Building that I knew of who got presents on both Christmas day AND *dia de Reyes,* the day when the Three Kings brought gifts to Christ and to Hispanic children.

Our supreme luxury in El Building was having our own television set. It must have been a result of Father's guilt feelings over the isolation he had imposed on us, but we were among the first in the barrio to have one. My brother quickly became an avid watcher of Captain Kangaroo and Jungle Jim, while I loved all the series showing families. By the time I started first grade, I could have drawn a map of Middle America as exemplified by the lives of characters in *Father Knows Best, The Donna Reed Show, Leave It to Beaver, My Three Sons,* and (my favorite) *Bachelor Father,* where John Forsythe treated his adopted teenage daughter like a princess because he was rich and had a Chinese houseboy to do everything for him. In truth, compared to our neighbors in El Building, *we* were rich. My father's Navy check provided us with financial security and a standard of life that the factory workers envied. The only thing his money could not buy us was a place to live away from the barrio—his greatest wish, Mother's greatest fear.

In the home movie the men are shown next, sitting around a card table set up in one corner of the living room, playing dominoes. The clack of the ivory pieces was a familiar sound. I heard it in many houses on the Island and in many apartments in Paterson. In "Leave It to Beaver," the Cleavers played bridge in every other episode; in my childhood, the men started every social occasion with a hotly debated round of dominoes. The women would sit around and watch, but they never participated in the games.

Here and there you can see a small child. Children were always brought to parties and, whenever they got sleepy, were put to bed in the host's bedroom. Babysitting was a concept unrecognized by the Puerto Rican women I knew: a responsible mother did not leave her children with any stranger. And in a culture where children are not considered intrusive, there was no need to leave the children at home. We went where our mother went.

Of my preschool years I have only impressions: the sharp bite of the wind in December as we walked with our parents toward the brightly lit stores downtown; how I felt like a stuffed doll in my heavy coat, boots, and mittens; how good it was to walk into the five-and-dime and sit at the counter drinking hot chocolate. On Saturdays our whole family would walk downtown to shop at the big department stores on Broadway. Mother bought all our clothes at Penney's and Sears, and she liked to buy her dresses at the women's specialty shops like Lerner's and Diana's. At some point we'd go into Woolworth's and sit at the soda fountain to eat.

We never ran into other Latinos at these stores or when eating out, and it became clear to me only years later that the women from El Building shopped mainly in other places—stores owned by other Puerto Ricans or by Jewish merchants who had philosophically accepted our presence in the city and decided to make us their good customers, if not real neighbors and friends. These establishments were located not downtown but in the blocks around our street, and they were referred to generically as *La Tienda, El Bazar, La Bodega, La Botánica*. Everyone knew what was meant. These were the stores where your face did not turn a clerk to stone, where your money was as green as anyone else's.

One New Year's Eve we were dressed up like child models in the Sears catalogue: my brother in a miniature man's suit and bow tie, and I in black patent-leather shoes and a frilly dress with several layers of crinoline underneath. My mother wore a bright red dress that night, I remember, and spike heels; her long black hair hung to her waist. Father, who usually wore his Navy uniform during his short visits home, had put on a dark civilian suit for the occasion: we had been invited to his uncle's house for a big celebration. Everyone was excited because my mother's brother Hernan—a bachelor who could indulge himself with luxuries—had bought a home movie camera, which he would be trying out that night.

Even the home movie cannot fill in the sensory details such a gathering left imprinted in a child's brain. The thick sweetness of women's perfumes mixing with the ever-present smells of food cooking in the kitchen: meat and plantain *pasteles,* as well as the ubiquitous rice dish made special with pigeon peas—*gandules*—and seasoned with precious *sofrito*[2] sent up from the Island by somebody's mother or smuggled in by a recent traveler. *Sofrito* was one of the items that women hoarded, since it was hardly ever in stock at La Bodega. It was the flavor of Puerto Rico.

The men drank Palo Viejo rum, and some of the younger ones got weepy. The first time I saw a grown man cry was at a New Year's Eve party: he had been reminded of his mother by the smells in the kitchen. But what I remember most were the boiled *pasteles*—plantain or yucca rectangles stuffed with corned beef or other meats, olives, and many other savory ingredients, all wrapped in banana leaves. Everybody had to fish one out with a fork. There was always a "trick" pastel—one without stuffing—and whoever got that one was the "New Year's Fool."

There was also the music. Long-playing albums were treated like precious china in these homes. Mexican recordings were popular, but the songs that brought tears to my mother's eyes were sung by the melancholy Daniel Santos, whose life as a drug addict was the stuff of legend. Felipe Rodríguez was a particular favorite of couples, since he sang about faithless women and brokenhearted men. There is a snatch of one lyric that has stuck in my mind like a needle on a worn groove: *De piedra ha de ser mi cama, de piedra la cabezera . . . la mujer que a mi me quiera . . . ha de quererme de veras. Ay, Ay,*

---

[2] *sofrito:* A cooked condiment. A sauce composed of a mixture of fatback, ham, tomatoes, and many island spices and herbs. It is added to many typical Puerto Rican dishes for a distinctive flavor.—COFERS NOTE.

Ay, corazón, porque no amas.[3] . . . I must have heard it a thousand times since the idea of a bed made of stone, and its connection to love, first troubled me with its disturbing images.

The five-minute home movie ends with people dancing in a circle—the creative filmmaker must have set it up, so that all of them could file past him. It is both comical and sad to watch silent dancing. Since there is no justification for the absurd movements that music provides for some of us, people appear frantic, their faces embarrassingly intense. It's as if you were watching sex. Yet for years I've had dreams in the form of this home movie. In a recurring scene, familiar faces push themselves forward into my mind's eyes, plastering their features into distorted close-ups. And I'm asking them: "Who is *she*? Who is the old woman I don't recognize? Is she an aunt? Somebody's wife? Tell me who she is."

"See the beauty mark on her cheek as big as a hill on the lunar landscape of her face—well, that runs in the family. The women on your father's side of the family wrinkle early; it's the price they pay for that fair skin. The young girl with the green stain on her wedding dress is *La Novia*—just up from the Island. See, she lowers her eyes when she approaches the camera, as she's supposed to. Decent girls never look at you directly in the face. *Humilde,* humble, a girl should express humility in all her actions. She will make a good wife for your cousin. He should consider himself lucky to have met her only weeks after she arrived here. If he marries her quickly, she will make him a good Puerto Rican–style wife; but if he waits too long, she will be corrupted by the city—just like your cousin there."

"She means me. I do what I want. This is not some primitive island I live on. Do they expect me to wear a black mantilla on my head and go to mass every day? Not me. I'm an American woman, and I will do as I please. I can type faster than anyone in my senior class at Central High, and I'm going to be a secretary to a lawyer when I graduate. I can pass for an American girl anywhere—I've tried it. At least for Italian, anyway—I never speak Spanish in public. I hate these parties, but I wanted the dress. I look better than any of these *humildes* here. My life is going to be different. I have an American boyfriend. He is older and has a car. My parents don't know it, but I sneak out of the house late at night sometimes to be

---

[3] *De piedra ha de ser . . . amas:* Lyrics from a popular romantic ballad (called a *bolero* in Puerto Rico). Freely translated: "My bed will be made of stone, of stone also my headrest (or pillow), the woman who (dares to) loves me, will have to love me for real. *Ay, Ay, Ay,* my heart, why can't you (let me) love. . . ."—COFER'S NOTE.

with him. If I marry him, even my name will be American. I hate rice and beans—that's what makes these women fat."

"Your *prima*[4] is pregnant by that man she's been sneaking around with. Would I lie to you? I'm your *Tía Política*,[5] your great-uncle's common-law wife—the one he abandoned on the Island to go marry your cousin's mother. *I* was not invited to this party, of course, but I came anyway. I came to tell you that story about your cousin that you've always wanted to hear. Do you remember the comment your mother made to a neighbor that has always haunted you? The only thing you heard was your cousin's name, and then you saw your mother pick up your doll from the couch and say: 'It was as big as this doll when they flushed it down the toilet.' This image has bothered you for years, hasn't it? You had nightmares about babies being flushed down the toilet, and you wondered why anyone would do such a horrible thing. You didn't dare ask your mother about it. She would only tell you that you had not heard her right, and yell at you for listening to adult conversations. But later, when you were old enough to know about abortions, you suspected.

"I am here to tell you that you were right. Your cousin was growing an *Americanito* in her belly when this movie was made. Soon after she put something long and pointy into her pretty self, thinking maybe she could get rid of the problem before breakfast and still make it to her first class at the high school. Well, *Niña*,[6] her screams could be heard downtown. Your aunt, her mamá, who had been a midwife on the Island, managed to pull the little thing out. Yes, they probably flushed it down the toilet. What else could they do with it—give it a Christian burial in a little white casket with blue bows and ribbons? Nobody wanted that baby—least of all the father, a teacher at her school with a house in West Paterson that he was filling with real children, and a wife who was a natural blonde.

"Girl, the scandal sent your uncle back to the bottle. And guess where your cousin ended up? Irony of ironies. She was sent to a village in Puerto Rico to live with a relative on her mother's side: a place so far away from civilization that you have to ride a mule to reach it. A real change in scenery. She found a man there—women like that cannot live without male company—but believe me, the men in Puerto Rico know how to put a saddle on a woman like her.

---

[4] *prima:* Female cousin.—COFER'S NOTE.

[5] *Tía Política:* Aunt by marriage.—COFER'S NOTE.

[6] *Niña:* Girl.—COFER'S NOTE.

La Gringa,[7] they call her. Ha, ha, ha. *La Gringa* is what she always wanted to be. . . ."

The old woman's mouth becomes a cavernous black hole I fall into. And as I fall, I can feel the reverberations of her laughter. I hear the echoes of her last mocking words: *La Gringa, La Gringa!* And the conga line keeps moving silently past me. There is no music in my dream for the dancers.

When Odysseus visits Hades to see the spirit of his mother, he makes an offering of sacrificial blood, but since all the souls crave an audience with the living, he has to listen to many of them before he can ask questions. I, too, have to hear the dead and the forgotten speak in my dream. Those who are still part of my life remain silent, going around and around in their dance. The others keep pressing their faces forward to say things about the past.

My father's uncle is last in line. He is dying of alcoholism, shrunken and shriveled like a monkey, his face a mass of wrinkles and broken arteries. As he comes closer I realize that in his features I can see my whole family. If you were to stretch that rubbery flesh, you could find my father's face, and deep within *that* face—my own. I don't want to look into those eyes ringed in purple. In a few years he will retreat into silence, and take a long, long time to die. *Move back, Tío,* I tell him. *I don't want to hear what you have to say. Give the dancers room to move. Soon it will be midnight. Who is the New Year's Fool this time?*

---

[7] *La Gringa:* Derogatory epithet used here to ridicule a Puerto Rican girl who wants to look like a blonde North American.—COFER'S NOTE.

Living Like Weasels
Annie Dillard

A weasel is wild. Who knows what he thinks? He sleeps in his underground den, his tail draped over his nose. Sometimes he lives in his den for two days without leaving. Outside, he stalks rabbits, mice, muskrats, and birds, killing more bodies than he can eat warm, and often dragging the carcasses home. Obedient to instinct, he bites his prey at the neck, either splitting the jugular vein at the throat or crunching the brain at the base of the skull, and he does not let go. One naturalist refused to kill a weasel who was socketed into his hand deeply as a rattlesnake. The man could in no way pry the tiny weasel off, and he had to walk half a mile in water, the weasel dangling from his palm, and soak him off like a stubborn label.

And once, says Ernest Thompson Seton—once, a man shot an eagle out of the sky. He examined the eagle and found the dry skull of a weasel fixed by the jaws to his throat. The supposition is that the eagle had pounced on the weasel and the weasel swiveled and bit as instinct taught him, tooth to neck, and nearly won. I would like to have seen that eagle from the air a few weeks or months before he was shot: was the whole weasel still attached to his feathered throat, a far pendant? Or did the eagle eat what he could reach, gutting the living weasel with his talons before his breast, bending his beak, cleaning the beautiful airborne bones?

I have been reading about weasels because I saw one last week. I startled a weasel who startled me, and we exchanged a long glance.

Twenty minutes from my house, through the woods by the quarry and across the highway, is Hollins Pond, a remarkable piece of shallowness, where I like to go at sunset and sit on a tree trunk. Hollins Pond is also called Murray's Pond; it covers two acres of bottomland near Tinker Creek with six inches of water and six thousand lily pads. In winter, brown-and-white steers stand in the middle of it, merely dampening their hooves; from the distant shore they look like miracle itself, complete with miracle's nonchalance. Now, in summer, the steers are gone. The water lilies have blossomed and spread to a green horizontal plane that is terra firma to plodding blackbirds, and tremulous ceiling to black leeches, crayfish, and carp.

This is, mind you, suburbia. It is a five-minute walk in three directions to rows of houses, though none is visible here. There's a 55 mph highway at one end of the pond, and a nesting pair of wood ducks at the other. Under every bush is a muskrat hole or a beer can. The far end is an alternating series of fields and woods, fields and woods, threaded everywhere with motorcycle tracks—in whose bare clay wild turtles lay eggs.

So. I had crossed the highway, stepped over two low barbed-wire fences, and traced the motorcycle path in all gratitude through the wild rose and poison ivy of the pond's shoreline up into high grassy fields. Then I cut down through the woods to the mossy fallen tree where I sit. This tree is excellent. It makes a dry, upholstered bench at the upper, marshy end of the pond, a plush jetty raised from the thorny shore between a shallow blue body of water and a deep blue body of sky. The sun had just set. I was relaxed on the tree trunk, ensconced in the lap of lichen, watching the lily pads at my feet tremble and part dreamily over the thrusting path of a carp. A yellow bird appeared to my right and flew behind me. It caught my eye; I swiveled around—and the next instant, inexplicably, I was looking down at a weasel, who was looking up at me.

Weasel! I'd never seen one wild before. He was ten inches long, thin as a curve, a muscled ribbon, brown as fruitwood, soft-furred, alert. His face was fierce, small and pointed as a lizard's; he would have made a good arrowhead. There was just a dot of chin, maybe two brown hairs' worth, and then the pure white fur began that spread down his underside. He had two black eyes I didn't see, any more than you see a window.

The weasel was stunned into stillness as he was emerging from beneath an enormous shaggy wild rose bush four feet away. I was stunned into stillness twisted backward on the tree trunk. Our eyes locked, and someone threw away the key.

Our look was as if two lovers, or deadly enemies, met unexpectedly on an overgrown path when each had been thinking of something else: a clearing blow to the gut. It was also a bright blow to the brain, or a sudden beating of brains, with all the charge and intimate grate of rubbed balloons. It emptied our lungs. It felled the forest, moved the fields, and drained the pond; the world dismantled and tumbled into that black hole of eyes. If you and I looked at each other that way, our skulls would split and drop to our shoulders. But we don't. We keep our skulls. So.

He disappeared. This was only last week, and already I don't remember what shattered the enchantment. I think I blinked, I think I retrieved my brain from the weasel's brain, and tried to memorize what I was seeing, and the weasel felt the yank of separation, the careening splashdown into real life and the urgent current of instinct. He vanished under the wild rose. I waited motionless, my mind suddenly full of data and my spirit with pleadings, but he didn't return.

Please do not tell me about "approach-avoidance conflicts." I tell you I've been in that weasel's brain for sixty seconds, and he was in mine. Brains are private places, muttering through unique and secret tapes—but the weasel and I both plugged into another tape simultaneously, for a sweet and shocking time. Can I help it if it was a blank?

What goes on in his brain the rest of the time? What does a weasel think about? He won't say. His journal is tracks in clay, a spray of feathers, mouse blood and bone: uncollected, unconnected, loose-leaf, and blown.

I would like to learn, or remember, how to live. I come to Hollins Pond not so much to learn how to live as, frankly, to forget about it. That is, I don't think I can learn from a wild animal how to live in particular—shall I suck warm blood, hold my tail high, walk with my footprints precisely over the prints of my hands?—but I might learn something of mindlessness, something of the purity of living in the physical senses and the dignity of living without bias or motive. The weasel lives in necessity and we live in choice, hating necessity and dying at the last ignobly in its talons. I would like to live as I should, as the weasel lives as he should. And I suspect that for me the way is like the weasel's: open to time and death painlessly, noticing everything, remembering nothing, choosing the given with a fierce and pointed will.

I missed my chance. I should have gone for the throat. I should have lunged for that streak of white under the weasel's chin and held on, held on through mud and into the wild rose, held on for a dearer life. We could live under the wild rose wild as weasels, mute and uncomprehending. I could very calmly go wild. I could live two days in the den, curled, leaning on mouse fur, sniffing bird bones, blinking, licking, breathing musk, my hair tangled in the roots of grasses. Down is a good place to go, where the mind is single. Down is out, out of your ever-loving mind and back to your careless senses. I remember muteness as a prolonged and giddy fast, where every moment is a feast of utterance received. Time and events are merely poured, unremarked, and ingested directly, like blood pulsed into my gut through a jugular vein. Could two live that way? Could two live under the wild rose, and explore by the pond, so that the smooth mind of each is as everywhere present to the other, and as received and as unchallenged, as falling snow?

We could, you know. We can live any way we want. People take vows of poverty, chastity, and obedience—even of silence—by choice. The thing is to stalk your calling in a certain skilled and supple way, to locate the most tender and live spot and plug into that pulse. This is yielding, not fighting. A weasel doesn't "attack" anything; a weasel lives as he's meant to, yielding at every moment to the perfect freedom of single necessity.

I think it would be well, and proper, and obedient, and pure, to grasp your one necessity and not let it go, to dangle from it limp wherever it takes you. Then even death, where you're going no matter how you live, cannot you part. Seize it and let it seize you up aloft even, till your eyes burn out and drop; let your musky flesh fall off in shreds, and let your very bones unhinge and scatter, loosened over fields, over fields and woods, lightly, thoughtless, from any height at all, from as high as eagles.

Somehow Form a Family

Tony Earley

In July 1969, I looked a lot like Opie in the second or third season of *The Andy Griffith Show*. I was a small boy with a big head. I wore blue jeans with the cuffs turned up and horizontally striped pullover shirts. I was the brother in a father-mother-brother-sister family. We lived in a four-room house at the edge of the country, at the foot of the mountains, outside a small town in North Carolina, but it could have been anywhere.

On one side of us lived Mr. and Mrs. White. They were old and rich. Their driveway was paved. Mrs. White was the president of the town garden club. When she came to visit Mama she brought her own ashtray. Mr. White was almost deaf. When he watched the news on television, it sounded like thunder in the distance. The Whites had an aluminum travel trailer in which you could see your reflection. One summer they hitched it to their Chrysler and pulled it all the way to Alaska.

On the other side of us lived Mack and Joan. They had just graduated from college. I thought Joan was beautiful, and still do. Mack had a bass boat and a three-tray tackle box in which lurked a bristling school of lures. On the other side of Mack and Joan lived Mrs. Taylor, who was old, and on the other side of Mrs. Taylor lived Mr. and Mrs. Frady, who had a fierce dog. My sister, Shelly, and I called it the Frady dog. The Frady dog lived a long and bitter life. It did not die until well after I had a driver's license.

On the far side of the Whites lived Mr. and Mrs. John Harris; Mr. and Mrs. Burlon Harris lived beyond them. John and Burlon were first cousins. John was a teacher who in the summers fixed lawn mowers, including ours, in a building behind his house. Burlon reminded me of Mr. Greenjeans on *Captain Kangaroo*. He kept horses and let us play in his barn. Shelly once commandeered one of his cats and brought it home to live with us. Burlon did not mind; he asked her if she wanted another one. We rode our bicycles toward Mr. Harris's house as if pulled there by gravity. We did not ride in the other direction; the Frady dog sat in its yard and watched for us.

In July 1969, we did not have much money, but in the hierarchy of southern poor, we were the good kind, the kind you would not mind living on your road. We were clean. Our clothes were clean. My parents worked. We went to church. Easter mornings, Mama stood us in front of the yellowbell bush and took our picture. We had meat at every meal—chicken and cube steak and pork chops and ham—and plenty of milk to drink. We were not trashy. Mrs. White would not sit with her ashtray in the kitchen of trashy people. Trashy people lived in the two houses around the curve past Mr. Harris's. When Daddy drove by those houses we could see that the kids in the yard had dirty faces. They were usually jabbing at something with a stick. Shelly and I were not allowed to ride our bicycles around the curve.

I knew we were poor only because our television was black and white. It was an old Admiral, built in the 1950s, with brass knobs the size of baseballs. Its cabinet was perfectly square, a cube of steel with a painted-on mahogany grain. Hoss on *Bonanza* could not have picked it up by himself. It was a formidable object, but its vertical hold was shot. We gathered around it the night Neil Armstrong walked on the moon, but we could not tell what was happening. The picture flipped up and down. We turned off the lights in the living room so we could see better. We listened to Walter Cronkite. In the distance we could hear Mr. White's color TV rumbling. We changed the channel and listened to Huntley and Brinkley. We could hear the scratchy radio transmissions coming down out of space, but we could not see anything. Daddy got behind the TV with a flashlight. He said, "Is that better? Is that better?" but it never was. Mama said, "Just be thankful you've got a television."

After the Eagle had landed but before the astronauts opened the door and came out, Mack knocked on the door and asked us if we wanted to look at the moon. He was an engineer for a power company and had set up his surveyor's transit in the backyard. Daddy and Shelly and I went with him. We left Mama sitting in the living room in the blue light of the TV. She said she did not want to miss anything. The moon, as I remember it, was full, although I have since learned that it wasn't. I remember that a galaxy of lightning bugs blinked against the black pine trees that grew between our yard and that of the Whites. Mack pointed the transit at the sky. Daddy held me up so I could see. The moon inside the instrument was startlingly bright; the man in the moon was clearly visible, although the men on the moon weren't. "You can't see them or anything," Mack said, which I already knew. I said, "I know that." I wasn't stupid and did not like to be talked to as if I were. Daddy put me down. He and Mack stood for a while and talked. Daddy smoked a cigarette. In the bright yard Shelly chased lightning bugs. She did not run, but instead jumped slowly, her feet together. I realized that she was pretending to walk on the moon, pretending that she was weightless. The moon was so bright, it cast a shadow at her feet. I remember these things for sure. I am tempted to say that she was beautiful in the moonlight, and I'm sure she was, but that isn't something I remember noticing that night, only a thing I need to say now.

Eight, maybe nine months later, Shelly and I rode the bus home from school. It was a Thursday, Mama's day off, Easter time. The cherry tree in the garden separating our driveway from that of the Whites was in brilliant, full bloom. We could hear it buzzing from the road. One of us checked the mailbox. We looked up the driveway at our house. Something was wrong with it, but we couldn't tell what. Daddy was adding four rooms on to the house, and we were used to it appearing large and unfinished. We stood in the driveway and stared. Black tar paper was tacked to the outside walls of the new part, but the old part was still covered with white asbestos shingles. In the coming summer, Daddy and a crew of brick masons would finish transforming the house into a split-level ranch style, remarkably similar to the one in which the Bradys would live. I loved the words *split-level ranch-style.* To me they meant "rich."

Shelly and I spotted what was wrong at the same time. A giant television antenna had attached itself to the roof of our house. It was shiny and tall as a young tree. It looked dangerous, as if it would bite, like a praying mantis. The antenna slowly began to turn, as if it had noticed us. Shelly and I looked quickly at each other, our mouths wide open, and then back at the antenna. We sprinted up the driveway.

In the living room, on the spot occupied by the Admiral that morning, sat a magnificent new color TV, a Zenith, with a twenty-one-inch screen. Its cabinet was made of real wood. *Gomer Pyle, U.S.M.C.* was on. I will never forget that. Gomer Pyle and Sergeant Carter were the first two people I ever saw on a color television. The olive green and khaki of their uniforms was dazzling. Above them was the blue sky of California. The sky in California seemed bluer than the sky in North Carolina.

We said, "Is that ours?"

Mama said, "I'm going to kill your daddy." He had charged the TV without telling her. Two men from Sterchi's Furniture had showed up at the house that morning with the TV on a truck. They climbed onto the roof and planted the antenna.

We said, "Can we keep it?"

Mama said, "I don't know," but I noticed she had written the numbers of the stations we could get on the dial of the Channel Master, the small box which controlled the direction the antenna pointed. Mama would never have written on anything she planned on taking back to the store.

The dial of the Channel Master was marked like a compass. Channel 3 in Charlotte lay to the east; Channel 13 in Asheville lay to the west. Channel 7 in Spartanburg and Channel 4 in Greenville rested side by side below them in the south. For years these cities would mark the outside edges of the world as I knew it. Shelly reached out and turned the dial. Mama smacked her on the hand. Gomer grew fuzzy and disappeared. I said, "Mama, she broke it." When the dial stopped turning, Mama carefully turned it back to the south. Gomer reappeared, resurrected. Jim Nabors probably never looked better to anyone, in his whole life, than he did to us right then.

Mama sat us down on the couch and laid down the law. Mama always laid down the law when she was upset. We were not to touch the TV. We could not turn it on, nor could we change the channel. Under no circumstances were we to touch the Channel Master. The Channel Master was very expensive. And if we so much as looked at the knobs that controlled the color, she would whip us. It had taken her all afternoon to get the color just right.

◦ ◦ ◦

We lived in a split-level ranch-style house, with two maple trees and a rose bush in the front yard, outside a town that could have been named Springfield. We had a color TV. We had a Channel Master antenna that turned slowly on top of our house until it found and pulled from the sky electromagnetic waves for our nuclear family.

We watched *Hee-Haw*, starring Buck Owens and Roy Clark; we watched *All in the Family*, *The Mary Tyler Moore Show*, *The Bob Newhart Show*, *The Carol Burnett Show*, and *Mannix*, starring Mike Connors with Gail Fisher as Peggy; we watched *Gunsmoke* and *Bonanza*, even after Adam left and Hoss died and Little Joe's hair turned gray; we watched *Adam-12* and *Kojak*, *McCloud*, *Colombo*, and *Hawaii Five-O*; we watched *Cannon*, a Quinn Martin production and *Barnaby Jones*, a Quinn Martin production, which co-starred Miss America and Uncle Jed from *The Beverly Hillbillies*. Daddy finished the new part of the house and moved out soon thereafter. He rented a trailer in town and took the old Admiral out of the basement with him. We watched *Mutual of Omaha's Wild Kingdom* and *The Wonderful World of Disney*. After school we watched *Gomer Pyle, U.S.M.C.*, *The Beverly Hillbillies*, *Gilligan's Island*, and *The Andy Griffith Show*. Upstairs, we had rooms of our own. Mama stopped taking us to church.

On Friday nights we watched *The Partridge Family*, *The Brady Bunch*, *Room 222*, *The Odd Couple*, and *Love American Style*. Daddy came to visit on Saturdays. We watched *The Little Rascals* on Channel 3 with Fred Kirby, the singing cowboy, and his sidekick, Uncle Jim. We watched *The Little Rascals* on Channel 4 with Monty Dupuy, the weatherman, and his sidekick, Doohickey. Mornings, before school, we watched *The Three Stooges* with Mr. Bill on Channel 13. Mr. Bill worked alone. The school year Daddy moved out, Mr. Bill showed Bible story cartoons instead of *The Three Stooges*. That year, we went to school angry.

After each of Daddy's visits, Mama said he was getting better. Shelly and I tried to imagine living with the Bradys but realized we would not fit in. They were richer and more popular at school. They did not have Southern accents. One Saturday Daddy brought me a set of golf clubs, which I had asked for but did not expect to get. It was raining that day. I took the clubs out in the yard and very quickly realized that golf was harder than it looked on television. I went back inside and wiped the mud and water off the clubs with Bounty paper towels, the quicker picker upper. Upstairs I heard Mama say, "Do you think he's stupid?" I spread the golf clubs on the floor around me. I tuned in *Shock Theater* on Channel 13 and turned it up loud.

Shelly had a crush on Bobby Brady; I had a crush on Jan. Jan had braces, I had braces. Jan had glasses, I had glasses. Their daddy was an architect. Our daddy lived in a trailer in town with a poster of Wile E. Coyote and the Road Runner on the living room wall. The Coyote held the Road Runner firmly by the neck. The caption on the poster said, "Beep, Beep your ass." I lay in bed at night and imagined being married to Jan Brady but having an affair with Marsha. I wondered how we would tell Jan, what Marsha and I would do then, where we would go. Greg Brady beat me up. I shook his hand and told him I deserved it. Alice refused to speak to me. During this time Mrs. White died. I heard the ambulance in the middle of the night. It sounded like the one on *Emergency*. I opened the door to Mama's room to see if she was OK. She was embarrassed because our dog barked and barked.

Rhoda left *The Mary Tyler Moore Show*. Maude and George Jefferson left *All in the Family;* Florida, Maude's maid, left *Maude*. Daddy moved back in. He watched the news during supper, the TV as loud as Mr. White's. We were not allowed to talk during the news. This was the law. After the news we watched *Rhoda* or *Maude* or *Good Times*. Daddy decided that cutting the grass should be my job. We had a big yard. I decided that I didn't want to do anything he said. Mr. White remarried. The new Mrs. White's daughter died of cancer. The new Mrs. White dug up every flower the old Mrs. White had planted; she cut down every tree and shrub, including the cherry tree in the garden between our driveways. Mama said the new Mrs. White broke her heart. Mr. White mowed and mowed and mowed their grass until it was smooth as a golf course. Mack and Joan paved their driveway.

What I'm trying to say is this: we lived in a split-level ranch-style house; we had a Zenith in the living room and a Channel Master attached to the roof. But Shelly and I fought like Thelma and J.J. on *Good Times*. I wanted to live in Hawaii and work for Steve McGarrett. No bad guy ever got away from McGarrett, except the Chinese master spy Wo Fat. Shelly said McGarrett would never give me a job. In all things Shelly was on Daddy's side; I lined up on Mama's. Friday evenings, when Daddy got home from work, I sneaked outside to snoop around in the glove compartment of his car. I pretended I had a search warrant, that I was Danno on a big case. Shelly reported my snooping to Daddy. I was trying to be a good son.

Every Saturday, before he went to work, Daddy left word that I was to cut the grass before he got home. I stayed in bed until lunch. Shelly came into my room and said, "You better get up." I flipped her the bird. She said, "I'm telling." I got up in time to watch professional wrestling on Channel 3. I hated the bad guys. They did not fight fair. They hid brass knuckles in their trunks and beat the good guys until they bled. They won too often. Mama brought me tomato and onion sandwiches. I could hear Mack on one side and Mr. White on the other mowing their grass. I could hear John Harris and Mr. Frady and Mrs. Taylor's daughter, Lucille, mowing grass. Lucille lived in Charlotte, but came home on weekends just to mow Mrs. Taylor's grass. We had the shaggiest lawn on the road. After wrestling, I watched the *Game of the Week* on Channel 4. Carl Yaztremski of the Boston Red Sox was my favorite baseball player. He had forearms like fenceposts. Nobody messed with him. I listened over the lawn mowers for the sound of Daddy's Volkswagen. Mama came in the living room and said, "Son, maybe you should mow some of the grass before your daddy gets home. You know what's going to happen." I knew what was going to happen.

I knew that eventually he would make me mow the grass. I knew that when I was through, Mack would come through the pine trees laughing. He would say, "Charles, I swear that is the laziest boy I have ever seen." Mack had a Snapper Comet riding mower, on which he sat like a king. I never saw him on it that I did not want to bean him with a rock. Daddy would shake his head and say, "Mack, dead lice wouldn't fall off that boy." Every Saturday night we ate out at Scoggin's Seafood and Steak House. *Hee-Haw* came on at seven; *All in the Family* came on at eight.

And then Shelly and I were in high school. We watched *M°A°S°H°* and *Lou Grant*, *Love Boat* and *Fantasy Island*. We watched *Dynasty* and *Dallas*. Opie was Richie Cunningham on *Happy Days*. Ben Cartwright showed up in a black bathrobe on *Battlestar Gallactica*. The Channel Master stopped working, but no one bothered to have it fixed. The antenna was left immobile on the roof in a compromised position: we could almost get most of the channels. One summer Mack built a pool in his backyard. Joan lay in a bikini beside the pool in the sun. The next summer Mack built a fence. This was during the late seventies. Shelly lay in her room with the lights turned off and listened to *Dark Side of the Moon*. On Friday nights she asked me to go out with her and her friends. I always said no. I did not want to miss *The Rockford Files*.

In those days Shelly and I watched *Guiding Light* when we got home from school. It was our soap. I remember that Ed Bauer's beautiful wife Rita left him because he was boring. Shelly said I reminded her of Ed Bauer. She wore her hair like Farrah Fawcett Majors on *Charlie's Angels*. After *Guiding Light* I changed the channel and watched *Star Trek*. I could not stay awake in school. I went to sleep during homeroom. During the day I woke up only long enough to change classes and eat lunch. I watched *Star Trek* when I got home as if it were beamed to our house by God. I did not want to be Captain Kirk, or any of the main characters. I just wanted to go with them. I wanted to wear a red jersey and walk the long, anonymous halls of the Starship Enterprise as it disappeared into space. One day *Star Trek* was preempted by an *ABC After School Special*. I tried to kick the screen out of the TV. I was wearing sneakers, so the glass would not break. Shelly hid in Mama and Daddy's room. I said, "Five-O. Open up." Then I kicked the door off the hinges.

Our family doctor thought I had narcolepsy. He sent me to a neurologist in Charlotte. Mama and Daddy went with me. In Charlotte, an EEG technician attached wires to my head. A small, round amber light glowed high up in the corner of the examination room. I watched the light until I went to sleep. The neurologist said that the EEG looked normal, but that he would talk to us more about the results in a few minutes. He led us to a private waiting room. It was small and bare and paneled with wood. In it were four chairs. Most of one wall was taken up by a darkened glass. I could not see what was on the other side of it. I studied our reflection. Mama and Daddy were trying to pretend that the glass wasn't there. I said, "Pa, when we get back to the Ponderosa, do you want me to round up those steers on the lower forty?"

Daddy said, "What?"

I said, "Damnit, Jim. I'm a doctor."

Daddy said, "What are you talking about?"

Mama said, "Be quiet. They're watching us."

Shelly died on Christmas Eve morning when I was a freshman in college. She had wrecked Mama's car. That night I stayed up late and watched the Pope deliver the Christmas mass from the Vatican. There was nothing else on. Daddy moved out again. My college almost shut down during the week *The Thorn Birds* was broadcast. Professors rescheduled papers and exams. In the basement of my dorm twenty-five nineteen-year-old guys shouted at the TV when the Richard Chamberlain character told the Rachel Ward character he loved God more than he loved her. At age nineteen, it was impossible to love God more than Rachel Ward. My best friend, a guy from Kenya, talked me into switching from *Guiding Light* to *General Hospital*. This was during the glory days of *General Hospital* when Luke and Scorpio roomed together on the Haunted Star. Laura was supposedly dead, but Luke knew in his heart she was still alive; every time he was by himself he heard a Christopher Cross song.

Going home was strange, as if the Mayberry I expected had become Mayberry, R.F.D. Shelly was gone. Daddy was gone. The second Mrs. White died, then Mr. White went away to a nursing home. The Fradys had moved away. John Harris had a heart attack and stopped fixing lawn mowers. Mama mowed our grass by herself with a rider. I stopped going to see Burlon Harris because he teared up every time he tried to talk about Shelly. Mack and Joan had a son named Timmy. Mack and Joan got a divorce. Mack moved to a farm out in the country; Joan moved to town.

Daddy fell in love with Mama my senior year and moved back in. The Zenith began slowly dying. Its picture narrowed into a greenly tinted slit. It stared like a diseased eye into the living room where Mama and Daddy sat. They turned off the lights so they could see better. I became a newspaper reporter. With my first Christmas bonus, I bought myself a television, a nineteen-inch GE. With my second Christmas bonus I bought Mama and Daddy one. They hooked it up to cable. When I visited them on Thursdays we watched *The Cosby Show, Family Ties, Cheers, Night Court,* and *Hill Street Blues*. Daddy gave up on broadcast TV when NBC cancelled *Hill Street Blues* and replaced it with *L.A. Law*. Now he mostly watches the Discovery Channel. Mama calls it the "airplanes and animals channel." They are in the eighteenth year of their new life together. I bear them no grudges. They were very young when I knew them best.

In grad school I switched back to *Guiding Light*. I had known Ed Bauer longer than I had known all but a few of my friends. It pleased me to see him in Springfield every afternoon, trying to do good. I watched *The Andy Griffith Show* twice a day. I could glance at Opie and tell you what year the episode was filmed. I watched the Gulf War from a stool in a bar.

Eventually I married a woman who grew up in a family that watched television only on special occasions—when Billie Jean King played Bobby Riggs, when Diana married Prince Charles. My wife was a student in a seminary. She did not want to meet Ed Bauer, nor could I explain, without sounding pathetic, why Ed Bauer was important to me. The first winter we were married I watched the winter Olympics huddled beneath a blanket in the frigid basement of the house we had rented. This was in a closed-down steel town near Pittsburgh, during the time I contemplated jumping from a bridge into the Ohio River. My wife asked the seminary community to pray for me. Ann B. Davis, who played Alice on *The Brady Bunch* was a member of that community. One day I saw her in the cafeteria at school. She looked much the same as when she played Alice, except that her hair was white, and she wore small, gold glasses. I didn't talk to her. I had heard that she didn't like talking about *The Brady Bunch,* and I could not think of anything to say to her about the world in which we actually lived. I sat in the cafeteria and stared at her as much as I could without anyone noticing. I don't know if she prayed for me or not, but I like to think that she did. I wanted to tell her that I grew up in a split-level ranch-style house outside a small town that could have been named Springfield, but that something had gone wrong inside it. I wanted to tell her that years ago Alice had been important to me, that my sister and I had looked to Alice for something we could not name, and had at least seen a picture of what love looked like. I wanted to tell her that no one in my family ever raised their voice while the television was on, that late at night even a bad television show could keep me from hearing the silence inside my own heart. I wanted to tell her that Ed Bauer and I were still alive, that both of us had always wanted to do what was right. Ann B. Davis stood, walked over to the trash can, and emptied her tray. She walked out of the cafeteria and into a small, gray town near Pittsburgh. I wanted her to *be* Alice. I wanted her to smile as if she loved me. I wanted her to say, "Buck up, kiddo, everything's going to be all right." And what I'm trying to tell you now is this: I grew up in a split-level ranch-style house outside a town that could have been anywhere. I grew up in front of a television. I would have believed her.

What They Don't Tell You About Hurricanes
Philip Gerard

*W*hat they don't tell you about hurricanes is the uncertainty.

First it's *whether.* As in *Weather* Channel. There's been a rumor of storm off the coast of Africa, and it's turned into a tropical depression. It churns across the Atlantic into the Caribbean and is upgraded to a Tropical Storm, winds at forty or fifty knots, and the person in charge of such things gives it an androgynous name: Fran.

Will it hit here on the south coast of North Carolina?

They can't tell. The experts. We've been through this before—Hugo, Felix, Marilyn, Edouard, Bertha. My wife, Kathleen, who grew up with California earthquakes, bridles at the lingering uncertainty, the waffling, a whole season of emergency. She wants it quick, bang, and over. But it doesn't happen that way. Hurricanes are big and slow and cyclone around offshore for a few thousand miles.

So the radar scope on the Weather Channel becomes familiar, part of the nightly ritual before going to bed, like taking out the dog and locking the front door. It becomes the first thing you do every morning, even before coffee. Watching the swirls of red and orange, a bright pinwheel of destruction. Checking the stats—wind speed, barometric pressure, latitude and longitude. We are at 34 degrees 12 minutes north latitude, 77 degrees 50 minutes west longitude. A degree of latitude equals sixty miles north or south. The arithmetic isn't hard.

Fran bangs into some islands from the vacation brochures and it's heading toward the U.S. mainland. But here in Wilmington, we just had Bertha, a direct hit. The eye sat over our backyard—you could look up and see the actual sky wound into a circular wall, like being down inside a black well, watching the stars out the top.

Surely, not twice in one season—what are the odds?

What they don't tell you is that hurricanes, like lightning, can strike exactly the same spot time and again. Fran is not the first storm. It's the second slam from a hurricane in eight weeks, and in the meantime it's rained torrentially almost every day. It's been a whole summer of violent storms, of lightning fires and local floods, of black line squalls that knock down fleets of sailboats racing off the beach. The ground is so saturated we have had the lawn sprinkler system turned off all summer. Starved of oxygen, tree roots are rotting in the ground.

The longleaf pines that ring our property stand sixty and seventy feet high, two feet in diameter, precarious upright tons of wet wood, swaying already in the breeze. Their roots are soft in the spongy ground.

We've been set up. It feels like there's a bull's-eye painted on the map next to the words "Cape Fear."

So it's *when*. Fran is moving at 14 knots, then 16, then wobbling slowly into a kind of hover. It's a monster storm, darkening the whole map of the Atlantic between Cape Fear and Bermuda, sucking up warm water and slinging it into windy horizontal rain. It's too big to miss us entirely.

It's Monday, the beginning of a long week. We fill up the bathtub, stockpile batteries and canned goods, locate flashlights and candles and matches, fill the truck with gas. Then we load all our important documents—passports, mortgage papers, insurance policies, marriage license—into a single attaché case and keep it handy. We take lots of cash out of the automatic teller.

Landfall of The Eye expected Wednesday night, late. Wednesday is good for us, because Wednesday means south. Good for us, bad for Charleston. Hugo country.

We wish it on them. Me, Kathleen, the neighbors who drift back and forth between houses just to talk out loud, just to look at the sky. We feel bad about it, but we wish it on them anyway. If we had real magic, we would make it happen to them, not to us.

But Fran wanders north, following Bertha's path, and on TV they change the *when*: Thursday night, after midnight. Because our Beneteau sloop *Savoir-Faire* is moored in a tidal harbor, we pay attention to the tides. Low tide will be at 9:34 P.M. From then on, the tide will rise one foot every two hours until 3:29 A.M. By mid-afternoon all of us whose boats remain in the community harbor at the end of our street are lashing on extra fenders, strapping lines to the pilings, watching the water lap at the bulkhead separating the marsh from the harbor.

I'd take the boat out of there, drive her to safety, but where? It would take eight hours to get down the waterway and up the Cape Fear River, and I don't know the hurricane holes there. I'd be stuck on the boat, away from my wife, in the low-country wilderness, with a three-to-five knot current pushing dangerous debris down the river at me all night long.

Full-force Fran aims for coast says the local newspaper front-page headline.

Everybody is thinking the same thing: *don't let it come ashore at high tide.*

We speculate nervously about how much the tidal surge will actually be in this protected harbor, blocked from the ocean by a large, developed barrier island—Wrightsville Beach—a channel, a spoil island, the Intracoastal Waterway, and finally a hundred yards of marsh that is dry land at low tide.

Nobody knows.

Our docks are the floating kind—they can float up on their pilings another nine feet, and all will be well. All of our boats made it through Bertha without a scratch—eighty-five knot winds and a tidal surge of six feet.

There's the standard hurricane drill: strip all sails, remove all windage-making gear—horseshoe buoy, man-overboard pole, life-sling. We all help one another. Nobody has to ask. While unbending the large full-battened mains'l, I bang my new racing watch on the boom gooseneck and break it. A bad portent.

We retreat across the causeway to our homes, where the power has already gone off, as the rain becomes torrential and the wind begins to blow in great twists of energy. It has started. So we have an answer to *when*. An hour later, when Fran comes howling down on us out of the ocean, it's *how hard*. As we huddle indoors and listen to the roaring, the question becomes *how long*.

When, How Hard, How Long: the trigonometry of catastrophe.

The answer is 8:05 P.M., almost dead low tide.

The answer is sixteen feet of surging water anyway and winds of 105 knots.

The answer is 15 hours.

Some of the clichés turn out to be true.

The rain really is *torrential,* as in *torrents.*

A hurricane *does* sound like a freight train. Exactly like. If you were lying between the rails and it went roaring along over your head all night long. It really does *roar.* Like whatever is holding the world together is coming apart, tonight, this minute, right here, and you're smack in the middle of the program.

And your mouth really does go so dry with fear you can hardly talk.

The great trees cracking and tumbling to the ground in the roaring darkness really do sound like an artillery barrage—*crack! crack! whump! whump!* It takes italics, exclamation points, boldface clichés to tell about it. The house shudders again and again. Our house has too many large windows, so we run next door to wait out Fran with our neighbors. We're sitting up with them in their living room drinking any liquor we can get our hands on—vodka, beer, wine, rum—and each shudder brings a sharp intake of breath, a little cry. You can't help it. You laugh and make jokes, but it feels bad and the feeling gets worse every minute. The kerosene lanterns don't help. They make Halloween light. Eerie, spooky light.

There are times when you have to dodge out into the maelstrom of wind and flying debris and back across the lawns to check the outside of your house, to clear the storm drain and prevent flooding of the lower story. It's stupid, especially in the pitch blackness, but it feels like something you have to do. The world is way out of control, but you're still responsible.

There are freaky contradictions of nature. Paradoxes of chance. A massive oak tree that has weathered three hundred years of storms is ripped apart by the wind, literally twisted out of the earth by the roots. The next lot over, a pair of forgotten work gloves left to dry on the spikes of a picket fence are still there in the morning, and so is the fence. Dry.

The wind blows strips of new caulking out from between the casement windows but leaves intact the plastic tarps you nailed over the open sides of the upstairs porch.

There are amazing feats of heroism and survival. A man on one of the beach islands sends his wife and kids to the shelter, remains behind with their dog to finish boarding up the house, then the only road off the island overwashes, and he's cut off. He grabs his dog in his arms and ropes himself to the house, and all night long he and the dog are bashed against the house by water and wind, but they make it through. The dog was a boxer.

Lightning strikes the home of an old couple and it catches fire. Two young men appear out of the storm, attack the fire with a garden hose and keep it from taking the house until the fire trucks arrive, then disappear. Nobody knows who they are or where they came from. The old couple believes they are angels.

There are tales of death. Another man is seen stepping onto his front porch as the hurricane hits. They find him in the morning miles away, floating face-down in the Intracoastal Waterway. A woman rescued from a mattress floating in the marsh dies anyway.

For a week afterward, urban rescue workers prowl the wrecked homes along the beach with dogs, sniffing out the bodies of the ones who wouldn't leave.

It's also true, the cliché about the capriciousness of nature and about blind luck. Three Marines in a Mustang are swept off the road by the rushing water. One is washed to the far shore and stumbles into a shelter. The second clings to a tree limb for nine hours until he is rescued. The third drowns.

There are things that are outrageously unfair. A family down the street gets flooded out on the ground floor. They scramble upstairs ahead of the surge. But the battery of their brand new car shorts out in the rising water, and it catches fire. The garage underneath the house burns. Soon the whole house is burning. Incredibly, at the height of the hurricane, the volunteer firemen arrive. They maneuver their pumper through waist-deep water. But they can't get the electric garage door open and have to axe it down. And by then the family is smoked out, the house is partly destroyed, the car is a hulk.

Hurricane, flood, fire, all at once.

Thunder and lightning come in ahead of the hurricane. Tornadoes spin off the leading edge like missiles, knocking out bridges, tearing holes in houses, twisting trees out of the earth and flinging them into power lines.

Biblical stuff.

Furious Fran unforgiving, the local newspaper says, again on page one, unable to let go of the corny habit of alliteration.

What they don't tell you about hurricanes is the heat.

The oppressive stillness of the stalled atmosphere the day before the winds start. The hundred degrees of swampy humidity the day after, before the torrential rains resume. The air-conditioning is off, the windows are latched down tight. An hour into the storm, everything you touch is greasy. You put on a fresh shirt and sweat it through before you can fasten the buttons.

And then the bees arrive. Swarming, disoriented, stinging, bees gone haywire. Bumblebees, wasps, yellow jackets, hornets. I'm no entomologist—they all sting.

After a hurricane, the radio warns, that's when the injuries start. Beestings are number one, followed by poisonous snakebites and chainsaw cuts.

When the rains resume a day and a half after Fran passes, the yard is jumping with frogs and toads. Little bright green tree frogs with suction cups on their feet, smaller than a penny. Black toads the size of your fist. Giant croaking bullfrogs that splash around like rocks. Rat snakes. Water moccasins. Copperheads.

What's next—locusts? Well, not exactly: crickets. By the millions. All over the debris, the backyard deck, the wrecked boats.

But the birds are gone.

The water is off.

After sweltering hours clearing the tree limbs out of the road, pulling limbs off cars and shrubs, dragging downed trees off the driveway, raking the mess off the steps and walks and deck, my wife and I shower by pouring buckets of cold water, saved in the bathtub, over our soapy heads and bodies. We are scraped and cut and bruised and stained with pine resin that does not wash off. Every pair of shoes we own is wet and muddy and will not dry. The house is tracked with mud and debris, and a lethargic depression sets in—part physical exhaustion from relentless manual labor in the heat, from two sleepless nights in a row. Part emotional exhaustion. Grief.

We were luckier than many. It just doesn't feel that way.

When the power comes back on, it's like a religious experience. Everything becomes possible again—bright lights, cool air, television news, ice.

Then after a few hours it goes off again.

What they don't tell you about hurricanes is that the Big Hit is the beginning, not the end. Fran has swept on up the coast, taking the Weather Channel and CNN with it. On the networks, things are happening in Bosnia, Chechnya, Indonesia.

Here in Hurricanelandia, it's raining eight inches in three hours on top of ten inches that came in with Fran. They predict it will rain for another week. All the low-country rivers are cresting, shouldering through the wreckage of human cities toward the sea.

Our house is an island surrounded by rushing water two feet deep, and it's back out into the storm wearing Red Ball boots, clearing out clogged gutters on an aluminum ladder, counting the seconds between lightning and thunder, counting how long to dare such foolishness. Then slogging out onto the muddy access road behind the house to rake out the clogged storm culvert, trying not to get carried into the muddy water.

On the local radio, the jocks are chatting about this and that and the other, but for hours nobody gives a weather report. When will it stop raining? *Will* it stop raining? The phone is working. A friend from across town, where they have power, calls. Look out your windows—is it raining there? The edge of the cloud is moving over us now, she says, and there's sun behind it.

The water recedes, and now it's time to clean out the flooded garage. At dusk, the generators go on. It gets dark and noisy. We will wake to the lumber-camp sound of chainsaws.

For weeks and weeks.

What they don't tell you about a hurricane is that it just seems to go on and on.

But the worst of it is not captured on the awesome helicopter videotape of destruction. The worst of it is waking up to the new stillness of the morning after, when the wind has finally quit and the rain has slacked and the sun may or may not be up yet, the sky is just a gray slate of clouds.

Overnight, the world has changed in some important, irrevocable way. You can just feel it.

My neighbor John is standing outside waiting. "You ready?" he says, and I nod.

Half a mile away, the approach to the harbor is littered with dock-boxes, paddles, small boats, lifejackets. Like a shipwreck has happened to the whole neighborhood. The houses by the harbor have taken a beating. A 44-foot sportfishing boat lies on its side on a front lawn, and my stomach turns. That's how high the water rose.

A few nights earlier, I had stood on our dock talking quietly with an old friend, admiring the sleek, trim lines of *Savoir-Faire* under starlight, feeling lucky. Thirty-two feet of beautiful racing yacht, a dream of fifteen years of saving come true. I'd take *Savoir-Faire* out onto the broad back of the Atlantic and race her hard, rail down, or just jog along in mild breezes, clearing my head, sharing her with friends, or filling up with the good strength that comes from working a yare boat alone.

The harbor was demolished. Boats and docks were piled up like a train wreck. Boats were crushed, sunk, broken, smashed, aground. Some were simply gone.

Out in the middle of the harbor, alone, *Savoir-Faire* lay impaled on a piling, sunk by the bows, only her mast and transom rising above the dirty water.

What they don't tell you about hurricanes is how many ways they can break your heart.

Mirrorings
Lucy Grealy

There was a long period of time, almost a year, during which I never looked in a mirror. It wasn't easy, for I'd never suspected just how omnipresent are our own images. I began by merely avoiding mirrors, but by the end of the year I found myself with an acute knowledge of the reflected image, its numerous tricks and wiles, how it can spring up at any moment: a glass tabletop, a well-polished door handle, a darkened window, a pair of sunglasses, a restaurant's otherwise magnificent brass-plated coffee machine sitting innocently by the cash register.

At the time, I had just moved, alone, to Scotland and was surviving on the dole, as Britain's social security benefits are called. I didn't know anyone and had no idea how I was going to live, yet I went anyway because by happenstance I'd met a plastic surgeon there who said he could help me. I had been living in London, working temp jobs. While in London, I'd received more nasty comments about my face than I had in the previous three years, living in Iowa, New York, and Germany. These comments, all from men and all odiously sexual, hurt and disoriented me. I also had journeyed to Scotland because after more than a dozen operations in the States my insurance had run out, along with my hope that further operations could make any *real* difference. Here, however, was a surgeon who had some new techniques, and here, amazingly enough, was a government willing to foot the bill: I didn't feel I could pass up yet another chance to "fix" my face, which I confusedly thought concurrent with "fixing" my self, my soul, my life.

Twenty years ago, when I was nine and living in America, I came home from school one day with a toothache. Several weeks and misdiagnoses later, surgeons removed most of the right side of my jaw in an attempt to prevent the cancer they found there from spreading. No one properly explained the operation to me, and I awoke in a cocoon of pain that prevented me from moving or speaking. Tubes ran in and out of my body, and because I was temporarily unable to speak after the surgery and could not ask questions, I made up my own explanations for the tubes' existence. I remember the mysterious manner the adults displayed toward me. They asked me to do things: lie still for x-rays, not cry for needles, and so on, tasks that, although not easy, never seemed equal to the praise I received in return. Reinforced to me again and again was how I was "a brave girl" for not crying, "a good girl" for not complaining, and soon I began defining myself this way, equating strength with silence.

Then the chemotherapy began. In the seventies chemo was even cruder than it is now, the basic premise being to poison patients right up to the very brink of their own death. Until this point I almost never cried and almost always received praise in return. Thus I got what I considered the better part of the deal. But now it was like a practical joke that had gotten out of hand. Chemotherapy was a nightmare and I wanted it to stop; I didn't want to be brave anymore. Yet I had grown so used to defining myself as "brave"—i.e., *silent*—that the thought of losing this sense of myself was even more terrifying. I was certain that if I broke down I would be despicable in the eyes of both my parents and the doctors.

The task of taking me into the city for the chemo injections fell mostly on my mother, though sometimes my father made the trip. Overwhelmed by the sight of the vomiting and weeping, my father developed the routine of "going to get the car," meaning that he left the doctor's office before the injection was administered, on the premise that then he could have the car ready and waiting when it was all over. Ashamed of my suffering, I felt relief when he was finally out of the room. When my mother took me, she stayed in the room, yet this only made the distance between us even more tangible. She explained that it was wrong to cry *before* the needle went in; afterward was one thing, but before, that was mere fear, and hadn't I demonstrated my bravery earlier? Every Friday for two and a half years I climbed up onto that big doctor's table and told myself not to cry, and every week I failed. The two large syringes were filled with chemicals so caustic to the vein that each had to be administered very slowly. The whole process took about four minutes; I had to remain utterly still. Dry retching began in the first fifteen seconds, then the throb behind my eyes gave everything a yellow-green aura, and the bone-deep pain of alternating extreme hot and cold flashes made me tremble, yet still I had to sit motionless and not move my arm. No one spoke to me—not the doctor, who was a paradigm of the cold-fish physician; not the nurse, who told my mother I reacted much more violently than many of "the other children"; and not my mother, who, surely overwhelmed by the sight of her child's suffering, thought the best thing to do was remind me to be brave, to try not to cry. All the while I hated myself for having wept before the needle went in, convinced that the nurse and my mother were right, that I was "overdoing it," that the throwing up was psychosomatic, that my mother was angry with me for not being good or brave enough.

Yet each week, two or three days after the injection, there came the first flicker of feeling better, the always forgotten and gratefully rediscovered understanding that to simply be well in my body was the greatest thing I could ask for. I thought other people felt this appreciation and physical joy all the time, and I felt cheated because I was able to feel it only once a week.

Because I'd lost my hair, I wore a hat constantly, but this fooled no one, least of all myself. During this time, my mother worked in a nursing home in a Hasidic community. Hasidic law dictates that married women cover their hair, and most commonly this is done with a wig. My mother's friends were now all willing to donate their discarded wigs, and soon the house seemed filled with them. I never wore one, for they frightened me even when my mother insisted I looked better in one of the few that actually fit. Yet we didn't know how to say no to the women who kept graciously offering their wigs. The cats enjoyed sleeping on them and the dogs playing with them, and we grew used to having to pick a wig up off a chair we wanted to sit in. It never struck us as odd until one day a visitor commented wryly as he cleared a chair for himself, and suddenly a great wave of shame overcame me. I had nightmares about wigs and flushed if I even heard the word, and one night I put myself out of my misery by getting up after everyone was asleep and gathering all the wigs except for one the dogs were fond of and that they had chewed up anyway. I hid all the rest in an old chest.

When you are only ten, which is when the chemotherapy began, two and a half years seem like your whole life, yet it finally did end, for the cancer was gone. I remember the last day of treatment clearly because it was the only day on which I succeeded in not crying, and because later, in private, I cried harder than I had in years; I thought now I would no longer be "special," that without the arena of chemotherapy in which to prove myself no one would ever love me, that I would fade unnoticed into the background. But this idea about *not being different* didn't last very long. Before, I foolishly believed that people stared at me because I was bald. After my hair eventually grew in, it didn't take long before I understood that I looked different for another reason. My face. People stared at me in stores, and other children made fun of me to the point that I came to expect such reactions constantly, wherever I went. School became a battleground.

Halloween, that night of frights, became my favorite holiday because I could put on a mask and walk among the blessed for a few brief, sweet hours. Such freedom I felt, walking down the street, my face hidden! Through the imperfect oval holes I could peer out at other faces, masked or painted or not, and see on those faces nothing but the normal faces of childhood looking back at me, faces I mistakenly thought were the faces everyone else but me saw all the time, faces that were simply curious and ready for fun, not the faces I usually braced myself for, the cruel, lonely, vicious ones I spent every day other than Halloween waiting to see around each corner. As I breathed in the condensed, plastic-scented air under the mask, I somehow thought that I was breathing in normality, that this joy and weightlessness were what the world was composed of, and that it was only my face that kept me from it, my face that was my own mask that kept me from knowing the joy I was sure everyone but me lived with intimately. How could the other children not know it? Not know that to be free of the fear of taunts and the burden of knowing no one would ever love you was all that anyone could ever ask for? I was a pauper walking for a short while in the clothes of the prince, and when the day ended I gave up my disguise with dismay.

○ ○ ○

I was living in an extreme situation, and because I did not particularly care for the world I was in, I lived in others, and because the world I did live in was dangerous now, I incorporated this danger into my secret life. I imagined myself to be an Indian. Walking down the streets, I stepped through the forest, my body ready for any opportunity to fight or flee one of the big cats that I knew stalked me. Vietnam and Cambodia, in the news then as scenes of catastrophic horror, were other places I walked through daily. I made my way down the school hall, knowing a land mine or a sniper might give themselves away at any moment with the subtle metal click I'd read about. Compared with a land mine, a mere insult about my face seemed a frivolous thing.

In those years, not yet a teenager, I secretly read—knowing it was some-how inappropriate—works by Primo Levi and Elie Wiesel, and every book by a survivor I could find by myself without asking the librarian. Auschwitz, Birkenau: I felt the blows of the capos and somehow knew that because any moment we might be called upon to live for a week on one loaf of bread and some water called soup, the peanut-butter sandwich I found on my plate was nothing less than a miracle, an utter and sheer miracle capable of making me literally weep with joy.

I decided to become a "deep" person. I wasn't exactly sure what this would entail, but I believed that if I could just find the right philosophy, think the right thoughts, my suffering would end. To try to understand the world I was in, I undertook to find out what was "real," and I quickly began seeing reality as existing in the lowest common denominator, that suffering was the one and only dependable thing. But rather than spend all of my time despairing, though certainly I did plenty of that, I developed a form of defensive egomania: I felt I was the only one walking about in the world who under-stood what was really important. I looked upon people complaining about the most mundane things—nothing on TV, traffic jams, the price of new clothes—and felt joy because I knew how unimportant those things really were and felt unenlightened superiority because other people didn't. Because in my fantasy life I had learned to be thankful for each cold, blan-ketless night that I survived on the cramped wooden bunks, my pain and despair were a stroll through the country in comparison. I was often miser-able, but I knew that to feel warm instead of cold was its own kind of joy, that to eat was a reenactment of the grace of some god whom I could only dimly define, and that to simply be alive was a rare, ephemeral gift.

As I became a teenager, my isolation began. My nonidentical twin sister started going out with boys, and I started—my most tragic mistake of all—to listen to and believe the taunts thrown at me daily by the very boys she and the other girls were interested in. I was a dog, a monster, the ugliest girl they had ever seen. Of all the remarks, the most damaging wasn't even directed at me but was really an insult to "Jerry," a boy I never saw because every day between fourth and fifth periods, when I was cornered by a particular group of kids, I was too ashamed to lift my eyes off the floor. "Hey, look, it's Jerry's girlfriend!" they shrieked when they saw me, and I felt such shame, knowing that this was the deepest insult to Jerry that they could imagine.

When pressed to it, one makes compensations. I came to love winter, when I could wrap up the disfigured lower half of my face in a scarf: I could speak to people and they would have no idea to whom and to what they were really speaking. I developed the bad habit of letting my long hair hang in my face and of always covering my chin and mouth with my hand, hoping it might be mistaken as a thoughtful, accidental gesture. I also became interested in horses and got a job at a rundown local stable. Having those horses to go to each day after school saved my life; I spent all of my time either with them or thinking about them. Completely and utterly repressed by the time I was sixteen, I was convinced that I would never want a boyfriend, not ever, and wasn't it convenient for me, even a blessing, that none would ever want me. I told myself I was free to concentrate on the "true reality" of life, whatever that was. My sister and her friends put on blue eye shadow, blowdried their hair, and spent interminable hours in the local mall, and I looked down on them for this, knew they were misleading themselves and being overly occupied with the "mere surface" of living. I'd had thoughts like this when I was younger, ten or twelve, but now my philosophy was haunted by desires so frightening I was unable even to admit they existed.

Throughout all of this, I was undergoing reconstructive surgery in an attempt to rebuild my jaw. It started when I was fifteen, two years after chemo ended. I had known for years I would have operations to fix my face, and at night I fantasized about how good my life would finally be then. One day I got a clue that maybe it wouldn't be so easy. An older plastic surgeon explained the process of "pedestals" to me, and told me it would take *ten years* to fix my face. Ten years? Why even bother, I thought; I'll be ancient by then. I went to a medical library and looked up the "pedestals" he talked about. There were gruesome pictures of people with grotesque tubes of their own skin growing out of their bodies, tubes of skin that were harvested like some kind of crop and then rearranged, with results that did not look at all normal or acceptable to my eye. But then I met a younger surgeon, who was working on a new way of grafting that did not involve pedestals, and I became more hopeful and once again began to await the fixing of my face, the day when I would be whole, content, loved.

Long-term plastic surgery is not like in the movies. There is no one single operation that will change everything, and there is certainly no slow unwrapping of the gauze in order to view the final, remarkable result. There is always swelling, sometimes to a grotesque degree, there are often bruises, and always there are scars. After each operation, too frightened to simply go look in the mirror, I developed an oblique method, with several stages. First, I tried to catch my reflection in an overhead lamp: the roundness of the metal distorted my image just enough to obscure details and give no true sense of size or proportion. Then I slowly worked my way up to looking at the reflection in someone's eyeglasses, and from there I went to walking as briskly as possible by a mirror, glancing only quickly. I repeated this as many times as it would take me, passing the mirror slightly more slowly each time until finally I was able to stand still and confront myself.

The theory behind most reconstructive surgery is to take large chunks of muscle, skin, and bone and slap them into the roughly appropriate place, then slowly begin to carve this mess into some sort of shape. It involves long, major operations, countless lesser ones, a lot of pain, and many, many years. And also, it does not always work. With my young surgeon in New York, who with each passing year was becoming not so young, I had two or three soft-tissue grafts, two skin grafts, a bone graft, and some dozen other operations to "revise" my face, yet when I left graduate school at the age of twenty-five I was still more or less in the same position I had started in: a deep hole in the right side of my face and a rapidly shrinking left side and chin, a result of the radiation I'd had as a child and the stress placed upon the bone by the other operations. I was caught in a cycle of having a big operation, one that would force me to look monstrous from the swelling for many months, then having the subsequent revision operations that improved my looks tremendously, and then slowly, over the period of a few months or a year, watching the graft reabsorb back into my body, slowly shrinking down and leaving me with nothing but the scarred donor site the graft had originally come from.

It wasn't until I was in college that I finally allowed that maybe, just maybe, it might be nice to have a boyfriend. I went to a small, liberal, predominantly female school and suddenly, after years of alienation in high school, discovered that there were other people I could enjoy talking to who thought me intelligent and talented. I was, however, still operating on the assumption that no one, not ever, would be physically attracted to me, and in a curious way this shaped my personality. I became forthright and honest in the way that only the truly self-confident are, who do not expect to be rejected, and in the way of those like me, who do not even dare to ask acceptance from others and therefore expect no rejection. I had come to know myself as a person, but I would be in graduate school before I was literally, physically able to use my name and the word "woman" in the same sentence.

Now my friends repeated for me endlessly that most of it was in my mind, that, granted, I did not look like everyone else, but that didn't mean I looked bad. I am sure now that they were right some of the time. But with the constant surgery I was in a perpetual state of transfiguration. I rarely looked the same for more than six months at a time. So ashamed of my face, I was unable even to admit that this constant change affected me; I let everyone who wanted to know that it was only what was inside that mattered, that I had "grown used to" the surgery, that none of it bothered me at all. Just as I had done in childhood, I pretended nothing was wrong, and this was constantly mistaken by others for bravery. I spent a great deal of time looking in the mirror in private, positioning my head to show off my eyes and nose, which were not only normal but quite pretty, as my friends told me often. But I could not bring myself to see them for more than a moment: I looked in the mirror and saw not the normal upper half of my face but only the disfigured lower half.

People still teased me. Not daily, as when I was younger, but in ways that caused me more pain than ever before. Children stared at me, and I learned to cross the street to avoid them; this bothered me, but not as much as the insults I got from men. Their taunts came at me not because I was disfigured but because I was a disfigured *woman*. They came from boys, sometimes men, and almost always from a group of them. I had long, blond hair, and I also had a thin figure. Sometimes, from a distance, men would see a thin blonde and whistle, something I dreaded more than anything else because I knew that as they got closer, their tune, so to speak, would inevitably change; they would stare openly or, worse, turn away quickly in shame or repulsion. I decided to cut my hair to avoid any misconception that anyone, however briefly, might have about my being attractive. Only two or three times have I ever been teased by a single person, and I can think of only one time when I was ever teased by a woman. Had I been a man, would I have had to walk down the street while a group of young women followed and denigrated my sexual worth?

Not surprisingly, then, I viewed sex as my salvation. I was sure that if only I could get someone to sleep with me, it would mean I wasn't ugly, that I was attractive, even lovable. This line of reasoning led me into the beds of several manipulative men who liked themselves even less than they liked me, and I in turn left each short-term affair hating myself, obscenely sure that if only I had been prettier it would have worked—he would have loved me and it would have been like those other love affairs that I was certain "normal" women had all the time. Gradually, I became unable to say "I'm depressed" but could say only "I'm ugly," because the two had become inextricably linked in my mind. Into that universal lie, that sad equation of "if only . . ." that we are all prey to, I was sure that if only I had a normal face, then I would be happy.

The new surgeon in Scotland, Oliver Fenton, recommended that I undergo a procedure involving something called a tissue expander, followed by a bone graft. A tissue expander is a small balloon placed under the skin and then slowly blown up over the course of several months, the object being to stretch out the skin and create room and cover for the new bone. It's a bizarre, nightmarish thing to do to your face, yet I was hopeful about the end results and I was also able to spend the three months that the expansion took in the hospital. I've always felt safe in hospitals: they're the one place I feel free from the need to explain the way I look. For this reason the first tissue expander was bearable—just—and the bone graft that followed it was a success; it did not melt away like the previous ones.

The surgical stress this put upon what remained of my original jaw instigated the deterioration of that bone, however, and it became unhappily apparent that I was going to need the same operation I'd just had on the right side done to the left. I remember my surgeon telling me this at an outpatient clinic. I planned to be traveling down to London that same night on an overnight train, and I barely made it to the station on time, such a fumbling state of despair I was in.

I could not imagine going through it *again*, and just as I had done all my life, I searched and searched through my intellect for a way to make it okay, make it bearable, for a way to *do* it. I lay awake all night on that train, feeling the tracks slip beneath me with an odd eroticism, when I remembered an afternoon from my three months in the hospital. Boredom was a big problem those long afternoons, the days marked by meals and television programs. Waiting for the afternoon tea to come, wondering desperately how I could make time pass, it had suddenly occurred to me that I didn't have to make time pass, that it would do it of its own accord, that I simply had to relax and take no action. Lying on the train, remembering that, I realized I had no obligation to improve my situation, that I didn't have to explain or understand it, that I could just simply let it happen. By the time the train pulled into King's Cross station, I felt able to bear it yet again, not entirely sure what other choice I had.

But there was an element I didn't yet know about. When I returned to Scotland to set up a date to have the tissue expander inserted, I was told quite casually that I'd be in the hospital only three or four days. Wasn't I going to spend the whole expansion time in the hospital? I asked in a whisper. What's the point of that? came the answer. You can just come in every day to the outpatient ward to have it expanded. Horrified by this, I was speechless. I would have to live and move about in the outside world with a giant balloon inside the tissue of my face? I can't remember what I did for the next few days before I went into the hospital, but I vaguely recall that these days involved a great deal of drinking alone in bars and at home.

I had the operation and went home at the end of the week. The only things that gave me any comfort during the months I lived with my tissue expander were my writing and Franz Kafka. I started a novel and completely absorbed myself in it, writing for hours each day. The only way I could walk down the street, could stand the stares I received, was to think to myself, "I'll bet none of them are writing a novel." It was that strange, old, familiar form of egomania, directly related to my dismissive, conceited thoughts of adolescence. As for Kafka, who had always been one of my favorite writers, he helped me in that I felt permission to feel alienated, and to have that alienation be okay, bearable, noble even. In the same way that imagining I lived in Cambodia helped me as a child, I walked the streets of my dark little Scottish city by the sea and knew without doubt that I was living in a story Kafka would have been proud to write.

The one good thing about a tissue expander is that you look so bad with it in that no matter what you look like once it's finally removed, your face has to look better. I had my bone graft and my fifth soft-tissue graft and, yes, even I had to admit I looked better. But I didn't look like me. Something was wrong: was *this* the face I had waited through eighteen years and almost thirty operations for? I somehow just couldn't make what I saw in the mirror correspond to the person I thought I was. It wasn't only that I continued to feel ugly; I simply could not conceive of the image as belonging to me. My own image was the image of a stranger, and rather than try to understand this, I simply stopped looking in the mirror. I perfected the technique of brushing my teeth without a mirror, grew my hair in such a way that it would require only a quick, simple brush, and wore clothes that were simply and easily put on, no complex layers or lines that might require even the most minor of visual adjustments.

On one level I understood that the image of my face was merely that, an image, a surface that was not directly related to any true, deep definition of the self. But I also knew that it is only through appearances that we experience and make decisions about the everyday world, and I was not always able to gather the strength to prefer the deeper world to the shallower one. I looked for ways to find a bridge that would allow me access to both, rather than riding out the constant swings between peace and anguish. The only direction I had to go in to achieve this was to strive for a state of awareness and self-honesty that sometimes, to this day, occasionally rewards me. I have found, I believe, that our whole lives are dominated, though it is not always so clearly translatable, by the question "How do I look?" Take all the many nouns in our lives—car, house, job, family, love, friends—and substitute the personal pronoun "I." It is not that we are all so self-obsessed; it is that all things eventually relate back to ourselves, and it is our own sense of how we appear to the world by which we chart our lives, how we navigate our personalities, which would otherwise be adrift in the ocean of *other* people's obsessions.

One evening toward the end of my year-long separation from the mirror, I was sitting in a café talking to someone—an attractive man, as it happened—and we were having a lovely, engaging conversation. For some reason I suddenly wondered what I looked like to him. What was he *actually* seeing when he saw me? So many times I've asked this of myself, and always the answer is this: a warm, smart woman, yes, but an unattractive one. I sat there in the café and asked myself this old question, and startlingly, for the first time in my life, I had no answer readily prepared. I had not looked in a mirror for so long that I quite simply had no clue as to what I looked like. I studied the man as he spoke; my entire life I had seen my ugliness reflected back to me. But now, as reluctant as I was to admit it, the only indication in my companion's behavior was positive.

And then, that evening in that café, I experienced a moment of the freedom I'd been practicing for behind my Halloween mask all those years ago. But whereas as a child I expected my liberation to come as a result of gaining something, a new face, it came to me now as the result of shedding something, of shedding my image. I once thought that truth was eternal, that when you understood something it was with you forever. I know now that this isn't so, that most truths are inherently unretainable, that we have to work hard all our lives to remember the most basic things. Society is no help; it tells us again and again that we can most be ourselves by looking like someone else, leaving our own faces behind to turn into ghosts that will inevitably resent and haunt us. It is no mistake that in movies and literature the dead sometimes know they are dead only after they can no longer see themselves in the mirror; and as I sat there feeling the warmth of the cup against my palm, this small observation seemed like a great revelation to me. I wanted to tell the man I was with about it, but he was involved in his own topic and I did not want to interrupt him, so instead I looked with curiosity toward the window behind him, its night-darkened glass reflecting the whole café, to see if I could, now, recognize myself.

Difficult Decisions

Lee Gutkind

The veterinarian guns the accelerator of her mobile clinic—a large pickup truck with a double cab, outfitted with a Fiberglas shell with drawers and compartments designed specifically for practicing veterinary medicine. She thunders out of the parking lot and down the road, her rear tires spitting gravel. As she drives, she fingers the stethoscope draped around her steering wheel and frequently turns to make eye contact. At first, her lack of attention to driving makes me nervous, but I soon note her uncanny ability to sense dips and turns in the road. Luckily there are only occasional oncoming vehicles, controlled primarily by people who seem to regard driving as an afterthought.

Although the veterinarian will treat a variety of animals on the many farms that dot this fertile valley, her specialty is "ruminants," sheep and goats especially, for which she possesses a special passion. A ruminant is a cloven-hoofed animal, with four compartments in their stomachs; they ruminate, meaning they eat food, regurgitate it back up, and eat it again. "From a treatment point of view, goats are pretty easy to handle. You can knock them down and flip them over. They're not going to kill you; they don't require a lot of equipment. Mostly, the diseases they get are straightforward and simple. If they end up having a serious enough disease, you euthanize them, because they're not worth a lot of money. It boils down to economics; a farmer looks at a sick animal and says, 'I can replace her for $50, why spend $500 trying to make her better?'"

She shrugs and turns toward me, as if she has said something that might offend. The veterinarian—her name is Wendy Freeman—has a well-scrubbed look: tall, slender, plain. Wearing faded, almost-white khakis, she is lean, freckled and boyish. I take off my baseball cap and toy with the brim while nodding in a reassuring manner, hoping she will not feel self-conscious. Working with animals, God's creatures, intrigues me. In fact, I am writing a book about veterinarians and how they interact with animals and people. Without the luxury of words, veterinarians mostly communicate with their patients in the special, silent language of touch. As any doctor, they may often save lives through technology and perseverance. But veterinarians also possess an invaluable escape clause. The ability to legally end life is perhaps the supreme privilege and the overwhelming psychic burden of their work and mission.

Euthanasia, the veterinarian says, is often difficult for clients to accept. Horses, such as the one she will be examining on her first stop that day, seem to generate an emotional attachment that makes an owner more sentimental than responsible. Ricki, who lives in a rambling brick ranch house on the edge of a lime green field dotted with a rainbow of summer wild flowers, is clearly perplexed over the fate of a thickset, whiskered twenty-eight-year-old mare named Honey, who is slowly and painfully dying from old age and arthritis.

Listening to Ricki talk about her daughter's unwillingness to even so much as discuss euthanasia and nodding frequently, the veterinarian removes the plastic cap of a needle by yanking it with her teeth and proceeds to vaccinate the horse for botulism and rabies. Because one hand is always holding down or caressing an animal, veterinarians, as a matter of course, employ their teeth as a third hand.

"Sometimes an old or sick horse like Honey will be 'cast,' that is, fall or lie down to sleep and be unable to lift themselves back up," the veterinarian tells me.

"We do sometimes find her wedged under the pasture gates or the stall door," Ricki replies. "But my daughter is twenty-five years old and has never known life without Honey. She won't come outside when the veterinarian is here because she refuses to enter into a discussion." Ricki throws up her hands and rolls her eyes. She is short, stocky, well-tanned, with Levi's, white sandals, and painted toes. "Do you ride?" she asks, motioning down at my boots.

"Motorcycles," I tell her. "Not horses."

The veterinarian continues down the line of Ricki's three other horses, yanking off the caps of needles with her teeth, patting and caressing each animal with gentle assurance before sinking the needle into a fleshy area at the nape of the neck.

"What do you think we should do about Honey?" Ricki asks. She gazes toward the silent house where her daughter is hiding, as if the question itself will bring her to the window.

"It's a quality of life issue," says the veterinarian. "Is Honey eating well, maintaining her weight? Ambulatory? I've seen some very lame horses that still had life quality; they're hobbling, but happy. When small animals are so sick they can't make it outside to go to the bathroom, they get upset, they have anxiety attacks. It is very painful and embarrassing."

"So do you think it is time this horse be put to sleep?" she asks, once more glancing toward the house.

"When you think the time has come, I'll support you. I'll do it here in Honey's home where she feels comfortable or I'll take her away and put her to sleep in the hospital, whatever is easier for you or your daughter."

"I don't want my horse to become a pasture potato," Ricki says.

"I understand," says the veterinarian. "It's a difficult decision."

"So then, what should we do?"

"I wish I had ten dollars for every person who wants me to make that decision for them."

○   ○   ○

On the average, Wendy Freeman will see eight cases a day, treating horses, goats, sheep, cows and an occasional llama. On an emergency basis, she'll see dystocias, which are difficult births, and pregnancy toxemia, common in ewes close to lambing—and the walking wounded from dog attacks. For horses, lameness and foot abscesses are common, as is colic—stomach pain. Cows get "milk fever," and when they get into the grain they will often overload, like a child with a stomachache after eating a package of cookies. Overeating could kill any farm animal.

Difficult pregnancies and deliveries are routine and troublesome. "I once chased a beef cow with a newborn calf hanging out of her by its feet. She was running wild in a two-acre field. The farmer and I tried to round her up with our trucks and push her into a shed. We gave up that idea when she smashed in the doors of both trucks with head butts. So we decided to rope her; took us an hour before we got the rope around her. We tied her leg to the bumper of my truck, stretched her out, knocked her down, pulled the calf out. It was rough work."

"Rough work" is an understatement in this particular instance and in calving generally, which is one of the most grueling aspects of her job, especially for a spare, slight woman like this veterinarian, who weighs all of 120 pounds. Sometimes even catching a wild and frightened cow in this bizarre drama is only the beginning. Sometimes a cow is so swollen with pregnancy and the calf wedged so deeply inside the womb that the struggling veterinarian, reaching and groping vainly for hour upon exhausting and frustrating hour on end, will lose her sense of time and grip on reality, and eventually begin to imagine the nightmarish possibility of literally losing herself—drowning inside the mother. Or inadvertently pushing rather than pulling and suffocating the almost born infant. Sometimes the veterinarian, shivering violently in the freezing night air, drained of all energy and spirit, will begin to envision the unmentionable but tempting notion of failure—of giving up—and the alluring rewards such a decision might bring: warmth, food, coffee, sleep.

But even in triumph, when the calf is finally pulled out, she will often experience a momentary and panicky feeling of failure. Calves in difficult births frequently look dead when they are first born. Their eyes are glassy; their tongues are bloated. The veterinarian knows she must encourage and coax life back, clear throats of possible obstructions, initiate artificial respiration—and pray through agonizingly long seconds until the animals can wrench their sticky eyes open and begin their tentative jerky attempts to communicate with the body and instigate control. In the end, the veterinarian says, she always experiences simultaneously fear, exhaustion, and frustration, along with an exhilarating feeling of triumph, which she carries with her—until the next long and endless night.

Recently, a cow decided to calf in a swamp two miles away from the nearest barn and in a pouring rain. The farmer, a stubborn and money-minded businessman, waited until 10:30 P.M. to telephone her. The veterinarian arrived within thirty minutes, helped hitch the cow to a tractor and drag her to solid ground. "I should say *solid mud*. We were covered in guck. Our rain gear was useless." She tried to deliver the calf, but it was breach, necessitating surgery.

The farmer wanted her to perform surgery in the field. It was the most economical approach, but not the safest for either mother or calf. When the veterinarian pointed out that it was pouring down rain, the farmer suggested pitching a tent. But she countered by stressing the need for electricity, so the farmer said he'd make a skid with the tractor—tomorrow—and take the mother down to the barn. The veterinarian refused to wait a day for the skid and persisted until the farmer agreed to call for the ambulance from a nearby animal clinic where the delivery could be made under safer conditions. In the end, her client—the farmer—had been cooperative, but some farmers are more difficult to deal with than their animals. Sometimes their eyes reflect dollar signs, their ears listen to the grunts and groans of the struggling vet, but only hear cash registers ringing. Farmers often think that they know more about their animals than veterinarians do.

A farmer telephoned one night and asked her to do a caesarean on a pregnant mare who was toxic and dying, in order to save the foal. This surgery took place in the field, lighted by the headlights from two pickup trucks. They put a catheter in the mare's neck so that the euthanization could come immediately after delivery, blocked out an area on her stomach, and cut her open. The foal came out easily, but the mare was dead. "It's pouring down rain," says the veterinarian, "lightning and thunder crackling everywhere. The mare's lying right along a major highway, and I said, 'You have to get this horse out of here. Nobody is going to want to see or smell this dead mare with all of her guts out when the sun comes up.'" Persisting, the veterinarian asked why the mare had been so sick in the first place. He was not a regular client; she had never met the man. The farmer said that the horse had been sick for three days, walking kind of funny, not eating well, acting strange. The veterinarian then asked the million dollar question. "No," the farmer replied, "she's not been vaccinated for rabies."

At this point, she knew that her dealings with this stubborn farmer were going to become considerably more difficult. "We need to take her head off and check for rabies," she said. "We argued for a while, but I insisted." Reluctantly agreeing, the farmer stepped back to watch. "So now I'm sawing her head off out in the middle of the rain. I finish, stick it in a bucket." The veterinarian's truck was parked on the other side of a fence dividing the field from the highway. Her plan was to hand the bucket over the fence to the farmer to put it on her truck, but now, suddenly, the farmer was nowhere to be found. So she balanced the bucket on top of the fence so that she could climb over and carry it to where her truck was parked. No sooner did she get on the fence, when the bucket fell over and the horse's head rolled into the middle of the highway. "I ran like hell, scooped the head up, threw it into my truck and jumped in. Whoever drove by during that whole fiasco probably thought *Godfather* was happening all over again." The animal was not rabid, but the veterinarian had been obliged to order the necessary tests.

The veterinarian locates a spot in the barn directly beside an electric outlet and plugs in the disbudding iron. She walks outside, opens a pen in which two calves are waiting, selects a brown spotted calf ("The kind that makes chocolate milk," she jokes) and brings it inside. Working quickly, she shaves the hair from around the horns, then reaches into her bag for Lidocaine, a pain blocker, which she has already siphoned into a hypodermic needle. She injects the Lidocaine directly around the horn. Next comes the electric disbudding iron, which resembles a branding iron, round, like a large "O," not unlike a packaged donut with a hole in the middle. She grabs the calf's ear, wedges its head against her body, inserts the "O" of the iron through the calf's horn, and then, bringing the iron slowly downward, digs the hot iron into the calf's little head.

First there is a wisp of bluish white smoke, and then the dank, stark stench of burning fur. Then comes the primeval aroma of roasting skin, followed by the sound of searing bone, as she applies increasing pressure. She twists the iron back and forth repeatedly until smoking copper-colored rings show through above the ears. It looks as if the smoke is emanating from the calf's head, as if the soul of this tiny helpless animal has suddenly been apprehended by the devil. "The horn is growing from cells within and below the hair, and so if you kill the skin around the horn, there will never be another horn returning. Animals sense the heat, but do not feel the pain," she adds. In the days of the wide-open range, horns were needed by livestock for protection. Today, horns serve no practical purpose and in fact may be used aggressively and cause harm to a farmer's valuable herd.

Veterinarians are asked to perform a number of such procedures, including the removal of waddles—appendages of skin that hang down from the necks of goats. For this procedure, she will snip off each waddle with a gigantic clipper, as if she were clipping fingernails. "The animal may not experience pain, although losing part of your anatomy can't be particularly pleasant." For cosmetic purposes, veterinarians may remove the third teat on the developing mammary gland of pygmy goats, a genetic flaw disqualifying the goat from competition or breeding. Using a local anesthetic to dull the pain and snipping the teat with a clipper resembling ordinary pliers, the procedure is completed in three minutes flat.

Disbudding of the second calf does not go as smoothly as in the first instance, perhaps because the first calf defecated on the floor during the procedure, and so now the second calf, an emaciated pale white baby of about four months, is slipping. As the calf struggles, its flying hooves pepper the veterinarian's khaki pants with feces and track it on her leather tennis shoes. "They love to stand on your feet," she says.

The veterinarian burns in the disbudding iron, twists it round and round, the calf jumping with each grinding twist. She blows a cloud of smoke away from her face. "It would be nice to have a little fan on your shoulder," she says. After the disbudding is finished, she rubs the hot circle of the iron on top of the tiny remaining buds, one at a time, to cauterize them. She sprays the burning circles with yellow anti-bacterial Furox and returns the calves to their pen. The horns will fall off in a couple of weeks. The calves will remember nothing, she says.

Back in the truck, the veterinarian picks up our conversation, as if the disbudding never occurred or was much too common and ordinary to discuss. "There was a woman at a riding stable where I was working, a schoolteacher named Pat. Her horse was old and thin, and very lame; she could no longer ride him. But every day, she went to that barn and took him for a walk and gave him carrots; she'd always be hanging out and letting him graze. And I would go over and pet him and say, 'Oh, Shadow looks good.' I never left the stable without saying hello or goodbye to Shadow.

"That year, I went away for the Christmas holidays, and while I was gone, Shadow had emergency surgery, and it turned out he was dying. But Pat wouldn't let anybody put him to sleep until I came back. She wanted me to drive to Limerick, a pet cemetery, and euthanize Shadow there so that we could bury him, but by the time I got back, it was too late. He needed to be euthanized immediately. I said, 'Pat, you need to say goodbye; he's suffered enough.'" When Pat walked into the stall and whispered his name, Shadow lifted his head, turned to look at her and started to nicker. "We all started to cry." Later, we loaded the horse on the trailer for her so that she could bury him.

"Not long afterward, the woman sent me a letter about how it meant so much to her that I would say 'hi' to Shadow. I remember reading the letter and thinking, 'Isn't that something? Just me stopping and saying hello to her horse made her feel like he was really important.' Those are the kinds of things that some clients want you to do; some clients want to feel that veterinarians really care about their animal.

"Four days before last Christmas, I had to put an old horse down for a little girl who had asthma. She would go the barn with a mask on her face every day and take care of that horse. He got real sick the weekend before Christmas; I was on duty, and I was up all night with him for two nights, and he wasn't getting better. She had run out of funds, and we decided to euthanize him. Even now I can picture that little girl's face as she walked into the barn with the little mask on and . . . I was the one who had to kill her horse. It was the worst Christmas of my life."

At the end of the day, back at her office, the veterinarian stoops on a patch of grass adjacent to the parking lot, examining a brown Nubian goat inflicted with a rare kidney disease far too expensive for its owner to treat. The goat's owner is a woman with whom she has worked for a half dozen years who is suffering from an increasingly debilitating case of multiple sclerosis. The conversation is short and to-the-point; the woman's options are significantly limited. "Okay," she says to the veterinarian, holding her hand like a traffic policeman, palm straight forward, signaling STOP. "That's enough talk." Looking back, I realize that the euthanasia happened quite quickly, but at the time it occurred, the process seemed agonizingly long. I watched it as if it were being played back to me in slow motion.

The veterinarian takes out a catheter with a long tube filled with pink liquid (sodium phenobarbital) and injects it into the goat's neck. First blood spatters onto the veterinarian's hand from the catheter. For an instant, the little goat seems to simultaneously inflate itself—and momentarily freeze—mid-air. Then comes a silent single shudder that ripples like quiet thunder through every dip and graceful curve of her dramatic and biblical body. Finally, the goat caves in, and collapses on the grass with a muffled thud.

Now the woman cries. She sits on the ground and pets her goat, stroking the goat's head and laying each ear, one at a time, on top of the forehead, tears streaming down her wrinkled cheeks. The veterinarian reaches down and attempts to close the goat's eyes with the palms of her hands. But the eyes open back up again, continuing to assert themselves. Those eyes are ice blue. They look like diamonds or stained glass glinting in the sun.

I don't know why the veterinarian selected such a public place to perform such a private act. Many people seemed to be going about their day as if nothing had changed, as if an animal hadn't lost a life and a woman, who herself is slowly dying, hadn't lost a friend. On the other side of the grass, a stable hand loading a horse on a trailer is talking loudly to a companion. Maintenance workers drive by, smiling and waving. The goat continues to shudder and groan, the woman stroking its ears.

"He's already dead," the woman says aloud. "Even though he's making these noises, I know they're involuntary. He's not coming back." Soon the woman struggles to her feet, hobbles back to the road and climbs shakily into her pickup truck. She starts the motor and drives away. I can see her watching us in her rearview mirror. Now the veterinarian and I are standing alone on the grass, staring quietly down at the goat. "It was a nice goat," the veterinarian says. "I wanted to tell the woman, 'Let's put her in the hospital and I'll pay the charges to fix her up.' It would have cost $300. But I do too much of that; I just didn't want to spend my own money this time." Soon the veterinarian disappears into her office. I sit down beside the brown goat; I stroke its ears and look into its ice-blue eyes.

Reading History to My Mother

Robin Hemley

Your silence will not protect you.

— AUDRE LOURDE

" Everything's mixed up in those boxes, the past and the present," my mother tells me. "Those movers made a mess of everything." I'm visiting her at the Leopold late on a Monday night after reading to my kids and being read to by my eldest, Olivia, who at six is rightfully proud of her newfound reading ability. My mother and I have been readers for many years, but in some ways, she finds it more difficult than does Olivia. At eighty-two, my mother's eyesight has deteriorated. Glaucoma. Severe optic nerve damage to her left eye. Macular degeneration. Tomorrow, I'm taking her to the doctor for a second laser operation to "relieve the pressure." We have been told by the doctor that the surgery won't actually improve her eyesight, but, with luck, will stop it from deteriorating any more. After that there's another operation she'll probably undergo, eighty miles south in Seattle. Another operation that won't actually make her see any better.

"I always had such good eyesight," she tells me. And then, "I wish there was something that could improve my eyesight." And then, "When are we going to go shopping for that new computer?"

"Well, let's make sure you can see the screen first," I say, which sounds cruel, but she has complained to me tonight that she wasn't able to see any of the words on her screen, though I think this has less to do with her eyesight than the glasses she's wearing. Unnaturally thick and foggy. My mother looks foggy, too, almost drunk, disheveled in her dirty sweater, though she doesn't drink. It's probably the medicine she's been taking for her many conditions.

My mother owns at least half a dozen glasses, and I know I should have sorted through them all by now (we tried once) but so many things have gone wrong in the last five months since my mother moved to Bellingham that sorting through her glasses is a side issue. I get up from the couch in the cramped living room of her apartment, step over the coffee table—careful not to tip over the cup of peppermint tea I'm drinking out of a beer stein, careful not to bump into my mother—and cross to the bedroom crammed with wardrobe boxes and too much furniture, though much less than what she's used to. On her dresser there are parts of various eyeglasses: maimed glasses, the corpses of eyeglasses, a dark orphaned lens here, a frame there, an empty case, and one case with a pair that's whole. This is the one I grab and take out to my mother who is waiting patiently, always patient these days, or perhaps so unnerved and exhausted that it passes for patience. She takes the case from me and takes off the old glasses, places them beside her beer mug of licorice tea, and puts on the new pair.

She rubs an eye, says, "This seems to be helping. Maybe these are my reading glasses." I should know, of course. I should have had them color-coded by now, but I haven't yet.

She bends down to the photo from the newsletter on the coffee table, and says. "Yes, that's William Carlos Williams."

A little earlier she told me about the photo. "It's in one of those boxes," she told me. "I saw it the other day. I thought I'd told you about it before," but she hadn't, this photo of her with William Carlos Williams, Theodore Roethke, and other famous writers. So I spent fifteen minutes rifling through her boxes of bills and old papers mixed up on the kitchen counter (a Cascade Gas Company bill, final payment requested for service at the apartment she moved into in December, when we still thought she could live on her own; a letter from the superintendent of public schools of New York City, dated 1959, addressed to my grandmother, a teacher at the time, telling her how many sick days she was allowed), looking for the photo, until she explained that it was actually part of a newsletter from the artists' colony, Yaddo, in Saratoga Springs, New York: Armed with that crucial bit of information, I found it.

The photo is captioned "Class picture, 1950."

"Can you pick me out?" she says.

Not many of these people are smiling. Eugenic Gershoy, seated next to Jessamyn West, has a little smirk, and Mitsu Yashima, seated next to Flossie Williams, smiles broadly, and also Cid Corman in the back row, whom I met in 1975, when I was a high school exchange student in Japan. My mother visited me in Osaka and we traveled by train to Kyoto, to Cid Corman's ice-cream parlor where I ate a hamburger, had an ice-cream cone and listened to a poetry reading while my mother and Cid reminisced.

"Don't I look prim?" my mother says, and she does. Or maybe it's something else. Scared? Intimidated? Shocked? My mother was 34 then. This was a year or so before she met my father. My sister, Nola, was three, and my mother was an up-and-coming young writer, one novel published in 1947. John Crowe Ransom liked her work, publishing several of her stories in the *Kenyon Review*. I wasn't born until 1958.

She stands up straight, hands behind her back, a scarf tied loosely around her neck, draping down over a breast, a flower pinned to the scarf. Theodore Roethke stands, huge, imposing, dour. In an accompanying article

Harvey Shapiro tells of how publicly Roethke liked to display his wounds, how he told Shapiro of his hurt that John Crowe Ransom had rejected "My Papa's Waltz," though Roethke was famous by then and the poem had been widely anthologized. What remained, still, was Roethke's pain, perhaps the pain of rejection meshed with the pain of the poem's subject matter—abuse at the hands of his drunken father. Shapiro also tells of Roethke's claim that he'd bummed his way to Yaddo after escaping in drag from a mental institution on the west coast earlier that summer. "He liked to romanticize his mental illness," Shapiro writes. Perhaps, but something honest still comes across in that picture, the despair clear for anyone to view head-on.

In the front row, William Carlos Williams sits cross-legged, dignified.

"He dreamed of my legs," my mother tells me.

"William Carlos Williams dreamed of your legs?" I ask.

"At breakfast one day he said he'd had a dream about my legs. 'That girl has nice legs,' he said."

We have to keep going back over histories, our own and the histories of others, constantly revising. There's no single truth . . . except that, perhaps. History is not always recorded and not always written by the victor. History is not always written. We carry our secret histories behind our words, in another room, in the eyeglass case on the dresser in the bedroom. Maybe someone comes along and finds the right pair. Maybe we have too many, unsorted.

My mother's former landlord, Loyce, wants to know the history of the "L." I was gone for the past week in Hawaii, and that's the only reason I haven't called before now. Loyce has left messages on my answering machine twice, ostensibly to see about getting my mother's deposit back to us: minus a charge for mowing, the ad for renting the apartment again, a reasonable charge for her time, and of course, for painting over the "L." She'd also like the keys back from us. But the "L" is the real reason she's called. My mother wrote an "L" on the wall of the apartment in indelible magic marker before she left. "I'm dying to know the story," Loyce says. "I know there's a good story behind it."

Loyce appreciates a good story, and this is one of the things I appreciate about Loyce, that and her compassion. She moved to Bellingham several years ago to take care of her ailing mother, and now lives in her mother's old house on top of a hill with a view of the bay and the San Juan Islands. So she understands our situation. She knows that my mother can't live alone anymore, that all of us were taken by surprise by her condition when she moved here five months ago. Until then, my mother had been living on her own in South Bend, Indiana, where she taught writing until ten years ago. She'd been living on her own since I moved out at the age of sixteen to go to boarding school, and had been taking care of herself since 1966 when my father died. But in the last several months things have fallen apart. Our first inkling was the mover, a man in his sixties who worked with his son. He took me aside on the first day and told me that in his thirty years of moving he'd never seen an apartment as messy as my mother's. When he and his son went to my mom's apartment in South Bend, they almost turned around. "You don't have to do this if you don't want," the mover told his son.

No, the first inkling was my brother's call from L.A., where my mother was visiting a few days prior to her big move. The van had loaded in South Bend and she'd flown off to L.A. to visit him and his family. The night before her flight from L.A. to Seattle he called me near midnight and said, "Mom's hallucinating."

I asked him what he meant, what she was seeing, and he told me that she was seeing all these people who didn't exist and making strange remarks. "When I picked her up at the airport, she said there was a group of Asians having a baby. She said they were a troupe of actors and they were doing a skit."

Still, the next day, he put her on the plane to me, and I picked her up and brought her to her new home. Since then, we have gone to three different doctors and my mother has had brain scans and blood tests and sonograms of her carotid arteries and been placed on a small dose of an anti-psychotic drug. One doctor says her cerebral cortex has shrunk and she's had a series of tiny strokes to individual arteries in her brain.

At three A.M. one morning, the police call me up and tell me that my mother thinks someone is trying to break into her apartment.

"Is there anyone living with her?" the policeman asks.

"No."

"She says a handicapped woman lives with her. You might want to see a doctor about this."

I take her to doctors and try to convince my mother that she needs to live where she can be safe, but she refuses to even consider it. "I should have stayed in New York," she tells me. "I never should have left." And then, "I should never have come here. Why can't you be on my side?" And then, "I'll move down to L.A. Your brother is much nicer than you are."

I spend a few nights at her apartment, and she tells me about the Middle Eastern couple who have taken over her bedroom and the children who are there, and the landlord comes over and puts a lock on the door from the kitchen to the garage, though we know no one was trying to break in. And homeless people are living on her back porch. And she keeps startling people in the garage who are removing her belongings.

But finally.

After my cousin David flies up from L.A. After visiting a dozen managed care facilities, after my brother says he thinks it's the medicine that's doing this and I talk to the doctors and the doctors talk to each other and they talk to my mother and she says, "The doctor says I'm fine," and I say "No, he doesn't," and she hangs up, turns off her hearing aid.

And coincidentally, a friend of my mother's in South Bend wins second place in a poetry competition run by the literary journal I edit. The poems were all anonymous, and I had nothing to do with the judging, but my mother's friend has won second prize for a poem about her delusional mother, called "My Mother and Dan Rather." I call her up to tell her the good news of her award, but she assumes, of course, I'm calling to talk about my mother. So that's what we do for half an hour. She tells me she's distanced herself over the last year from my mother because she seemed too much like her own mother, and she tells me that several of my mother's friends wondered if they should call me and let me know what was going on.

I almost forget to tell her about her prize.

No, the first inkling was two years ago. My wife, Beverly, wondered aloud about my mother's memory, her hold on reality. I told Beverly my mother had always been kind of scattered, messy, unfocused.

And finally. After I come into her apartment one day and feel the heat. I go to the stove and turn off the glowing burners. My mother has a blister on her hand the size of a walnut. Beverly tells me that it's insane for my mother to live alone, that somehow we have to force her to move. "What if she sets the apartment on fire? She might not only kill herself, but the people next door."

"I know," I tell her. "I'm trying," but I also know that short of a court order, short of being declared her legal guardian, I can't force her.

And finally. I convince my mother to come with me to the Leopold, an historic hotel in downtown Bellingham that has been converted into apartments for seniors, one wing assisted living, the other independent. We have lunch there one day. My mother likes the food.

And finally, she agrees to spend a couple of weeks there in a guest room.

Famous people stayed at the Leopold, I tell my mother. Rutherford B. Hayes, Jenny Lind, the Swedish Nightingale. This doesn't impress her, of course. She has known more famous people than can fit on a plaque. But she has a nice view of the bay, somewhat blocked by the Georgia Pacific Paper Mill. And she likes the food but the apartment is only two cramped rooms, and across the street at the Greek restaurant, people party until two each night and climb trees and conduct military rituals. And the Iraqi Army rolled through the streets one night. And a truck dumped two bodies, a man and a woman dressed in formal evening attire.

"They sometimes flood the parking lot," she tells me, "and use it as a waterway."

Or, "Look at that," pointing, reaching for nothing.

She keeps returning to the apartment, driven by the woman I've hired to clean it. My mother wants to drive again, and I tell her no, she can't possibly, and I read articles and watch programs that tell me not to reverse roles, not to become the parent, and I wonder how that's possible to avoid. One day, I walk into her apartment and find signs she's posted all around on the bed, in the guest room, on the kitchen counter. "Keep off." "Stay out." "Go away." I ask her about these signs and she tells me they're just a joke. She's become wary of me. I tell her she's safe, ask her why she feels so threatened. She tells me, "I've never felt safe in my life."

During this period, my mother writes her "L" on the wall of the kitchen.

And the weeks at the Leopold have turned to months, and now most of her belongings are stuffed into a heated mini-storage unit. More of her belongings are stuffed into the basement of The Leopold.

Finally.

I almost don't want to tell Loyce the story of the "L" when she calls. I'd like to keep her in suspense, because sometimes that's stronger than the truth. She probably thinks it's about her, that the "L" stands for Loyce, but it doesn't. It stands for Leopold. One day my mother was at the apartment, after we finally convinced her she had to move, and I gave her a magic marker and asked her to mark the boxes she'd like taken to the Leopold. Apparently, she thought she was marking a box, but she was really marking the wall. This is what she really wanted. That was not lost on me. She loved that apartment. She wanted her independence, but this was just too much for me to move.

Loyce and I say goodbye after I assure her I'll return the keys and she assures me she'll return most of the deposit. It's already eight-thirty and I told my mother I'd be over around eight, but I had to read to my kids first. I haven't see them in a week. I've just returned from Hawaii.

In Hawaii, where I've been researching a new book, I probably had more fun than I should have. Not the kind of fun with life-bending consequences, but fun nonetheless, hanging out with a former student, eating out every night, smoking cigars, drinking. For ten dollars a day more, I was told at the airport, I could rent a convertible—a Ford Mustang, or a Caddie, and I'm not ready for that, so I take the Mustang. Stupid. The wife of the friend I'm staying with laughed when she saw it in her driveway. "Oh," she tells me. "I thought maybe Robbie was having a mid-life crisis." No, it's me probably, even though I hate to admit it. I refuse to believe such a thing could happen to me at this pre-ordained age, a month from forty, that I could be saddled with such a cliché crisis, such mediocre regrets.

Olivia wants to read to *me* tonight, all seven stories from an Arnold Lobel book. "They're short," she assures me. We compromise on three, her three favorites. One of these she read last week to her class while I was in Hawaii. Beverly, who sometimes works in Olivia's class as a volunteer, has already told me that the class was enthralled by Olivia. "She acted so confident. She took her time and showed them the pictures."

The one she read to her class, "The Journey," is about a mouse who wants to visit his mother, and in a sequence of transactions, acquires a car, roller skates, boots, sneakers and finally a new set of feet. When he reaches his mother she hugs him, kisses him and says, "Hello, my son, you are looking fine—and what nice new feet you have!" Olivia's whole class broke out in hysterical laughter, she assured me.

◊   ◊   ◊

I've brought my mother a box of chocolate-covered macadamia nuts. She looks at it, bewildered. "Oh, I thought it was a book," she says.

I make tea for us, but she only has a few tea mugs and they're dirty, so we have to use beer steins. "I've ended up with such an odd assortment of things," she tells me, and she blames this on the movers.

A week before my trip to Hawaii, I visited her and she showed me a notebook in which she'd kept a journal during the mid-seventies. My mother has kept journals from the time she was sixteen, a series of secret histories written in any notebook she can find. But now, she cannot read these histories, and she asks me to read this one to her.

"I might use it in a story," she tells me. "It's about Moe and Helen." Moe is Moe Howard, of the Three Stooges. He was a cousin of ours by marriage, and whenever she visited California, she'd stop by to see them. Moe, who had such a violent on-screen persona: Think of him saying, "Wise guy, eh?" Poking the eyes of Larry, Curly, Shemp, or one of the later pseudo-Stooges, Curly Joe and Joe Besser. I met him once, a frail old man with white hair, too quiet to seem like Moe. Off-screen, he was a gentle family man, kind and grateful to his fans, never refusing to sign an autograph. What my mother wants me to read to her is an account of the last time she saw Moe and his wife Helen, when they were both dying.

> Seeing Moe and Helen was touching—a beautiful hill of purple flowers outside that Moe said was all theirs—a beautifully furnished, expensively comfortable house through which they glide, ghost-like. They don't kiss me because of the possibility of germs. Helen is in a loose purple nylon dressing gown. She has been recuperating from a breast operation and says in a slightly quaking voice that she will be going to the doctor soon and will probably have cobalt.
>
> Moe is red-faced and very thin. His thinness, wispiness, makes him look elfin—because he used to be heavier, he seemed bigger. His hair is white. He smiles proudly, talking about his appearances at colleges and his memoirs which comprise many books. Talk about the film I am supposed to have made with him. He reminds me that I acted in it (at the age of about 19) 8mm, I think, with his children. But it is packed somewhere with thousands of feet of other film.

As I'm reading this to my mother I feel odd, wondering if she notices the similarities between this passage and her own present life—the things packed away, the memories, the frailty—but I say nothing about this, though it moves me. Instead, I ask her about this film she was in, and she tells me it was an impromptu home movie in which Moe was cast as the villain, of course, and she was the protector of his children. She has never seen it but it exists somewhere. Moe's daughter, Joan, once showed me the huge roll of home movies in her attic. Towards the end of his life, Moe took every home movie he made and spliced them all together onto one monstrous cumbersome roll that no one could ever possibly watch in its entirety. Somewhere on this roll exists a movie with my mother, age nineteen, circa 1935.

Silently, I flip through other pages in my mother's journal, as she sits near me, lost in her memories, needing no journal really.

> I am not in fantasy land. I am painfully living out my loneliness and nostalgia. I dream of my son every night and wish he were here. Those who have died are intolerably absent and I feel that all the love I need and want will not come because I had my chance and lost it, and what man will be responsible for or will react to my aging, my passion, my intolerable loneliness . . . ?

I am with her now, but not. We see each other through veils. We have battled for this moment, and neither sees the other as we would like.

William Carlos Williams dreamed of my mother's legs, as did other men that summer of 1950 at Yaddo.

As we bend over the class photo, circa 1950, she tells me the official history of that summer, how special it was for her, how it was so exciting to be around such vital intellects, such talented writers. "It was really something, going down to breakfast and having conversations with all these people. The talent was never quite the same after that."

I tell her I'd love to have a copy of this picture. "You could write to Yaddo," she says, "They use it for publicity," She tells me I could write to one of the writers pictured with her. "It's the least he could do," she says, with what seems like bitterness, and I let this remark wash over me because I think I know what's behind it.

Once, a number of years ago, Beverly and my mother and I were on a drive, and I was telling her about a friend of mine who'd done his dissertation on the poetry of one of the poets pictured in the photo. From the back seat my mother blurted, "You know, he raped me."

Beverly and I looked at one another. We didn't say anything. We didn't know what to say. The remark was so sudden, so unexpected, we hardly knew how to react. We were silent, all three of us. Neither Beverly nor I mentioned this to each other later.

My mother starts talking about him now, though I haven't asked. She says, "One time, he invited me to a private party, and innocent that I was, I went there." In memory, she's lucid. Only the present is slippery, tricky, untrustworthy.

"There were all these men there. They were all leches. Ted Roethke kept lunging for me, just making grabs. He really had problems," and she laughs. She mentions the name of the poet who was her friend, whom she trusted.

He was younger than her, than all these other famous men. "I thought he'd protect me." She laughs again. This time, there's no mistaking the bitterness.

I think about asking her. What term to use? "He assaulted you?"

"Yes," she says.

"Did it happen at Yaddo?" I ask.

She nods.

"Did you ever confront him?"

"No," she says. "I don't want to talk about it."

But then she says, "There wasn't much I could do. In those days, there wasn't much to do. I just pretended it didn't happen. For a little while, he became my boyfriend."

I don't know what to say. I probably shouldn't say anything. I sigh. "He should have been locked up. How could he be your boyfriend after that?"

"He was drunk when it happened," and I want to say that's no excuse, but I keep my mouth shut and let her talk. "I left the party early and he followed me back to my room. I tried to lock the door, but the lock was broken.

"I turned things around. I had to. I was confused. In my mind, he became my protector from the other men there."

I study the picture again. My mother's expression and the expressions of the men. I wonder when this photo was taken, before or after the assault my mother describes. The photo has taken on the quality of a group mug shot to me, I think they look like jerks, most of them—except for Cid Corman, whom my mother says is a wonderful person, and maybe some others, too, maybe William Carlos Williams, who dreamed of my mother's legs and "had an eye for the ladies" as my mother says. Maybe even dour Theodore Roethke, though he lunged at her as though she was something being wheeled by on a dessert tray.

"They weren't famous for their personalities," she tells me.

I think about these people in the photo, how unfair it seems to me that someone can go on to have a career, hide behind his smirk, have dissertations written about him, how the actions of some people seem to have no visible consequences. I think of my mother's secret histories, her journals, her blurted comments, her assertion that she has never felt safe.

I flip the newsletter over to the section titled "Recent Works Produced by Yaddo Fellows," and see that the latest works reported are from 1987. For an absurd moment, I believe that none of the Fellows at Yaddo have been productive for over ten years, and this makes me happy, but then I realize the newsletter itself is ten years old.

My mother has taken to carrying a picture of me, Ideal Robin, I call it, skinny, sitting languorously, smiling beside a life-size cardboard cutout of Rudolph Valentino. The son she longed for in her journal perhaps hardly exists anymore—I was away at boarding school that year, my choice, not hers, and I never returned.

I have come to visit her now. I've knocked lightly. I've used my key. She can barely see me when I walk into her apartment. I've told her I've returned from Hawaii, that she can expect me around eight, but I'm late and as I push open the door she's looking at me almost suspiciously, because really her eyesight is that bad, and until I speak she has no idea who's entering. The Iraqi army? A stranger who wants her belongings? A poet she thinks is her "protector" but means her harm? I half expect to see signs. "Keep Off," "Stay Out," "Go Away." I have brought a box of chocolate-covered macadamia nuts. I am wearing new feet, but she doesn't notice. Tomorrow she will have surgery on her eyes that will not improve anything, but keep things from getting worse. How much worse could things get for this woman who loves words, but can neither see nor write them anymore? Does her history go on inside her, on some gigantic roll of spliced-together home movies? Tell me the story of the "L." Tell me the story of the wall of your apartment. Tell me the story of those talented writers who publicly display their wounds and the writers who secretly wound others. Tell me which is worse. She kisses me lightly and I give her her gift. And she says, once, only once, though I keep hearing it, the disappointment, and strangely, even fear. "Oh, I thought it was a book."

The Courage of Turtles
Edward Hoagland

$\mathcal{T}$urtles are a kind of bird with the governor turned low. With the same attitude of removal, they cock a glance at what is going on, as if they need only to fly away. Until recently they were also a case of virtue rewarded, at least in the town where I grew up, because, being humble creatures, there were plenty of them. Even when we still had a few bobcats in the woods the local snapping turtles, growing up to forty pounds, were the largest carnivores. You would see them through the amber water, as big as greeny wash basins at the bottom of the pond, until they faded into the inscrutable mud as if they hadn't existed at all.

When I was ten I went to Dr. Green's Pond, a two-acre pond across the road. When I was twelve I walked a mile or so to Taggart's Pond, which was lusher, had big water snakes and a waterfall; and shortly after that I was bicycling way up to the adverturesome vastness of Mud Pond, a lake-sized body of water in the reservoir system of a Connecticut city, possessed of cat-backed little islands and empty shacks and a forest of pines and hardwoods along the shore. Otters, foxes and mink left their prints on the bank; there were pike and perch. As I got older, the estates and forgotten back lots in town were parceled out and sold for nice prices, yet, though the woods had shrunk, it seemed that fewer people walked in the woods. The new residents didn't know how to find them. Eventually, exploring, they did find them, and it required some ingenuity and doubling around on my part to go for eight miles without meeting someone. I was grown by now, I lived in New York, and that's what I wanted on the occasional weekends when I came out.

Since Mud Pond contained drinking water I had felt confident nothing untoward would happen there. For a long while the developers stayed away, until the drought of the mid–1960s. This event, squeezing the edges in, convinced the local water company that the pond really wasn't a necessity as a catch basin, however; so they bulldozed a hole in the earthen dam, bulldozed the banks to fill in the bottom, and landscaped the flow of water that remained to wind like an English brook and provide a domestic view for the houses which were planned. Most of the painted turtles of Mud Pond, who had been inaccessible as they sunned on their rocks, wound up in boxes in boys' closets within a matter of days. Their footsteps in the dry leaves gave them away as they wandered forlornly. The snappers and the little musk turtles, neither of whom leave the water except once a year to lay their eggs, dug into the drying mud for another siege of hot weather, which they were accustomed to doing whenever the pond got low. But this time it was low for good; the mud baked over them and slowly entombed them. As for the ducks, I couldn't stroll in the woods and not feel guilty, because they were crouched beside every stagnant pothole, or were slinking between the bushes with their heads tucked into their shoulders so that I wouldn't see them. If they decided I had, they beat their way up through the screen of trees, striking their wings dangerously, and wheeled about with that headlong, magnificent velocity to locate another poor puddle.

I used to catch possums and black snakes as well as turtles, and I kept dogs and goats. Some summers I worked in a menagerie with the big personalities of the animal kingdom, like elephants and rhinoceroses. I was twenty before these enthusiasms began to wane, and it was then that I picked turtles as the particular animal I wanted to keep in touch with. I was allergic to fur, for one thing, and turtles need minimal care and not much in the way of quarters. They're personable beasts. They see the same colors we do and they seem to see just as well, as one discovers in trying to sneak up on them. In the laboratory they unravel the twists of a maze with the hot-blooded rapidity of a mammal. Though they can't run as fast as a rat, they improve on their errors just as quickly, pausing at each crossroads to look left and right. And they rock rhythmically in place, as we often do, although they are hatched from eggs, not the womb. (A common explanation psychologists give for our pleasure in rocking quietly is that it recapitulates our mother's heartbeat *in utero*.)

Snakes, by contrast, are dryly silent and priapic. They are smooth movers, legalistic, unblinking, and they afford the humor which the humorless do. But they make challenging captives; sometimes they don't eat for months on a point of order—if the light isn't right, for instance. Alligators are sticklers too. They're like war-horses, or German shepherds, and with their bar-shaped, vertical pupils adding emphasis, they have the *idée fixe* of eating, eating, even when they choose to refuse all food and stubbornly die. They delight in tossing a salamander up towards the sky and grabbing him in their long mouths as he comes down. They're so eager that they get the jitters, and they're too much of a proposition for a casual aquarium like mine. Frogs are depressingly defenseless: that moist, extensive back, with the bones almost sticking through. Hold a frog and you're holding its skeleton. Frogs' tasty legs are the staff of life to many animals—herons, raccoons, ribbon snakes—though they themselves are hard to feed. It's not an enviable role to be the staff of life, and after frogs you descend down the evolutionary ladder a big step to fish.

Turtles cough, burp, whistle, grunt and hiss, and produce social judgments. They put their heads together amicably enough, but then one drives the other back with the suddenness of two dogs who have been conversing in tones too low for an onlooker to hear. They pee in fear when they're first caught, but exercise both pluck and optimism in trying to escape, walking for hundreds of yards within the confines of their pen, carrying the weight of that cumbersome box on legs which are cruelly positioned for walking. They don't feel that the contest is unfair; they keep plugging, rolling like sailorly souls—a bobbing, infirm gait, a brave, sea-legged momentum—stopping occasionally to study the lay of the land. For me, anyway, they manage to contain the rest of the animal world. They can stretch out their necks like a giraffe, or loom underwater like an apocryphal hippo. They browse on lettuce thrown on the water like a cow moose which is partly submerged. They have a penguin's alertness, combined with a build like a Brontosaurus when they rise up on tiptoe. Then they hunch and ponderously lunge like a grizzly going forward.

Baby turtles in a turtle bowl are a puzzle in geometrics. They're as decorative as pansy petals, but they are also self-directed building blocks, propping themselves on one another in different arrangements, before upending the tower. The timid individuals turn fearless, or vice versa. If one gets a bit arrogant he will push the others off the rock and afterwards climb down into the water and cling to the back of one of those he has bullied, tickling him with his hind feet until he bucks like a bronco. On the other hand, when this same milder-mannered fellow isn't exerting himself, he will stare right into the face of the sun for hours. What could be more lionlike? And he's at home in or out of the water and does lots of metaphysical tilting. He sinks and rises, with an infinity of levels to choose from; or, elongating himself, he climbs out on the land again to perambulate, sits boxed in his box, and finally slides back in the water, submerging into dreams.

I have five of these babies in a kidney-shaped bowl. The hatchling, who is a painted turtle, is not as large as the top joint of my thumb. He eats chicken gladly. Other foods he will attempt to eat but not with sufficient perseverance to succeed because he's so little. The yellow-bellied terrapin is probably a yearling, and he eats salad voraciously, but no meat, fish or fowl. The Cumberland terrapin won't touch salad or chicken but eats fish and all of the meats except for bacon. The little snapper, with a black crenelated shell, feasts on any kind of meat, but rejects greens and fish. The fifth of the turtles is African. I acquired him only recently and don't know him well. A mottled brown, he unnerves the green turtles, dragging their food off to his lairs. He doesn't seem to want to be green—he bites the algae off his shell, hanging meanwhile at daring, steep, head-first angles.

The snapper was a Ferdinand until I provided him with deeper water. Now he snaps at my pencil with his downturned and fearsome mouth, his swollen face like a napalm victim's. The Cumberland has an elliptical red mark on the side of his green-and-yellow head. He is benign by nature and ought to be as elegant as his scientific name (*Pseudemys scripta elegans*), except he has contracted a disease of the air bladder which has permanently inflated it; he floats high in the water at an undignified slant and can't go under. There may have been internal bleeding, too, because his carapace is stained along its ridge. Unfortunately, like flowers, baby turtles often die. Their mouths fill up with a white fungus and their lungs with pneumonia. Their organs clog up from the rust in the water, or diet troubles, and, like a dying man's, their eyes and heads become too prominent. Toward the end, the edge of the shell becomes flabby as felt and folds around them like a shroud.

While they live they're like puppies. Although they're vivacious, they would be a bore to be with all the time, so I also have an adult wood turtle about six inches long. Her shell is the equal of any seashell for sculpturing, even a Cellini shell; it's like an old, dusty, richly engraved medallion dug out of a hillside. Her legs are salmon-orange bordered with black and protected by canted, heroic scales. Her plastron—the bottom shell—is splotched like a margay cat's coat, with black ocelli on a yellow background. It is convex to make room for the female organs inside, whereas a male's would be concave to help him fit tightly on top of her. Altogether, she exhibits every camouflage color on her limbs and shells. She has a turtleneck neck, a tail like an elephant's, wise old pachydermous hind legs, and the face of a turkey—except that when I carry her she gazes at the passing ground with a hawk's eyes and mouth. Her feet fit to the fingers of my hand, one to each one, and she rides looking down. She can walk on the floor in perfect silence, but usually she lets her shell knock portentously, like a footstep, so that she resembles some grand, concise, slow-moving id. But if an earthworm is presented, she jerks swiftly ahead, poises above it, and strikes like a mongoose, consuming it with wild vigor. Yet she will climb on my lap to eat bread or boiled eggs.

If put into a creek, she swims like a cutter, nosing forward to intercept a strange turtle and smell him. She drifts with the current to go downstream, maneuvering behind a rock when she wants to take stock, or sinking to the nether levels, while bubbles float up. Getting out, choosing her path, she will proceed a distance and dig into a pile of humus, thrusting herself to the coolest layer at the bottom. The hole closes over her until it's as small as a mouse's hole. She's not as aquatic as a musk turtle, not quite as terrestrial as the box turtles in the same woods, but because of her versatility she's marvelous, she's everywhere. And though she breathes the way we breathe, with scarcely perceptible movements of her chest, sometimes instead she pumps her throat ruminatively, like a pipe smoker sucking and puffing. She waits and blinks, pumping her throat, turning her head, then sets off like a loping tiger in slow motion, hurdling the jungly lumber, the pea vine and twigs. She estimates angles so well that when she rides over the rocks, sliding down a drop-off with her rugged front legs extended, she has the grace of a rodeo mare.

But she's well off to be with me rather than at Mud Pond. The other turtles have fled—those that aren't baked into the bottom. Creeping up the brooks to sad, constricted marshes, burdened as they are with that box on their backs, they're walking into a setup where all their enemies move thirty times faster than they. It's like the nightmare most of us have whimpered through, where we are weighted down disastrously while trying to flee; fleeing our home ground, we try to run.

I've seen turtles in still worse straits. On Broadway, in New York, there is a penny arcade which used to sell baby terrapins that were scrawled with bon mots in enamel paint, such as KISS ME BABY. The manager turned out to be a wholesaler as well, and once I asked him whether he had any larger turtles to sell. He took me upstairs to a loft room devoted to the turtle business. There were desks for the paper work and a series of racks that held shallow tin bins atop one another, each with several hundred babies crawling around in it. He was a smudgy-complexioned, serious fellow and he did have a few adult terrapins, but I was going to school and wasn't actually planning to buy; I'd only wanted to see them. They were aquatic turtles, but here they went without water, presumably for weeks, lurching about in those dry bins like handicapped citizens, living on gumption. An easel where the artist worked stood in the middle of the floor. She had a palette and a clip attachment for fastening the babies in place. She wore a smock and a beret, and was homely, short, and eccentric-looking, with funny black hair, like some of the ladies who show their paintings in Washington Square in May. She had a cold, she was smoking, and her hand wasn't very steady, although she worked quickly enough. The smile that she produced for me would have looked giddy if she had been happier, or drunk. Of course the turtles' doom was sealed when she painted them, because their bodies inside would continue to grow but their shells would not. Gradually, invisibly, they would be crushed. Around us their bellies—two thousand belly shells—rubbed on the bins with a mournful, momentous hiss.

Somehow there were so many of them I didn't rescue one. Years later, however, I was walking on First Avenue when I noticed a basket of living turtles in front of a fish store. They were as dry as a heap of old bones in the sun; nevertheless, they were creeping over one another gimpily, doing their best to escape. I looked and was touched to discover that they appeared to be wood turtles, my favorites, so I bought one. In my apartment I looked closer and realized that in fact this was a diamondback terrapin, which was bad news. Diamondbacks are tidewater turtles from brackish estuaries, and I had no sea water to keep him in. He spent his days thumping interminably against the baseboards, pushing for an opening through the wall. He drank thirstily but would not eat and had none of the hearty, accepting qualities of wood turtles. He was morose, paler in color, sleeker and more Oriental in the carved ridges and rings that formed his shell. Though I felt sorry for him, finally I found his unrelenting presence exasperating. I carried him, struggling in a paper bag, across town to the Morton Street Pier on the Hudson. It was August but gray and windy. He was very surprised when I tossed him in; for the first time in our association, I think, he was afraid. He looked afraid as he bobbed about on top of the water, looking up at me from ten feet below. Though we were both accustomed to his resistance and rigidity, seeing him still pitiful, I recognized that I must have done the wrong thing. At least the river was salty, but it was also bottomless; the waves were too rough for him, and the tide was coming in, bumping him against the pilings underneath the pier. Too late, I realized that he wouldn't be able to swim to a peaceful inlet in New Jersey, even if he could figure out which way to swim. But since, short of diving in after him, there was nothing I could do, I walked away.

Where Worlds Collide

Pico Iyer

*T*hey come out, blinking, into the bleached, forgetful sunshine, in Dodgers caps and Rodeo Drive T-shirts, with the maps their cousins have drawn for them and the images they've brought over from *Cops* and *Terminator 2;* they come out, dazed, disoriented, heads still partly in the clouds, bodies still several time zones—or centuries—away, and they step into the Promised Land.

In front of them is a Van Stop, a Bus Stop, a Courtesy Tram Stop, and a Shuttle Bus Stop (the shuttles themselves tracing circuits A, B, and C). At the Shuttle Bus Stop, they see the All American Shuttle, the Apollo Shuttle, Celebrity Airport Livery, the Great American Stageline, the Movie Shuttle, the Transport, Ride-4-You, and forty-two other magic buses waiting to whisk them everywhere from Bakersfield to Disneyland. They see Koreans piling into the Taeguk Airport Shuttle and the Seoul Shuttle, which will take them to Koreatown without their ever feeling they've left home; they see newcomers from the Middle East disappearing under the Arabic script of the Sahara Shuttle. They see fast-talking, finger-snapping, palm-slapping jive artists straight from their TV screens shouting incomprehensible slogans about deals, destinations, and drugs. Over there is a block-long white limo, a Lincoln Continental, and, over there, a black Chevy Blazer with Mexican stickers all over its windows, being towed. They have arrived in the Land of Opportunity, and the opportunities are swirling dizzily, promiscuously, around them.

They have already braved the ranks of Asian officials, the criminal-looking security men in jackets that say "Elsinore Airport Services," the men shaking tins that say "Helping America's Hopeless." They have already seen the tilting mugs that say "California: a new slant on life" and the portable fruit machines in the gift shop. They have already, perhaps, visited the rest room where someone has written, "Yes on Proposition 187. Mexicans go home," the snack bar where a slice of pizza costs $3.19 (18 quetzals, they think in horror, or 35,000 dong), and the sign that urges them to try the Cockatoo Inn Grand Hotel. The latest arrivals at Los Angeles International Airport are ready now to claim their new lives.

Above them in the terminal, voices are repeating, over and over, in Japanese, Spanish, and unintelligible English, "Maintain visual contact with your personal property at all times." Out on the sidewalk, a man's voice and a woman's voice are alternating an unending refrain: "The white zone is for loading and unloading of passengers only. No parking." There are "Do Not Cross" yellow lines cordoning off parts of the sidewalk and "Wells Fargo Alarm Services" stickers on the windows; there are "Aviation Safeguard" signs on the baggage carts and "Beware of Solicitors" signs on the columns; there are even special phones "To Report Trouble." More male and female voices are intoning, continuously, "Do not leave your car unattended" and "Unattended cars are subject to immediate tow-away." There are no military planes on the tarmac here, the newcomers notice, no khaki soldiers in fatigues, no instructions not to take photographs, as at home; but there are civilian restrictions every bit as strict as in many a police state.

"This Terminal Is in a Medfly Quarantine Area," says the sign between the terminals. "Stop the Spread of Medfly!" If, by chance, the new Americans have to enter a parking lot on their way out, they will be faced with "Cars left over 30 days may be impounded at Owner's Expense" and "Do not enter without a ticket." It will cost them $16 if they lose their parking ticket, they read, and $56 if they park in the wrong zone. Around them is an unending cacophony of antitheft devices, sirens, beepers, and car-door openers; lights are flashing everywhere, and the man who fines them $16 for losing their parking ticket has the tribal scars of Tigre across his forehead.

The blue skies and palm trees they saw on TV are scarcely visible from here: just an undifferentiated smoggy haze, billboards advertising Nissan and Panasonic and Canon, and beyond those an endlessly receding mess of gray streets. Overhead, they can see the all-too-familiar signs of Hilton and Hyatt and Holiday Inn; in the distance, a sea of tract houses, mini-malls, and highrises. The City of Angels awaits them.

It is a commonplace nowadays to say that cities look more and more like airports, cross-cultural spaces that are a gathering of tribes and races and variegated tongues; and it has always been true that airports are in many ways like miniature cities, whole, self-sufficient communities, with their own chapels and museums and gymnasiums. Not only have airports colored our speech (teaching us about being upgraded, bumped, and put on standby, coaching us in the ways of fly-by-night operations, holding patterns, and the Mile High Club); they have also taught us their own rules, their own codes, their own customs. We eat and sleep and shower in airports; we pray and weep and kiss there. Some people stay for days at a time in these perfectly convenient, hermetically sealed, climate-controlled duty-free zones, which offer a kind of caesura from the obligations of daily life.

Airports are also, of course, the new epicenters and paradigms of our dawning post-national age—not just the bus terminals of the global village but the prototypes, in some sense, for our polyglot, multicolored, user-friendly future. And in their very universality—like the mall, the motel, or the McDonald's outlet—they advance the notion of a future in which all the world's a multiculture. If you believe that more and more of the world is a kind of mongrel hybrid in which many cities (Sydney, Toronto, Singapore) are simply suburbs of a single universal order, then Los Angeles's LAX, London's Heathrow, and Hong Kong's Kai Tak are merely stages on some great global Circle Line, shuttling variations on a common global theme. Mass travel has made L.A. contiguous to Seoul and adjacent to São Paulo, and has made all of them now feel a little like bedroom communities for Tokyo.

And as with most social trends, especially the ones involving tomorrow, what is true of the world is doubly true of America, and what is doubly true of America is quadruply true of Los Angeles. L.A., legendarily, has more Thais than any city but Bangkok, more Koreans than any city but Seoul, more El Salvadorans than any city outside of San Salvador, more Druze than anywhere but Beirut; it is, at the very least, the easternmost outpost of Asia and the northernmost province of Mexico. When I stopped at a Traveler's Aid desk at LAX recently, I was told I could request help in Khamu, Mien, Tigrinya, Tajiki, Pashto, Dari, Pangasinan, Pampangan, Waray-Waray, Bambara, Twi, and Bicolano (as well, of course, as French, German, and eleven languages from India). LAX is as clear an image as exists today of the world we are about to enter, and of the world that's entering us.

For me, though, LAX has always had a more personal resonance: it was in LAX that I arrived myself as a new immigrant, in 1966; and from the time I was in the fourth grade, it was to LAX that I would go three times a year, as an "unaccompanied minor," to fly to school in London—and to LAX that I returned three times a year for my holidays. Sometimes it seems as if I have spent half my life in LAX. For me, it is the site of my liberation (from school, from the Old World, from home) and the place where I came to design my own new future.

Often when I have set off from L.A. to some distant place—Havana, say, or Hanoi, or Pyongyang—I have felt that the multicultural drama on display in LAX, the interaction of exoticism and familiarity, was just as bizarre as anything I would find when I arrived at my foreign destination. The airport is an Amy Tan novel, a short story by Bharati Mukherjee, a Henry James sketch set to an MTV beat; it is a cross-generational saga about Chang Hsieng meeting his daughter Cindy and finding that she's wearing a nose ring now and is shacked up with a surfer from Berlin. The very best kind of airport reading to be found in LAX these days is the triple-decker melodrama being played out all around one—a complex tragicomedy of love and war and exile, about people fleeing centuries-old rivalries and thirteenth-century mullahs and stepping out into a fresh, forgetful, born-again city that is rewriting its script every moment.

Not long ago I went to spend a week in LAX. I haunted the airport by day and by night, I joined the gloomy drinkers listening to air-control-tower instructions on earphones at the Proud Bird bar. I listened each morning to

Airport Radio (530 AM), and I slept each night at the Airport Sheraton or the Airport Hilton. I lived off cellophaned crackers and Styrofoam cups of tea, browsed for hours among Best Actor statuettes and Beverly Hills magnets, and tried to see what kinds of America the city presents to the new Americans, who are remaking America each day.

It is almost too easy to say that LAX is a perfect metaphor for L.A., a flat, spaced-out desert kind of place, highly automotive, not deeply hospitable, with little reading matter and no organizing principle. (There are eight satellites without a center here, many international arrivals are shunted out into the bleak basement of Terminal 2, and there is no airline that serves to dominate LAX as Pan Am once did JFK.) Whereas "SIN" is a famously ironical airline code for Singapore, cathedral of puritanical rectitude, "LAX" has always seemed perilously well chosen for a city whose main industries were traditionally thought to be laxity and relaxation. LAX is at once a vacuum waiting to be colonized and a joyless theme park—Tomorrowland, Adventureland, and Fantasyland all at once.

The postcards on sale here (made in Korea) dutifully call the airport "one of the busiest and most beautiful air facilities in the world," and it is certainly true that LAX, with thirty thousand international arrivals each day— roughly the same number of tourists that have visited the Himalayan country of Bhutan in its entire history—is not uncrowded. But bigger is less and less related to better: in a recent survey of travel facilities, *Business Traveller* placed LAX among the five worst airports in the world for customs, luggage retrieval, and passport processing.

LAX is, in fact, a surprisingly shabby and hollowed-out kind of place, certainly not adorned with the amenities one might expect of the world's strongest and richest power. When you come out into the Arrivals area in the International Terminal, you will find exactly one tiny snack bar, which serves nine items; of them, five are identified as Cheese Dog, Chili Dog, Chili Cheese Dog, Nachos with Cheese, and Chili Cheese Nachos. There is a large panel on the wall offering rental-car services and hotels, and the newly deplaned American dreamer can choose between the Cadillac Hotel, the Banana Bungalow (which offers a Basketball Court, "Free Toast," "Free Bed Sheets," and "Free Movies and Parties"), and the Backpacker's Paradise (with "Free Afternoon Tea and Crumpets" and "Free Evening Party Including Food and Champagne").

Around one in the terminal is a swirl of priests rattling cans, Iranians in suits brandishing pictures of torture victims, and Japanese girls in Goofy hats. "I'm looking for something called Clearasil," a distinguished-looking Indian man diffidently tells a cashier. "Clearasil?" shouts the girl. "For your face?"

Upstairs, in the Terrace Restaurant, passengers are gulping down "Dutch Chocolate" and "Japanese Coffee" while students translate back and forth between English and American, explaining that "soliciting" loses something of its cachet when you go across the Atlantic. A fat man is nuzzling the neck of his outrageously pretty Filipina companion, and a few Brits are staring doubtfully at the sign that assures them that seafood is "cheerfully served at your table!" Only in America, they are doubtless thinking. A man goes from table to table, plunking down on each one a key chain attached to a globe. As soon as an unsuspecting customer picks one up, touched by the largesse of the New World and convinced now that there is such a thing as a free lunch in America, the man appears again, flashes a sign that says "I Am a Deaf," and requests a dollar for the gift.

At a bank of phones, a saffron-robed monk gingerly inserts a credit card, while schoolkids page Jesse Jackson at the nearest "white courtesy telephone." One notable feature of the modern airport is that it is wired, with a vengeance: even in a tiny, two-urinal men's room, I found two telephones on offer; LAX bars rent out cellular phones; and in the Arrivals area, as you come out into the land of plenty, you face a bank of forty-six phones of every kind, with screens and buttons and translations, from which newcomers are calling direct to Bangalore or Baghdad. Airports are places for connections of all kinds and *loci classici*, perhaps, for a world ruled by IDD and MCI, DOS and JAL.

Yet for all these grounding reminders of the world outside, everywhere I went in the airport I felt myself in an odd kind of twilight zone of consciousness, that weightless limbo of a world in which people are between lives and between selves, almost sleepwalking, not really sure of who or where they are. Light-headed from the trips they've taken, ears popping and eyes about to do so, under a potent foreign influence, people are at the far edge of themselves in airports, ready to break down or through. You see strangers pouring out their life stories to strangers here, or making new life stories with other strangers. Everything is at once intensified and slightly unreal. One L.A. psychiatrist advises shy women to practice their flirting here, and religious groups circle in the hope of catching unattached souls.

Airports, which often have a kind of perpetual morning-after feeling (the end of the holiday, the end of the affair), are places where everyone is ruled by the clock, but all the clocks show different times. These days, after all, we fly not only into yesterday or this morning when we go across the world but into different decades, often, of the world's life and our own: in ten or fifteen hours, we are taken back into the twelfth century or into worlds we haven't seen since childhood. And in the process we are subjected to transitions more jolting than any imagined by Oscar Wilde or Sigmund Freud: if the average individual today sees as many images in a day as a Victorian saw in a lifetime, the average person today also has to negotiate switches between continents inconceivable only fifty years ago. Frequent fliers like Ted Turner have actually become ill from touching down and taking off so often; but, in less diagnosable ways, all of us are being asked to handle difficult suspensions of the laws of Nature and Society when moving between competing worlds.

This helps to compound the strange statelessness of airports, where all bets are off and all laws are annulled—modern equivalents, perhaps, to the hundred yards of no-man's-land between two frontier crossings. In airports we are often in dreamy, floating, out-of-body states, as ready to be claimed as that suitcase on Carousel C. Even I, not traveling, didn't know sometimes if I was awake or asleep in LAX, as I heard an announcer intone, "John Cheever, John Cheever, please contact a Northwest representative in the Baggage Claim area. John Cheever, please contact a service representative at the Northwest Baggage Claim area."

As I started to sink into this odd, amphibious, bipolar state, I could begin to see why a place like LAX is a particular zone of fear, more terrifying to many people than anywhere but the dentist's office. Though dying in a plane is, notoriously, twenty times less likely than dying in a car, every single airline crash is front-page news and so dramatic—not a single death but three hundred—that airports are for many people killing grounds. Their runways are associated in the mind's (televisual) eye with hostages and hijackings; with bodies on the tarmac or antiterrorist squads storming the plane.

That general sense of unsettledness is doubtless intensified by all the people in uniform in LAX. There are ten different security agencies working the Tom Bradley Terminal alone, and the streets outside are jam-packed with Airport Police cars, FBI men, and black-clad airport policemen on bicycles. All of them do as much, I suspect, to instill fear as to still it. "People are scared here," a gloomy Pakistani security guard told me, "because under-cover are working. Police are working. You could be undercover, I could be undercover. Who knows?"

And just as L.A. is a province of the future in part because so many people take it to be the future, so it is a danger zone precisely because it is imagined to be dangerous. In Osaka's new $16 billion airport recently, I cross-examined the Skynet computer (in the Departures area) about what to expect when arriving at LAX or any other foreign airport. "Guard against theft in the arrival hall," it told me (and, presumably, even warier Japanese). "A thief is waiting for a chance to take advantage of you." Elsewhere it added, "Do not dress too touristy," and, "Be on your guard when approached by a group of suspicious-looking children, such as girls wearing bright-colored shirts and scarves." True to such dark prognostications, the side doors of the Airport Sheraton at LAX are locked every day from 8:00 P.M. to 6:00 A.M., and you cannot even activate the elevators without a room key ."Be extra careful in parking garages and stairwells," the hotel advises visitors. "Always try to use the main entrance to your hotel, particularly late in the evening. Never answer your hotel room door without verifying who is there."

One reason airports enjoy such central status in our imaginations is that they play such a large part in forming our first (which is sometimes our last) impression of a place; this is the reason that poor countries often throw all their resources into making their airports sleek, with beautifully landscaped roads leading out of them into town. L.A., by contrast, has the bareness of arrogance, or simple inhospitability. Usually what you see as you approach the city is a grim penitential haze through which is visible nothing but rows of gray buildings, a few dun-hued warehouses, and ribbons of dirty freeway: a no-colored blur without even the comforting lapis ornaments of the swimming pools that dot New York or Johannesburg. (Ideally, in fact, one should enter L.A. by night, when the whole city pulses like an electric grid of lights—or the back of a transistor radio, in Thomas Pynchon's inspired metaphor. While I was staying in LAX, Jackie Collins actually told *Los Angeles* magazine that "Flying in [to LAX] at night is just an orgasmic thrill.") You land, with a bump, on a mess of gray runways with no signs of welcome, a hangar that says "T ans W rld Airlines," another broken sign that announces "Tom Bradl y International Ai port," and an air-control tower under scaffolding.

The first thing that greeted me on a recent arrival was a row of Asians sitting on the floor of the terminal, under a sign that told them of a $25,000 fine for bringing in the wrong kinds of food. As I passed through endless corridors, I was faced with almost nothing except long escalators (a surprisingly high percentage of the accidents recorded at airports comes from escalators, bewildering to newcomers) and bare hallways. The other surprise, for many of my fellow travelers, no doubt, was that almost no one we saw looked like Robert Redford or Julia Roberts or, indeed, like anyone belonging to the race we'd been celebrating in our in-flight movies. As we passed into the huge, bare assembly hall that is the Customs and Immigration Center here, I was directed into one of the chaotic lines by a Noriko and formally admitted to the country by a C. Chen. The man waiting to transfer my baggage (as a beagle sniffed around us in a coat that said "Agriculture's Beagle Brigade" on one side and "Protecting American Agriculture" on the other) was named Yoji Yosaka. And the first sign I saw, when I stepped into America, was a big board being waved by the "Executive Sedan Service" for one "Mr. T. Ego."

For many immigrants, in fact, LAX is quietly offering them a view of their own near futures: the woman at the Host Coffee Shop is themselves, in a sense, two years from now, and the man sweeping up the refuse is the American dream in practice. The staff at the airport seems to be made up almost entirely of recent immigrants: on my very first afternoon there, I was served by a Hoa, an Ephraim, and a Glinda; the waitpeople at a coffee shop in Terminal 5 were called Ignacio, Ever, Aura, and Erick. Even at the Airport Sheraton (where the employees all wear nameplates), I was checked in by Viera (from "Bratislavia") and ran into Hasmik and Yovik (from Ethiopia), Faye (from Vietnam), Ingrid (from Guatemala City), Khrystyne (from Long Beach, by way of Phnom Penh, I think), and Moe (from West L.A., she said). Many of the bright-eyed dreamers who arrive at LAX so full of hope never actually leave the place.

The deeper drama of any airport is that it features a kind of interaction almost unique in our lives, wherein many of us do not know whom we are going to meet or whom others are going to meet in us. You see people standing at the barriers outside the Customs area looking into their pasts, while wide-open newcomers drift out, searching for their futures. Lovers do not know if they will see the same person who kissed them good-bye a month ago; grandparents wonder what the baby they last saw twenty years ago will look like now.

In L.A. all of this has an added charge, because unlike many cities, it is not a hub but a terminus: a place where people come to arrive. Thus many of the meetings you witness are between the haves and the hope-to-haves, between those who are affecting a new ease in their new home and those who are here in search of that ease. Both parties, especially if they are un-American by birth, are eager to stress their Americanness or their fitness for America; and both, as they look at each other's made-up self, see themselves either before or after a stay in L.A.'s theater of transformation. And so they stream in, wearing running shoes or cowboy hats or 49ers jackets, anxious to make a good first impression; and the people who wait for them, under a halfhearted mural of Desertland, are often American enough not to try to look the part. Juan and Esperanza both have ponytails now, and Kimmie is wearing a Harley-Davidson cap backward and necking with a Japanese guy; the uncle from Delhi arrives to find that Rajiv not only has grown darker but has lost weight, so that he looks more like a peasant from back home than ever.

And the newcomers pour in in astonishing numbers. A typical Sunday evening, in a single hour, sees flights arriving from England, Taiwan, the Philippines, Indonesia, Mexico, Austria, Germany, Spain, Costa Rica, and Guatemala; and each new group colors and transforms the airport: an explosion of tropical shades from Hawaiian Air, a rash of blue blazers and white shirts around the early flight from Tokyo. Red-haired Thais bearing pirated Schwarzenegger videos, lonely Africans in Aerial Assault sneakers, farmers from changeless Confucian cultures peering into the smiles of a Prozac city, children whose parents can't pronounce their names. Many of them are returning, like Odysseus, with the spoils of war: young brides from Luzon, business cards from Shanghai, boxes of macadamia nuts from Oahu. And for many of them the whole wild carnival will feature sights they have never seen before: Japanese look anxiously at the first El Salvadorans they've ever seen, and El Salvadorans ogle sleek girls from Bangkok in thigh-high boots. All of them, moreover, may not be pleased to realize that the America they've dreamed of is, in fact, a land of tacos and pita and pad thai—full, indeed, of the very Third World cultures that other Third Worlders look down upon.

One day over lunch I asked my Ethiopian waitress about her life here. She liked it well enough, she said, but still she missed her home. And yet, she added, she couldn't go back. "Why not?" I asked, still smiling. "Because they killed my family," she said. "Two years back. They killed my father. They killed my brother." "They," I realized, referred to the Tigreans—many of them working just down the corridor in other parts of the hotel. So, too, Tibetans who have finally managed to flee their Chinese-occupied homeland arrive at

LAX to find Chinese faces everywhere; those who fled the Sandinistas find themselves standing next to Sandinistas fleeing their successors. And all these people from ancient cultures find themselves in a country as amnesiac as the morning, where World War II is just a rumor and the Gulf War a distant memory. Their pasts are escaped, yes, but by the same token they are unlikely to be honored.

It is dangerously tempting to start formulating socioeconomic principles in the midst of LAX: people from rich countries (Germany and Japan, say) travel light, if only because they are sure that they can return any time; those from poor countries come with their whole lives in cardboard boxes imperfectly tied with string. People from poor countries are often met by huge crowds—for them each arrival is a special occasion—and stagger through customs with string bags and Gold Digger apple crates, their addresses handwritten on them in pencil; the Okinawan honeymooners, by contrast, in the color-coordinated outfits they will change every day, somehow have packed all their needs into a tiny case.

If airports have some of the excitement of bars, because so many people are composing (and decomposing) selves there, they also have some of the sadness of bars, the poignancy of people sitting unclaimed while everyone around them has paired off. A pretty girl dressed in next to nothing sits alone in an empty Baggage Claim area, waiting for a date who never comes; a Vietnamese man, lost, tells an official that he has friends in Orange County who can help him, but when the friends are contacted, they say they know no one from Vietnam. I hear of a woman who got off and asked for "San Mateo," only to learn that she was meant to disembark in San Francisco; and a woman from Nigeria who came out expecting to see her husband in Monroe, Louisiana, only to learn that someone in Lagos had mistaken "La." on her itinerary for "L.A."

The greetings I saw in the Arrivals area were much more tentative than I had expected, less passionate—as ritualized in their way as the kisses placed on Bob Barker's cheek—and much of that may be because so many people are meeting strangers, even if they are meeting people they once knew. Places like LAX—places like L.A.—perpetuate the sense that everyone is a stranger in our new floating world. I spent one afternoon in the airport with a Californian blonde, and I saw her complimented on her English by a sweet Korean woman and asked by an Iranian if she was Indian. Airports have some of the unsteady brashness of singles bars, where no one knows quite what is expected of them. "Mike, is that you?" "Oh, I didn't recognize you." "I'd have known you anywhere." "It's so kind of you to come and pick me up." And already at a loss, a young Japanese girl and a broad, lonely-looking man head off toward the parking lot, not knowing, in any sense, who is going to be in the driver's seat.

The driving takes place, of course, in what many of the newcomers, primed by video screenings of *L.A. Law* and *Speed*, regard as the ultimate heart of darkness, a place at least as forbidding and dangerous as Africa must have seemed to the Victorians. They have heard about how America is the murder capital of the world; they have seen Rodney King get pummeled by L.A.'s finest; they know of the city as the site of drive-by shootings and freeway snipers, of riots and celebrity murders. The "homeless" and the "tempest-tost" that the Statue of Liberty invites are arriving, increasingly, in a city that is itself famous for its homeless population and its fires, floods, and earthquakes.

In that context, the ideal symbol of LAX is, perhaps, the great object that for thirty years has been the distinctive image of the place: the ugly white quadruped that sits in the middle of the airport like a beached white whale or a jet-age beetle featuring a 360-degree circular restaurant that does not revolve and an observation deck from which the main view is of twenty-three thousand parking places. The Theme Building, at 201 World Way, is a sad image of a future that never arrived, a monument to Kennedy-era idealism and the thrusting modernity of the American empire when it was in its prime; it now has the poignancy of an abandoned present with its price tag stuck to it. When you go there (and almost nobody does) you are greeted by photos of Saturn's rings and Jupiter and its moons by a plaque laid down by L.B.J. and a whole set of symbols from the time when NASA was shooting for the heavens. Now the "landmark" building, with its "gourmet-type restaurant," looks like a relic from a time long past, when it must have looked like the face of the future.

Upstairs, a few desperately merry waiters are serving nonalcoholic drinks and cheeseburgers to sallow diners who look as if they've arrived at the end of the world; on the tarmac outside, speedbirds inch ahead like cars in a traffic jam. "Hello All the New People of LAX—Welcome," says the graffiti on the elevator.

The Theme Restaurant comes to us from an era when L.A. was leading the world. Nowadays, of course, L.A. is being formed and reformed and led by the world around it. And as I got ready to leave LAX, I could not help but feel that the Theme Building stands, more and more, for a city left behind by our accelerating planet. LAX, I was coming to realize, was a good deal scruffier than the airports even of Bangkok or Jakarta, more chaotic, more suggestive of Third World lawlessness. And the city around it is no more golden than Seoul, no more sunny than Taipei, and no more laid-back than Moscow. Beverly Hills, after all, is largely speaking Farsi now. Hollywood Boulevard is sleazier than 42nd Street. And Malibu is falling into the sea.

Yet just as I was about to give up on L.A. as yesterday's piece of modernity, I got on the shuttle bus that moves between the terminals in a never-ending loop. The seats next to me were taken by two tough-looking dudes from nearby South Central, who were riding the free buses and helping people on and off with their cases (acting, I presumed, on the safe assumption that the Japanese, say, new to the country and bewildered, had been warned beforehand to tip often and handsomely for every service they received). In between terminals, as a terrified-looking Miss Kudo and her friend guarded their luggage, en route from Nagoya to Las Vegas, the two gold-plated sharks talked about the Raiders' last game and the Lakers' next season. Then one of them, without warning, announced, "The bottom line is the spirit is with you. When you work out, you chill out and, like, you meditate in your spirit. You know what I mean? Meditation is recreation. Learn math, follow your path. That's all I do, man, that's all I live for: learnin' about God, learnin' about Jesus. I am *possessed* by that spirit. You know, I used to have all these problems, with the flute and all, but when I heard about God, I learned about the body, the mind, and the flesh. People forget, they don't know, that the Bible isn't talkin' about the flesh, it's talkin' about the spirit. And I was reborn again in the spirit."

His friend nodded. "When you recreate, you meditate. Recreation is a spiritually uplifting experience."

"Yeah. When you do that, you allow the spirit to breathe."

"Because you're gettin' into the physical world. You're lettin' the spirit flow. You're helpin' the secretion of the endorphins in the brain."

Nearby, the Soldiers of the Cross of Christ Church stood by the escalators, taking donations, and a man in a dog collar approached another stranger.

I watched the hustlers allowing the spirit to breathe, I heard the Hare Krishna devotees plying their wares, I spotted some Farrakhan flunkies collecting a dollar for a copy of their newspaper, *The Final Call*—redemption and corruption all around us in the air—and I thought: welcome to America, Miss Kudo, welcome to L.A.

Biography of a Dress

Jamaica Kincaid

The dress I am wearing in this black-and-white photograph, taken when I was two years old, was a yellow dress made of cotton poplin (a fabric with a slightly unsmooth texture first manufactured in the French town of Avignon and brought to England by the Huguenots, but I could not have known that at the time), and it was made for me by my mother. This shade of yellow, the color of my dress that I am wearing when I was two years old, was the same shade of yellow as boiled cornmeal, a food that my mother was always eager for me to eat in one form (as a porridge) or another (as fongie, the starchy part of my midday meal) because it was cheap and therefore easily available (but I did not know that at the time), and because she thought that foods bearing the colors yellow, green or orange were particularly rich in vitamins and so boiled cornmeal would be particularly good for me. But I was then (not so now) extremely particular about what I would eat, not knowing then (but I do now) of shortages and abundance, having no consciousness of the idea of rich and poor (but I know now that we were poor then), and would eat only boiled beef (which I required my mother to chew for me first and, after she had made it soft, remove it from her mouth and place it in mine), certain kinds of boiled fish (doctor or angel), hard-boiled eggs (from hens, not ducks), poached calf's liver and the milk from cows, and so would not even look at the boiled cornmeal (porridge or fongie). There was not one single thing that I could isolate and say I did not like about the boiled cornmeal (porridge or fongie) because I could not isolate parts of things then (though I can and do now), but whenever I saw this bowl of trembling yellow substance before me I would grow still and silent, I did not cry, that did not make me cry. My mother told me this then (she does not tell me this now, she does not remember this now, she does not remember telling me this now): she knew of a man who had eaten boiled cornmeal at least once a day from the time he was my age then, two years old, and he lived for a very long time, finally dying when he was almost one hundred years old, and when he died he had looked rosy and new, with the springy wrinkles of the newborn, not the slack pleats of skin of the aged; as he lay dead his stomach was cut open, and all his insides were a beautiful shade of yellow, the same shade of yellow as boiled cornmeal. I was powerless then (though not so now) to like or dislike this story; it was beyond me then (though not so now) to understand the span of my lifetime then, two years old, and it was beyond me then (though not so now), the span of time called almost one hundred years old;

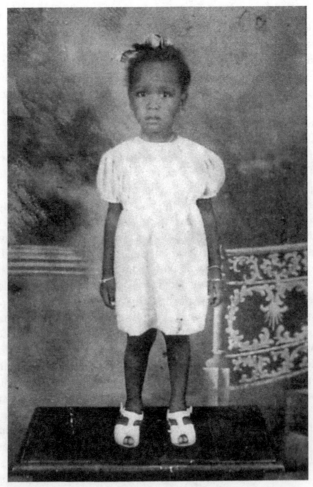

© 1992 by Jamaica Kincaid. Reprinted with permission of The Wylie Agency.

I did not know then (though I do now) that there was such a thing as an inside to anybody, and that this inside would have a color, and that if the insides were the same shade of yellow as the yellow of boiled cornmeal my mother would want me to know about it.

On a day when it was not raining (that would have been unusual, that would have been out of the ordinary, ruining the fixed form of the day), my mother walked to one of the Harneys stores (there were many Harneys who owned stores, and they sold the same things, but I did not know then and I do not know now if they were all of the same people) and bought one-and-a-half yards of this yellow cotton poplin to make a dress for me, a dress I would wear to have my picture taken on the day I turned two years old. Inside, the store was cool and dark, and this was a good thing because outside was hot and overly bright. Someone named Harney did not wait on my mother, but some-one named Miss Verna did and she was very nice still, so nice that she tickled my cheek as she spoke to my mother, and I reached forward as if to kiss her, but when her cheek met my lips I opened my mouth and bit her hard with my small child's teeth. Her cry of surprise did not pierce the air, but she looked at me hard, as if she knew me very, very well; and later, much later, when I was about twelve years old or so and she was always in and out of the crazy house, I would pass her on the street and throw stones at her, and she would turn and look at me hard, but she did not know who I was, she did not know who any-one was at all, not at all. Miss Verna showed my mother five flat thick bolts of cloth, white, blue (sea), blue (sky), yellow and pink, and my mother chose the yellow after holding it up against the rich copper color that my hair was then (it is not so now); she paid for it with a one-pound note that had an engraving of the king George Fifth on it (an ugly man with a cruel, sharp, bony nose, not the kind, soft, fleshy noses I was then used to), and she received change that included crowns, shillings, florins and farthings.

My mother, carrying me and the just-bought piece of yellow poplin wrapped in coarse brown paper in her arms, walked out of Mr. Harney's store, up the street a few doors away, and into a store called Murdoch's (because the family who owned it were the Murdochs), and there my mother bought two skeins of yellow thread, the kind used for embroidering and a shade of yellow almost identical to the yellow poplin. My mother not only took me with her everywhere she went, she carried me, sometimes in her arms, sometimes on her back; for this errand she carried me in her arms; she did not complain, she never complained (but later she refused to do it anymore and never gave an explanation, at least not one that I can remember now); as usual, she spoke to me and sang to me in French patois (but I did not understand French patois then and I do not now and so I can never know what exactly she said to me then). She walked back to our house on Dickenson Bay Street, stopping often to hold conversations with people (men and women) she knew, speaking to them sometimes in English, sometimes in French; and if after they said how beautiful I was (for people would often say that about me then but they do not say that about me now), she would laugh and say that I did not like to be kissed (and I don't know if that was really true then but it is not so now). And that night after we had eaten our supper (boiled fish in a butter-and-lemon-juice sauce) and her husband (who was not my father but I did not know that at the time, I know that now) had gone for a walk (to the jetty), she removed her yellow poplin from its brown wrapper and folded and made creases in it and with scissors made holes (for the arms and neck) and slashes (for an opening in the back and the shoulders); she then placed it along with some ordinary thread (yellow), the thread for embroidering, the scissors and a needle in a basket that she had brought with her from her home in Dominica when she first left it at sixteen years of age.

For days afterward, my mother, after she had finished her usual chores (clothes washing, dish washing, floor scrubbing, bathing me, her only child, feeding me a teaspoon of cod-liver-oil), sat on the sill of the doorway, half in the sun, half out of the sun, and sewed together the various parts that would make up altogether my dress of yellow poplin; she gathered and hemmed and made tucks; she was just in the early stages of teaching herself how to make smocking and so was confined to making straight stitches (up-cable, down-cable, outline, stem, chain); the bodice of the dress appeared simple, plain, and the detail and pattern can only be seen close up and in real life, not from far away and not in a photograph; and much later, when she grew in confidence with this craft, the bodice of my dresses became overburdened with the stitches, chevron, trellis, diamonds, Vandyke, and species of birds she had never seen (swan) and species of flowers she had never seen (tulip) and species of animals she had never seen (bear) in real life, only in a picture in a book.

My skin was not the color of cream in the process of spoiling, my hair was not the texture of silk and the color of flax, my eyes did not gleam like blue jewels in a crown, the afternoons in which I sat watching my mother make me this dress were not cool, and verdant lawns and pastures and hills and dales did not stretch out before me; but it was the picture of such a girl at two years old—a girl whose skin was the color of cream in the process of spoiling, whose hair was the texture of silk and the color of flax, a girl whose eyes gleamed like blue jewels in a crown, a girl whose afternoons (and mornings and nights) were cool, and before whom stretched verdant lawns and pastures and hills and dales—that my mother saw, a picture on an almanac advertising a particularly fine and scented soap (a soap she could not afford to buy then but I can now), and this picture of this girl wearing a yellow dress with smocking on the front bodice perhaps created in my mother the desire to have a daughter who looked like that or perhaps created the desire in my mother to try and make the daughter she already had look like that. I do not know now and I did not know then. And who was that girl really? (I did not ask then because I could not ask then but I ask now.) And who made her dress? And this girl would have had a mother; did the mother then have some friends, other women, did they sit together under a tree (or sit somewhere else) and compare strengths of potions used to throw away a child, or weigh the satisfactions to be had from the chaos of revenge or the smooth order of forgiveness; and this girl with skin of cream on its way to spoiling and hair the color of flax, what did her insides look like, what did she eat? (I did not ask then because I could not ask then and I ask now but no one can answer me, really answer me.)

My second birthday was not a major event in anyone's life, certainly not my own (it was not my first and it was not my last, I am now forty-three years old), but my mother, perhaps because of circumstances (I would not have known then and to know now is not a help), perhaps only because of an established custom (but only in her family, other people didn't do this), to mark the occasion of my turning two years old had my ears pierced. One day, at dusk (I would not have called it that then), I was taken to someone's house (a woman from Dominica, a woman who was as dark as my mother was fair, and yet they were so similar that I am sure now as I was then that they shared the same tongue), and two thorns that had been heated in a fire were pierced through my earlobes. I do not now know (and could not have known then) if the pain I experienced resembled in any way the pain my mother experienced while giving birth to me or even if my mother, in having my ears bored in that way, at that time, meant to express hostility or aggression toward me (but without meaning to and without knowing that it was possible to mean to). For days afterward my earlobes were swollen and covered with a golden crust (which might have glistened in the harsh sunlight, but I can only imagine that now), and the pain of my earlobes must have filled up all that made up my entire being then and the pain of my earlobes must have been unbearable, because it was then that was the first time that I separated myself from myself, and I became two people (two small children then, I was two years old), one having the experience, the other observing the one having the experience. And the observer, perhaps because it was an act of my own will (strong then, but stronger now), my first and only real act of self-invention, is the one of the two I most rely on, the one of the two whose voice I believe to be the true voice; and of course it is the observer who cannot be relied on as the final truth to be believed, for the observer has woven between myself and the person who is having an experience a protective membrane, which allows me to see but only feel as much as I can handle at any given moment. And so . . .

. . . On the day I turned two years old, the twenty-fifth of May 1951, a pair of earrings, small hoops made of gold from British Guiana (it was called that then, it is not called that now), were placed in the bored holes in my earlobes (which by then had healed); a pair of bracelets made of silver from someplace other than British Guiana (and that place too was called one thing then, something else now) was placed one on each wrist; a pair of new shoes bought from Bata's was placed on my feet. That afternoon, I was bathed and powdered, and the dress of yellow poplin, completed, its seams all stitched together with a certainty found only in the natural world (I now realize), was placed over my head, and it is quite possible that this entire act had about it the feeling of being draped in a shroud. My mother, carrying me in her arms (as usual), took me to the studio of a photographer, a man named Mr. Walker, to have my picture taken. As she walked along with me in her arms (not complaining), with the heat of the sun still so overwhelming that it, not gravity, seemed to be the force that kept us pinned to the earth's surface, I placed my lips against one side of her head (the temple) and could feel the rhythm of the blood pulsing through her body; I placed my lips against her throat and could hear her swallow saliva that had collected in her mouth; I placed my face against her neck and inhaled deeply a scent that I could not identify then (how could I, there was nothing to compare it to) and cannot now, because it is not of animal or place or thing, it was (and is) a scent unique to her, and it left a mark of such depth that it eventually became a part of my other senses, and even now (yes, now) that scent is also taste, touch, sight and sound.

And Mr. Walker lived on Church Street in a house that was mysterious to me (then, not now) because it had a veranda (unlike my own house) and it had many rooms (unlike my own house, but really Mr. Walker's house had only four rooms, my own house had one) and the windows were closed (the windows in my house were always open). He spoke to my mother, I did not understand what they said, they did not share the same tongue. I knew Mr. Walker was a man, but how I knew that I cannot say (now, then, sometime to come). It is possible that because he touched his hair often, smoothing down, caressing, the forcibly straightened strands, and because he admired and said that he admired my dress of yellow poplin with its simple smocking (giving to me a false air of delicacy), and because he admired and said that he admired the plaid taffeta ribbon in my hair, I thought that he perhaps wasn't a man at all, I had never seen a man do or say any of those things, I had then only seen a woman do or say those things. He (Mr. Walker) stood next to a black box which had a curtain at its back (this was his camera but I did not know that at the time, I only know it now) and he asked my mother to stand me on a table, a small table, a table that made me taller, because the scene in the background, against which I was to be photographed, was so vast, it overwhelmed my two-year-old frame, making me seem a mere figurine, not a child at all; and when my mother picked me up, holding my by the armpits with her hands, her thumb accidentally (it could have been deliberate, how could someone who loved me inflict so much pain just in passing?) pressed deeply into my shoulder, and I cried out and then (and still now) looked up at her face and couldn't find any reason in it, and could find no malice in it, only that her eyes were full of something, a feeling that I thought then (and am convinced now) had nothing to do with me; and of course it is possible that just at that moment she had realized that she was exhausted, not physically, but just exhausted by this whole process, celebrating my second birthday, commemorating an event, my birth, that she may not have wished to occur in the first place and may have tried repeatedly to prevent, and then, finally, in trying to find some beauty in it, ended up with a yard and a half of yellow poplin being shaped into a dress, teaching herself smocking and purchasing gold hoops from places whose names never remained the same and silver bracelets from places whose names never remained the same. And Mr. Walker, who was not at all interested in my mother's ups and downs and would never have dreamed of taking in the haphazard mess of her life (but there was nothing so unusual about that, every life, I now know, is a haphazard mess), looked on for a moment as my mother, belying the look in her eyes, said kind and loving words to me in a kind and loving voice, and he then walked over to a looking glass that hung on a wall and squeezed with two of his fingers a lump the size of a pinch of sand that was on his cheek; the lump had a shiny white surface and it broke, emitting a tiny plap sound, and from it came a long ribbon of thick, yellow pus that curled on Mr. Walker's cheek imitating, almost, the decoration on the birthday cake that awaited me at home, and my birthday cake was decorated with a series of species of flora and fauna my mother had never seen (and still has not seen to this day, she is seventy-three years old).

After that day I never again wore my yellow poplin dress with the smocking my mother had just taught herself to make. It was carefully put aside, saved for me to wear to another special occasion; but by the time another special occasion came (I could say quite clearly then what the special occasion was and can say quite clearly now what the special occasion was but I do not want to), the dress could no longer fit me, I had grown too big for it.

Brothers

Bret Lott

This much is fact: There is a home movie of the two of us sitting on the edge of the swimming pool at our grandma and grandpa's old apartment building in Culver City. The movie, taken sometime in early 1960, is in color, though the color has faded, leaving my brother Brad and me milk white and harmless children, me a year and a half old, Brad almost four, our brown hair faded to only the thought of brown hair. Our mother, impossibly young, sits next to me on the right of the screen. Her hair, for all the fading of the film, is coal black, shoulder length, and parted in the middle, curled up on the sides. She has on a bathing suit covered in purple and blue flowers, the color in them nearly gone. Next to me on the left of the screen is Brad, in his white swimming trunks. I am in the center, my fat arms up, bent at the elbows, fingers curled into fists, my legs kicking away at the water, splashing and splashing. I am smiling, the baby of the family, the center of the world at that very instant, though my little brother, Tim, is only some six or seven months off, and my little sister, Leslie, the last child, just three years distant. The pool water before us is only a thin sky blue, the bushes behind us a dull and lifeless light green. There is no sound.

My mother speaks to me, points at the water, then looks up. She lifts a hand to block the sun, says something to the camera. Her skin is the same white as ours, but her lips are red, a sharp cut of lipstick moving as she speaks. I am still kicking. Brad is looking to his right, off the screen, his feet in the water, too, but moving slowly. His hands are on the edge of the pool, and he leans forward a little, looks down into the water. My mother still speaks to the camera, and I give an extra-hard kick, splash up shards of white water.

Brad flinches at the water, squints his eyes, while my mother laughs, puts a hand to her face. She looks back to the camera, keeps talking, a hand low to the water to keep more from hitting her. I still kick hard, still send up bits of water, and I am laughing a baby's laugh, mouth open and eyes nearly closed, arms still up, fingers still curled into fists.

More water splashes at Brad, who leans over to me, says something. Nothing about me changes: I only kick, laugh. He says something again, his face leans a little closer to mine. Still I kick.

This is when he lifts his left hand from the edge of the pool, places it on my right thigh, and pinches hard. It's not a simple pinch, not two fingers on a fraction of skin, but his whole hand, all his fingers grabbing the flesh just above my knee and squeezing down hard. He grimaces, his eyes on his hand, on my leg.

My expression changes, of course: In an instant I go from a laughing baby to a shocked one, my mouth a perfect O, my body shivering so that my legs kick even harder, even quicker, but just this one last time. They stop, and I cry, my mouth open even more, my eyes all the way closed. My hands are still in fists.

Then Brad's hand is away, and my mother turns from speaking to the camera to me. She leans in close, asking, I am certain, what's wrong. The movie cuts then to my grandma, white skin and silver hair, seated on a patio chair by the pool, above her a green-and-white-striped umbrella. She has a cigarette in one hand, waves off the camera with the other. Though she died eight years ago, and though she, too, loses color with each viewing, she is still alive up there, still waves, annoyed, at my grandpa and his camera, the moment my brother pinched hell out of me already gone.

This much is fact, too: Thumbtacked to the wall of my office is a photograph of Brad and me taken by my wife in November 1980, the date printed on the border. In it we stand together, me a good six inches taller than him, my arm around his shoulder. The photograph is black and white, as though the home movie and its sinking colors were a prophecy pointing to this day twenty years later: We are at the tidepools at Portuguese Bend, out on the Palos Verdes Peninsula; in the background are the stone-gray bluffs, to the left of us the beginning of the black rocks of the pools, above us the perfect white of an overcast sky.

Brad has on a white Panama hat, a collarless shirt beneath a gray hooded sweatshirt. His face is smooth shaven, and he is grinning, lips together, eyes squinted nearly shut beneath the brim of the hat. It is a goofy smile, but a real one.

I have on a cardigan with an alpine design around the shoulders, the rest of it white, the shawl collar on it black here, though I know it to have been navy blue. I have on a buttondown Oxford shirt, sideburns almost to my earlobes. I have a mustache, a pair of glasses too large for my face; and I am smiling, my mouth open to reveal my big teeth. It isn't my goofy smile, but it's a real one too.

These are the facts of my brother: the four-year-old pinching me, the twenty-four-year-old leaning into me, grinning.

But between the fact of these two images lie twenty years of the play of memory, the dark and bright pictures my mind has retained, embroidered upon, made into things they are and things they are not. There are twenty years of things that happened between my brother and me, from the fistfight we had in high school over who got the honey bun for breakfast, to his phone call to me from a tattoo parlor in Hong Kong where he'd just gotten a Chinese junk stitched beneath the skin of his right shoulder blade; from his showing me one summer day how to do a death drop from the jungle gym at Elizabeth Dickerson Elementary, to him watching while his best friend and our next-door neighbor, Lynn Tinton, beat me up on the driveway of our home in a fight over whether I'd fouled Lynn or not at basketball. I remember—no true picture, necessarily, but what I have made the truth by holding tight to it, playing it back in my head at will and in the direction I wish it to go—I remember lying on my back, Lynn's knees pinning my shoulders to the driveway while he hit my chest, and looking up at Brad, the basketball there at his hip, him watching.

I have two children now. Both boys, born two and a half years apart. I showed the older one, Zeb—almost eight—the photograph, asked him who those two people were. He held it in his hands a long while.

We were in the kitchen. The bus comes at seven-twenty each morning, and I have to have lunches made and breakfasts set out—all before that bus comes and before Melanie takes off for work, Jacob in tow, to be dropped off at the Montessori school on her way in to her office.

I waited, and waited, finally turned from him to get going on his lunch.

"It's you," he said. "You have a lot of hair," he said.

"Who's the other guy?" I said. I looked back at him, saw the concentration on his face, the way he brought the photograph close, my son's eyes taking in his uncle as best he could.

He said, "I don't know."

"That's your uncle Brad," I said. "Your mom took that picture ten years ago, long before you were ever born."

He still looked at the picture. He said, "He has a beard now."

I turned from him, finished with the peanut butter, and spread jelly on the other piece of bread. This is the only kind of sandwich he will eat at school. He said from behind me, "Only three years before I was born. That's not a long time." I stopped, turned again to him. He touched the picture with a finger. He said, "Three years isn't a long time, Dad."

But I was thinking of my question: *Who's the other guy?* and of the truth of his answer: *I don't know.*

Zeb and Jake fight. Melanie and I were upstairs wrapping Christmas presents in my office, a room kept locked the entire month of December for the gifts piled up in there. We heard Jake wailing, dropped the bucket of Legos and the red-and-green HO! HO! HO! paper, ran for the hall and down the stairs.

There in the kitchen stood my two sons, Jacob's eyes wet, him whimpering now, a hand to his bottom lip. I made it first, yelled, "What happened?"

"I didn't do it," Zeb said, and backed away from me, there with my hand to Jacob's jaw.

Melanie stroked Jacob's hair, whispered, "What's wrong?"

Jacob opened his mouth then, showed us the thick wash of blood between his bottom lip and his tongue, a single tooth, horribly white, swimming up from it. "We were playing Karate Kid," Zeb said, and now he was crying. "I didn't do it," he said, and backed away even farther.

One late afternoon a month or so ago, Melanie backed the van into the driveway to make it easier to unload all the plastic bags of groceries. When we'd finished we let the boys play outside, glad for them to be out of the kitchen while we sorted through the bags heaped on the counter, put everything away. Melanie's last words to the two of them, her leaning out the front door into the near-dark: "Don't play in the van!"

Not ten minutes later Jacob came into the house, slammed shut the front door like he always does. He walked into the kitchen, his hands behind him. He said, "Zeb's locked in the van." His face takes on the cast of the guilty when he knows he's done something wrong: His mouth gets pursed, his eyebrows go up, his eyes look right into mine. He doesn't know enough yet to look away. "He told me to come get you." He turned, headed for the door, and I followed him out onto the porch, where, before I could even see the van in the dark, I heard Zeb screaming.

I went to the van, tried one of the doors. It was locked, and Zeb was still screaming.

"Get the keys!" he was saying. "Get the keys!" I pressed my face to the glass of the back window, saw Zeb inside jumping up and down. "My hand's caught," he cried.

I ran into the house, got the keys from the hook beneath the cupboard, only enough time for me to say to Melanie, "Zeb's hand's closed in the back door," and turn, run back out. I made it to the van, unlocked the big back door, and pushed it up as quick as I could, Melanie already beside me.

Zeb stood holding the hand that'd been closed in the door. Melanie and I both took his hand, gently examined the skin, wiggled the fingers, and in the dull glow of the dome light we saw that nothing'd been broken, no skin torn. The black foam lining the door had cushioned his fingers, so that they'd only been smashed a little, but a little enough to scare him, and to make blue bruises there the next day. Beneath the dome light there was the sound of his weeping, then the choked words, "Jacob pulled the door down on me."

From the darkness just past the line of light from inside the van came my second son's voice: "I didn't do it."

I have no memory of the pinch Brad gave me on the edge of that apartment-complex pool, no memory of my mother's black hair—now it's a sort of brown—nor even any memory of the pool itself. There is only that bit of film.

But I can remember putting my arm around his shoulder in 1980, leaning into him, the awkward and alien comfort of that touch. In the photograph we are both smiling, me a newlywed with a full head of hair, him only a month or so back from working a drilling platform in the Gulf of Mexico. He'd missed my wedding six months before, stranded on the rig, he'd told us, because of a storm.

What I believe is this: That pinch was entry into our childhood; my arm around him, our smiling, is the proof of us two surfacing, alive but not unscathed.

And here are my own two boys, already embarked.

The Search for Marvin Gardens

John McPhee

Go. I roll the dice—a six and a two. Through the air I move my token, the flatiron, to Vermont Avenue, where dog packs range.

The dogs are moving (some are limping) through ruins, rubble, fire damage, open garbage. Doorways are gone. Lath is visible in the crumbling walls of the buildings. The street sparkles with shattered glass. I have never seen, anywhere, so many broken windows. A sign—"Slow, Children at Play"—has been bent backward by an automobile. At the lighthouse, the dogs turn up Pacific and disappear. George Meade, Army engineer, built the lighthouse— brick upon brick, six hundred thousand bricks, to reach up high enough to throw a beam twenty miles over the sea. Meade, seven years later, saved the Union at Gettysburg.

I buy Vermont Avenue for $100. My opponent is a tall, shadowy figure, across from me, but I know him well, and I know his game like a favorite tune. If he can, he will always go for the quick kill. And when it is foolish to go for the quick kill he will be foolish. On the whole, though, he is a master assessor of percentages. It is a mistake to underestimate him. His eleven carries his top hat to St. Charles Place, which he buys for $140.

The sidewalks of St. Charles Place have been cracked to shards by through-growing weeds. There are no buildings. Mansions, hotels once stood here. A few street lamps now drop cones of light on broken glass and vacant space behind a chain-link fence that some great machine has in places bent to the ground. Five plane trees—in full summer leaf, flecking the light—are all that live on St. Charles Place.

Block upon block, gradually, we are cancelling each other out—in the blues, the lavenders, the oranges, the greens. My opponent follows a plan of his own devising. I use the Hornblower & Weeks opening and the Zuricher defense. The first game draws tight, will soon finish. In 1971, a group of people in Racine, Wisconsin, played for seven hundred and sixty-eight hours. A game begun a month later in Danville, California, lasted eight hundred and twenty hours. These are official records, and they stun us. We have been playing for eight minutes. It amazes us that Monopoly is thought of as a long game. It is possible to play to a complete, absolute, and final conclusion in less than fifteen minutes, all within the rules as written. My opponent and I have done so thousands of times. No wonder we are sitting across from each other now in this best-of-seven series for the international singles championship of the world.

On Illinois Avenue, three men lean out from second-story windows. A girl is coming down the street. She wears dungarees and a bright-red shirt, has ample breasts and a Hadendoan Afro, a black halo, two feet in diameter. Ice rattles in the glasses in the hands of the men.

"Hey, sister!"

"Come on up!"

She looks up, looks from one to another to the other, looks them flat in the eye.

"What for?" she says, and she walks on.

I buy Illinois for $240. It solidifies my chances, for I already own Kentucky and Indiana. My opponent pales. If he had landed first on Illinois, the game would have been over then and there, for he has houses built on Boardwalk and Park Place, we share the railroads equally, and we have cancelled each other everywhere else. We never trade.

In 1852, R. B. Osborne, an immigrant Englishman, civil engineer, surveyed the route of a railroad line that would run from Camden to Absecon Island, in New Jersey, traversing the state from the Delaware River to the barrier beaches of the sea. He then sketched in the plan of a "bathing village" that would surround the eastern terminus of the line. His pen flew glibly, framing and naming spacious avenues parallel to the shore—Mediterranean, Baltic, Oriental, Ventnor—and narrower transsecting avenues: North Carolina, Pennsylvania, Vermont, Connecticut, States, Virginia, Tennessee, New York, Kentucky, Indiana, Illinois. The place as a whole had no name, so when he had completed the plan Osborne wrote in large letters over the ocean, "Atlantic City." No one ever challenged the name, or the names of Osborne's streets. Monopoly was invented in the early nineteen-thirties by Charles B. Darrow, but Darrow was only transliterating what Osborne had created. The railroads, crucial to any player, were the making of Atlantic City. After the rails were down, houses and hotels burgeoned from Mediterranean and Baltic to New York and Kentucky. Properties—building lots—sold for as little as six dollars apiece and as much as a thousand dollars. The original investors in the railroads and the real estate called themselves the Camden & Atlantic Land Company. Reverently, I repeat their names: Dwight Bell, William Coffin, John DaCosta, Daniel Deal, William Fleming, Andrew Hay, Joseph Porter, Jonathan Pitney, Samuel Richards—founders, fathers, forerunners, archetypical masters of the quick kill.

My opponent and I are now in a deep situation of classical Monopoly. The torsion is almost perfect—Boardwalk and Park Place versus the brilliant reds.

His cash position is weak, though, and if I escape him now he may fade. I land on Luxury Tax, contiguous to but in sanctuary from his power. I have four houses on Indiana. He lands there. He concedes.

Indiana Avenue was the address of the Brighton Hotel, gone now. The Brighton was exclusive—a word that no longer has retail value in the city. If you arrived by automobile and tried to register at the Brighton, you were sent away. Brighton-class people came in private railroad cars. Brighton-class people had other private railroad cars for their horses—dawn rides on the firm sand at water's edge, skirts flying. Colonel Anthony J. Drexel Biddle— the sort of name that would constrict throats in Philadelphia—lived, much of the year, in the Brighton.

Colonel Sanders' fried chicken is on Kentucky Avenue. So is Clifton's Club Harlem, with the Sepia Revue and the Sepia Follies, featuring the Honey Bees, the Fashions, and the Lords.

My opponent and I, many years ago, played 2,428 games of Monopoly in a single season. He was then a recent graduate of the Harvard Law School, and he was working for a downtown firm, looking up law. Two people we knew—one from Chase Manhattan, the other from Morgan, Stanley— tried to get into the game, but after a few rounds we found that they were not in the conversation and we sent them home. Monopoly should always be *mano a mano* anyway. My opponent won 1,199 games, and so did I. Thirty were ties. He was called into the Army, and we stopped just there. Now, in Game 2 of the series, I go immediately to jail, and again to jail while my opponent seines property. He is dumbfoundingly lucky. He wins in twelve minutes.

Visiting hours are daily, eleven to two; Sunday, eleven to one; evenings, six to nine. "NO MINORS, NO FOOD, Immediate Family Only Allowed in Jail." All this above a blue steel door in a blue cement wall in the windowless interior of the basement of the city hall. The desk sergeant sits opposite the door to the jail. In a cigar box in front of him are pills in every color, a banquet of fruit salad an inch and a half deep—leapers, co-pilots, footballs, truck drivers, peanuts, blue angels, yellow jackets, redbirds, rainbows. Near the desk are two soldiers, waiting to go through the blue door. They are about eighteen years old. One of them is trying hard to light a cigarette. His wrists are in steel cuffs. A military policeman waits, too. He is a year or so older than the soldiers, taller, studious in appearance, gentle, fat. On a bench against a wall sits a good-looking girl in slacks. The blue door rattles, swings heavily open. A turnkey stands in the doorway. "Don't you guys kill yourselves back there now," says the sergeant to the soldiers.

"One kid, he overdosed himself about ten and a half hours ago," says the M.P.

The M.P., the soldiers, the turnkey, and the girl on the bench are white. The sergeant is black. "If you take off the handcuffs, take off the belts," says the sergeant to the M.P. "I don't want them hanging themselves back there." The door shuts and its tumblers move. When it opens again, five minutes later, a young white man in sandals and dungarees and a blue polo shirt emerges. His hair is in a ponytail. He has no beard. He grins at the good-looking girl. She rises, joins him. The sergeant hands him a manila envelope. From it he removes his belt and a small notebook. He borrows a pencil, makes an entry in the notebook. He is out of jail, free. What did he do? He offended Atlantic City in some way. He spent a night in the jail. In the nineteen-thirties, men visiting Atlantic City went to jail, directly to jail, did not pass Go, for appearing in topless bathing suits on the beach. A city statute requiring all men to wear full-length bathing suits was not seriously chal-lenged until 1937, and the first year in which a man could legally go bare-chested on the beach was 1940.

Game 3. After seventeen minutes, I am ready to begin construction on over-priced and sluggish Pacific, North Carolina, and Pennsylvania. Nothing else being open, opponent concedes.

The physical profile of streets perpendicular to the shore is something like a playground slide. It begins in the high skyline of Boardwalk hotels, plummets into warrens of "side-avenue" motels, crosses Pacific, slopes through church missions, convalescent homes, burlesque houses, rooming houses, and liquor stores, crosses Atlantic, and runs level through the bombed-out ghetto as far—Baltic, Mediterranean—as the eye can see. North Carolina Avenue, for example, is flanked at its beach end by the Chalfonte and the Haddon Hall (908 rooms, air-conditioned), where, according to one biographer, John Philip Sousa (1854–1932) first played when he was twenty-two, insisting, even then, that everyone call him by his entire name. Behind these big hotels, motels—Barbizon, Catalina—crouch. Between Pacific and Atlantic is an occasional house from 1910—wooden porch, wooden mullions, old yellow paint—and two churches, a package store, a strip show, a dealer in fruits and vegetables. Then, beyond Atlantic Avenue, North Carolina moves on into the vast ghetto, the bulk of the city, and it looks like Metz in 1919, Cologne in 1944. Nothing has actually exploded. It is not bomb damage. It is deep and complex decay. Roofs are off. Bricks are scattered in the street. People sit on porches, six deep, at nine on a Monday morning. When they go off to wait in unemployment lines, they wait sometimes two hours. Between Mediterranean and Baltic runs a chain-link fence, enclosing rubble. A patrol car sits idling by the curb. In the back seat is a German shepherd. A sign on the fence says, "Beware of Bad Dogs."

Mediterranean and Baltic are the principal avenues of the ghetto. Dogs are everywhere. A pack of seven passes me. Block after block, there are three-story brick row houses. Whole segments of them are abandoned, a thousand broken windows. Some parts are intact, occupied. A mattress lies in the street, soaking in a pool of water. Wet stuffing is coming out of the mattress. A postman is having a rye and a beer in the Plantation Bar at nine-fifteen in the morning. I ask him idly if he knows where Marvin Gardens is. He does not. "HOOKED AND NEED HELP? CONTACT N.A.R.C.O." "REVIVAL NOW GOING ON, CONDUCTED BY REVEREND H. HENDERSON OF TEXAS." These are signboards on Mediterranean and Baltic. The second one is upside down and leans against a boarded-up window of the Faith Temple Church of God in Christ. There is an old peeling poster on a warehouse wall showing a figure in an electric chair. "The Black Panther Manifesto" is the title of the poster, and its message is, or was, that "the fascists have already decided in advance to murder Chairman Bobby Seale in the electric chair." I pass an old woman who carries a bucket. She wears blue sneakers, worn through. Her feet spill out. She wears red socks, rolled at the knees. A white handkerchief, spread over her head, is knotted at the corners. Does she know where Marvin Gardens is? "I sure don't know," she says, setting down the bucket. "I sure don't know. I've heard of it somewhere, but I just can't say where." I walk on, through a block of shattered glass. The glass crunches underfoot like coarse sand. I remember when I first came here—a long train ride from Trenton, long ago, games of poker in the train—to play basketball against Atlantic City. We were half black, they were all black. We scored forty points, they scored eighty, or something like it. What I remember most is that they had glass backboards—glittering, pendent, expensive glass backboards, a rarity then in high schools, even in colleges, the only ones we played on all year.

I turn on Pennsylvania, and start back toward the sea. The windows of the Hotel Astoria, on Pennsylvania near Baltic, are boarded up. A sheet of unpainted plywood is the door, and in it is a triangular peephole that now frames an eye. The plywood door opens. A man answers my question. Rooms there are six, seven, and ten dollars a week. I thank him for the information and move on, emerging from the ghetto at the Catholic Daughters of America Women's Guest House, between Atlantic and Pacific. Between Pacific and the Boardwalk are the blinking vacancy signs of the Aristocrat and Colton Manor motels. Pennsylvania terminates at the Sheraton-Seaside—thirty-two dollars a day, ocean corner. I take a walk on the Boardwalk and into the Holiday Inn (twenty-three stories). A guest is registering. "You reserved for Wednesday, and this is Monday," the clerk tells him. "But that's all right. We have *plenty* of rooms." The clerk is very young, female, and has soft brown hair that hangs below her waist. Her superior kicks her.

He is a middle-aged man with red spiderwebs in his face. He is jacketed and tied. He takes her aside. "Don't say 'plenty,'" he says. "Say 'You are fortunate, sir. We have rooms available.'"

The face of the young woman turns sour. "We have all the rooms you need," she says to the customer, and, to her superior, "How's that?"

Game 4. My opponent's luck has become abrasive. He has Boardwalk and Park Place, and has sealed the board.

Darrow was a plumber. He was, specifically, a radiator repairman who lived in Germantown, Pennsylvania. His first Monopoly board was a sheet of linoleum. On it he placed houses and hotels that he had carved from blocks of wood. The game he thus invented was brilliantly conceived, for it was an uncannily exact reflection of the business milieu at large. In its depth, range, and subtlety, in its luck-skill ratio, in its sense of infrastructure and socio-economic parameters, in its philosophical characteristics, it reached to the profundity of the financial community. It was as scientific as the stock market. It suggested the manner and means through which an underdeveloped world had been developed. It was chess at Wall Street level. "Advance token to the nearest Railroad and pay owner twice the rental to which he is otherwise entitled. If Railroad is unowned, you may buy it from the Bank. Get out of Jail, free. Advance token to nearest Utility. If unowned, you may buy it from Bank. If owned, throw dice and pay owner a total ten times the amount thrown. You are assessed for street repairs: $40 per house, $115 per hotel. Pay poor tax of $15. Go to Jail. Go directly to Jail. Do not pass Go. Do not collect $200."

The turnkey opens the blue door. The turnkey is known to the inmates as Sidney K. Above his desk are ten closed-circuit-TV screens—assorted view-points of the jail. There are three cellblocks—men, women, juvenile boys. Six days is the average stay. Showers twice a week. The steel doors and the equipment that operates them were made in San Antonio. The prisoners sleep on bunks of butcher block. There are no mattresses. There are three prisoners to a cell. In winter, it is cold in here. Prisoners burn newspapers to keep warm. Cell corners are black with smudge. The jail is three years old. The men's block echoes with chatter. The man in the cell nearest Sidney K. is pacing. His shirt is covered with broad stains of blood. The block for juvenile boys is, by contrast, utterly silent—empty corridor, empty cells. There is only one prisoner. He is small and black and appears to be thirteen. He says he is sixteen and that he has been alone in here for three days.
"Why are you here? What did you do?"
"I hit a jitney driver."

The series stands at three all. We have split the fifth and sixth games. We are scrambling for property. Around the board we fairly fly. We move so fast because we do our own banking and search our own deeds. My opponent grows tense.

Ventnor Avenue, a street of delicatessens and doctors' offices, is leafy with plane trees and hydrangeas, the city flower. Water Works is on the mainland. The water comes over in submarine pipes. Electric Company gets power from across the state, on the Delaware River, in Deepwater. States Avenue, now a wasteland like St. Charles, once had gardens running down the middle of the street, a horse-drawn trolley, private homes. States Avenue was as exclusive as the Brighton. Only an apartment house, a small motel, and the All Wars Memorial Building—monadnocks spaced widely apart—stand along States Avenue now. Pawnshops, convalescent homes, and the Paradise Soul Saving Station are on Virginia Avenue. The soul-saving station is pink, orange, and yellow. In the windows flanking the door of the Virginia Money Loan Office are Nikons, Polaroids, Yashicas, Sony TVs, Underwood typewriters, Singer sewing machines, and pictures of Christ. On the far side of town, beside a single track and locked up most of the time, is the new railroad station, a small hut made of glazed firebrick, all that is left of the lines that built the city. An authentic phrenologist works on New York Avenue close to Frank's Extra Dry Bar and a church where the sermon today is "Death in the Pot." The church is of pink brick, has blue and amber windows and two red doors. St. James Place, narrow and twisting, is lined with boarding houses that have wooden porches on each of three stories, suggesting a New Orleans made of salt-bleached pine. In a vacant lot on Tennessee is a white Ford station wagon stripped to the chassis. The windows are smashed. A plastic Clorox bottle sits on the driver's seat. The wind has pressed newspaper against the chain-link fence around the lot. Atlantic Avenue, the city's principal thoroughfare, could be seventeen American Main Streets placed end to end—discount vitamins and Vienna Corset shops, movie theatres, shoe stores, and funeral homes. The Boardwalk is made of yellow pine and Douglas fir, soaked in pentachlorophenol. Downbeach, it reaches far beyond the city. Signs everywhere—on windows, lampposts, trash baskets—proclaim "Bienvenue Canadiens!" The salt air is full of Canadian French. In the Claridge Hotel, on Park Place, I ask a clerk if she knows where Marvin Gardens is. She says, "Is it a floral shop?" I ask a cabdriver, parked outside. He says, "Never heard of it." Park Place is one block long, Pacific to Boardwalk. On the roof of the Claridge is the Solarium, the highest point in town—panoramic view of the ocean, the bay, the salt-water ghetto. I look down at the rooftops of the side-avenue motels and into swimming pools. There are hundreds of people around the rooftop pools, sunbathing, reading—many more people than are on the beach. Walls, windows, and a block of sky are all that is visible from these pools—no sand, no sea. The pools are craters, and with the people around them they are countersunk into the motels.

The seventh, and final, game is ten minutes old and I have hotels on Oriental, Vermont, and Connecticut. I have Tennessee and St. James. I have North Carolina and Pacific. I have Boardwalk, Atlantic, Ventnor, Illinois, Indiana. My fingers are forming a "V." I have mortgaged most of these properties in order to pay for others, and I have mortgaged the others to pay for the hotels. I have seven dollars. I will pay off the mortgages and build my reserves with income from the three hotels. My cash position may be low, but I feel like a rocket in an underground silo. Meanwhile, if I could just go to jail for a time I could pause there, wait there, until my opponent, in his inescapable rounds, pays the rates of my hotels. Jail, at times, is the strategic place to be. I roll boxcars from the Reading and move the flatiron to Community Chest. "Go to Jail. Go directly to Jail."

The prisoners, of course, have no pens and no pencils. They take paper napkins, roll them tight as crayons, char the ends with matches, and write on the walls. The things they write are not entirely idiomatic; for example, "In God We Trust." All is in carbon. Time is required in the writing. "Only humanity could know of such pain." "God So Loved the World." "There is no greater pain than life itself." In the women's block now, there are six blacks, giggling, and a white asleep in red shoes. She is drunk. The others are pushers, prostitutes, an auto thief, a burglar caught with pistol in purse. A sixteen-year-old accused of murder was in here last week. These words are written on the wall of a now empty cell: "Laying here I see two bunks about six inches thick, not counting the one I'm laying on, which is hard as brick. No cushion for my back. No pillow for my head. Just a couple scratchy blankets which is best to use it's said. I wake up in the morning so shivery and cold, waiting and waiting till I am told the food is coming. It's on its way. It's not worth waiting for, but I eat it anyway. I know one thing when they set me free I'm gonna be good if it kills me."

How many years must a game be played to produce an Anthony J. Drexel Biddle and chestnut geldings on the beach? About half a century was the original answer, from the first railroad to Biddle at his peak. Biddle, at his peak, hit an Atlantic City streetcar conductor with his fist, laid him out with one punch. This increased Biddle's legend. He did not go to jail. While John Philip Sousa led his band along the Boardwalk playing "The Stars and Stripes Forever" and Jack Dempsey ran up and down in training for his fight with Gene Tunney, the city crossed the high curve of its parabola. Al Capone held conventions here—upstairs with his sleeves rolled, apportioning among his lieutenant governors the states of the Eastern seaboard. The natural history of an American resort proceeds from Indians to French Canadians via Biddies and Capones. French Canadians, whatever they may be at home, are Visigoths here. Bienvenue Visigoths!

My opponent plods along incredibly well. He has got his fourth railroad, and patiently, unbelievably, he has picked up my potential winners until he has blocked me everywhere but Marvin Gardens. He has avoided, in the fifty-dollar zoning, my increasingly petty hotels. His cash flow swells. His railroads are costing me two hundred dollars a minute. He is building hotels on States, Virginia, and St. Charles. He has temporarily reversed the current. With the yellow monopolies and my blue monopolies, I could probably defeat his lavenders and his railroads. I have Atlantic and Ventnor. I need Marvin Gardens. My only hope is Marvin Gardens.

There is a plaque at Boardwalk and Park Place, and on it in relief is the leonine profile of a man who looks like an officer in a metropolitan bank—Charles B. Darrow, 1889–1967, inventor of the game of Monopoly." "Darrow," I address him, aloud. "Where is Marvin Gardens?" There is, of course, no answer. Bronze, impassive, Darrow looks south down the Boardwalk. "Mr. Darrow, please, where is Marvin Gardens?" Nothing. Not a sign. He just looks south down the Boardwalk.

My opponent accepts the trophy with his natural ease, and I make, from notes, remarks that are even less graceful than his.

Marvin Gardens is the one color-block Monopoly property that is not in Atlantic City. It is a suburb within a suburb, secluded. It is a planned compound of seventy-two handsome houses set on curvilinear private streets under yews and cedars, poplars and willows. The compound was built around 1920, in Margate, New Jersey, and consists of solid buildings of stucco, brick, and wood, with slate roofs, tile roofs, multimullioned porches, Giraldic towers, and Spanish grilles. Marvin Gardens, the ultimate outwash of Monopoly, is a citadel and sanctuary of the middle class. "We're heavily patrolled by police here. We don't take no chances. Me? I'm living here nine years. I paid seventeen thousand dollars and I've been offered thirty. Number one, I don't want to move. Number two, I don't need the money. I have four bedrooms, two and a half baths, front den, back den. No basement. The Atlantic is down there. Six feet down and you float. A lot of people have a hard time finding this place. People that lived in Atlantic City all their life don't know how to find it. They don't know where the hell they're going. They just know it's south, down the Boardwalk."

Three Pokes of a Thistle
Naomi Shihab Nye

Hiding Inside the Good Girl

" She has the devil inside her," said my first report card from first grade. I walked home slowly, holding it out from my body, a thistle, a thorn, to my mother, who read the inside, then the note on the back. She cried mightily, heaves of underground rivers, we stood looking deep into the earth as water rushed by.

I didn't know who he was.

One day I'd smashed John's nose on the pencil sharpener and broken it. Stood in the cloakroom smelling the rust of coats. I said No. No thank you. I already read that and it's not a very good story. Jane doesn't do much. I want the spider who talks. The family of little women and their thousand days. No. What I had for breakfast is a secret. I didn't want to tell them I ate dried apricots. I listened to their lineage of eggs. I listened to the bacon crackle in everyone else's pail. Thank you.

What shall we do, what shall we do? Please, *I beg you.* Our pajamas were flying from the line, waists pinned, their legs fat with fabulous air. My mother peeled beets, her fingers stained deep red. She was bleeding dinner for us. She was getting up and lying down.

Once I came home from school in the middle of the day in a taxi. School gave me a stomachache. I rode in the front passenger seat. It would be expensive. My mother stood at the screen door peering out, my baby brother perched on her hip. She wore an apron. The taxi pulled up in front of the blue mailbox I viewed as an animal across from our house—his opening mouth. Right before I climbed out, another car hit the taxi hard from behind so my mother saw me fly from the front seat to the back. Her mouth wide open, the baby dangling from her like fringe. She came toward us running. I climbed up onto the ledge inside the back window to examine the wreckage. The taxi driver's visored cap had blown out the window. He was shaking his head side to side as if he had water in his ears.

You, you, look what a stomachache gets you. Whiplash.

The doctor felt my neck.

Later I sat on the front steps staring at the spot where it had happened. What about that other driver? He cried when the policeman arrived. He was an old man coming to mail a letter. I was incidental to the scene, but it couldn't have happened without me. *If you had just stayed where you belonged. . . .* My classmates sealed into their desks laboring over pages or subtraction, while out in the world, cars were banging together. Yellow roses opened slowly on a bush beside my step. I was thinking how everything looked from far away.

Then I was old. A hundred years before I found it, Mark Twain inscribed the front of his first-edition leatherbound book, "BE GOOD—AND YOU WILL BE LONESOME." In black ink, with a flourish. He signed his name. My friend had the book in a box in her attic and did not know. It was from her mother's collection. I carried it down the stairs, trembling. My friend said, "Do you think it is valuable?"

Language Barrier

Basically our father spoke English perfectly, though he still got his *b*s and *p*s mixed up. He had a gentle, deliberate way of choosing words. I could feel him reaching up into the air to find them. At night, he told us whimsical, curling "Joha" stories which hypnotized us to sleep. I especially liked the big cooking pan that gave birth to the little pan. My friend Marcia's father who grew up in the United States hardly talked. He built airplanes. I didn't think I would want to fly in anything he made. When Marcia asked him a question, he grunted a kind of pig sound. He sank his face into the paper. My father spilled out musical lines, a horizon of graceful buildings standing beside one another in a distant city. You could imagine people living inside one of my father's words.

He said a few things to us in Arabic—fragrant syllables after we ate, blessings when he hugged us. He hugged us all the time. He said, "I love you" all the time. But I didn't learn how to say "Thank you" in Arabic till I was fourteen, which struck me, even then, as a preposterous omission.

Marcia's father seemed tired. He had seven children because he was a Catholic, Marcia said. I didn't get it. Marcia's mother threw away the leftovers from their table after dinner. My mother carefully wrapped the last little mound of mashed potato inside waxed paper. We'd eat it later.

I felt comfortable in the world of so many different people. Their voices floated around the neighborhood like pollen. On the next block, French-Canadians made blueberry pie. I wanted a slice. It is true that a girl knocked on our door one day and asked to "see the Arab," but I was not insulted. I was mystified. Who?

Sometimes Marcia and I slept together on our screened-in back porch, or in a big green tent in her yard. She was easy to scare. I said the giant harvest moon was coming to eat her and she hid under her pillow. She told me spider stories. We had fun trading little terrors.

When I was almost ready to move away, Marcia and I stood in Dade Park together one last time. I said good-bye to the swings and benches and wooden seesaws with chipped red paint. Two bigger boys rode up on bicycles and circled us. We'd never seen them before. One of them asked if we knew how to do the F-word. I had no idea what they were talking about. Marcia said she knew, but wouldn't tell me. The boys circled the basketball courts, eyeing us strangely. Walking home with Marcia, I felt almost glad to be moving away from her. She stuck her chest out. She said, "Did you ever wish someone would touch you in a private place?"

I looked in the big dictionary at home. Hundreds of F-words I didn't know reached their hands out so it took a long time. And I asked my mother, whose face was so smooth and beautiful and filled with sadness because nothing was quite as good as it could be.

She didn't know either.

Bra Strap

It felt like a taunt, the elastic strap of Karen's bra visible beneath her white blouse in front of me in fifth grade. I saw it even before Douglas snapped it. Who did she think she was, growing older without me?

I spent the night with her one Saturday. In the bathtub together, we splashed and soaped, jingling our talk of teachers, boys, and holidays. But my eyes were on her chest, the great pale fruits growing there. Already they mounded toward stems.

She caught me looking and said, "So?" Sighing, as if she were already tired. Said, "In my family they grow early." Downstairs her bosomy mother stacked cups in a high old cabinet that smelled of grandmother's hair. I could hear her clinking. In my family they barely grew at all. I had been proud of my mother's boyishness, her lithe trunk and straight legs.

Now I couldn't stop thinking about it: what was there, what wasn't there. The mounds on the fronts of certain dolls with candy-coated names. One by one, watching the backs of my friends' blouses, I saw them all fall under the spell. I begged my mother, who said, "For what? Just to be like everybody else?"

Pausing near the underwear displays at Famous and Barr, I asked to be measured, sizing up boxes. "Training Bra"—what were we in training for?

When Louise fell off her front porch and a stake went all the way through her, I heard teachers whispering, "Hope this doesn't ruin her for the future." We discussed the word "impaled." What future? The mysteries of ovaries had not yet been explained. Little factories for eggs. Little secret nests. On the day we saw the film, I didn't like it. If that was what the future meant, I didn't want it anymore. As I was staring out the window afterwards, my mouth tasted like pennies, my throat closed up. The leaves on the trees blurred together so they could carry me.

I sat on a swivel chair practicing handwritings. The backwards slant, the loopy up-and-down. Who would I ever be? My mother was inside the lawyer's office signing papers about the business. That waiting room, with its dull wooden side tables and gloomy magazines, had absolutely nothing to do with me. Never for a second was I drawn toward the world of the dreary professional. I would be a violinist with the Zurich symphony. I would play percussion in a traveling band. I would bake zucchini muffins in Yarmouth, Nova Scotia.

In the car traveling slowly home under a thick gray sky, I worked up courage. Rain, rain, the intimacy of cars. At a stoplight, staring hard at my mother, I asked, "What really happens between men and women to make babies?"

She jumped as if I'd thrown ice at her.

"Not *that!* Not *now!*" From red to green, the light, the light. "There is *oh so much you do not know.*"

It was all she ever told me. The weight of my ignorance pressed upon us both.

Later she slipped me a book, *Little Me, Big Me.* One of the more incomprehensible documents of any childhood: "When a man and a woman love one another enough, he puts his arms around her and part of him goes into part of her and the greatness of their love for one another causes this to feel pleasurable."

On my twelfth birthday, my father came home with our first tape recorder. My mother produced a bouquet of shiny boxes, including a long, slim one. My Lutheran grandparents sat neatly on the couch as the heavy reels wound up our words. "Do you like it? Is it just what you've been waiting for?"

They wanted me to hold it up to my body, the way I would when I put it on. My mother shushing, "Oh, I guess it's private!"

Later the tape would play someone's giggles in the background. My brother? Or the gangs of little girl angels that congregate around our heads, chanting, "Don't grow up, don't grow up!"

I never liked wearing it as much as I did thinking about it.

Buckeye

Scott Russell Sanders

Years after my father's heart quit, I keep in a wooden box on my desk the two buckeyes that were in his pocket when he died. Once the size of plums, the brown seeds are shriveled now, hollow, hard as pebbles, yet they still gleam from the polish of his hands. He used to reach for them in his overalls or suit pants and click them together, or he would draw them out, cupped in his palm, and twirl them with his blunt carpenter's fingers, all the while humming snatches of old tunes.

"Do you really believe buckeyes keep off arthritis?" I asked him more than once.

He would flex his hands and say, "I do so far."

My father never paid much heed to pain. Near the end, when his worn knee often slipped out of joint, he would pound it back in place with a rubber mallet. If a splinter worked into his flesh beyond the reach of tweezers, he would heat the blade of his knife over a cigarette lighter and slice through the skin. He sought to ward off arthritis not because he feared pain but because he lived through his hands, and he dreaded the swelling of knuckles, the stiffening of fingers. What use would he be if he could no longer hold a hammer or guide a plow? When he was a boy he had known farmers not yet forty years old whose hands had curled into claws, men so crippled up they could not tie their own shoes, could not sign their names.

"I mean to tickle my grandchildren when they come along," he told me, "and I mean to build doll houses and turn spindles for tiny chairs on my lathe."

So he fondled those buckeyes as if they were charms, carrying them with him when our family moved from Ohio at the end of my childhood, bearing them to new homes in Louisiana, then Oklahoma, Ontario, and Mississippi, carrying them still on his final day when pain a thousand times fiercer than arthritis gripped his heart.

The box where I keep the buckeyes also comes from Ohio, made by my father from a walnut plank he bought at a farm auction. I remember the auction, remember the sagging face of the widow whose home was being sold, remember my father telling her he would prize that walnut as if he had watched the tree grow from a sapling on his own land. He did not care for pewter or silver or gold, but he cherished wood. On the rare occasions when my mother coaxed him into a museum, he ignored the paintings or porcelain and studied the exhibit cases, the banisters, the moldings, the parquet floors.

I remember him planing that walnut board, sawing it, sanding it, joining piece to piece to make foot stools, picture frames, jewelry boxes. My own box, a bit larger than a soap dish, lined with red corduroy, was meant to hold earrings and pins, not buckeyes. The top is inlaid with pieces fitted so as to bring out the grain, four diagonal joints converging from the corners toward the center. If I stare long enough at those converging lines, they float free of the box and point to a center deeper than wood.

I learned to recognize buckeyes and beeches, sugar maples and shagbark hickories, wild cherries, walnuts, and dozens of other trees while tramping through the Ohio woods with my father. To his eyes, their shapes, their leaves, their bark, their winter buds were as distinctive as the set of a friend's shoulders. As with friends, he was partial to some, craving their company, so he would go out of his way to visit particular trees, walking in a circle around the splayed roots of a sycamore, laying his hand against the trunk of a white oak, ruffling the feathery green boughs of a cedar.

"Trees breathe," he told me. "Listen."

I listened, and heard the stir of breath.

He was no botanist; the names and uses he taught me were those he had learned from country folks, not from books. Latin never crossed his lips. Only much later would I discover that the tree he called ironwood, its branches like muscular arms, good for axe handles, is known in the books as hophornbeam; what he called tuliptree or canoewood, ideal for log cabins, is officially the yellow poplar; what he called hoop ash, good for barrels and fence posts, appears in books as hackberry.

When he introduced me to the buckeye, he broke off a chunk of the gray bark and held it to my nose. I gagged.

"That's why the old-timers called it stinking buckeye," he told me. "They used it for cradles and feed troughs and peg legs."

"Why for peg legs?" I asked.

"Because it's light and hard to split, so it won't shatter when you're clumping around."

He showed me this tree in late summer, when the fruits had fallen and the ground was littered with prickly brown pods. He picked up one, as fat as a lemon, and peeled away the husk to reveal the shiny seed. He laid it in my palm and closed my fist around it so the seed peeped out from the circle formed by my index finger and thumb. "You see where it got the name?" he asked.

I saw: what gleamed in my hand was the eye of a deer, bright with life. "It's beautiful," I said.

"It's beautiful," my father agreed, "but also poisonous. Nobody eats buckeyes, except maybe a fool squirrel."

I knew the gaze of deer from living in the Ravenna Arsenal, in Portage County, up in the northeastern corner of Ohio. After supper we often drove the Arsenal's gravel roads, past the munitions bunkers, past acres of rusting tanks and wrecked bombers, into the far fields where we counted deer. One June evening, while mist rose from the ponds, we counted three hundred and eleven, our family record. We found the deer in herds, in bunches, in amorous pairs. We came upon lone bucks, their antlers lifted against the sky like the bare branches of dogwood. If you were quiet, if your hands were empty, if you moved slowly, you could leave the car and steal to within a few paces of a grazing deer, close enough to see the delicate lips, the twitching nostrils, the glossy, fathomless eyes.

The wooden box on my desk holds these grazing deer, as it holds the buck-eyes and the walnut plank and the farm auction and the munitions bunkers and the breathing forests and my father's hands. I could lose the box, I could lose the polished seeds, but if I were to lose the memories I would become a bush without roots, and every new breeze would toss me about. All those memories lead back to the northeastern corner of Ohio, the place where I came to consciousness, where I learned to connect feelings with words, where I fell in love with the earth.

It was a troubled love, for much of the land I knew as a child had been ravaged. The ponds in the Arsenal teemed with bluegill and beaver, but they were also laced with TNT from the making of bombs. Because the wolves and coyotes had long since been killed, some of the deer, so plump in the June grass, collapsed on the January snow, whittled by hunger to racks of bones. Outside the Arsenal's high barbed fences, many of the farms had failed, their barns caving in, their topsoil gone. Ravines were choked with swollen couches and junked washing machines and cars. Crossing fields, you had to be careful not to slice your feet on tin cans or shards of glass. Most of the rivers had been dammed, turning fertile valleys into scummy playgrounds for boats.

One free-flowing river, the Mahoning, ran past the small farm near the Arsenal where our family lived during my later years in Ohio. We owned just enough land to pasture three ponies and to grow vegetables for our table, but those few acres opened onto miles of woods and creeks and secret meadows. I walked that land in every season, every weather, following animal trails. But then the Mahoning, too, was doomed by a government decision; we were forced to sell our land, and a dam began to rise across the river.

If enough people had spoken for the river, we might have saved it. If enough people had believed that our scarred country was worth defending, we might have dug in our heels and fought. Our attachments to the land were all private. We had no shared lore, no literature, no art to root us there, to give us courage, to help us stand our ground. The only maps we had were those issued by the state, showing a maze of numbered lines stretched over empti-ness. The Ohio landscape never showed up on postcards or posters, never unfurled like tapestry in films, rarely filled even a paragraph in books. There were no mountains in that place, no waterfalls, no rocky gorges, no vistas. It was a country of low hills, cut over woods, scoured fields, villages that had lost their purpose, roads that had lost their way.

"Let us love the country of here below," Simone Weil urged. "It is real; it offers resistance to love. It is this country that God has given us to love. He has willed that it should be difficult yet possible to love it." Which is the deeper truth about buckeyes, their poison or their beauty? I hold with the beauty; or rather, I am held by the beauty, without forgetting the poison. In my corner of Ohio the gullies were choked with trash, yet cedars flickered up like green flames from cracks in stone; in the evening bombs exploded at the ammunition dump, yet from the darkness came the mating cries of owls. I was saved from despair by knowing a few men and women who cared enough about the land to clean up trash, who planted walnuts and oaks that would long outlive them, who imagined a world that would have no call for bombs.

How could our hearts be large enough for heaven if they are not large enough for earth? The only country I am certain of is the one here below. The only paradise I know is the one lit by our everyday sun, this land of difficult love, shot through with shadow. The place where we learn this love, if we learn it at all, shimmers behind every new place we inhabit.

A family move carried me away from Ohio thirty years ago; my schooling and marriage and job have kept me away ever since, except for visits in memory and in flesh. I returned to the site of our farm one cold November day, when the trees were skeletons and the ground shone with the yellow of fallen leaves. From a previous trip I knew that our house had been bulldozed, our yard and pasture had grown up in thickets, and the reservoir had flooded the woods. On my earlier visit I had merely gazed from the car, too numb with loss to climb out. But on this November day, I parked the car, drew on my hat and gloves, opened the door, and walked.

I was looking for some sign that we had lived there, some token of our affection for the place. All that I recognized, aside from the contours of the land, were two weeping willows that my father and I had planted near the road. They had been slips the length of my forearm when we set them out, and now their crowns rose higher than the telephone poles. When I touched them last, their trunks had been smooth and supple, as thin as my wrist, and now they were furrowed and stout. I took off my gloves and laid my hands against the rough bark. Immediately I felt the wince of tears. Without knowing why, I said hello to my father, quietly at first, then louder and louder, as if only shouts could reach him through the bark and miles and years.

Surprised by sobs, I turned from the willows and stumbled away toward the drowned woods, calling to my father. I sensed that he was nearby. Even as I called, I was wary of grief's deceptions. I had never seen his body after he died. By the time I reached the place of his death, a furnace had reduced him to ashes. The need to see him, to let go of him, to let go of this land and time, was powerful enough to summon mirages; I knew that. But I also knew, stumbling toward the woods, that my father was here.

At the bottom of a slope where the creek used to run, I came to an expanse of gray stumps and withered grass. It was a bay of the reservoir from which the water had retreated, the level drawn down by engineers or drought. I stood at the edge of this desolate ground, willing it back to life, trying to recall the woods where my father had taught me the names of trees. No green shoots rose. I walked out among the stumps. The grass crackled under my boots, breath rasped in my throat, but otherwise the world was silent.

Then a cry broke overhead and I looked up to see a red-tailed hawk launching out from the top of an oak. I recognized the bird from its band of dark feathers across the creamy breast and the tail splayed like rosy fingers against the sun. It was a red-tailed hawk for sure; and it was also my father. Not a symbol of my father, not a reminder, not a ghost, but the man himself, right there, circling in the air above me. I knew this as clearly as I knew the sun burned in the sky. A calm poured through me. My chest quit heaving. My eyes dried.

Hawk and father wheeled above me, circle upon circle, wings barely moving, head still. My own head was still, looking up, knowing and being known. Time scattered like fog. At length, father and hawk stroked the air with those powerful wings, three beats, then vanished over a ridge.

The voice of my education told me then and tells me now that I did not meet my father, that I merely projected my longing onto a bird. My education may well be right; yet nothing I heard in school, nothing I've read, no lesson reached by logic has ever convinced me as utterly or stirred me as deeply as did that red-tailed hawk. Nothing in my education prepared me to love a piece of the earth, least of all a humble, battered country like northeastern Ohio; I learned from the land itself.

Before leaving the drowned woods, I looked around at the ashen stumps, the wilted grass, and for the first time since moving from this place I was able to let it go. This ground was lost; the flood would reclaim it. But other ground could be saved, must be saved, in every watershed, every neighborhood. For each home ground we need new maps, living maps, stories and poems, photographs and paintings, essays and songs. We need to know where we are, so that we may dwell in our place with a full heart.

The Drama Bug

David Sedaris

The man was sent to our class to inspire us, and personally speaking, I thought he did an excellent job. After introducing himself in a relaxed and genial manner, he started toward the back of the room, only to be stopped midway by what we came to know as "the invisible wall," that transparent barrier realized only by psychotics, drug fiends, and other members of the show business community.

I sat enthralled as he righted himself and investigated the imaginary wall with his open palms, running his hands over the seemingly hard surface in hopes of finding a way out. Moments later he was tugging at an invisible rope, then struggling in the face of a violent, fantastic wind.

You know you're living in a small town when you can reach the ninth grade without ever having seen a mime. As far as I was concerned, this man was a prophet, a genius, a pioneer in the field of entertainment—and here he was in Raleigh, North Carolina! It was a riot, the way he imitated the teacher, turning down the corners of his mouth and riffling through his imaginary purse in search of gum and aspirin. Was this guy funny or what!

I went home and demonstrated the invisible wall for my two-year-old brother, who pounded on the very real wall beside his playpen, shrieking and wailing in disgust. When my mother asked what I'd done to provoke him, I threw up my hands in mock innocence before lowering them to retrieve the imaginary baby that lay fussing at my feet. I patted the back of my little ghost to induce gas and was investigating its soiled diaper when I noticed my mother's face assume an expression she reserved for unspeakable horror. I had seen this look only twice before: once when she was caught in the path of a charging, rabid pig and then again when I told her I wanted a peach-colored velveteen blazer with matching slacks.

"I don't know who put you up to this," she said, "but I'll kill you myself before I watch you grow up to be a clown. If you want to paint your face and prance around on street corners, then you'll have to find some other place to live because I sure as hell won't have it in my house." She turned to leave. "*Or in my yard,*" she added.

Fearful of her retribution, I did as I was told, ending my career in mime with a whimper rather than the silent bang I had hoped for.

The visiting actor returned to our classroom a few months later, removing his topcoat to reveal a black body stocking worn with a putty-colored neck brace, the result of a recent automobile accident. This afternoon's task was to introduce us to the works of William Shakespeare, and once again I was completely captivated by his charm and skill. When the words became confusing, you needed only to pay attention to the actor's face and hands to understand that this particular character was not just angry, but vengeful. I loved the undercurrent of hostility that lay beneath the surface of this deceptively beautiful language. It seemed a shame that people no longer spoke this way, and I undertook a campaign to reintroduce Elizabethan English to the citizens of North Carolina.

"Perchance, fair lady, thou dost think me unduly vexed by the sorrowful state of thine quarters," I said to my mother as I ran the vacuum cleaner over the living-room carpet she was inherently too lazy to bother with. "These foul specks, the evidence of life itself, have sullied not only thine shag-tempered mat but also thine character. Be ye mad, woman? Were it a punishable crime to neglect thine dwellings, you, my feeble-spirited mistress, would hang from the tallest tree in penitence for your shameful ways. Be there not garments to launder and iron free of turbulence? See ye not the porcelain plates and hearty mugs waiting to be washed clean of evidence? Get thee to thine work, damnable lady, and quickly, before the products of thine very loins raise their collected fists in a spirit born both of rage and indignation, forcibly coaxing the last breath from the foul chamber of thine vain and upright throat. Go now, wastrel, and get to it!"

My mother reacted as if I had whipped her with a short length of yarn. The intent was there, but the weapon was strange and inadequate. I could tell by the state of my room that she spent the next day searching my dresser for drugs. The clothes I took pride in neatly folding were crammed tight into their drawers with no regard for color or category. I smelled the evidence of cigarettes and noticed the coffee rings on my desk. My mother had been granted forgiveness on several previous occasions, but mess with mine drawers and ye have just made thyself an enemy for life. Tying a feather to the shaft of my ballpoint pen, I quilled her a letter. "The thing that ye search for so desperately," I wrote, "resideth not in mine well-ordered chamber, but in the questionable content of thine own character." I slipped the note into her purse, folded twice and sealed with wax from the candles I now used to light my room. I took to brooding, refusing to let up until I received a copy of Shakespeare's collected plays. Once they were acquired, I discovered them dense and difficult to follow. Reading the words made me feel dull and stupid, but speaking them made me feel powerful. I found it best to simply carry the book from room to room, occasionally skimming for fun words I might toss into my ever fragrant vocabulary. The dinner hour became either unbearable or excruciating, depending on my mood.

"Methinks, kind sir, most gentle lady, fellow siblings all, that this barnyard fowl be most tasty and succulent, having simmered in its own sweet juices for such a time as it might take the sun to pass, rosy and full-fingered, across the plum-colored sky for the course of a twilight hour. 'Tis crisp yet juicy, this plump bird, satisfied in the company of such finely roasted neighbors. Hear me out, fine relations, and heed my words, for methinks it adventurous, and fanciful, too, to saddle mine fork with both fowl *and* carrot at the exact same time, the twin juices blending together in a delicate harmony which doth cajole and enliven mine tongue in a spirit of unbridled merriment! What say ye, fine father, sisters, and infant brother, too, that we raise our flagons high in celebration of this hearty feast, prepared lovingly and with utmost grace by this dutiful woman we have the good fortune to address as wife, wench, or mother!"

My enthusiasm knew no limits. Soon my mother was literally begging me to wait in the car while she stepped into the bank or grocery store.

I was at the orthodontist's office, placing a pox upon the practice of dentistry, when the visiting actor returned to our classroom.

"You missed it," my friend Lois said. "The man was so indescribably powerful that I was practically crying, that's how brilliant he was." She positioned her hands as if she were supporting a tray. "I don't know what more I can say. The words, they just don't exist. I could try to explain his realness, but you'd never be able to understand it. Never," she repeated. "Never, never, never."

Lois and I had been friends for six months when our relationship suddenly assumed a competitive edge. I'd never cared who made better grades or had more spending money. We each had our strengths; the important thing was to honor each other for the thing that person did best. Lois held her Chablis better than I, and I respected her for that. Her frightening excess of self-confidence allowed her to march into school wearing a rust-colored Afro wig, and I stood behind her one hundred percent. She owned more records than I did, and because she was nine months older, also knew how to drive a car and did so as if she were rushing to put out a fire. *Fine,* I thought, *good for her.* My superior wisdom and innate generosity allowed me to be truly happy for Lois up until the day she questioned my ability to understand the visiting actor. The first few times he visited, she'd been just like the rest of them, laughing at his neck brace and rolling her eyes at the tangerine-sized lump in his tights. *I* was the one who first identified his brilliance, and now she was saying I couldn't understand him? Methinks not.

"Honestly, woman," I said to my mother on our way to the dry cleaner, "to think that this low-lying worm might speak to me of greatness as though it were a thing invisible to mine eyes is more than I can bear. Her words doth strike mine heart with the force of a punishing blow, leaving me both stunned and highly vexed, too. Hear me, though, for I shall bide my time, quietly, and with cunning, striking back at the very hour she doth least expect it. Such an affront shall not go unchallenged, of that you may rest assured, gentle lady. My vengeance will hold the sweet taste of the ripest berry; and I shall savor it slowly."

"You'll get over it," my mother said. "Give it a week or two and I'm sure everything will be back to normal. I'm going in now to get your father's shirts and I want you to wait here, *in the car.* Trust me, this whole thing will be forgotten about in no time."

This had become her answer to everything. She'd done some asking around and concluded I'd been bitten by what her sister referred to as "the drama bug." My mother was convinced that this was a phase, just like all the others. A few weeks of fanfare and I'd drop show business, just like I had the guitar and my private detective agency. I hated having my life's ambition reduced to the level of a common cold. This wasn't a bug, but a full-fledged virus. It might lay low for a year or two, but this little germ would never go away. It had nothing to do with talent or initiative. Rejection couldn't weaken it, and no amount of success would ever satisfy it. Once diagnosed, the prognosis was terminal.

The drama bug seemed to strike hardest with Jews, homosexuals, and portly girls, whose faces were caked with acne medication. These were individuals who, for one reason or another, desperately craved attention. I would later discover it was a bad idea to gather more than two of these people in an enclosed area for any length of time. The stage was not only a physical place but also a state of mind, and the word *audience* was defined as anyone forced to suffer your company. We young actors were a string of lightbulbs left burning twenty-four hours a day, exhausting ourselves and others with our self-proclaimed brilliance.

I had the drama bug and Lois had a car. Weighing the depth of her momentary transgression against the rich rewards of her private chariot, I found it within my bosom to forgive my wayward friend. I called her the moment I learned the visiting actor had scheduled a production of *Hamlet* set to take place in the amphitheater of the Raleigh Rose Garden. He himself would direct and play the title role, but the other parts were up for grabs. We auditioned, and because we were the youngest and least experienced, Lois and I were assigned the roles of the traveling players Hamlet uses to bait his uncle Claudius. It wasn't the part I was hoping for, but I accepted my role with quiet dignity. I had a few decent speeches and planned to work them to the best of my ability.

Our fellow cast members were in their twenties and thirties and had wet their feet in such long-running outdoor dramas as *The Lost Colony* and *Tender Is the Lamb.* These were professionals, and I hoped to benefit from their experience, sitting literally at their feet as the director paced the lip of the stage addressing his clenched fist as "poor Yorick."

I worshiped these people. Lois slept with them. By the second week of rehearsal, she had abandoned Fortinbras in favor of Laertes, who, she claimed, had a "real way with the sword." Unlike me, she was embraced by the older crowd, attending late-night keg parties with Polonius and Ophelia and driving to the lake with the director while Gertrude and Rosencrantz made out in the backseat. The killer was that Lois was nowhere near as committed as I was. Her drama bug was the equivalent of a twenty-four-hour flu, yet there she was, playing bumper pool with Hamlet himself while I practiced lines alone in my room, dreaming up little ways to steal the show.

It was decided that as traveling players, Lois and I would make our entrance tumbling onto the outdoor stage. When she complained that the grass was irritating her skin, the director examined the wee pimples on her back and decided that, from this point on, the players would enter skipping. I had rehearsed my tumble until my brain lost its mooring and could be heard rattling inside my skull, and now, on the basis of one complaint, we were skipping? He'd already cut all my speeches, leaving me with the one line "Aye, my lord." That was it, three lousy syllables. A person could wrench more emotion out of a sneeze than all my dialogue put together. While the other actors strolled the Rose Garden memorizing their vengeful soliloquies, I skipped back and forth across the parking lot repeating, "Aye, my lord," in a voice that increasingly sounded like that of a trained parrot. Lois felt silly skipping and spoke to the director, who praised her instincts and announced that, henceforth, the players would enter walking.

The less I had to do, the more my fellow actors used me as a personal slave. I would have been happy to help them run lines, but instead, they wanted me to polish their crowns or trot over to a car, searching the backseat for a misplaced dagger.

"Looking for something to do? You can help Doogan glow-tape the props," the director said. "You can chase the spiders out of the dressing room, or better yet, why don't you run down to the store and get us some drinks."

For the most part, Lois sat in the shade doing nothing. Not only did she refuse to help out, but she was always the first one to hand me a large bill when placing an order for a thirty-cent diet soda. She'd search through her purse, bypassing the singles in favor of a ten or a twenty. "I need to break this anyway," she'd say. "If they charge you extra for a cup of ice, tell them to fuck themselves." During the rehearsal breaks she huddled in the stands, gossiping with the other actors while I was off anchoring ladders for the technicians.

When it came time for our big scene, Lois recited her lines as if she were reading the words from the surface of some distant billboard. She squinted and paused between syllables, punctuating each word with a question mark. "Who this? Has seen with tongue? In venom steeped?"

If the director had a problem with her performance, he kept it to himself. I, on the other hand, was instructed to remove the sweater from around my neck, walk slower, and drop the accent. It might have been easier to accept the criticism had he spread it around a little, but that seemed unlikely. She could enter the scene wearing sunglasses and eating pizza and that was "fine, Lois. Great work, babe."

By this time I was finding my own way home from rehearsal. Lois couldn't give me a ride, as she was always running off to some party or restaurant with what she referred to as "the gang from Elsinore."

"I can't go," I'd say, pretending I had been invited. "I really need to get home and concentrate on my line. You go ahead, though. I'll just call my mother. She'll pick me up."

"Are we vexed?" my mother would ask, pulling her station wagon into the parking lot.

"We are indeed," I answered. "And highly so."

"Let it go," she said. "Ten years from now I guarantee you won't remember any of these people. Time passes, you'll see." She frowned, studying her face in the rearview mirror. "Enough liquor, and people can forget anything. Don't let it get to you. If nothing else, this has taught you to skim money while buying their drinks."

I didn't appreciate her flippant attitude, but the business with the change was insightful.

"Round everything off to the nearest dollar," she said. "Hand them their change along with their drinks so they'll be less likely to count it—and never fold the bills, keep the money in a wad."

My mother had the vengeful part down. It was the craft of acting I thought she knew nothing about.

We were in dress rehearsal when the director approached Lois regarding a new production he hoped to stage that coming fall. It was to be a musical based on the lives of roving Gypsies. "And you," he said, "shall be my lusty bandit queen."

Lois couldn't sing; everyone knew that. Neither could she act or play the tambourine. "Yours is the heart of a Gypsy," he said, kneeling in the grass. "The vibrant soul of a nomad."

When I expressed an interest, he suggested I might enjoy working behind the scenes. He meant for me to hang lights or lug scenery, to become one of those guys with the low-riding pants, their tool belts burdened with heavy wrenches and thick rolls of gaffer tape. Anyone thinking I might be trusted with electrical wiring had to be a complete idiot, and that's what this man was. I looked at him clearly then, noticing the way his tights made a mockery of his slack calves and dumpy little basket. Vibrant soul of a nomad, indeed. If he were such a big stinking deal, what was he doing in Raleigh? His blow-dried hair, the cheap Cuban-heeled shoes, and rainbow-striped suspenders—it was all a sham. Why wear tights with suspenders when their only redeeming feature was that they stayed up on their own—that's how they got their name, tights. And acting? The man performed as if the audience were deaf. He shouted his lines, grinning like a jack-o'-lantern and flailing his arms as if his sleeves were on fire. His was a form of acting that never fails to embarrass me. Watching him was like opening the door to a singing telegram: you know it's supposed to be entertaining, but you can't get beyond the sad fact that this person actually thinks he's bringing some joy into your life. Somewhere he had a mother who sifted through a shoe box of mimeographed playbills, pouring herself another drink and wondering when her son would come to his senses and swallow some drain cleaner.

I finally saw Hamlet for who he really was and recognized myself as the witless Yorick who had blindly followed along behind him.

My mother attended the opening-night performance. Following my leaden "Aye, my lord," I lay upon the grassy stage as Lois poured a false vial of poison into my ear. As I lay dying, I opened my eyes just a crack, catching sight of my mother stretched out on her hard, stone pew, fighting off the moths that, along with a few dozen seniors, had been attracted by the light.

There was a cast party afterward, but I didn't go. I changed my clothes in the dressing room, where the actors stood congratulating one another, repeating the words "brilliant" and "intense" as if they were describing the footlights. Horatio asked me to run to the store for cigarettes, and I pocketed his money, promising to return "with lightning speed, my lord."

"You were the best in the whole show," my mother said, stopping for frozen pizza on our way home. "I mean it, you walked onto that stage and all eyes went right to you."

It occurred to me then that my mother was a better actor than I could ever hope to be. Acting is different than posing or pretending. When done with precision, it bears a striking resemblance to lying. Stripped of the costumes and grand gestures, it presents itself as an unquestionable truth. I didn't envy my mother's skill, neither did I contradict her. That's how convincing she was. It seemed best, sitting beside her with a frozen pizza thawing on my lap, to simply sit back and learn.

The Knife

Richard Selzer

One holds the knife as one holds the bow of a cello or a tulip—by the stem. Not palmed nor gripped nor grasped, but lightly, with the tips of the fingers. The knife is not for pressing. It is for drawing across the field of skin. Like a slender fish, it waits, at the ready, then, go! It darts, followed by a fine wake of red. The flesh parts, falling away to yellow globules of fat. Even now, after so many times, I still marvel at its power—cold, gleaming, silent. More, I am still struck with a kind of dread that it is I in whose hand the blade travels, that my hand is its vehicle, that yet again this terrible steel-bellied thing and I have conspired for a most unnatural purpose, the laying open of the body of a human being.

A stillness settles in my heart and is carried to my hand. It is the quietude of resolve layered over fear. And it is this resolve that lowers us, my knife and me, deeper and deeper into the person beneath. It is an entry into the body that is nothing like a caress; still, it is among the gentlest of acts. Then stroke and stroke again, and we are joined by other instruments, hemo-stats and forceps, until the wound blooms with strange flowers whose looped handles fall to the sides in steely array.

There is sound, the tight click of clamps fixing teeth into severed blood vessels, the snuffle and gargle of the suction machine clearing the field of blood for the next stroke, the litany of monosyllables with which one prays his way down and in: *clamp, sponge, suture, tie, cut.* And there is color. The green of the cloth, the white of the sponges, the red and yellow of the body. Beneath the fat lies the fascia, the tough fibrous sheet encasing the muscles. It must be sliced and the red beef of the muscles separated. Now there are retractors to hold apart the wound. Hands move together, part, weave. We are fully engaged, like children absorbed in a game or the craftsmen of some place like Damascus.

Deeper still. The peritoneum, pink and gleaming and membranous, bulges into the wound. It is grasped with forceps, and opened. For the first time we can see into the cavity of the abdomen. Such a primitive place. One expects to find drawings of buffalo on the walls. The sense of trespassing is keener now, height-ened by the world's light illuminating the organs, their secret colors revealed—maroon and salmon and yellow. The vista is sweetly vulnerable at this moment, a kind of welcoming. An arc of the liver shines high and on the right, like a dark sun. It laps over the pink sweep of the stomach, from whose lower border the gauzy omentum is draped, and through which veil one sees, sinuous, slow as just-fed snakes, the indolent coils of the intestine.

You turn aside to wash your gloves. It is a ritual cleansing. One enters this temple doubly washed. Here is man as microcosm, representing in all his parts the earth, perhaps the universe.

I must confess that the priestliness of my profession has ever been impressed on me. In the beginning there are vows, taken with all solemnity. Then there is the endless harsh novitiate of training, much fatigue, much sacrifice. At last one emerges as celebrant, standing close to the truth lying curtained in the Ark of the body. Not surplice and cassock but mask and gown are your regalia. You hold no chalice, but a knife. There is no wine, no wafer. There are only the facts of blood and flesh.

And if the surgeon is like a poet, then the scars you have made on count-less bodies are like verses into the fashioning of which you have poured your soul. I think that if years later I were to see the trace from an old incision of mine, I should know it at once, as one recognizes his pet expressions.

But mostly you are a traveler in a dangerous country, advancing into the moist and jungly cleft your hands have made. Eyes and ears are shuttered from the land you left behind; mind empties itself of all other thought. You are the root of groping fingers. It is a fine hour for the fingers, their sense of touch so enhanced. The blind must know this feeling. Oh, there is risk every-where. One goes lightly. The spleen. No! No! Do not touch the spleen that lurks below the left leaf of the diaphragm, a manta ray in a coral cave, its bloody tongue protruding. One poke and it might rupture, exploding with sudden hemorrhage. The filmy omentum must not be torn, the intestine scraped or denuded. The hand finds the liver, palms it, fingers running along its sharp lower edge, admiring. Here are the twin mounds of the kidneys, the apron of the omentum hanging in front of the intestinal coils. One lifts it aside and the fingers dip among the loops, searching, mapping territory, establishing boundaries. Deeper still, and the womb is touched, then held like a small muscular bottle—the womb and its earlike appendages, the ovaries. How they do nestle in the cup of a man's hand, their power all dormant. They are frailty itself.

There is a hush in the room. Speech stops. The hands of the others, assistants and nurses, are still. Only the voice of the patient's respiration remains. It is the rhythm of a quiet sea, the sound of waiting. Then you speak, slowly, the terse entries of a Himalayan climber reporting back.

"The stomach is okay. Greater curvature clean. No sign of ulcer. Pylorus, duodenum fine. Now comes the gall-bladder. No stones. Right kidney, left, all right. Liver . . . uh-oh."

Your speech lowers to a whisper, falters, stops for a long, long moment, then picks up again at the end of a sigh that comes through your mask like a last exhalation.

"Three big hard ones in the left lobe, one on the right. Metastatic deposits. Bad, bad. Where's the primary? Got to be coming from somewhere."

The arm shifts direction and the fingers drop lower and lower into the pelvis—the body impaled now upon the arm of the surgeon to the hilt of the elbow.

"Here it is."

The voice goes flat, all business now.

"Tumor in the sigmoid colon, wrapped all around it, pretty tight. We'll take out a sleeve of the bowel. No colostomy. Not that, anyway. But, God, there's a lot of it down there. Here, you take a feel."

You step back from the table, and lean into a sterile basin of water, resting on stiff arms, while the others locate the cancer.

When I was a small boy, I was taken by my father, a general practitioner in Troy, New York, to St. Mary's Hospital, to wait while he made his rounds. The solarium where I sat was all sunlight and large plants. It smelled of soap and starch and clean linen. In the spring, clouds of lilac billowed from the vases; and in the fall, chrysanthemums crowded the magazine tables. At one end of the great high-ceilinged, glass-walled room was a huge cage where colored finches streaked and sang. Even from the first, I sensed the nearness of that other place, the Operating Room, knew that somewhere on these premises was that secret dreadful enclosure where *surgery* was at that moment happening. I sat among the cut flowers, half drunk on the scent, listening to the robes of the nuns brush the walls of the corridor, and felt the awful presence of *surgery.*

Oh, the pageantry! I longed to go there. I feared to go there. I imagined surgeons bent like storks over the body of the patient, a circle of red painted across the abdomen. Silence and dignity and awe enveloped them, these surgeons; it was the bubble in which they bent and straightened. Ah, it was a place I would never see, a place from whose walls the hung and suffering Christ turned his affliction to highest purpose. It is thirty years since I yearned for that old Surgery. And now I merely break the beam of an electric eye, and double doors swing open to let me enter, and as I enter, always, I feel the surging of a force that I feel in no other place. It is as though I am suddenly stronger and larger, heroic. Yes, that's it!

The operating room is called a theatre. One walks onto a set where the cupboards hold tanks of oxygen and other gases. The cabinets store steel cutlery of unimagined versatility, and the refrigerators are filled with bags of blood. Bodies are stroked and penetrated here, but no love is made. Nor is it ever allowed to grow dark, but must always gleam with a grotesque brightness. For the special congress into which patient and surgeon enter, the one must have his senses deadened, the other his sensibilities restrained. One lies naked, blind, offering; the other stands masked and gloved. One yields; the other does his will.

I said no love is made here, but love happens. I have stood aside with lowered gaze while a priest, wearing the purple scarf of office, administers Last Rites to the man I shall operate upon. I try not to listen to those terrible last questions, the answers, but hear, with scorching clarity, the words that formalize the expectation of death. For a moment my resolve falters before the resignation, the *attentiveness,* of the other two. I am like an executioner who hears the cleric comforting the prisoner. For the moment I am excluded from the centrality of the event, a mere technician standing by. But it is only for the moment.

The priest leaves, and we are ready. Let it begin.

Later, I am repairing the strangulated hernia of an old man. Because of his age and frailty, I am using local anesthesia. He is awake. His name is Abe Kaufman, and he is a Russian Jew. A nurse sits by his head, murmuring to him. She wipes his forehead. I know her very well. Her name is Alexandria, and she is the daughter of Ukrainian peasants. She has a flat steppe of a face and slanting eyes. Nurse and patient are speaking of blintzes, borscht, piroshki—Russian food that they both love. I listen, and think that it may have been her grandfather who raided the shtetl where the old man lived long ago, and in his high boots and his blouse and his fury this grandfather pulled Abe by his side curls to the ground and stomped his face and kicked his groin. Perhaps it was that ancient kick that caused the hernia I am fixing. I listen to them whispering behind the screen at the head of the table. I listen with breath held before the prism of history.

"Tovarich," she says, her head bent close to his.

He smiles up at her, and forgets that his body is being laid open.

"You are an angel," the old man says.

One can count on absurdity. There, in the midst of our solemnities, appears, small and black and crawling, an insect: The Ant of the Absurd. The belly is open; one has seen and felt the catastrophe within. It seems the patient is already vaporizing into angelhood in the heat escaping therefrom. One could warm one's hands in that fever. All at once that ant is there, emerging from beneath one of the sterile towels that border the operating field. For a moment one does not really see it, or else denies the sight, so impossible it is, marching precisely, heading briskly toward the open wound.

Drawn from its linen lair, where it snuggled in the steam of the great sterilizer, and survived, it comes. Closer and closer, it hurries toward the incision. Ant, art thou in the grip of some fatal *ivresse?* Wouldst hurtle over these scarlet cliffs into the very boil of the guts? Art mad for the reek we handle? Or in some secret act of formication engaged?

The alarm is sounded. An ant! An ant! And we are unnerved. Our fear of defilement is near to frenzy. It is not the mere physical contamination that we loathe. It is the evil of the interloper, that he scurries across our holy place, and filthies our altar. He *is* disease—that for whose destruction we have gathered. Powerless to destroy the sickness before us, we turn to its incarnation with a vengeance, and pluck it from the lip of the incision in the nick of time. Who would have thought an ant could move so fast?

Between thumb and forefinger, the intruder is crushed. It dies as quietly as it lived. Ah, but now there is death in the room. It is a perversion of our purpose. Albert Schweitzer would have spared it, scooped it tenderly into his hand, and lowered it to the ground.

The corpselet is flicked into the specimen basin. The gloves are changed. New towels and sheets are placed where it walked. We are pleased to have done something, if only a small killing. The operation resumes, and we draw upon ourselves once more the sleeves of office and rank. Is our reverence for life in question?

In the room the instruments lie on trays and tables. They are arranged precisely by the scrub nurse, in an order that never changes, so that you can reach blindly for a forceps or hemostat without looking away from the operating field. The instruments lie *thus!* Even at the beginning, when all is clean and tidy and no blood has been spilled, it is the scalpel that dominates. It has a figure the others do not have, the retractors and the scissors. The scalpel is all grace and line, a fierceness. It grins. It is like a cat—to be respected, deferred to, but which returns no amiability. To hold it above a belly is to know the knife's force—as though were you to give it slightest rein, it would pursue an intent of its own, driving into the flesh, a wild energy.

In a story by Borges, a deadly knife fight between two rivals is depicted. It is not, however, the men who are fighting. It is the knives themselves that are settling their own old score. The men who hold the knives are mere adjuncts to the weapons. The unguarded knife is like the unbridled warhorse that not only carries its helpless rider to his death, but tramples all beneath its hooves. The hand of the surgeon must tame this savage thing. He is a rider reining to capture a pace.

So close is the joining of knife and surgeon that they are like the Centaur—the knife, below, all equine energy, the surgeon, above, with his delicate art. One holds the knife back as much as advances it to purpose. One is master of the scissors. One is partner, sometimes rival, to the knife. In a moment it is like the long red fingernail of the Dragon Lady. Thus does the surgeon curb in order to create, restraining the scalpel, governing it shrewdly, setting the action of the operation into a pattern, giving it form and purpose.

It is the nature of creatures to live within a tight cuirass that is both their constriction and their protection. The carapace of the turtle is his fortress and retreat, yet keeps him writhing on his back in the sand. So is the surgeon rendered impotent by his own empathy and compassion. The surgeon cannot weep. When he cuts the flesh, his own must not bleed. Here it is all work. Like an asthmatic hungering for air, longing to take just one deep breath, the surgeon struggles not to feel. It is suffocating to press the feeling out. It would be easier to weep or mourn—for you know that the lovely precise world of proportion contains, just beneath, *there*, all disaster, all disorder. In a surgical operation, a risk may flash into reality: the patient dies . . . of *complication*. The patient knows this too, in a more direct and personal way, and he is afraid.

And what of that *other*, the patient, you, who are brought to the operating room on a stretcher, having been washed and purged and dressed in a white gown? Fluid drips from a bottle into your arm, diluting you, leaching your body of its personal brine. As you wait in the corridor, you hear from behind the closed door the angry clang of steel upon steel, as though a battle were being waged. There is the odor of antiseptic and ether, and masked women hurry up and down the halls, in and out of rooms. There is the watery sound of strange machinery, the tinny beeping that is the transmitted heartbeat of yet another *human being*. And all the while the dreadful knowledge that soon you will be taken, laid beneath great lamps that will reveal the secret linings of your body. In the very act of lying down, you have made a declaration of surrender. One lies down gladly for sleep or for love. But to give over one's body and will for surgery, to *lie down* for it, is a yielding of more than we can bear.

Soon a man will stand over you, gowned and hooded. In time the man will take up a knife and crack open your flesh like a ripe melon. Fingers will rummage among your viscera. Parts of you will be cut out. Blood will run free. Your blood. All the night before you have turned with the presentiment of death upon you. You have attended your funeral, wept with your mourners. You think, "I should never have had surgery in the springtime." It is too cruel. Or on a Thursday. It is an unlucky day.

Now it is time. You are wheeled in and moved to the table. An injection is given. "Let yourself go," I say. "It's a pleasant sensation," I say. "Give in," I say.

Let go? Give in? When you know that you are being tricked into the hereafter, that you will end when consciousness ends? As the monstrous silence of anesthesia falls discourteously across your brain, you watch your soul drift off.

Later, in the recovery room, you awaken and gaze through the thickness of drugs at the world returning, and you guess, at first dimly, then surely, that you have not died. In pain and nausea you will know the exultation of death averted, of life restored.

What is it, then, this thing, the knife, whose shape is virtually the same as it was three thousand years ago, but now with its head grown detachable? Before steel, it was bronze. Before bronze, stone—then back into unremembered time. Did man invent it or did the knife precede him here, hidden under ages of vegetation and hoofprints, lying in wait to be discovered, picked up, used?

The scalpel is in two parts, the handle and the blade. Joined, it is six inches from tip to tip. At one end of the handle is a narrow notched prong upon which the blade is slid, then snapped into place. Without the blade, the handle has a blind, decapitated look. It is helpless as a trussed maniac. But slide on the blade, click it home, and the knife springs instantly to life. It is headed now, edgy, leaping to mount the fingers for the gallop to its feast.

Now is the moment from which you have turned aside, from which you have averted your gaze, yet toward which you have been hastened. Now the scalpel sings along the flesh again, its brute run unimpeded by germs or other frictions. It is a slick slide home, a barracuda spurt, a rip of embedded talon. One listens, and almost hears the whine—nasal, high, delivered through that gleaming metallic snout. The flesh splits with its own kind of moan. It is like the penetration of rape.

The breasts of women are cut off, arms and legs sliced to the bone to make ready for the saw, eyes freed from sockets, intestines lopped. The hand of the surgeon rebels. Tension boils through his pores, like sweat. The flesh of the patient retaliates with hemorrhage, and the blood chases the knife wherever it is withdrawn.

Within the belly a tumor squats, toadish, fungoid. A gray mother and her brood. The only thing it does not do is croak. It too is hacked from its bed as the carnivore knife lips the blood, turning in it in a kind of ecstasy of plenty, a gluttony after the long fast. It is just for this that the knife was created, tempered, heated, its violence beaten into paper-thin force.

At last a little thread is passed into the wound and tied. The monstrous booming fury is stilled by a tiny thread. The tempest is silenced. The operation is over. On the table, the knife lies spent; on its side, the bloody meal smear-dried upon its flanks. The knife rests.

And waits.

42 Tattoos

David Shields

A tattoo is ink stored in scar tissue.

*

Archeologists believe, based on marks they've seen on mummies, that human beings had tattoos between 4000–2000 B.C. in Egypt. Around 2000 B.C., tattooing spread to southern Asia to Japan and from there to Burma and Scythia.

*

In 1998, 35% of NBA players had tattoos. Now, well over 50% have tattoos. According to the *Christian Science Monitor,* that arbiter of the down-and-dirty, the number of Americans with tattoos is "as high as 15 percent."

*

Asked by *Playboy* what he'd like people to know, Allen Iverson said, "Tell them not to believe what they read or hear. Tell them to read my body. I wear my story every day, man." At the very end of the interview, Iverson said, "The minister at [his close friend] Rah's funeral said to look at your life as a book and stop wasting pages complaining, worrying, and gossiping. That's some deep shit right there."

*

In body-contact sports, such as basketball or football, there's a much higher percentage of tattooed players than in "cerebral" sports such as baseball, golf, or tennis.

*

Last year, while watching a basketball game on TV, Dakkan Abbe, a marketing executive with the advertising firm Fifty Rubies, came up with the idea of NBA players selling space on their bodies to plug products with temporary tattoos. Abbe wanted someone with "bad-boy" appeal, so he approached Rasheed Wallace, who two years ago set an NBA record for the most technical fouls in a season, about a candy-bar tattoo. Wallace's agent, Bill Strickland, said there's "nothing in any basic agreement [between the players' association and the league] that forbids advertising on the human body." An NBA spokesman said, "We don't allow commercial advertising on our uniforms, our coaches, or our playing floors, so there's no reason to think we'll allow it on our players." Abbe said, "The NBA is defining tattoos as part of the players' uniforms, but a player's skin is not part of his uniform. I find it offensive that the league would not allow something on someone's skin. Whenever the topic of taboos comes up, the league says things like, 'We prefer if players didn't have tattoos.'" It's interesting which stars don't have tattoos: Kobe Bryant, Ray Allen—pretty boys with all the endorsement deals. Abbe continued: "The NBA scared people off. The very nature of tattoos is disturbing to the NBA. The league is a little bit out of touch with the players and fans. Tattoos are a very explicit example of that. They just don't understand what tattoos are about." Strickland said, "Being a lawyer, I thought it presented some free-speech issues," but he finally decided not to press the case. Stephon Marbury of the Phoenix Suns, asked if he'd wear a tattoo advertisement, said, "Depends on how much money they'd pay. If they're paying the right money: yeah." Selling, say, his left shoulder to a shoe company, would Stephon Marbury be losing control over his body or exerting control over capitalism?

*

In the *Tattoo* Magazine supplement to the New Orleans tattoo convention, an inordinately buxom but somehow slightly demure-looking blonde babe is on the cover, wearing a sailor hat, fishnet stockings, a short red skirt, white gloves, a bra top, and a couple of tattoos. Behind her in black shadow is a dark-haired woman dressed in a leopard costume. The function of the blonde babe's tattoo is to portray her in the process of being transfigured from sailor-girl to jungle-cat and back again (and to portray as well the eros of this tension between civilization and savagery).

*

"As for the primitive, I hark back to it because we are still very primitive. How many thousands of years of culture, think you, have rubbed and polished at our raw edges? One probably; at the best, no more than two. And that takes us back to screaming savagery, when, gross of body and deed, we drank blood from the skulls of our enemies and hailed as highest paradise the orgies and carnage of Valhalla."—Jack London

*

According to a third-century account of the Sycthians' defeat of the Thracians, the Sycthians tattooed symbols of defeat upon the Thracians, but as a way of turning "the stamp of violence and shame into beautiful ornaments," the Thracian women covered the rest of their bodies with tattoos.

*

On my thirtieth birthday, under my girlfriend's influence, I got my left ear pierced and bought a diamond earring. I wore various earrings over the next ten years or so, but wearing an earring never really worked for me, and on my fortieth birthday, under the influence of my daughter, who thought it made me look like a pirate, I took out the earring I was then wearing—a gold hoop—and haven't worn an earring since. Earrings forced me to confront the nature of my style, or lack of style. I'm certainly not macho enough to wear an earring as if I were a tough guy, but neither am I effeminate enough to wear an earring in my right ear as if I were maybe gay-in-training. Instead, I'm just me, muddling through in the middle, and the earring forced me, over time, to see this, acknowledge it, and respond to it.

Marcus Camby's first name is tattooed on his arm; Kirby Puckett also has his first name tattooed on his arm. Scottie Pippen has small tattoos on his biceps and legs. Michael Jordan has a horseshoe-shaped fraternity tattoo. Dennis Rodman's tattoos include a Harley, a shark, a cross (the loop of which encircles his pierced navel), and a photo of his daughter. Mike Tyson has a tattoo of Che Guevara on his abdomen, a tattoo of Mao on his right hand, and one of Arthur Ashe on his left shoulder. Shaquille O'Neal has a Superman tattoo on his left shoulder. Detroit Pistons center Ben Wallace has a tattoo of the Big Ben clock tower on his right bicep, with basketballs for clock faces; he also has two tattoos of Taz, the Tasmanian devil from "Bugs Bunny."

*

"Human barcodes are hip," declared that arbiter of hip, the *Wall Street Journal*. "Heavy-metal band Slipknot has a barcode logo, with the stripes emblazoned across their prison-jumpsuit outfits. Barcode tattoos are also big, says New York tattoo tycoon Carlo Fodera."

*

Who owns these words?

*

In Galatians 6.17, St. Paul says, "From this time onward let no one trouble me; for, as for me, I bear, branded on my body, the scars of Jesus as my Master."

*

"Since a tattoo to certain levels of society is the mark of a thug, it becomes also the sign of inarticulate revolt, often producing its only possible result: violence."—Amy Krakow

*

In order to demonstrate their corporate loyalty, many Nike employees wear on their leg a tattoo of a swoosh.

*

The Greek philosopher Bion of Borysthenes (ca. 300 B.C.) described the brutally tattooed face of his father, a former slave, as "a narrative of his master's harshness."

*

Jason Richardson, a Michigan State University basketball player, said, "If you're a good basketball player, you've got to have some tattoos to go with the package. Basketball players have tattoos; that's the way it is. It's a way of showing who I am."

*

Asked what his tattoos mean, Iverson replied, "I got CRU THIK in four places—that's my crew, that's what we call ourselves, me and the guys I grew up with, the guys I'm loyal to. I got my kids' names, Tiaura and Deuce [Allen II], 'cause they're everything to me. I got my wife's name, Tawanna, on my stomach. A set of praying hands between my grandma's initials—she died when I was real young—and my mom's initials, Ethel Ann Iverson. I put shit on my body that means something to me. Here, on my left shoulder, I got a cross of daggers knitted together that says ONLY THE STRONG SURVIVE, because that's the one true thing I've learned in this life. On the other arm, I got a soldier's head. I feel like my life has been a war and I'm a soldier in it. Here, on my left forearm, it says NBN—for 'Newport Bad News.' That's what we call our hometown of Newport News, Virginia, because a lot of bad shit happens there. On the other arm, I got the Chinese symbol for respect, because I feel that where I come from deserves respect—being from there, surviving from there, and staying true to everybody back there. I got one that says FEAR NO ONE, a screaming skull with a red line through it—'cause you'll never catch me looking scared."

*

Iverson's Philadelphia 76er teammate Aaron McKie said, "A lot of guys get tattoos because they think they look nice and sexy wearing them. But I don't need them. One reason is because of my old college coach, John Cheney. He didn't allow players to wear tattoos or earrings or stuff like that. The other reason is because I guess I'm old-fashioned. I don't see any good reason to pierce or paint my body. I'm comfortable with my natural look."

*

"The publication of 'International Archives of Body Techniques' would be of truly international benefit, providing an inventory of all the possibilities of the human body and of the methods of apprenticeship and training employed to build up each technique, for there is not one human group in the world which could not make an original contribution to such an enterprise. It would also be a project eminently well fitted to counteracting racial prejudices, since it would contradict the racialist conceptions which try to make out that man is a product of his body, by demonstrating that it is the other way around: man has, at all times and in all places, been able to turn his body into a product of his techniques and his representations."—Claude Levi-Strauss

*

What Levi-Strauss means, I think, is this: before we started, she said she needed to tell me something. She had herpes. Madly in love with her witchy bitchiness, I found occasional enforced celibacy insanely erotic, the way a chastity belt glamorizes what it locks out. We wound up living together, and as we fell out of love with each other, her herpes became a debate point between us. She suggested that we just get married and then if I got it, I got it, and who would care? I suggested she at least explore some of the possibilities of which modern medicine avails us. For a multitude of reasons, the two of us didn't belong together, but what interests me now is what, for a lack of a better term, a free-floating signifier the virus was. When I was in love with her, it eroticized her. When I wasn't, it repelled me. The body has no meanings. We bring meanings to it.

*

Detroit Lions fullback Brock Olivo, who has only one tattoo—an Italian flag, on his back, to honor his ancestry—said, "That's my last tattoo. No more.

I don't want to scare my kids or affect things in the business world by having all kinds of crazy stuff on me."

*

According to *Rolling Stone*, Paul Booth is "the tattoo artist of choice for rock stars who love death, perversion, and torture." His "black-and-gray tattoos of blasphemous violence echo the same nihilist madness of the metalheads he inks," musicians from Slipknot, Mudvayne, Slayer, Pantera, and Soulfly. His East Village shop features cobwebs, rusty meat hooks, a moose head, a mummified cat, medieval torture devices, a gynecologist's black leather chair with silver stirrups, a human skull given to him by a Swedish gravedigger, a note from a customer written in blood. His arms are covered in tattoos, his face is studded with silver loops, and he's enormously fat. Some of his most popular tattoos are "weeping demons, decapitated Christ figures, transvestite nuns severing their own genitals, cascading waves of melting skulls, muscled werewolves raping bare-chested women." He has a two-year waiting list. His clients—including the "hardcore-metal elite"—come to him "because they share his frustration and rage, his feelings of anger and alienation. He understands those emotions and brings them to the surface with his needle. His gift lies in transforming the dark side of his clients—their hurt, their torments—into flesh." Evan Seinfeld, the bassist for Biohazard, says, "We're all trying to release our negative energy, our frustration with the world. Through our art and our music, we're getting it all out. Shawn Crahan of Slipknot says, "I have a lot of dark ideas in my head. Paul develops these same emotions in very powerful pieces." Booth says, "If I woke up one day and became happy, I probably wouldn't tattoo anymore, because I wouldn't see a need to do it. I would lose my art if I became happy."

*

"In Samoa there is a legend that tattooing was introduced there by the goddesses of tattooing. They swam to Samoa from Fiji, singing on the way their divine message: 'Tattoo the women but not the men.' With constant repetition the message became confused and twisted. When the goddesses finally arrived on the Samoan shore, they found themselves singing just the reverse, and so, says the legend, the tattoo became the undeserved prerogative of the men and not the women."—Albert Parry

*

Who owns these paragraphs?

*

Revelation 17.5 says of the Scarlet Woman: "And upon her forehead was a name written, MYSTERY, BABYLON THE GREAT, THE MOTHER OF HARLOTS AND ABOMINATIONS OF THE EARTH."

*

NBA veteran Jud Buechler, now with the Orlando Magic, said Michael Jordan wanted "me and Steve Kerr [Jordan's then teammates] to get tattoos" after the Bulls won their fourth championship. "I thought about it but didn't do it because I knew my mom, wife, and mother-in-law would kill me."

*

"The human body is always treated as an image of society."—Mary Douglas

*

"By the early seventeenth century [in Japan], a generally recognized codification of tattoo marks was widely used to identify criminals and outcasts. Outcasts were tattooed on the arms: a cross might be tattooed on the inner forearm, or a straight line on the outside of the forearm or on the upper arm. Criminals were marked with a variety of symbols that designated the places where the crimes were committed. In one region, the pictograph for 'dog' was tattooed on the criminal's forehead. Other marks included such patterns as bars, crosses, double lines, and circles on the face and arms. Tattooing was reserved for those who had committed serious crimes, and individuals bearing tattoo marks were ostracized by their families and denied all participation in the life of the community. For the Japanese, who valued family membership and social position above all things, tattooing was a particularly severe and terrible form of punishment. By the end of the seventeenth century, penal tattooing had been largely replaced by other forms of punishment. One reason for this is said to be that about that time decorative tattooing became popular, and criminals covered their penal tattoos with larger decorative patterns. This is also thought to be the historical origin of the association of tattooing with organized crime in Japan. In spite of efforts by the government to suppress it, tattooing continued to flourish among firemen, laborers, and others at the lower end of the social scale. It was particularly favored by gangs of itinerant gamblers called Yakuza. Members of these gangs were recruited from the underworld of outlaws, penniless peasants, laborers, and misfits who migrated to Edo in the hope of improving their lot. Although the Yakuza engaged in a variety of semi-legal and illegal activities, they saw themselves as champions of the common people and adhered to a strict code of honor that specifically prohibited crimes against people, such as rape and theft. Like Samurai, they prided themselves on being able to endure pain and privation without flinching. And when loyalty required it, they were willing to sacrifice themselves by facing imprisonment or death to protect the gang. The Yakuza expressed these ideals in tattooing: because it was painful, it was proof of courage; because it was permanent, it was evidence of lifelong loyalty to the group; and because it was illegal, it made them forever outlaws."—Steve Gilbert

*

"You put a tattoo on yourself with the knowledge that this body is yours to have and enjoy while you're here. You have fun with it, and nobody else can control (supposedly) what you do with it. That's why tattooing is such a big thing in prison: it's an expression of freedom—one of the only expressions of freedom there. They can lock you down, control everything, but 'I've got my mind, and I can tattoo my body, alter it my way as an act of personal will.' "—Don Ed Hardy

*

Weren't American slaves branded by masters to identify them like cattle? I've always thought there was a connection between the gold jewelry worn by rap artists and the chains of slavery—transformation of bondage into gold, escape from slavery, but not quite. . . .

*

During the early Roman Empire, slaves exported to Asia were tattooed with the words "tax paid." Words, acronyms, sentences, and doggerel were inscribed on the bodies of slaves and convicts, both as identification and punishment. A common phrased etched on the forehead of Roman slaves was "Stop me—I'm a runaway."

Peter Trachtenberg, the author of *Seven Tattoos: A Memoir in the Flesh,* told me: "The most obvious reason African Americans didn't get tattooed until recently was that the old inks didn't show up on black skin. Newer, clearer pigments didn't come into use until the mid- to late eighties, which coincides with the introduction of tattoos into the African-American community. I also wouldn't be surprised if tattooing's association with working-class culture—redneck culture in particular—made it unpopular with African Americans. You don't come across many black country & western fans, either. Charlie Pride's fan base is entirely white. My guess is that there were two principal routes of diffusion: the first from rap, the second from black college fraternities (some of which also used branding as an initiation rite). Starting in the late '80s, a number of gangsta rappers adopted tattoos, most notably Tupac Shakur, who had THUG LIFE tattooed in block letters down his torso. It would be interesting to go back through magazines of that period and see if photos of tattooed rappers predate those of tattooed ballplayers." They do. "Also, to find out what percentage of NBA players belonged to black college fraternities." Some, but not a lot. "There's some irony at work here. The tattoos mark their wearers as gangstas or gangsta-wannabes, but one of the hallmarks of black gangsta rap is its appropriation of white organized-crime terminology, e.g., the group BLACK M.A.F.I.A. and admiring references to John Gotti in several songs."

*

"White folks are not going to come to see a bunch of guys with tattoos, with cornrows. I'm sorry, but anyone who thinks different, they're stupid."—Charles Barkley

*

A few years ago, the shoe company And I created a controversial advertisement in which Latrell Sprewell, who was suspended from the NBA for a year for choking his coach, says, "People say I'm America's worst nightmare;

I say I'm the American dream." In the background a blues guitar plays "The Star-Spangled Banner" in imitation of Jimi Hendrix's version of the anthem (And I couldn't afford the rights to the original). Seth Berger, the president of the company, said that MTV created a youth market in which blacks and whites are indifferent to color: "It's a race-neutral culture that is open to endorsers and heroes that look different. These people are comfortable with tattoos and cornrows."

*

Who owns these statements—the people who said them or the people who wrote them down or the person who has gathered them together here or the person who reads them?

*

Concerning the people who are featured in the book *Modern Primitives* and who are devoted to body modification, mutilation, scarification, tattoos, *Whole Earth Review* said: "Through 'primitive' modifications, they are taking possession of the only thing that any of us will ever really own: our bodies."

*

In the 1890s, socialite Ward McAllister said about tattoos: "It is certainly the most vulgar and barbarous habit the eccentric mind of fashion ever invented. It may do for an illiterate seaman, but hardly for an aristocrat."

*

Upon hearing that the NBA's *Hoop* magazine had airbrushed his tattoos off the photograph of him on the cover of the magazine, Allen Iverson responded: "Hey, you can't do that. That's not right. I am who I am. You can't change that. Who gives them the authority to remake me? Everybody knows who Allen Iverson is. That's wild. That's kind of crazy. I personally am offended that somebody would do something like that. They don't have the right to try to present me in another way to the public than the way I truly am without my permission. It's an act of freedom and a form of self-expression. That's why I got mine."

*

John Allen, a Philadelphia high-school basketball star, said, "I think that on the court, if I didn't have as many tattoos as I do, people would look at me as—not being soft—but people would look at me as average. When they see me come in with my tattoos and the big name that I've got, before you even play a game, it's like, 'Whoa, this guy, he must be for real.'"

*

In the nineteenth century, Earl Roberts, Field Marshall of the British Army, said that "every officer in the British Army should be tattooed with his regimental crest. Not only does this encourage *esprit de corps* but also assists in the identification of casualties."

*

I broke my leg as a sophomore in high school, spending the summer in traction and then in a body cast, but when the doctor misread the x-rays and removed the body cast too early, I had to have a metal pin inserted to stabilize my left leg. I recently had the pin removed, for no particularly compelling reason of any kind other than it spooked me to think of one day being buried with a "foreign object" in my body (for one thing, it's a violation of Jewish law). Not that I'll be buried; I'll be cremated. Not that I'm religious; I'm an atheist. Still, leaving the pin in seemed to me some obscure violation of the order of things. As one tattoo artist has said, "The permanence really hits other people, and that is linked to mortality. And that is why skull tattoos really ice it."

*

Who owns this body, this body of work?

Mother Tongue

Amy Tan

$\mathcal{I}$am not a scholar of English or literature. I cannot give you much more than personal opinions on the English language and its variations in this country or others.

I am a writer. And by that definition, I am someone who has always loved language. I am fascinated by language in daily life. I spend a great deal of my time thinking about the power of language—the way it can evoke an emotion, a visual image, a complex idea, or a simple truth. Language is the tool of my trade. And I use them all—all the Englishes I grew up with.

Recently, I was made keenly aware of the different Englishes I do use. I was giving a talk to a large group of people, the same talk I had already given to half a dozen other groups. The nature of the talk was about my writing, my life, and my book, *The Joy Luck Club*. The talk was going along well enough, until I remember one major difference that made the whole talk sound wrong. My mother was in the room. And it was perhaps the first time she had heard me give a lengthy speech, using the kind of English I have never used with her. I was saying things like, "The intersection of memory upon imagination" and "There is an aspect of my fiction that relates to thus-and-thus"—a speech filled with carefully wrought grammatical phrases, burdened, it suddenly seemed to me, with nominalized forms, past perfect tenses, conditional phrases, all the forms of standard English that I had learned in school and through books, the forms of English I did not use at home with my mother.

Just last week, I was walking down the street with my mother, and I again found myself conscious of the English I was using, the English I do use with her. We were talking about the price of new and used furniture and I heard myself saying this: "Not waste money that way." My husband was with us as well, and he didn't notice any switch in my English. And then I realized why. It's because over the twenty years we've been together I've often used that same kind of English with him, and sometimes he even uses it with me. It has become our language of intimacy, a different sort of English that relates to family talk, the language I grew up with.

So you'll have some idea of what this family talk I heard sounds like, I'll quote what my mother said during a recent conversation which I videotaped and then transcribed. During this conversation, my mother was talking about a political gangster in Shanghai who had the same last name as her family's, Du, and how the gangster in his early years wanted to be adopted by her family, which was rich by comparison. Later, the gangster became more powerful, far richer than my mother's family, and one day showed up at my mother's wedding to pay his respects. Here's what she said in part:

"Du Yusong having business like fruit stand. Like off the street kind. He is Du like Du Zong—but not Tsung-ming Island people. The local people call putong, the river east side, he belong to that side local people. That man want to ask Du Zong father take him in like become own family. Du Zong father wasn't look down on him, but didn't take seriously, until that man big like become a mafia. Now important person, very hard to inviting him. Chinese way, came only to show respect, don't stay for dinner. Respect for making big celebration, he shows up. Mean give lots of respect. Chinese custom. Chinese social life that way. If too important won't have to stay too long. He come to my wedding. I didn't see, I heard it. I gone to boy's side, they have YMCA dinner. Chinese age I was nineteen."

You should know that my mother's expressive command of English belies how much she actually understands. She reads the *Forbes* report, listens to *Wall Street Week,* converses daily with her stockbroker, reads all of Shirley MacLaine's books with ease—all kinds of things I can't begin to understand. Yet some of my friends tell me they understand 50 percent of what my mother says. Some say they understand 80 to 90 percent. Some say they understand none of it, as if she were speaking pure Chinese. But to me, my mother's English is perfectly clear, perfectly natural. It's my mother tongue. Her language, as I hear it, is vivid, direct, full of observation and imagery. That was the language that helped shape the way I saw things, expressed things, made sense of the world.

Lately, I've been giving more thought to the kind of English my mother speaks. Like others, I have described it to people as "broken" or "fractured" English. But I wince when I say that. It has always bothered me that I can think of no way to describe it other than "broken," as if it were damaged and needed to be fixed, as if it lacked a certain wholeness and soundness. I've heard other terms used, "limited English," for example. But they seem just as bad, as if everything is limited, including people's perceptions of the limited English speaker.

I know this for a fact, because when I was growing up, my mother's "limited" English limited *my* perception of her. I was ashamed of her English. I believed that her English reflected the quality of what she had to say. That is, because she expressed them imperfectly her thoughts were imperfect. And I had plenty of empirical evidence to support me: the fact that people in department stores, at banks, and at restaurants did not take her seriously, did not give her good service, pretended not to understand her, or even acted as if they did not hear her.

My mother has long realized the limitations of her English as well. When I was fifteen, she used to have me call people on the phone to pretend I was she. In this guise, I was forced to ask for information or even to complain and yell at people who had been rude to her. One time it was a call to her stockbroker in New York. She had cashed out her small portfolio and it just happened we were going to go to New York the next week, our very first trip outside California. I had to get on the phone and say in an adolescent voice that was not very convincing, "This is Mrs. Tan."

And my mother was standing in the back whispering loudly, "Why he don't send me check, already two weeks late. So mad he lie to me, losing me money."

And then I said in perfect English, "Yes, I'm getting rather concerned. You had agreed to send the check two weeks ago, but it hasn't arrived."

Then she began to talk more loudly. "What he want, I come to New York tell him front of his boss, you cheating me?" And I was trying to calm her down, make her be quiet, while telling the stockbroker, "I can't tolerate any more excuses. If I don't receive the check immediately, I am going to have to speak to your manager when I'm in New York next week." And sure enough, the following week there we were in front of this astonished stockbroker, and I was sitting there red-faced and quiet, and my mother, the real Mrs. Tan, was shouting at his boss in her impeccable broken English.

We used a similar routine just five days ago, for a situation that was far less humorous. My mother had gone to the hospital for an appointment, to find out about a benign brain tumor a CAT scan had revealed a month ago. She said she had spoken very good English, her best English, no mistakes. Still, she said, the hospital did not apologize when they said they had lost the CAT scan and she had come for nothing. She said they did not seem to have any sympathy when she told them she was anxious to know the exact diagnosis, since her husband and son had both died of brain tumors. She said they would not give her any more information until the next time and she would have to make another appointment for that. So she said she would not leave until the doctor called her daughter. She wouldn't budge. And when the doctor finally called her daughter, me, who spoke in perfect English—lo and behold—we had assurances the CAT scan would be found, promises that a conference call on Monday would be held, and apologies for any suffering my mother had gone through for a most regrettable mistake.

I think my mother's English almost had an effect on limiting my possibilities in life as well. Sociologists and linguists probably will tell you that a person's developing language skills are more influenced by peers. But I do think that the language spoken in the family, especially in immigrant families which are more insular, plays a large role in shaping the language of the child. And I believe that it affected my results on achievement tests, IQ tests, and the SAT. While my English skills were never judged as poor, compared to math, English could not be considered my strong suit. In grade school I did moderately well, getting perhaps B's, sometimes B-pluses, in English and scoring perhaps in the sixtieth or seventieth percentile on achievement tests. But those scores were not good enough to override the opinion that my true abilities lay in math and science, because in those areas I achieved A's and scored in the ninetieth percentile or higher.

This was understandable. Math is precise; there is only one correct answer. Whereas, for me at least, the answers on English tests were always a judgment call, a matter of opinion and personal experience. Those tests were constructed around items like fill-in-the-blank sentence completion, such as, "Even though Tom was _____, Mary thought he was _____." And the correct answer always seemed to be the most bland combinations of thoughts, for example, "Even though Tom was shy, Mary thought he was charming," with the grammatical structure "even though" limiting the correct answer to some sort of semantic opposites, so you wouldn't get answers like, "Even though Tom was foolish, Mary thought he was ridiculous." Well, according to my mother, there were very few limitations as to what Tom could have been and what Mary might have thought of him. So I never did well on tests like that.

The same was true with word analogies, pairs of words in which you were supposed to find some sort of logical, semantic relationship—for example, "*Sunset* is to *nightfall* as _____ is to _____." And here you would be presented with a list of four possible pairs, one of which showed the same kind of relationship: *red* is to *stoplight, bus* is to *arrival, chills* is to *fever, yawn* is to *boring.* Well, I could never think that way. I knew what the tests were asking, but I could not block out of my mind the images already created by the first pair, "*sunset* is to *nightfall*"—and I would see a burst of colors against a darkening sky, the moon rising, the lowering of a curtain of stars. And all the other pairs of words—red, bus, stoplight, boring—just threw up a mass of confusing images, making it impossible for me to sort out something as logical as saying: "A sunset precedes nightfall" is the same as "a chill precedes a fever." The only way I would have gotten that answer right would have been to imagine an associative situation, for example, my being disobedient and staying out past sunset, catching a chill at night, which turns into feverish pneumonia as punishment, which indeed did happen to me.

I have been thinking about all this lately, about my mother's English, about achievement tests. Because lately I've been asked as a writer, why there are not more Asian Americans represented in American literature. Why are there few Asian Americans enrolled in creative writing programs? Why do so many Chinese students go into engineering? Well, these are broad sociological questions I can't begin to answer. But I have noticed in surveys—in fact, just last week—that Asian students, as a whole, always do significantly better on math achievement tests than in English. And this makes me think that there are other Asian-American students whose English spoken in the home might also be described as "broken" or "limited." And perhaps they also have teachers who are steering them away from writing and into math and science, which is what happened to me.

Fortunately, I happen to be rebellious in nature and enjoy the challenge of disproving assumptions made about me. I became an English major my first year in college, after being enrolled as pre-med. I started writing nonfiction as a freelancer the week after I was told by my former boss that writing was my worst skill and I should hone my talents toward account management.

But it wasn't until 1985 that I finally began to write fiction. And at first I wrote using what I thought to be wittily crafted sentences, sentences that would finally prove I had mastery over the English language. Here's an example from the first draft of a story that later made its way into *The Joy Luck Club,* but without this line: "That was my mental quandary in its nascent state." A terrible line, which I can barely pronounce.

Fortunately, for reasons I won't get into today, I later decided I should envision a reader for the stories I would write. And the reader I decided upon was my mother, because these were stories about mothers. So with this reader in mind—and in fact she did read my early drafts—I began to write stories using all the Englishes I grew up with: the English I spoke to my mother, which for lack of a better term might be described as "simple"; the English she used with me, which for lack of a better term might be described as "broken"; my translation of her Chinese, which could certainly be described as "watered down"; and what I imagined to be her translation of her Chinese if she could speak in perfect English, her internal language, and for that I sought to preserve the essence, but neither an English nor a Chinese structure. I wanted to capture what language ability tests can never reveal: her intent, her passion, her imagery, the rhythms of her speech and the nature of her thoughts.

Apart from what any critic had to say about my writing, I knew I had succeeded where it counted when my mother finished reading my book and gave me her verdict: "So easy to read."

The Clan of One-Breasted Women

Terry Tempest Williams

I belong to a Clan of One-Breasted Women. My mother, my grandmothers, and six aunts have all had mastectomies. Seven are dead. The two who survive have just completed rounds of chemotherapy and radiation.

I've had my own problems: two biopsies for breast cancer and a small tumor between my ribs diagnosed as a "borderline malignancy."

This is my family history.

Most statistics tell us breast cancer is genetic, hereditary, with rising percentages attached to fatty diets, childlessness, or becoming pregnant after thirty. What they don't say is living in Utah may be the greatest hazard of all.

We are a Mormon family with roots in Utah since 1847. The "word of wisdom" in my family aligned us with good foods—no coffee, no tea, tobacco, or alcohol. For the most part, our women were finished having their babies by the time they were thirty. And only one faced breast cancer prior to 1960. Traditionally, as a group of people, Mormons have a low rate of cancer.

Is our family a cultural anomaly? The truth is, we didn't think about it. Those who did, usually the men, simply said, "bad genes." The women's attitude was stoic. Cancer was part of life. On February 16, 1971, the eve of my mother's surgery, I accidentally picked up the telephone and overheard her ask my grandmother what she could expect.

"Diane, it is one of the most spiritual experiences you will ever encounter."

I quietly put down the receiver.

Two days later, my father took my brothers and me to the hospital to visit her. She met us in the lobby in a wheelchair. No bandages were visible. I'll never forget her radiance, the way she held herself in a purple velvet robe, and how she gathered us around her.

"Children, I am fine. I want you to know I felt the arms of God around me."

We believed her. My father cried. Our mother, his wife, was thirty-eight years old.

A little over a year after Mother's death, Dad and I were having dinner together. He had just returned from St. George, where the Tempest Company was completing the gas lines that would service southern Utah. He spoke of his love for the country, the sandstoned landscape, bare-boned and beautiful. He had just finished hiking the Kolob trail in Zion National Park. We got caught up in reminiscing, recalling with fondness our walk up Angel's Landing on his fiftieth birthday and the years our family had vacationed there.

Over dessert, I shared a recurring dream of mine. I told my father that for years, as long as I could remember, I saw this flash of light in the night in the desert—that this image had so permeated my being that I could not venture south without seeing it again, on the horizon, illuminating buttes and mesas.

"You did see it," he said.

"Saw what?"

"The bomb. The cloud. We were driving home from Riverside, California. You were sitting on Diane's lap. She was pregnant. In fact, I remember the day, September 7, 1957. We had just gotten out of the Service. We were driving north, past Las Vegas. It was an hour or so before dawn, when this explosion went off. We not only heard it, but felt it. I thought the oil tanker in front of us had blown up. We pulled over and suddenly, rising from the desert floor, we saw it, clearly, this golden-stemmed cloud, the mushroom. The sky seemed to vibrate with an eerie pink glow. Within a few minutes, a light ash was raining on the car."

I stared at my father.

"I thought you knew that," he said. "It was a common occurrence in the fifties."

It was at this moment that I realized the deceit I had been living under. Children growing up in the American Southwest, drinking contaminated milk from contaminated cows, even from the contaminated breasts of their mothers, my mother—members, years later, of the Clan of One-Breasted Women.

It is a well-known story in the Desert West, "The Day We Bombed Utah," or more accurately, the years we bombed Utah: above ground atomic testing in Nevada took place from January 27, 1951 through July 11, 1962. Not only were the winds blowing north covering "low-use segments of the population" with fallout and leaving sheep dead in their tracks, but the climate was right. The United States of the 1950s was red, white, and blue. The Korean War was raging. McCarthyism was rampant. Ike was it, and the cold war was hot. If you were against nuclear testing, you were for a communist regime.

Much has been written about this "American nuclear tragedy." Public health was secondary to national security. The Atomic Energy Commissioner, Thomas Murray, said, "Gentlemen, we must not let anything interfere with this series of tests, nothing."

Again and again, the American public was told by its government, in spite of burns, blisters, and nausea, "It has been found that the tests may be conducted with adequate assurance of safety under conditions prevailing at the bombing reservations." Assuaging public fears was simply a matter of public relations. "Your best action," an Atomic Energy Commission booklet read, "is not to be worried about fallout." A news release typical of the times stated, "We find no basis for concluding that harm to any individual has resulted from radioactive fallout."

On August 30, 1979, during Jimmy Carter's presidency, a suit was filed, *Irene Allen v. The United States of America*. Mrs. Allen's case was the first on an alphabetical list of twenty-four test cases, representative of nearly twelve hundred plaintiffs seeking compensation from the United States government for cancers caused by nuclear testing in Nevada.

Irene Allen lived in Hurricane, Utah. She was the mother of five children and had been widowed twice. Her first husband, with their two oldest boys, had watched the tests from the roof of the local high school. He died of leukemia in 1956. Her second husband died of pancreatic cancer in 1978.

In a town meeting conducted by Utah Senator Orrin Hatch, shortly before the suit was filed, Mrs. Allen said, "I am not blaming the government, I want you to know that, Senator Hatch. But I thought if my testimony could help in any way so this wouldn't happen again to any of the generations coming up after us . . . I am happy to be here this day to bear testimony of this."

God-fearing people. This is just one story in an anthology of thousands.

On May 10, 1984, Judge Bruce S. Jenkins handed down his opinion. Ten of the plaintiffs were awarded damages. It was the first time a federal court had determined that nuclear tests had been the cause of cancers. For the remaining fourteen test cases, the proof of causation was not sufficient. In spite of the split decision, it was considered a landmark ruling. It was not to remain so for long.

In April 1987, the Tenth Circuit Court of Appeals overturned Judge Jenkins's ruling on the ground that the United States was protected from suit by the legal doctrine of sovereign immunity, a centuries-old idea from England in the days of absolute monarchs.

In January 1988, the Supreme Court refused to review the Appeals Court decision. To our court system it does not matter whether the United States government was irresponsible, whether it lied to its citizens, or even that citizens died from the fallout of nuclear testing. What matters is that our government is immune: "The King can do no wrong."

In Mormon culture, authority is respected, obedience is revered, and independent thinking is not. I was taught as a young girl not to "make waves" or "rock the boat."

"Just let it go," Mother would say. "You know how you feel, that's what counts."

For many years, I have done just that—listened, observed, and quietly formed my own opinions, in a culture that rarely asks questions because it has all the answers. But one by one, I have watched the women in my family die common, heroic deaths. We sat in waiting rooms hoping for good news, but always receiving the bad. I cared for them, bathed their scarred bodies, and kept their secrets. I watched beautiful women become bald as Cytoxan, cisplatin, and Adriamycin were injected into their veins. I held their foreheads as they vomited green-black bile, and I shot them with morphine when the pain became inhuman. In the end, I witnessed their last peaceful breaths, becoming a midwife to the rebirth of their souls.

The price of obedience has become too high.

The fear and inability to question authority that ultimately killed rural communities in Utah during atmospheric testing of atomic weapons is the same fear I saw in my mother's body. Sheep. Dead sheep. The evidence is buried.

I cannot prove that my mother, Diane Dixon Tempest, or my grandmothers, Lettie Romney Dixon and Kathryn Blackett Tempest, along with my aunts developed cancer from nuclear fallout in Utah. But I can't prove they didn't.

My father's memory was correct. The September blast we drove through in 1957 was part of Operation Plumbbob, one of the most intensive series of bomb tests to be initiated. The flash of light in the night in the desert, which I had always thought was a dream, developed into a family nightmare. It took fourteen years, from 1957 to 1971, for cancer to manifest in my mother—the same time, Howard L. Andrews, an authority in radioactive fallout at the National Institutes of Health, says radiation cancer requires to become evident. The more I learn about what it means to be a "downwinder," the more questions I drown in.

What I do know, however, is that as a Mormon woman of the fifth generation of Latter-day Saints, I must question everything, even if it means losing my faith, even if it means becoming a member of a border tribe among my own people. Tolerating blind obedience in the name of patriotism or religion ultimately takes our lives.

When the Atomic Energy Commission described the country north of the Nevada Test Site as "virtually uninhabited desert terrain," my family and the birds at Great Salt Lake were some of the "virtual uninhabitants."

One night, I dreamed women from all over the world circled a blazing fire in the desert. They spoke of change, how they hold the moon in their bellies and wax and wane with its phases. They mocked the presumption of even-tempered beings and made promises that they would never fear the witch inside themselves. The women danced wildly as sparks broke away from the flames and entered the night sky as stars.

And they sang a song given to them by Shoshone grandmothers:

Ah ne nah, nah	Consider the rabbits
nin nah nah—	How gently they walk on the earth—
ah ne nah, nah	Consider the rabbits
nin nah nah—	How gently they walk on the earth—
Nyaga mutzi	We remember them
oh ne nay—	We can walk gently also—
Nyaga mutzi	We remember them
oh ne nay—	We can walk gently also—

The women danced and drummed and sang for weeks, preparing themselves for what was to come. They would reclaim the desert for the sake of their children, for the sake of the land.

A few miles downwind from the fire circle, bombs were being tested. Rabbits felt the tremors. Their soft leather pads on paws and feet recognized the shaking sands, while the roots of mesquite and sage were smoldering. Rocks were hot from the inside out and dust devils hummed unnaturally. And each time there was another nuclear test, ravens watched the desert heave. Stretch marks appeared. The land was losing its muscle.

The women couldn't bear it any longer. They were mothers. They had suffered labor pains but always under the promise of birth. The red hot pains beneath the desert promised death only, as each bomb became a stillborn. A contract had been made and broken between human beings and the land. A new contract was being drawn by the women, who understood the fate of the earth as their own.

Under the cover of darkness, ten women slipped under a barbed-wire fence and entered the contaminated country. They were trespassing. They walked toward the town of Mercury, in moonlight, taking their cues from coyote, kit fox, antelope squirrel, and quail. They moved quietly and deliberately through the maze of Joshua trees. When a hint of daylight appeared they rested, drinking tea and sharing their rations of food. The women closed their eyes. The time had come to protest with the heart, that to deny one's genealogy with the earth was to commit treason against one's soul.

At dawn, the women draped themselves in mylar, wrapping long streamers of silver plastic around their arms to blow in the breeze. They wore clear masks, that became the faces of humanity. And when they arrived at the edge of Mercury, they carried all the butterflies of a summer day in their wombs. They paused to allow their courage to settle.

The town that forbids pregnant women and children to enter because of radiation risks was asleep. The women moved through the streets as winged messengers, twirling around each other in slow motion, peeking inside homes and watching the easy sleep of men and women. They were astonished by each stillness and periodically would utter a shrill note or low cry just to verify life.

The residents finally awoke to these strange apparitions. Some simply stared. Others called authorities, and in time the women were apprehended by wary soldiers dressed in desert fatigues. They were taken to a white, square building on the other edge of Mercury. When asked who they were and why they were there, the women replied, "We are mothers and we have come to reclaim the desert for our children."

The soldiers arrested them. As the ten women were blindfolded and handcuffed, they began singing:

You can't forbid us everything
You can't forbid us to think—
You can't forbid our tears to flow
And you can't stop the songs that we sing.

The women continued to sing louder and louder, until they heard the voices of their sisters moving across the mesa:

Ah ne nah, nah
nin nah nah—
Ah ne nah, nah
nin nah nah—
Nyaga mutzi
oh ne nay—
Nyaga mutzi
oh ne nay—

"Call for reinforcements," one soldier said.

"We have," interrupted one woman, "we have—and you have no idea of our numbers."

I crossed the line at the Nevada Test Site and was arrested with nine other Utahns for trespassing on military lands. They are still conducting nuclear tests in the desert. Ours was an act of civil disobedience. But as I walked toward the town of Mercury, it was more than a gesture of peace. It was a gesture on behalf of the Clan of One-Breasted Women.

As one officer cinched the handcuffs around my wrists, another frisked my body. She found a pen and a pad of paper tucked inside my left boot.

"And these?" she asked sternly.

"Weapons," I replied.

Our eyes met. I smiled. She pulled the leg of my trousers back over my boot.

"Step forward, please," she said as she took my arm.

We were booked under an afternoon sun and bused to Tonopah, Nevada. It was a two-hour ride. This was familiar country. The Joshua trees standing their ground had been named by my ancestors, who believed they looked like prophets pointing west to the Promised Land. These were the same trees that bloomed each spring, flowers appearing like white flames in the Mojave. And I recalled a full moon in May, when Mother and I had walked among them, flushing out mourning doves and owls.

The bus stopped short of town. We were released.

The officials thought it was a cruel joke to leave us stranded in the desert with no way to get home. What they didn't realize was that we were home, soul-centered and strong, women who recognized the sweet smell of sage as fuel for our spirits.

Essays on the Craft of Creative Nonfiction

Seeing

Annie Dillard

When I was six or seven years old, growing up in Pittsburgh, I used to take a precious penny of my own and hide it for someone else to find. It was a curious compulsion; sadly, I've never been seized by it since. For some reason I always "hid" the penny along the same stretch of sidewalk up the street. I would cradle it at the roots of a sycamore, say, or in a hole left by a chipped-off piece of sidewalk. Then I would take a piece of chalk, and, starting at either end of the block, draw huge arrows leading up to the penny from both directions. After I learned to write I labeled the arrows: SURPRISE AHEAD or MONEY THIS WAY. I was greatly excited, during all this arrow-drawing, at the thought of the first lucky passer-by who would receive in this way, regardless of merit, a free gift from the universe. But I never lurked about. I would go straight home and not give the matter another thought, until, some months later, I would be gripped again by the impulse to hide another penny.

It is still the first week in January, and I've got great plans. I've been thinking about seeing. There are lots of things to see, unwrapped gifts and free surprises. The world is fairly studded and strewn with pennies cast broadside from a generous hand. But—and this is the point—who gets excited by a mere penny? If you follow one arrow, if you crouch motionless on a bank to watch a tremulous ripple thrill on the water and are rewarded by the sight of a muskrat kit paddling from its den, will you count that sight a chip of copper only, and go your rueful way? It is dire poverty indeed when a man is so malnourished and fatigued that he won't stoop to pick up a penny. But if you cultivate a healthy poverty and simplicity, so that finding a penny will literally make your day, then, since the world is in fact planted in pennies, you have with your poverty bought a lifetime of days. It is that simple. What you see is what you get.

I used to be able to see flying insects in the air. I'd look ahead and see, not the row of hemlocks across the road, but the air in front of it. My eyes would focus along that column of air, picking out flying insects. But I lost interest, I guess, for I dropped the habit. Now I can see birds. Probably some people can look at the grass at their feet and discover all the crawling creatures. I would like to know grasses and sedges—and care. Then my least journey into the world would be a field trip, a series of happy recognitions. Thoreau, in an expansive mood, exulted, "What a rich book might be made about buds, including, perhaps, sprouts!" It would be nice to think so. I cherish mental images I have of three perfectly happy people. One collects stones. Another—an Englishman, say—watches clouds. The third lives on a coast and collects drops of seawater which he examines microscopically and mounts. But I don't see what the specialist sees, and so I cut myself off, not only from the total picture, but from the various forms of happiness.

Unfortunately, nature is very much a now-you-see-it, now-you-don't affair. A fish flashes, then dissolves in the water before my eyes like so much salt. Deer apparently ascend bodily into heaven; the brightest oriole fades into leaves. These disappearances stun me into stillness and concentration; they say of nature that it conceals with a grand nonchalance, and they say of vision that it is a deliberate gift, the revelation of a dancer who for my eyes only flings away her seven veils. For nature does reveal as well as conceal: now-you-don't-see-it, now-you-do. For a week last September migrating red-winged blackbirds were feeding heavily down by the creek at the back of the house. One day I went out to investigate the racket; I walked up to a tree, an Osage orange, and a hundred birds flew away. They simply materialized out of the tree. I saw a tree, then a whisk of color, then a tree again. I walked closer and another hundred blackbirds took flight. Not a branch, not a twig budged: the birds were apparently weightless as well as invisible. Or, it was as if the leaves of the Osage orange had been freed from a spell in the form of red-winged blackbirds; they flew from the tree, caught my eye in the sky, and vanished. When I looked again at the tree the leaves had reassembled as if nothing had happened. Finally I walked directly to the trunk of the tree and a final hundred, the real diehards, appeared, spread, and vanished. How could so many hide in the tree without my seeing them? The Osage orange, unruffled, looked just as it had looked from the house, when three hundred redwinged blackbirds cried from its crown. I looked downstream where they flew, and they were gone. Searching, I couldn't spot one. I wandered downstream to force them to play their hand, but they'd crossed the creek and scattered. One show to a customer. These appearances catch at my throat; they are the free gifts, the bright coppers at the roots of trees.

It's all a matter of keeping my eyes open. Nature is like one of those line drawings of a tree that are puzzles for children: Can you find hidden in the leaves a duck, a house, a boy, a bucket, a zebra, and a boot? Specialists can find the most incredibly well-hidden things. A book I read when I was young recommended an easy way to find caterpillars to rear: you simply find some fresh caterpillar droppings, look up, and there's your caterpillar. More recently an author advised me to set my mind at ease about those piles of cut stems on the ground in grassy fields. Field mice make them; they cut the grass down by degrees to reach the seeds at the head. It seems that when the grass is tightly packed, as in a field of ripe grain, the blade won't topple at a single cut through the stem; instead, the cut stem simply drops vertically, held in the crush of grain. The mouse severs the bottom again and again, the stem keeps dropping an inch at a time, and finally the head is low enough for the mouse to reach the seeds. Meanwhile, the mouse is positively littering the field with its little piles of cut stems into which, presumably, the author of the book is constantly stumbling.

If I can't see these minutiae, I still try to keep my eyes open. I'm always on the lookout for antlion traps in sandy soil, monarch pupae near milkweed, skipper larvae in locust leaves. These things are utterly common, and I've not seen one. I bang on hollow trees near water, but so far no flying squirrels have appeared. In flat country I watch every sunset in hopes of seeing the green ray. The green ray is a seldom-seen streak of light that rises from the sun like a spurting fountain at the moment of sunset; it throbs into the sky for two seconds and disappears. One more reason to keep my eyes open. A photography professor at the University of Florida just happened to see a bird die in midflight; it jerked, died, dropped, and smashed on the ground. I squint at the wind because I read Steward Edward White: "I have always maintained that if you looked closely enough you could *see* the wind—the dim, hardly-made-out, fine debris fleeing high in the air." White was an excellent observer, and devoted an entire chapter of *The Mountains* to the subject of seeing deer: "As soon as you can forget the naturally obvious and construct an artificial obvious, then you too will see deer."

But the artificial obvious is hard to see. My eyes account for less than one percent of the weight of my head; I'm bony and dense; I see what I expect. I once spent a full three minutes looking at a bullfrog that was so unexpectedly large I couldn't see it even though a dozen enthusiastic campers were shouting directions. Finally I asked, "What color am I looking for?" and a fellow said, "Green." When at last I picked out the frog, I saw what painters are up against: the thing wasn't green at all, but the color of wet hickory bark.

The lover can see, and the knowledgeable. I visited an aunt and uncle at a quarterhorse ranch in Cody, Wyoming. I couldn't do much of anything useful, but I could, I thought, draw. So, as we all sat around the kitchen table after supper, I produced a sheet of paper and drew a horse. "That's one lame horse," my aunt volunteered. The rest of the family joined in: "Only place to saddle that one is his neck"; "Looks like we better shoot the poor thing, on account of those terrible growths." Meekly, I slid the pencil and paper down the table. Everyone in that family, including my three young cousins, could draw a horse.

Beautifully. When the paper came back it looked as though five shining, real quarter horses had been corralled by mistake with a papier-mâché moose; the real horses seemed to gaze at the monster with a steady, puzzled air. I stay away from horses now, but I can do a creditable goldfish. The point is that I just don't know what the lover knows; I just can't see the artificial obvious that those in the know construct. The herpetologist asks the native, "Are there snakes in that ravine?" "Nosir." And the herpetologist comes home with, yessir, three bags full. Are there butterflies on that mountain? Are the bluets in bloom, are there arrowheads here, or fossil shells in the shale?

Peeping through my keyhole I see within the range of only about thirty percent of the light that comes from the sun; the rest is infrared and some little ultraviolet, perfectly apparent to many animals, but invisible to me. A nightmare network of ganglia, charged and firing without my knowledge, cuts and splices what I do see, editing it for my brain. Donald E. Carr points out that the sense impressions of one-celled animals are *not* edited for the brain: "This is philosophically interesting in a rather mournful way, since it means that only the simplest animals perceive the universe as it is."

A fog that won't burn away drifts and flows across my field of vision. When you see fog move against a backdrop of deep pines, you don't see the fog itself, but streaks of clearness floating across the air in dark shreds. So I see only tatters of clearness through a pervading obscurity. I can't distinguish the fog from the overcast sky; I can't be sure if the light is direct or reflected. Everywhere darkness and the presence of the unseen appalls. We estimate now that only one atom dances alone in every cubic meter of intergalactic space. I blink and squint. What planet or power yanks Halley's Comet out of orbit? We haven't seen that force yet; it's a question of distance, density, and the pallor of reflected light. We rock, cradled in the swaddling band of darkness. Even the simple darkness of night whispers suggestions to the mind. Last summer, in August, I stayed at the creek too late.

Where Tinker Creek flows under the sycamore log bridge to the tear-shaped island, it is slow and shallow, fringed thinly in cattail marsh. At this spot an astonishing bloom of life supports vast breeding populations of insects, fish, reptiles, birds, and mammals. On windless summer evenings I stalk along the creek bank or straddle the sycamore log in absolute stillness, watching for muskrats. The night I stayed too late I was hunched on the log staring spellbound at spreading, reflected stains of lilac on the water. A cloud in the sky suddenly lighted as if turned on by a switch; its reflection just as suddenly materialized on the water upstream, flat and floating, so that I couldn't see the creek bottom, or life in the water under the cloud. Downstream, away from the cloud on the water, water turtles smooth as beans were gliding down with the current in a series of easy, weightless push-offs, as men bound on the moon. I didn't know whether to trace the progress of one turtle I was sure of, risking sticking my face in one of the bridge's spider webs made invisible by the gathering dark, or take a chance on seeing the carp, or scan the mudbank in hope of seeing a muskrat, or follow the last of the swallows who caught at my heart and trailed it after them like streamers as they appeared from directly below, under the log, flying upstream with their tails forked, so fast.

But shadows spread, and deepened, and stayed. After thousands of years we're still strangers to darkness, fearful aliens in an enemy camp with our arms crossed over our chests. I stirred. A land turtle on the bank, startled, hissed the air from its lungs and withdrew into its shell. An uneasy pink here, an unfathomable blue there, gave great suggestion of lurking beings. Things were going on. I couldn't see whether that sere rustle I heard was a distant rattlesnake, slit-eyed, or a nearby sparrow kicking in the dry flood debris slung at the foot of a willow. Tremendous action roiled the water everywhere I looked, big action, inexplicable. A tremor welled up beside a gaping muskrat burrow in the bank and I caught my breath, but no muskrat appeared. The ripples continued to fan upstream with a steady, powerful thrust. Night was knitting over my face an eyeless mask, and I still sat transfixed. A distant airplane, a delta wing out of nightmare, made a gliding shadow on the creek's bottom that looked like a stingray cruising upstream. At once a black fin slit the pink cloud on the water, shearing it in two. The two halves merged together and seemed to dissolve before my eyes. Darkness pooled in the cleft of the creek and rose, as water collects in a well. Untamed, dreaming lights flickered over the sky. I saw hints of hulking underwater shadows, two pale splashes out of the water, and round ripples rolling close together from a blackened center.

At last I stared upstream where only the deepest violet remained of the cloud, a cloud so high its underbelly still glowed feeble color reflected from a hidden sky lighted in turn by a sun halfway to China. And out of that violet, a sudden enormous black body arced over the water. I saw only a cylindrical sleekness. Head and tail, if there was a head and tail, were both submerged in cloud. I saw only one ebony fling, a headlong dive to darkness; then the waters closed, and the lights went out.

I walked home in a shivering daze, up hill and down. Later I lay open-mouthed in bed, my arms flung wide at my sides to steady the whirling darkness. At this latitude I'm spinning 836 miles an hour round the earth's axis; I often fancy I feel my sweeping fall as a breakneck arc like the dive of dolphins, and the hollow rushing of wind raises hair on my neck and the side of my face. In orbit around the sun I'm moving 64,800 miles an hour. The solar system as a whole, like a merry-go-round unhinged, spins, bobs, and blinks at the speed of 43,200 miles an hour along a course set east of Hercules. Someone has piped, and we are dancing a tarantella until the sweat pours. I open my eyes and I see dark, muscled forms curl out of water, with flapping gills and flattened eyes. I close my eyes and I see stars, deep stars giving way to deeper stars, deeper stars bowing to deepest stars at the crown of an infinite cone.

"Still," wrote van Gogh in a letter, "a great deal of light falls on everything." If we are blinded by darkness, we are also blinded by light. When too much light falls on everything, a special terror results. Peter Freuchen describes the notorious kayak sickness to which Greenland Eskimos are prone. "The Greenland fjords are peculiar for the spells of completely quiet weather, when there is not enough wind to blow out a match and the water is like a sheet of glass. The kayak hunter must sit in his boat without stirring a finger so as not to scare the shy seals away. . . . The sun, low in the sky, sends a glare into his eyes, and the landscape around moves into the realm of the unreal. The reflex from the mirror-like water hypnotizes him, he seems to be unable to move, and all of a sudden it is as if he were floating in a bottomless void, sinking, sinking, and sinking. . . . Horror-stricken, he tries to stir, to cry out, but he cannot, he is completely paralyzed, he just falls and falls." Some hunters are especially cursed with this panic, and bring ruin and sometimes starvation to their families.

Sometimes here in Virginia at sunset low clouds on the southern or northern horizon are completely invisible in the lighted sky. I only know one is there because I can see its reflection in still water. The first time I discovered this mystery I looked from cloud to no-cloud in bewilderment, checking my bearings over and over, thinking maybe the ark of the covenant was just passing by south of Dead Man Mountain. Only much later did I read the explanation: polarized light from the sky is very much weakened by reflection, but the light in clouds isn't polarized. So invisible clouds pass among visible clouds, till all slide over the mountains; so a greater light extinguishes a lesser as though it didn't exist.

In the great meteor shower of August, the Perseid, I wail all day for the shooting stars I miss. They're out there showering down, committing harakiri in a flame of fatal attraction, and hissing perhaps at last into the ocean. But at dawn what looks like a blue dome clamps down over me like a lid on a pot. The stars and planets could smash and I'd never know. Only a piece of ashen moon occasionally climbs up or down the inside of the dome, and our local star without surcease explodes on our heads. We have really only that one light, one source for all power, and yet we must turn away from it by universal decree. Nobody here on the planet seems aware of this strange, powerful taboo, that we all walk about carefully averting our faces, this way and that, lest our eyes be blasted forever.

Darkness appalls and light dazzles; the scrap of visible light that doesn't hurt my eyes hurts my brain. What I see sets me swaying. Size and distance and the sudden swelling of meanings confuse me, bowl me over. I straddle the sycamore log bridge over Tinker Creek in the summer. I look at the lighted creek bottom: snail tracks tunnel the mud in quavering curves. A crayfish jerks, but by the time I absorb what has happened, he's gone in a billowing smokescreen of silt. I look at the water: minnows and shiners. If I'm thinking minnows, a carp will fill my brain till I scream. I look at the water's surface: skaters, bubbles, and leaves sliding down. Suddenly, my own face, reflected, startles me witless. Those snails have been tracking my face! Finally, with a shuddering wrench of the will, I see clouds, cirrus clouds. I'm dizzy, I fall in. This looking business is risky.

Once I stood on a humped rock on nearby Purgatory Mountain, watching through binoculars the great autumn hawk migration below, until I discovered that I was in danger of joining the hawks on a vertical migration of my own. I was used to binoculars, but not, apparently, to balancing on humped rocks while looking through them. I staggered. Everything advanced and receded by turns; the world was full of unexplained foreshortenings and depths. A distant huge tan object, a hawk the size of an elephant, turned out to be the browned bough of a nearby loblolly pine. I followed a sharp-shinned hawk against a featureless sky, rotating my head unawares as it flew, and when I lowered the glass a glimpse of my own looming shoulder sent me staggering. What prevents the men on Palomar from falling, voiceless and blinded, from their tiny, vaulted chairs?

I reel in confusion; I don't understand what I see. With the naked eye I can see two million light-years to the Andromeda galaxy. Often I slop some creek water in a jar and when I get home I dump it in a white china bowl. After the silt settles I return and see tracings of minute snails on the bottom, a planarian or two winding round the rim of water, roundworms shimmying frantically, and finally, when my eyes have adjusted to these dimensions, amoebae. At first the amoebae look like muscae volitantes, those curled moving spots you seem to see in your eyes when you stare at a distant wall. Then I see the amoebae as drops of water congealed, bluish, translucent, like chips of sky in the bowl. At length I choose one individual and give myself over to its idea of an evening. I see it dribble a grainy foot before it on its wet, unfathomable way. Do its unedited sense impressions include the fierce focus of my eyes? Shall I take it outside and show it Andromeda, and blow its little endoplasm? I stir the water with a finger, in case it's running out of oxygen. Maybe I should get a tropical aquarium with motorized bubblers and lights, and keep this one for a pet. Yes, it would tell its fissioned descendants, the universe is two feet by five, and if you listen closely you can hear the buzzing music of the spheres.

Oh, it's mysterious lamplit evenings, here in the galaxy, one after the other. It's one of those nights when I wander from window to window, looking for a sign. But I can't see. Terror and a beauty insoluble are a ribband of blue woven into the fringes of garments of things both great and small. No culture explains, no bivouac offers real haven or rest. But it could be that we are not seeing something. Galileo thought comets were an optical illusion. This is fertile ground: since we are certain that they're not, we can look at what our scientists have been saying with fresh hope. What if there are *really* gleaming, castellated cities hung upside-down over the desert sand? What limpid lakes and cool date palms have our caravans always passed untried?

Until, one by one, by the blindest of leaps, we light on the road to these places, we must stumble in darkness and hunger. I turn from the window. I'm blind as a bat, sensing only from every direction the echo of my own thin cries.

I chanced on a wonderful book by Marius von Senden, called *Space and Sight*. When Western surgeons discovered how to perform safe cataract operations, they ranged across Europe and America operating on dozens of men and women of all ages who had been blinded by cataracts since birth. Von Senden collected accounts of such cases; the histories are fascinating. Many doctors had tested their patients' sense perceptions and ideas of space both before and after the operations. The vast majority of patients, of both sexes and all ages, had, in von Senden's opinion, no idea of space whatsoever. Form, distance, and size were so many meaningless syllables. A patient "had no idea of depth, confusing it with roundness." Before the operation a doctor would give a blind patient a cube and a sphere; the patient would tongue it or feel it with his hands, and name it correctly. After the operation the doctor would show the same objects to the patient without letting him touch them; now he had no clue whatsoever what he was seeing. One patient called lemonade "square" because it pricked on his tongue as a square shape pricked on the touch of his hands. Of another postoperative patient, the doctor writes, "I have found in her no notion of size, for example, not even within the narrow limits which she might have encompassed with the aid of touch. Thus when I asked her to show me how big her mother was, she did not stretch out her hands, but set her two index-fingers a few inches apart." Other doctors reported their patients' own statements to similar effect. "The room he was in . . . he knew to be but part of the house, yet he could not conceive that the whole house could look bigger"; "Those who are blind from birth . . . have no real conception of height or distance. A house that is a mile away is thought of as nearby, but requiring the taking of a lot of steps. . . . The elevator that whizzes him up and down gives no more sense of vertical distance than does the train of horizontal."

For the newly sighted, vision is pure sensation unencumbered by meaning: "The girl went through the experience that we all go through and forget, the moment we are born. She saw, but it did not mean anything but a lot of different kinds of brightness." Again, "I asked the patient what he could see; he answered that he saw an extensive field of light, in which everything appeared dull, confused, and in motion. He could not distinguish objects." Another patient saw "nothing but a confusion of forms and colours." When a newly sighted girl saw photographs and paintings, she asked, " 'Why do they put those dark marks all over them?' 'Those aren't dark marks,' her mother explained, 'those are shadows. That is one of the ways the eye knows that things have shape. If it were not for shadows many things would look flat.' 'Well, that's how things do look,' Joan answered. 'Everything looks flat with dark patches.' "

But it is the patients' concepts of space that are most revealing. One patient, according to his doctor, "practiced his vision in a strange fashion; thus he takes off one of his boots, throws it some way off in front of him, and then attempts to gauge the distance at which it lies; he takes a few steps towards the boot and tries to grasp it; on failing to reach it, he moves on a step or two and gropes for the boot until he finally gets hold of it." "But even at this stage, after three weeks' experience of seeing," von Senden goes on, "'space,' as he conceives it, ends with visual space, i.e., with colour-patches that happen to bound his view. He does not yet have the notion that a larger object (a chair) can mask a smaller one (a dog), or that the latter can still be present even though it is not directly seen."

In general the newly sighted see the world as a dazzle of color-patches. They are pleased by the sensation of color, and learn quickly to name the colors, but the rest of seeing is tormentingly difficult. Soon after his operation a patient "generally bumps into one of these colour-patches and observes them to be substantial, since they resist him as tactual objects do. In walking about it also strikes him—or can if he pays attention—that he is continually passing in between the colours he sees, that he can go past a visual object, that a part of it then steadily disappears from view; and that in spite of this, however he twists and turns—whether entering the room from the door, for example, or returning back to it—he always has a visual space in front of him. Thus he gradually comes to realize that there is also a space behind him, which he does not see."

The mental effort involved in these reasonings proves overwhelming for many patients. It oppresses them to realize, if they ever do at all, the tremendous size of the world, which they had previously conceived of as something touchingly manageable. It oppresses them to realize that they have been visible to people all along, perhaps unattractively so, without their knowledge or consent. A disheartening number of them refuse to use their new vision, continuing to go over objects with their tongues, and lapsing into apathy and despair. "The child can see, but will not make use of his sight. Only when pressed can he with difficulty be brought to look at objects in his neighbourhood; but more than a foot away it is impossible to bestir him to the necessary effort." Of a twenty-one-year-old girl, the doctor relates, "Her unfortunate father, who had hoped for so much from this operation, wrote that his daughter carefully shuts her eyes whenever she wishes to go about the house, especially when she comes to a staircase, and that she is never happier or more at ease than when, by closing her eyelids, she relapses into her former state of total blindness." A fifteen-year-old boy, who was also in love with a girl at the asylum for the blind, finally blurted out, "No, really, I can't stand it any more; I want to be sent back to the asylum again. If things aren't altered, I'll tear my eyes out."

Some do learn to see, especially the young ones. But it changes their lives. One doctor comments on "the rapid and complete loss of that striking and wonderful serenity which is characteristic only of those who have never yet seen." A blind man who learns to see is ashamed of his old habits. He dresses up, grooms himself, and tries to make a good impression. While he was blind he was indifferent to objects unless they were edible; now, "a sifting of values sets in . . . his thoughts and wishes are mightily stirred and some few of the patients are thereby led into dissimulation, envy, theft and fraud."

On the other hand, many newly sighted people speak well of the world, and teach us how dull is our own vision. To one patient, a human hand, unrecognized, is "something bright and then holes." Shown a bunch of grapes, a boy calls out, "It is dark, blue and shiny. . . . It isn't smooth, it has bumps and hollows." A little girl visits a garden. "She is greatly astonished, and can scarcely be persuaded to answer, stands speechless in front of the tree, which she only names on taking hold of it, and then as 'the tree with the lights in it.'" Some delight in their sight and give themselves over to the visual world. Of a patient just after her bandages were removed, her doctor writes, "The first things to attract her attention were her own hands; she looked at them very closely, moved them repeatedly to and fro, bent and stretched the fingers, and seemed greatly astonished at the sight." One girl was eager to tell her blind friend that "men do not really look like trees at all," and astounded to discover that her every visitor had an utterly different face. Finally, a twenty-two-year-old girl was dazzled by the world's brightness and kept her eyes shut for two weeks. When at the end of that time she opened her eyes again, she did not recognize any objects, but, "the more she now directed her gaze upon everything about her, the more it could be seen how an expression of gratification and astonishment overspread her features; she repeatedly exclaimed: 'Oh God! How beautiful!'"

I saw color-patches for weeks after I read this wonderful book. It was summer; the peaches were ripe in the valley orchards. When I woke in the morning, color-patches wrapped round my eyes, intricately, leaving not one unfilled spot. All day long I walked among shifting color-patches that parted before me like the Red Sea and closed again in silence, transfigured, whenever I looked back. Some patches swelled and loomed, while others vanished utterly, and dark marks flitted at random over the whole dazzling sweep. But I couldn't sustain the illusion of flatness. I've been around for too long. Form is condemned to an eternal danse macabre with meaning: I couldn't unpeach the peaches. Nor can I remember ever having seen without understanding; the color-patches of infancy are lost. My brain then must have been smooth as any balloon. I'm told I reached for the moon; many babies do. But the color-patches of infancy swelled as meaning filled them; they arrayed themselves in solemn ranks down distances which unrolled and stretched before me like a plain. The moon rocketed away. I live now in a world of shadows that shape and distance color, a world where space makes a kind of terrible sense. What gnosticism is this, and what physics? The fluttering patch I saw in my nursery window—silver and green and shape-shifting blue—is gone; a row of Lombardy poplars takes its place, mute, across the distant lawn. That humming oblong creature pale as light that stole along the walls of my room at night, stretching exhilaratingly around the corners, is gone, too, gone the night I ate of the bittersweet fruit, put two and two together and puckered forever my brain. Martin Buber tells this tale: "Rabbi Mendel once boasted to his teacher Rabbi Elimelekh that evenings he saw the angel who rolls away the light before the darkness, and mornings the angel who rolls away the darkness before the light. 'Yes,' said Rabbi Elimelekh, 'in my youth I saw that too. Later on you don't see these things any more.'"

Why didn't someone hand those newly sighted people paints and brushes from the start, when they still didn't know what anything was? Then maybe we all could see color-patches too, the world unraveled from reason, Eden before Adam gave names. The scales would drop from my eyes; I'd see trees like men walking; I'd run down the road against all orders, hallooing and leaping.

Seeing is of course very much a matter of verbalization. Unless I call my attention to what passes before my eyes, I simply won't see it. It is, as Ruskin says, "not merely unnoticed, but in the full, clear sense of the word, unseen." My eyes alone can't solve analogy tests using figures, the ones which show, with increasing elaborations, a big square, then a small square in a big square, then a big triangle, and expect me to find a small triangle in a big triangle. I have to say the words, describe what I'm seeing. If Tinker Mountain erupted, I'd be likely to notice. But if I want to notice the lesser cataclysms of valley life, I have to maintain in my head a running description of the present. It's not that I'm observant; it's just that I talk too much. Otherwise, especially in a strange place, I'll never know what's happening. Like a blind man at the ball game, I need a radio.

When I see this way I analyze and pry. I hurl over logs and roll away stones; I study the bank a square foot at a time, probing and tilting my head. Some days when a mist covers the mountains, when the muskrats won't show and the microscope's mirror shatters, I want to climb up the blank blue dome as a man would storm the inside of a circus tent, wildly, dangling, and with a steel knife claw a rent in the top, peep, and, if I must, fall.

But there is another kind of seeing that involves a letting go. When I see this way I sway transfixed and emptied. The difference between the two ways of seeing is the difference between walking with and without a camera. When I walk with a camera, I walk from shot to shot, reading the light on a calibrated meter. When I walk without a camera, my own shutter opens, and the moment's light prints on my own silver gut. When I see this second way I am above all an unscrupulous observer.

It was sunny one evening last summer at Tinker Creek; the sun was low in the sky, upstream. I was sitting on the sycamore log bridge with the sunset at my back, watching the shiners the size of minnows who were feeding over the muddy sand in skittery schools. Again and again, one fish, then another turned for a split second across the current and flash! the sun shot out from its silver side. I couldn't watch for it. It was always just happening somewhere else, and it drew my vision just as it disappeared: flash, like a sudden dazzle of the thinnest blade, a sparking over a dun and olive ground at chance intervals from every direction. Then I noticed white specks, some sort of pale petals, small, floating from under my feet on the creek's surface, very slow and steady. So I blurred my eyes and gazed towards the brim of my hat and saw a new world. I saw the pale white circles roll up, roll up, like the world's turning, mute and perfect, and I saw the linear flashes, gleaming silver, like stars being born at random down a rolling scroll of time. Something broke and something opened. I filled up like a new wineskin. I breathed an air like light; I saw a light like water. I was the lip of a fountain the creek filled forever; I was ether, the leaf in the zephyr; I was flesh-flake, feather, bone.

When I see this way I see truly. As Thoreau says, I return to my senses. I am the man who watches the baseball game in silence in an empty stadium. I see the game purely; I'm abstracted and dazed. When it's all over and the white-suited players lope off the green field to their shadowed dugouts, I leap to my feet; I cheer and cheer.

But I can't go out and try to see this way. I'll fail, I'll go mad. All I can do is try to gag the commentator, to hush the noise of useless interior babble that keeps me from seeing just as surely as a newspaper dangled before my eyes. The effort is really a discipline requiring a lifetime of dedicated struggle; it marks the literature of saints and monks of every order East and West, under every rule and no rule, discalced and shod. The world's spiritual geniuses seem to discover universally that the mind's muddy river, this ceaseless flow of trivia and trash, cannot be dammed, and that trying to dam it is a waste of effort that might lead to madness. Instead you must allow the muddy river to flow unheeded in the dim channels of consciousness; you raise your sights; you look along it, mildly, acknowledging its presence without interest and gazing beyond it into the realm of the real where subjects and objects act and rest purely, without utterance. "Launch into the deep," says Jacques Ellul, "and you shall see."

The secret of seeing is, then, the pearl of great price. If I thought he could teach me to find it and keep it forever I would stagger barefoot across a hundred deserts after any lunatic at all. But although the pearl may be found, it may not be sought. The literature of illumination reveals this above all: although it comes to those who wait for it, it is always, even to the most prac-ticed and adept, a gift and a total surprise. I return from one walk knowing where the killdeer nests in the field by the creek and the hour the laurel blooms. I return from the same walk a day later scarcely knowing my own name. Litanies hum in my ears; my tongue flaps in my mouth Ailinon, alleluia! I cannot cause light; the most I can do is try to put myself in the path of its beam. It is possible, in deep space, to sail on solar wind. Light, be it particle or wave, has force: you rig a giant sail and go. The secret of seeing is to sail on solar wind. Hone and spread your spirit till you yourself are a sail, whetted, translucent, broadside to the merest puff.

When her doctor took her bandages off and led her into the garden, the girl who was no longer blind saw "the tree with the lights in it." It was for this tree I searched through the peach orchards of summer, in the forests of fall and down winter and spring for years. Then one day I was walking along Tinker Creek thinking of nothing at all and I saw the tree with the lights in it. I saw the backyard cedar where the mourning doves roost charged and transfigured, each cell buzzing with flame. I stood on the grass with the lights in it, grass that was wholly fire, utterly focused and utterly dreamed. It was less like seeing than like being for the first time seen, knocked breathless by a powerful glance. The flood of fire abated, but I'm still spending the power. Gradually the lights went out in the cedar, the colors died, the cells unflamed and disappeared. I was still ringing. I had been my whole life a bell, and never knew it until at that moment I was lifted and struck. I have since only very rarely seen the tree with the lights in it. The vision comes and goes, mostly goes, but I live for it, for the moment when the mountains open and a new light roars in spate through the crack, and the mountains slam.

Making the Truth Believable
Tracy Kidder

*W*hen I started writing nonfiction a couple of decades ago there was an idea in the air, which for me had the force of a revelation: that all journalism was inevitably subjective. I was in my 20s then, and although my behavior was somewhat worse than it has been recently, I was quite a moralist. I decided that writers of nonfiction had a moral obligation to write in the first person—really write in the first person, making themselves characters on the page. In this way, I would disclose my biases. I would not hide the truth from the reader. I would proclaim that what I wrote was just my own impression of events. In retrospect it seems clear that this prescription for honesty often served as a license for self-absorption on the page. I was too young and self-absorbed to realize what should have been obvious: that I was less likely to write honestly about myself than about anyone else on earth.

I wrote a book about a murder case in a swashbuckling first person. After it was published and disappeared without a trace, I went back to writing nonfiction articles for the *Atlantic Monthly,* under the tutelage of Richard Todd, then a young editor there. For about 5 years, during which I didn't dare attempt another book, I worked on creating what many writer friends of mine call "voice." I didn't do this consciously. If I had, I probably wouldn't have gotten anywhere. But gradually, I think, I found a writing voice, the voice of a person who was informed, fair-minded, and always temperate—the voice, not of the person I was, but of the person I wanted to be. Then I went back to writing books, and discovered other points of view besides the first person.

Choosing a point of view is a matter of finding the best place to stand, from which to tell a story. The process shouldn't be determined by theory, but driven by immersion in the material itself. The choice of point of view, I've come to think, has nothing to do with morality. It's a choice among tools. On the other hand, the wrong choice can lead to dishonesty. Point of view is primary; it affects everything else, including voice. I've made my choices by instinct sometimes and sometimes by experiment. Most of my memories of time spent writing have merged together in a blur, but I remember vividly my first attempts to find a way to write *Among Schoolchildren,* a book about an inner-city teacher. I had spent a year inside her classroom. I intended, vaguely, to fold into my account of events I'd witnessed there a great deal about the lives of particular children and about the problems of education in

America. I tried every point of view that I'd used in previous books, and every page I wrote felt lifeless and remote. Finally, I hit on a restricted third-person narration.

That approach seemed to work. The world of that classroom seemed to come alive when the view of it was restricted mainly to observations of the teacher and to accounts of what the teacher saw and heard and smelled and felt. This choice narrowed my options. I ended up writing something less comprehensive than I'd planned. The book became essentially an account of a year in the emotional life of a schoolteacher.

My choice of the restricted third person also obliged me to write parts of the book as if from within the teacher's mind. I wrote many sentences that contained the phrase "she thought." I felt I could do so because the teacher had told me how she felt and what she thought about almost every thing that happened in her classroom. And her descriptions of her thoughts and feeling never seemed self-serving. Believing in them myself, I thought that I could make them believable on the page.

For me, part of the pleasure of reading comes from the awareness that an author stands behind the scenes adroitly pulling the strings. But the pleasure quickly palls at painful reminders of that presence—the times when, for instance, I sense that the author strains to produce yet another clever metaphor. Then I stop believing in what I read, and usually stop reading. Belief is what a reader offers an author, what Coleridge famously called "That willing suspension of disbelief for the moment, which constitutes poetic faith." All writers have to find ways to do their work without disappointing readers into withdrawing belief.

In fiction, believability may have nothing to do with reality or even plausibility. In nonfiction it has everything to do with those things.

I think that the nonfiction writer's fundamental job is to make what is true believable. But for some writers lately the job has clearly become more varied: to make believable what the writer thinks is true (if the writer wants to be scrupulous); to make believable what the writer wishes were true (if the writer isn't interested in scrupulosity); or to make believable what the writer thinks might be true (if the writer couldn't get the story and had to make it up).

I figure that if I call a piece of my own writing nonfiction it ought to be about real people, with their real names attached whenever possible, who say and do in print nothing that they didn't actually say and do. On the cover page of my new book I put a note that reads, "This is a work of nonfiction," and I listed the several names that I was obliged to change in the text. I feared that a longer note would stand between the reader and the spell that I wanted to create, inviting the reader into the world of a nursing home. But the definition of "nonfiction" has become so slippery that I wonder if I shouldn't have written more. So now I'll take this opportunity to explain that I spent a year doing research, that the name of the place I wrote about is its real name, that I didn't change the names of any major characters, and that I didn't invent dialogue or put any thoughts in characters minds that the characters themselves didn't confess to.

I no longer care what rules other writers set for themselves. If I don't like what someone has written, I can stop reading, which is, after all, the worst punishment a writer can suffer. But the expanded definitions of "nonfiction" have created problems for those writers who define the term narrowly. Many readers now view with suspicion every narrative that claims to be nonfiction. But not all writers make up their stories or the details in them. In fact, scores of very good writers do not—writers such as John McPhee (*Coming into the Country*), Jane Kramer (*The Last Cowboy*), J. Anthony Lukas (*Common Ground*). There are also special cases, which confound categories and all attempts to lay down rules for narrative. I have in mind especially Norman Mailer's *Executioner's Song*, a hybrid of fact and fiction, labeled as such, which I loved reading.

Most writers lack Mailer's powers of invention. Some nonfiction writers do not lack his willingness to invent, but the candor to admit it. Some writers proceed by trying to discover the truth about a situation, and then invent the facts as necessary. Even in these suspicious times, a writer can get away with this. Often no one will know, and the subjects of the story may not care. They may approve. They may not notice. But the writer always knows. I believe in immersion in the events of a story. I take it on faith that the truth lies in the events somewhere, and that immersion in those real events will yield glimpses of that truth. I try to hew to a narrow definition of nonfiction partly in that faith and partly out of fear. I'm afraid that if I started making things up in a story that purported to be about real events and people, I'd stop believing it myself. And I imagine that such a loss of conviction would infect every sentence and make each one unbelievable.

I don't mean to imply that all a person has to do to write good nonfiction is to take accurate notes and reproduce them. The kind of nonfiction I like to read is at bottom storytelling, as gracefully accomplished as good fiction. I don't think any technique should be ruled out to achieve it well. For myself, I rule out only invention. But I don't think that honesty and artifice are contradictory. They work together in good writing of every sort. Artfulness and an author's justified belief in a story can produce the most believable nonfiction.

Toward a Definition of Creative Nonfiction
Bret Lott

The Reverend Francis Kilvert, an English curate in the Welsh Border region, kept a journal of his life—where he went, what he did, what he dreamt, who he knew, and what he thought—from 1870 to 1879. In the journal he wrote, "Why do I keep this voluminous journal! I can hardly tell. Partly because life appears to me such a curious and wonderful thing that it almost seems a pity that even such a humble and uneventful life as mine should pass altogether away without some record such as this." *Kilvert's Diary*, published in 1941 and reprinted in 1960, serves as a beautiful, moving, and genuine glimpse into country life of that time nonetheless. All well and good, but how does it help define what creative nonfiction is?

That passage serves, I hold, to illuminate as best as any passage from any piece of literature I can find the longing each of us carries, or ought to carry, in our hearts as human beings first, and as writers second. Creative nonfiction is, in one form or another, for better and worse, in triumph and failure, the attempt to keep from passing altogether away the lives we have lived.

And though that may sound like a definitive pronouncement on what creative nonfiction is, I mean what I say in giving this essay the title it has: *Toward a Definition of Creative Nonfiction*. We aren't going to arrive anywhere here. We can no more understand what creative nonfiction is by trying to define it than we can learn how to ride a bike by looking at a bicycle tire, a set of handlebars, the bicycle chain itself. Sure, we'll have something of an idea, maybe a glimpse into the importance of finding your balance when we look at how narrow those tires are. But until we get on that thing and try to steer it with this weirdly twisted metal tube and actually try to synchronize pushing down on the pedals and pushing forward at the same time, we won't have a clue.

Any definition of true worth to you as a writer will and must come to you experientially. What creative nonfiction is will reveal itself to you only at the back end of things, once you have written it. Kilvert wrote his journal in the midst of his life, looking back at what had happened that day, trying to piece together the meaning of his life from the shards of it, however exquisitely beautiful or sharply painful they were. It was the piecing together of it that mattered, and that matters to us here, today.

And because we are human beings, as such we are pattern makers, a species desirous of order, no matter how much we as "artists" may masquerade otherwise. Yet looking back at our lives to find that order—and here is the sticky part—must *not* be an effort to reorder our lives as we want them to be seen; rather, we are after, in creative nonfiction, an understanding of what it is that has happened, and in that way to see order, however chaotic it may be.

Frank O'Connor, arguably the most important and influential short story writer of this century, wrote in a letter to a friend, " . . . there are occasions when we all feel guilt and remorse; we all want to turn back time. But even if we were able, things would go in precisely the same way, because the mistakes we make are not in our judgments but in our natures. It is only when we do violence to our natures that we are justified in our regrets. . . . We are what we are, and within our limitations we have made our own efforts. They seem puny in the light of eternity, but they didn't at the time, and they weren't."

It is in creative nonfiction we try to divine from what we have done, who we have known, what we have dreamt and how we have failed, an order to our lives. "The test of a first-rate intelligence," F. Scott Fitzgerald wrote in his landmark essay "The Crack-Up," "is the ability to hold two opposed ideas in the mind at the same time, and still retain the ability to function." The two opposed ideas of creative nonfiction are finding order in chaos without reforming chaos into order; retaining the ability to function is the act of writing all this down for someone else to understand.

So let's begin with just that much: a desire not to let slip altogether away our lives as we have known them, and to put an order—again, for better and worse—to our days.

Creative nonfiction can take any form, from the letter to the list, from the biography to the memoir, from the journal to the obituary. When I say we are trying to find order in what has happened, I do *not* mean creative nonfiction is simply writing about what happened to me. Rather, it is writing about oneself *in relation to* the subject at hand. A book review is creative nonfiction in that it is a written record of the reviewer *in relation to* the book in question; John Krakauer's fantastic book *Into the Wild* is a biography of an idealistic young man, Chris McCandless, who upon graduation from college disappeared into the wild, his decomposed body found four months later in an abandoned bus in the Alaskan wilderness. The biography becomes creative nonfiction as the author increasingly identifies himself with the young man, increasingly recognizing in the stupidity of the boy's folly his own reckless self—Krakauer sees himself *in relation to* the subject at hand: the death of Chris McCandless. This essay itself is a form of creative nonfiction in that it is my attempt at defining an abstract through the smallest of apertures: my own experience *in relation to* creative nonfiction. So creative nonfiction is not solely, What happened to me today, and why is it important?

Creative nonfiction can be and often is a euphemism for the personal essay, and my earlier assertion that creative nonfiction's being understood only through its being written is borne out rather handily in the meaning of the word *essay* itself.

The French word *essai* means to attempt something, to give something a trial run, to test. Michel de Montaigne, considered the writer who identified if not invented the form, was the first to use the word *essai* to describe his writings, the first collection of which was entitled strangely enough *Essais,* and which was written between 1572 and 1574. This notion of the attempt, of testing one's words lined up in an order one deems close enough to reveal a personal understanding so that all may have that same understanding is, and will always be, only an attempt. The essay as trial run is inherent to any definition of creative nonfiction; you will only come to know this form by running your own tests.

Montaigne, a landowner and lawyer from a nominally wealthy family in the Perigord region of France, wrote out of his own interests, but wrote convinced that it was his own interest as a human being in a matter or topic at hand that made his attempts universal: "Each man bears the entire form of man's estate," he wrote, and therefore, he reasoned, what he was attempting to render in words might make his attempts of interest to all. Philip Lopate, in his indispensable anthology *The Art of the Personal Essay,* writes, "What Montaigne tells us about himself is peculiarly, charmingly specific and daily: he is on the short side, has a loud, abrasive voice, suffers from painful kidney stones, scratches his ears a lot (the insides itch), loves sauces, is not sure radishes agree with him, does his best thinking on horseback, prefers glass to metal cups, moves his bowels regularly in the morning, and so on. It is as if the self were a new continent, and Montaigne its first explorer."

The self as continent, and you its first explorer: another definition of creative nonfiction. For self, however at the center of what you are writing or however tangential, must inform the heart of the tale you are telling. It is indeed *self* that is the *creative* element of creative nonfiction. Without you and who you are, a piece of writing that tells what happened is simply nonfiction: a police report. But when I begin to incorporate the sad and glorious fact that the way I see it shapes and forms what it is to be seen, I end up with creative nonfiction.

As a kind of sidebar, I'd like to interject here the fact that one doesn't have to have had a bizarre life before that life becomes worthy of writing about. Contrary to popular belief, that belief borne out by even the most cursory look at the lineup of victim-authors on afternoon and morning TV talk shows and evening newsmagazines, one's life needn't have been wracked by incest or murder or poorly executed plastic surgery to be worthy of examination. Which is, of course, not to say that those lives are not worth writing about. They most certainly are. But E. B. White's words from the introduction to his *Letters of E .B. White* speak as eloquently as I have seen to this matter of whether or not one's life has been miserable enough to record: "If an unhappy childhood is indispensable for a writer, I am ill-equipped: I missed out on all that and was neither deprived nor unloved. It would be inaccurate, however, to say that my childhood was untroubled. The normal fears and worries of every child were in me developed to a high degree; every day was an awesome prospect. I was uneasy about practically everything: the uncertainty of the future, the dark of the attic, the panoply and discipline of school, the transitoriness of life, the mystery of the church and of God, the frailty of the body, the sadness of afternoon, the shadow of sex, the distant challenge of love and marriage, the far-off problem of a livelihood."

These normal fears, if we have been paying the least bit of attention to our lives, inform us all; and if E. B. White, who is the greatest American essayist of this century, found in that uneasiness the material for a lifetime, we too have all we need.

But *how* do we look at ourselves in order best to inform our readers that who we are matters, and is worthy of their attention? In the Tyndale commentary on the Book of Proverbs, Derek Kidner writes that the sayings and aphorisms of King Solomon, and to a lesser degree Lemuel and Agur, constitute "not a portrait album of a book of manners: [the Book of Proverbs] offers a key to life. The samples of behavior which it holds up to view are all assessed by one criterion, which could be summed up in the question, 'Is this wisdom, or is this folly?'" I believe that this same criterion is one that helps define creative nonfiction as well. In examining the self as continent, in seeing the way self shades and informs the meaning of what has happened, the writer must be inquiring of himself, Is this wisdom, or is this folly? The self as inquisitor of self is integral to an examination of one's life; it calls for a kind of ruthlessness about seeing oneself in relation to others: Why did I do that? What was I thinking? Who was I trying to kid? What did I hope to achieve? These questions must be asked, and asked with all the candor and courage and objectivity one can muster, though objectivity is an abstract to be hoped for, and not to be achieved; it is, after all, *you* who is writing about you.

Which brings me to another major point on our way toward a definition: creative nonfiction cannot at any time be self-serving. There is no room here for grandstanding of oneself. To my way of thinking—and this is me speaking as a follower of Christ, and therefore one well aware of my transgressions, my iniquities, my falling short of the glory of God—ninety-nine times out of a hundred the answer to the question, Is this wisdom, or is this folly? is, Folly. Hands down.

Phillip Lopate writes, "The enemy of the personal essay is self-righteousness, not just because it is tiresome and ugly in itself, but because it slows down the dialectic of self-questioning. . . . The essayist is someone who lives with the guilty knowledge that he is 'prejudiced' (Mencken called his essay collections *Prejudices*) and has a strong predisposition for or against certain everyday phenomena. It then becomes his business to attend to these inner signals, these stomach growls, these seemingly indefensible intuitions, and try to analyze what lies underneath them, the better to judge them."

So, our definition thus far: a desire not to let slip altogether away our lives as we have known them; to put an order, for better and worse, to our days; this is only a test; the self as continent, you its first explorer; is this wisdom, or is this folly?; no self-righteousness.

This last point, however, seems at odds with the entire notion of the personal essay, all this business about me: isn't talk about myself in relation to others by definition egotistical? Wasn't I taught in seventh grade never to include "I" in an essay? Who cares about what I think in the first place?

Thoreau, in answer to this assertion we have had pounded into our heads most of our lives, wrote in the opening of *Walden*, "In most books the I, or first person, is omitted; in this it will be retained; that, in respect to egotism, is the main difference. We commonly do not remember that it is, after all, always the first person that is speaking." And if one is honestly seeking to understand, circling with a cold eye one's relation to events, places, people—whatever the subject of the essay—then that search's chances of being construed as egotistical will be dismissed. Seventeenth-century English writer Alexander Smith wrote, "The speaking about one self is not necessarily offensive. A modest, truthful man speaks better about himself than about anything else, and on that subject his speech is likely to be most profitable to his hearers. . . . If he be without taint of boastfulness, of self-sufficiency, of hungry vanity, the world will not press the charge home."

Another element of any definition of creative nonfiction must include the form's circling bent, its way of looking again and again at itself from all angles in order to see itself most fully. The result is literary triangulation, a finding of the subject in a three-dimensional grid through digression, full-frontal assault, guerrilla tactics and humble servitude, all in an effort, simply, to see. The creative nonfiction form attempts in whatever way it can to grab hold hard and sure its subject in any manner possible. Eudora Welty writes in *One Writer's Beginnings*, "In writing, as in life, the connections of all sorts of relationships and kinds lie in wait of discovery, and give out their signals to the Geiger counter of the charged imagination, once it is drawn into the right field. . . . What I do make my stories out of is the whole fund of my feelings, my responses to the real experiences of my own life, to the relationships that formed and changed it, that I have given most of myself to, and so learned my way toward a dramatic counterpart." The dramatic counterpart of which she here writes is, of course, her stories—fiction—but I maintain that this "whole fund" of feelings, the complete range of our responses to our own real experiences, must inform creative nonfiction as well. Only when we use our "whole fund" can we circle our subjects in the most complete way, wringing from our stores of knowledge and wisdom and the attendant recognition of how little we have of both—*the essence of who we are*—then coupling those recognitions with what in fact we do not know altogether, will we find what we have come looking for: ourselves and, by grace and by luck, the larger world perhaps we hadn't seen before.

Lopate writes, "The personal essay is the reverse of that set of Chinese boxes that you keep opening, only to find a smaller one within. Here you start with the small—the package of flaws and limits—and suddenly find a slightly larger container, insulated by the essay's successful articulation and the writer's self-knowledge."

284 PART IV ANTHOLOGY

I agree with Lopate in how the essay reveals larger and larger selves in itself, but rather than the Chinese box, the image that comes to my mind is that of the Russian nesting dolls, one person inside another inside another. But instead of finding smaller selves inside the self, the opposite occurs, as with Lopate's boxes: we find nested inside that smallest of selves a larger self, and a larger inside that, until we come to the whole of humanity within our own hearts.

Now back to our definition: a desire not to let slip altogether away our life as we have known it; to put an order, for better and worse, to our days; this is only a test; the self as continent, you its first explorer; is this wisdom, or is this folly?; no self-righteousness, though it is always the first person talking; circle the subject to see it most whole.

I'm saving perhaps the most conundrum-like element for nearly last. What role, we have to ask once all these prior elements are taken into account, does *truth* have here? If you look at the pieces of our definition thus far, each one contains within it the angle of perception: the fact that it is only me who is seeing. That is, I don't want to let slip away my life as I have seen it, but who is to say I am telling the truth? In my attempt to put order to my days, am I deluding myself, inflicting an order that was and is now nowhere to be seen? If this is only a test, who is to say I pass? If I am the explorer of my self as continent, what does my discovery matter—didn't Leif Erikson set up shop in North America 500 years before Columbus discovered the place? Isn't one man's wisdom another man's folly? How do I know if I'm not being self-righteous unless there's somebody outside myself to cut me down to size? In circling my subject, isn't it me who determines my course, my longitude and latitude, and therefore am I, by definition, being the most subjective of anyone on planet earth when it comes to my subject?

The answer to each and every one of these questions is: continue to question. Only through rigorous and ruthless questioning of the self can we hope to arrive at any kind of truth.

If you wish to understand creative nonfiction, hope to find a definition, then it is up to you to embrace the fact that, as Montaigne saw, "Each man bears the entire form of man's estate." Inherent to that form are the eccentricities, egotism, foolishness, and fraud of all mankind; inherent as well are the wisdom and self-recognition, the worth and value and merit available to mankind, once enough scouring of what we know and do not know has taken place. V. S. Pritchett, in his memoir *Midnight Oil*, wrote, "The true autobiography of this egotist is exposed in all its intimate foliage in his work. But there is a period when a writer has not yet become one, or, just having become one, is struggling to form his talent, and it is from this period that I have selected most of the scenes and people in this book. It *is* a selection, and it is neither a confession nor a volume of literary reminiscences, but as far as I am able I have put in my 'truth.'"

Pritchett puts the word *truth* in quotation marks; he predicates it with the possessive pronoun *my*. We must recognize that this is the deepest truth we can hope to attain on our own: quotation marks, calling it our own. Only when we have scoured as clean as possible by self-inquiry, even interrogation, what we *perceive,* can we approach calling it *truth*; and even then that crutch of the quotation marks and the assignation of who it belongs to—me—must be acknowledged.

Finally, we have to try and further illuminate *why* we write creative nonfiction. Certainly that first element—a desire not to let slip altogether away our lives as we have known them—is a beginning point, but simply trying to capture our lives before they slip away seems more *reactive* than *proactive.* Writing is, I believe, both, and so any definition must encompass both the reactive and the proactive.

Karen Blixen, AKA Isak Dinesen, in a dinner meeting speech she gave in 1959 at the National Institute of Arts and Letters in New York, addressed the subject, "On Mottoes of My Life." In it she said, "The family of Finch Hatton, of England, have on their crest the device *Je responderay,* 'I will answer.' . . . I liked it so much I asked Denys . . . if I might have it for my own. He generously made me a present of it and even had a seal cut for me, with the words carved on it. The device was meaningful and dear to me for many reasons, two in particular. The first . . . was its high evaluation of the idea of the answer in itself. For an answer is a rarer thing than is generally imagined. There are many highly intelligent people who have no answer at all in them. . . . Secondly, I liked the Finch Hatton device for its ethical content. I will answer *for* what I say or do; I will answer *to* the impression I make. I will be responsible."

This is the proactive element of creative nonfiction, and the final element of my *essai* to define creative writing: *our responsibility as human beings to answer for and to our lives.* It is a responsibility that must encompass all the elements laid out in all this talk about definitions; it is a responsibility that must be woven through the recognition of the fleeting nature of this span of days we have been given, woven through our attempt to see order in chaos, through our understanding that we are only attempting this test and through our being the first explorers of the continent of ourselves. This responsibility to answer for and to ourselves must be woven through the interrogation of self as to whether this is folly or wisdom, through the pledge to humility and to avoiding the abyss of self-righteousness, through the recognition that it is always and only me—the first person—talking, and through the relentless circling of the subject to see it most completely. And this responsibility to answer for and to ourselves must be woven through our recognition that the only truth I can hope to approach will finally and always and only be *my truth.*

But if we are rigorous enough, fearless enough, and humble enough to attempt this responsibility, this way of seeing—for creative nonfiction, like fiction, like poetry, is simply and complexly a way of seeing—the rewards we will reap will be great: we will *understand.* To understand, and nothing more, and that is everything.

Memoir? Fiction? Where's the Line?

Mimi Schwartz

"It was very cold the night my mother died . . ."
> —Anna Quindlen

I don't remember what my second grade teacher wore! How can I recall the dialogue when my Dad left 10 years ago? All my summers in Maine blur together. That's what my students will say tomorrow when I return their first efforts at turning memories into memoir. They are mostly 21- and 22-year-old college seniors, plus a few retirees and second careerists, all eager to explore their lives on paper for themselves, friends and the world. No one is famous, although one woman said she won the lottery.

The memory worries will come mainly from marine biologists, psychology and history majors who deal in term papers and lab reports, rarely from poets and fiction writers who have taken enough creative writing workshops to understand, as V. S. Pritchett once wrote about memoir, "It's all in the art. You get no credit for living."

Some of these "creative" writers assume such advice excludes their boring lives, and so I have written "Great detail!" in many margins of first essays only to find out that the date rape or house burning down didn't happen. No, no, you can't do that, I say. That's fiction, not memoir. You have to play by the rules; there's a line you can't cross. And where is that? they ask. I don't know, only that if you make up too much, you've crossed it. The murkiness makes writer Anna Quindlen choose fiction over memoir. In "How Dark? How Stormy? I Can't Recall!" (*New York Times Book Review*), she says that the newspaper reporter in her made her check old weather charts before she could publish the line, "It was very cold the night my mother died." Like my fact-conscious students, she worries: "Was it very cold or was that just the trick memory played on a girl who was sick and shivering, at least metaphorically?" and this worry, combined with a lousy memory, makes Quindlen avoid memoir, "a terrain too murky for me to tread." She says she can't, like Frank McCourt in *Angela's Ashes*, "remember half a century later the raw, itching sore that erupted between his eyebrows when he was a boy." So she writes fiction, preferring to create a world "from the ground up, the imagined minutiae of the lives of characters I invent from my knowledge of characters."

"But what about your *true* stories?" I would ask, if Anna were in my class. Don't you tell your friends, family, especially your children, about who you were, who your family was once upon a time? And do you want those stories to last more than one minute? If we stick only to facts, our past is as skeletal as black-and-white line drawings in a coloring book. We must color it in.

I tell the Annas in my class what I tell myself as memoir writer: Go for the emotional truth, that's what matters. Yes, gather the facts by all means. Look at old photos, return to old places, ask family members what they remember, look up time-line books for the correct songs and fashion styles, read old newspapers, encyclopedias, whatever—and then use the imagination to fill in the remembered experience. You don't need a tape recording of what your parents said to "remember" what they said that day. You don't need a photo of your kindergarten teacher to describe her; the clothes you imagine will match your feeling about her. Maybe you see a red, mini-suited girl; maybe you see a woman in a thick, long black dress with white cuffs. Either way, we see the teacher as you saw her. And who knows? She might even have worn those white cuffs! The subconscious is remembering.

That's also what I told my mother last week when she called to tell me that an essay I'd sent her about my love affair with horses was wrong. "I picked you up that day you fell off that horse, Sultan."

"You did not. I still remember everyone staring because my pants were ripped, my knee all bloody on the bus ride home."

"You were crying in the Pontiac."

"I was not."

It was her memory against mine with no one else to ask, so I wasn't changing my story. It was true for me—the humiliation following my glory riding Sultan—and she could tell her version, I said. That's what Rosemary Wolff threatened when her two sons, Geoffrey and Tobias, wrote separate and conflicting memoirs of their youth. (Or so Geoffrey Wolff said once in a workshop I took in Aspen.)

How subjective can you be in memoir, accidentally or on purpose? That is a central question, and different writers have different solutions. I teach the possibilities. You might start with a disclaimer the way John Irving did in "Trying to Save Piggy Sneed." He warns readers up front to "Please remember that all memoir is fiction," and then tells a wonderful story about how a retarded garbage man started him on his career as a writer. You might hint a disclaimer in your title, as Mary Carr does in *The Liar's Club*, and leave the reader wondering. You might tip off the reader with phrases such as "I imagine her . . ." or "Perhaps he said . . .", the way Jane Bernstein does in her retelling of her sister's murder 2,000 miles away and 20 years before. You might use exaggeration as Russell Baker does in *Growing Up*, so that the dialogue of his interview to become a paperboy sounds as if he were being interviewed to head up IBM.

You might even give a lament that you don't remember, as Bret Lott does in his book *Fathers, Sons, and Brothers,* before he gives a rich description of the morning that his son stopped calling him Mommy:

> The sad thing, though, is that I can't recall the first day he called me Daddy when I went into his room. I could make up a story about it, here and now; I could tell you how it was on a Tuesday—Melanie's morning—and how there seemed something different in his voice as I came up from sleep.

Whatever else, there's always Joan Didion's wonderful permission in "On Reading a Notebook"—that if you remember it, it's true. I use it often.

> Perhaps it never did snow that August in Vermont; perhaps there never were flurries in the night wind, and maybe no one else felt the ground hardening and summer already dead even as we pretended to bask in it, but that was how it felt to me, and it might as well have snowed, could have snowed, did snow.

How it felt to me! What a relief to memoir writers who want to explore the emotional truth of memory. It may be "murky terrain," you may cross the line into fiction and have to step back reluctantly into what really happened—the struggle creates the tension that makes memoir either powerfully true or hopelessly phony. The challenge of this genre is that it hands you characters, plot and setting, and says, "Go figure them out!"—using fact, memory and imagination to recreate the complexity of real moments, big and small, with no invented rapes or houses burning down. If the challenge intrigues you, imaginatively and emotionally, and you find the right voice—one savvy and appealing enough to make the reader say, "Yes. I've been there. I know what you mean!"—you have something good. But if the voice you adopt annoys, embarrasses or bores because of lack of insight, then beware. The reader will say, "So what? I don't care about you!" often in anger.[1]

It's that personal, the judgment. It's YOU, not some anonymous character they are talking about. Like a smile at a cocktail party, the voice of memoir—far more than in fiction—can evoke a quick response. Phony or real. I like this person. I hate this person. Nothing lukewarm or impersonal about it.

That vulnerability—more than a bad memory, I suspect—makes many agree with writer Pam Houston: "I write fiction to tell the truth." The seeming

---

[1] James Woolcott's recent article, "Me, Myself and I," in *Vanity Fair* is a good example of that anger. He attacks Anne Roiphe as "the true queen of the daytime soaps," creative nonfiction as "civic journalism for the soul," and others like Laurie Stone as "navel gazers"—as if the person, genre and subject ("no detail is too mundane to share") and not the art sinks the "I" of true stories.

anonymity of fiction, even autobiographical fiction, can be creatively freeing, as Jamaica Kincaid shows in *Annie John*. She makes her real-life, older brothers disappear so that the emotional focus is on a girl and her mother, and she calls the story fiction—even though other basics are true. (Kincaid, like the main character, Annie, grew up on the island of Antigua and left at 17.) But if your story is really about Mom in Iowa, why turn her into a half-sister in New York—unless in the transformation, you, like Kincaid, tap into the real story you need to tell?

One essay, out of the 25 I just finished reading, does hook me with its savvy. This young woman of 22, Nicole Ross, already knows what it has taken me years to figure out: that the ambiguity of memoir, its shifting planes of truth and memory, can take you somewhere important:

> I want to remember a childhood brimming with sunlight, with just enough suffering to make it seem real. Each Christmas becomes bleaker than the last; it always seems as if there are fewer presents under the tree, and less laughter as my grandparents grow older. Ironically, the Christmases of my childhood have become lavish feasts of endless caroling because I don't remember them any more. I think that my collection of memories is nothing more than a soothing deception; many details have been supplied by a fertile imagination. It can't be all bad, though, because my parents still smile at me the way they do in my memories of those early Christmases.

Unlike Anna, Nicole is comfortable with how memory, fact and imagination mix up her Christmases; she trusts the process. I wrote "Great!" in every margin of her six pages. I believed every word, heard the caroling, saw her parents smile.

There *is* one reason not to write memoir, aside from worries about memory and the restraints on creative freedom: Mom may not speak to you again if you write her story, and you care. Frank McCourt waited to publish his memoir until after his mother died because he didn't want to hurt her. Others don't wait and call their story fiction, so they can tell Mom, family, friends, anyone real who appears on the page: "Of course that isn't you. I made that part up." No one is fooled, but you save face, maybe a lawsuit.

A writer does have some fictive leeway even in memoir, I believe—*if* you are cautious (and not too famous). Tomorrow I will tell the student who wrote about her bulimic roommate that her profile could be just as powerful and less hurtful if she moved the girl next door, changed her hair color and did not call her Kimmie.[2] I will tell the class that in a memoir about six months in my

---

[2] This anonymity is essential if, like me, you have students share their work in progress in class. Why should the roommate's problems become public knowledge?

marriage, I made a few composite characters of minor characters and wrote this disclaimer in my introduction: "The story is 90 percent factual; the rest is made up to protect those who didn't ask to be in this book." The problem was not my husband and my children (I was willing to take my chances with them); it was my friends, like the one who was leaving her husband just as I was deciding to stay with mine. In fact, I had three friends who were thinking about divorce, so in the book, I made a composite character and we met for cappuccino.

Depending on the story's focus, you sometimes collapse time and characters as well, I will tell my students, and still are "true" on my truth scale. Writer Jack Connor, in a personal essay about a weekend of watching eagles, collapsed three days into one morning and mentioned only two of the four students who accompanied him on that trip. He wanted to capture how young people reawakened in him the simple pleasure of birding even in a mid-January freeze, and the number of days, the number of people, didn't matter—although in a scientific field report they would. I will show my students how his original journal entry of facts and private observations evolved many drafts later into a published story ("A Lesson from Mott's Creek") with a voice and a point of view.

Journal Entry:

1/11/94   —eagle weekend—
one of the best birding experiences of the last year this weekend—
the eagle survey with Jerry Liguori, Brian Sullivan, two folks from Ocean City (mcdermotts?), and on Sunday with Joe Mangion and Bil Seng.
. . . both days cold—and windy. temp in teens, with wind chill, probably below 10, maybe even bordering on zero. but blue sky, growing cloudy on saturday around one and then mostly cloudy. Sunday, blue until 2 or so and only partly cloudy after that.

Essay Opening:

Binoculars in my fingers, tears in my eyes from the January glare, face stiff from the hard wind, I am standing between Brian Sullivan and Jerry Liguori and wonder, "Why don't I come out here every single day?

I will also tell my students about a friend who is writing about her aunt who had a lobotomy 50 years ago. My friend visited the mental institution where it happened, looked up records, talked to a nurse and doctor who remembered her aunt and tried writing what her aunt's life was like. But those "facts" weren't enough to recreate the story. She must take an imaginative leap, our writing group told her, imagine herself as her aunt and what would it feel like, maybe write in first person. Draft in hand, my friend can then check with a psychiatrist—"Does this ring true?"—and with relatives, before revising for more accuracy.

The Joan Didions and John Irvings in tomorrow's class will nod their heads in agreement. The Anna Quindlens will not. They want clear-cut boundaries and would side with my writer friend, Andrea Herrmann, who warns me: "If the writer can make a composite character, what prevents her from making up scenes, blending parts of places together, switching historical time frames?" Making up anything, for them, is crossing the line into fiction and should be called that. But I disagree. If the main plot, characters, and setting are true, if the intent is to make honest sense of "how it felt to me" and tell that true story well (with disclaimers as needed), it's memoir to me.

In "Why Memoir Now?" Vivian Gornick writes, "What happened to the writer is not what matters; what matters is the larger sense that the writer is able to make of what happened. For that the power of a writing imagination is required." Use that imagination in memoir, I tell myself and my students, to find the language and complexity of real lives, not imagined ones. It's OK to trust yourself (with a bit of Quindlen's and Herrmann's wariness)—even if you can't remember the temperature on the night Mom died.

Notes on the Authors

Jane Armstrong's work has appeared in *Newsweek, The North American Review,* the *Beloit Fiction Journal,* and elsewhere. She is an assistant editor for *The Mississippi Review.*

James Baldwin was a distinguished novelist, essayist, and playwright. He was the author of the novel *Go Tell It on the Mountain,* as well as nonfiction books, including *The Fire Next Time* and *Notes of a Native Son.* Baldwin is considered one of the principal literary voices informing the civil rights struggles of the 1950s and 1960s.

Jo Ann Beard is the author of *The Boys of My Youth.* Her work has appeared in *The New Yorker, Story,* and many other magazines.

Norma Elia Cantú, author of *Canícula: Snapshots of a Girlhood en la Frontera,* is a recognized expert in the fields of Chicana/o and Latina/o literature, folklore, and borderland studies.

Judith Ortiz Cofer is the author of *Silent Dancing* and *Woman in Front of the Sun: On Becoming a Writer.* Born in Puerto Rico, she is an accomplished novelist, poet, and essayist.

Joan Didion is the author of *The White Album, Slouching Toward Bethlehem,* and numerous other books of fiction and nonfiction. Didion has also written numerous screenplays and contributes to *The New Yorker* and *The New York Review of Books.*

Annie Dillard is the author of *The Living, An American Childhood,* and many other books. Her memoir, *Pilgrim at Tinker Creek,* won the Pulitzer Prize for nonfiction in 1975.

Brian Doyle is author of *The Wet Engine: Exploring the Mad Wild Miracle of the Heart* and *Leaping: Revelations & Epiphanies.* He is editor of *Portland Magazine.*

Laurie Lynn Drummond's short story collection, *Anything You Say Can and Will Be Used Against You,* was a finalist for the 2005 PEN/Hemingway Award. Her work has appeared in *Story, The Southern Review, Fiction,* and *Creative Nonfiction.*

Tony Earley is the author of *Somehow Form a Family: Stories That Are Mostly True*, as well as a novel and a book of stories. He has twice been included in the notable anthology *Best American Short Stories*.

James Galvin is the author of *The Meadow* as well as numerous books of poetry. Galvin lives in Laramie, Wyoming, where he works as a rancher part of each year, and also in Iowa City.

Henry Louis Gates is the author of *Thirteen Ways of Looking at a Black Man*, *America Behind the Color Line: Dialogues with African Americans*, and many other books. A noted African-American scholar, Gates is the chair of Harvard's African and African American Studies program.

Philip Gerard is the author of *Writing a Book that Makes a Difference* and *Secret Soldiers: The Story of World War II's Heroic Army of Deception*. His work has appeared in numerous magazines and his radio essays are heard regularly on National Public Radio's *All Things Considered*.

Lucy Grealy authored *Autobiography of a Face* and *As Seen on TV*. After a lifelong struggle with facial bone cancer (Ewing's sarcoma), Grealy died in 2002.

Lee Gutkind is the author of *Forever Fat: Essays by the Godfather*, *The Veterinarian's Touch: Profiles of Life among Animals*, and more than a dozen other books. He is also founder and editor of the acclaimed journal *Creative Nonfiction*.

Robin Hemley is a novelist, short story writer, and essayist. His books include *Nola: A Memoir of Faith, Art, and Madness* and *Invented Eden: The Elusive, Disputed History of the Tasaday*.

Edward Hoagland has written nearly twenty books, including *Walking the Dead Diamond River*, *African Calliope*, and *The Tugman's Passage*. Hoagland is considered one of the finest contemporary American essayists, especially for his nature and travel writing.

Art Homer is author of the memoir *The Drownt Boy: An Ozark Tale*, as well as poetry collections, including *Skies of Such Valuable Glass*.

Pico Iyer's books include *Sun After Dark: Flights into the Foreign*, *Falling Off the Map*, and *The Global Soul*. Iyer works as a freelance journalist, and has contributed to publications such as *Time* magazine, *Harper's*, *Conde Nast Traveler*, and *The New York Review of Books*.

Lori Jakiela is author of the memoir *Miss New York Has Everything*. Her work has appeared in various newspapers and literary magazines, including *Doubletake*, *River Styx*, *Nerve Cowboy*, *Pittsburgh City Paper*, and *In Pittsburgh*.

Tracy Kidder is the author of numerous books, including *House, Among Schoolchildren,* and *Home Town. The Soul of a New Machine*—a book celebrated for its insight into the world of corporate, high-technology America—earned him a Pulitzer and a National Book Award in 1982.

Jamaica Kincaid's most recent work is the novel *The Autobiography of My Mother.* Her first three books—*At the Bottom of the River, Annie John,* and *A Small Place*—focus on life in her birthplace, Antigua, West Indies.

Sonja Livingston's essays have appeared in *The Iowa Review, Alaska Quarterly Review, Gulf Coast, Blue Mesa Review, Puerto del Sol, Apalachee Review,* and *Short Takes,* an anthology of brief nonfiction.

Bret Lott is author of the novels *The Man Who Owned Vermont, A Stranger's House, Jewel, Reed's Beach,* and *The Hunt Club,* and the memoir *Fathers, Sons and Brothers.* He also edits the *Southern Review.*

Lee Martin's memoir *From Our House* was a Barnes and Noble Discover Great New Writers selection in 2000. He is also the author of the novel *The Bright Forever.*

Patricia Ann McNair's fiction and creative nonfiction has appeared in various anthologies, journals, and magazines, including *American Fiction: Best Unpublished Short Stories by Emerging Writers, Other Voices, River Teeth, Fourth Genre,* and Air Canada's *enRoute* magazine.

John McPhee is the author of more than two dozen books, including *Coming into the Country, The Founding Fish,* and *Oranges.* His book *Annals of the Former World* was awarded the Pulitzer Prize in 1999.

Naomi Shihab Nye, born to a Palestinian father and an American mother, is the author of numerous books of poems, including *19 Varieties of Gazelle: Poems of the Middle East, Fuel, Red Suitcase,* and *Hugging the Jukebox.*

Scott Russell Sanders' books include *Writing from the Center, Hunting for Hope,* and *A Private History of Awe.* His writing appears regularly in the *Georgia Review, Orion, Audubon,* and numerous anthologies, and he has been awarded fellowships from the Guggenheim Foundation and the National Endowment for the Arts.

Mimi Schwartz's essays have appeared in *The Fourth Genre, Creative Nonfiction, The New York Times,* and *The Philadelphia Inquirer,* among others. She is the author of the memoir, *Thoughts from a Queen-Sized Bed.*

David Sedaris is the author of the bestsellers *Barrel Fever* and *Holidays on Ice,* as well as collections of personal essays, including *Naked* and *Me Talk Pretty One Day.* His work appears regularly in *Esquire* and *The New Yorker,* and his original radio pieces can often be heard on *This American Life.*

Richard Selzer, a surgeon and the son of a family doctor, has published numerous essays on the art of medicine in such magazines as *Redbook*, *Esquire*, and *Harper's*. His essays are collected in *Mortal Lessons* and *Confessions of a Knife*.

David Shields is the author of eight books, including *Black Planet: Facing Race During an NBA Season* and *Remote: Reflections on Life in the Shadow of Celebrity*. His essays and stories have appeared in *The New York Times Magazine*, *Harper's*, *Village Voice*, *Salon*, *Slate*, *McSweeney's*, and *Utne Reader*.

Deborah Tall is the author of four books of poems, most recently *Summons*. She has also written two books of nonfiction, *The Island of the White Cow: Memories of an Irish Island* and *From Where We Stand: Recovering a Sense of Place*.

Amy Tan is the author of *The Joy Luck Club*, an international best-selling novel that explores the relationships between Chinese women and their Chinese-American daughters. She is also author of *The Kitchen God's Wife*, *The Hundred Secret Senses*, *The Bonesetter's Daughter*, and two books for children.

Richard Terrill is the author of a collection of poems, *Coming Late to Rachmaninoff*, and three books of creative nonfiction, including *Fakebook: Improvisations on a Journey Back to Jazz* and *Saturday Night in Baoding: A China Memoir*, winner of the Associated Writing Programs Award for Nonfiction.

Terry Tempest Williams is known for works such as *Refuge: An Unnatural History of Family and Place*, *Red: Patience and Passion in the Desert*, *Coyote's Canyon*, and *An Unspoken Hunger: Stories from the Field*. An outspoken environmental activist, she has been a fellow for the John Simon Guggenheim Memorial Foundation and received a Lannan Literary Fellowship in Creative Nonfiction.

CREDITS

Index

"Alive" (Drummond), 103–104
Alliteration, 44
Armstrong, Jane, 24–25, 47

Baldwin, James, 97, 111–126
Beard, Jo Ann, 127–131
"Biography of a Dress" (Kincaid), 200–206
Braided essay, 95–98
Brief essay, 6–7
"Brothers" (Lott), 207–210
"Buckeye" (Sanders), 224–228

Cantú, Norma Elia, 58–60, 98
Characterization
 round vs. flat, 37–38
 and action, 34–38
 and dialogue, 29–34
"The Clan of One-Breasted Women" (Williams), 257–262
Cofer, Judith Ortiz, 96, 132–139
Collage essay, 96–97
"The Courage of Turtles" (Hoagland), 184–188

Dialogue, 29–34
Didion, Joan, 9, 53, 86–90,
"Difficult Decisions" (Gutkind), 167–173
Dillard, Annie, 140–142, 263–275
Doyle, Brian, 43–45, 76–78, 80–81
"The Drama Bug" (Sedaris), 229–235
"A Dramatic Dogalog" (Homer), 32–33
"Drink It" (Livingston), 35–36
Drummond, Laurie Lynn, 13–14, 103–104
"Dumber Than" (Martin), 107–108

Earley, Tony, 143–150
Experimental essay, 98

"42 Tattoos" (Shields), 243–251
Framed essay, 97

Galvin, James, 85–86
Gates, Henry Louis, 49–51
"Genesis" (Lott), 68–67
Gerard, Philip, 43, 51, 98, 151–156
Gornick, Vivian, 4
Grealy, Lucy, 97, 157–166
Greene, Melissa Faye, 47
Gutkind, Lee, 75, 167–173

Hemley, Robin, 96, 174–183
Hoagland, Edward, 184–188
Homer, Art, 32–34
"Hope" (Doyle), 76–77

Immersion, 75–76
"In Bed" (Didion), 86–89
"Injection" (Armstrong), 24–25
Iyer, Pico, 78–80, 189–199

Jakiela, Lori, 105–106

Kidder, Tracy, 47, 276–278
Kincaid, Jamaica, 45, 200–206
"The Knife" (Selzer), 236–242

Literary journalism, 4, 74–83
"Living Like Weasels" (Dillard), 140–142
Livingston, Sonja, 68–69
Lopate, Phillip, 41, 84, 91

Lott, Bret, 45–46, 66–68, 207–210, 279–285
Lyric essay, 90

"Making the Truth Believable" (Kidder), 276–278
Martin, Lee, 107–108
McNair, Patricia Ann, 35–37
McPhee, John, 211–219
"The Meadow" (Galvin), 85–86
Memoir, 4, 65–73
"Memoir? Fiction? Where's the Line?" (Schwartz), 286–291
Memory, 6, 14–17, 22–23, 31–32
Metaphor, 44
"Mirrorings" (Grealy), 157–166
Montaigne, Michel de, 10, 71
"Mother Tongue" (Tan), 252–256

Narrative structure, 93–98
Newman, Naomi, 98
"Notes of a Native Son" (Baldwin), 111–126
Nye, Naomi Shihab, 97, 220–223

"Out There" (Beard), 127–131

Personal essay, 4, 84–92
Plutarch, 10
Point of view, 46–52
"Pop Art" (Doyle), 43

"Reading History to My Mother" (Hemley), 174–183
Research, 81–82
Revision
and narrative structure, 93–98
for detail and description, 26–28
for discovery, 60–62
for scene, 39–40
for voice and point of view, 51–52
Ritea, Steve, 12–13
Robinson, Roxanna, 92
Round vs. flat characters, 37–38

Sanders, Scott Russell, 71, 84, 224–228
Scene, 38–39

Schwartz, Mimi, 286–291
Sedaris, David, 71, 229–235
"The Search for Marvin Gardens" (McPhee), 211–219
"Seeing" (Dillard), 263–275
Selzer, Richard, 10–11, 91, 236–242
Seneca, 10
Shields, David, 97, 243–251
"Silent Dancing" (Cofer), 132–139
"Solstice" (Terrill), 55–57
"Somehow Form a Family" (Earley), 143–150
"The Stories Tell the Land" (Tall), 109–110
"Sunday" (Gates), 49

Talese, Gay, 9
Tall, Deborah, 109–110
Tan, Amy, 51, 252–256
Terrill, Richard, 55–58, 96
Thompson, Hunter S., 10
Thoreau, Henry David, 10, 84
"Three Pokes of a Thistle" (Nye), 220–223
"Thumb-Sucking Girl" (Livingston), 68–69
"Tino & Papi" (Cantú), 58–59
"Toward a Definition of Creative Nonfiction" (Lott), 279–285
Truth in nonfiction, 6, 14–17, 32

Voice, 43–46
Vonnegut, Kurt, 52

"What They Don't Tell You About Hurricanes" (Gerard), 151–156
"Where Worlds Collide" (Iyer), 78–79, 189–199
Williams, Terry Tempest, 257–262

Yellow pen test, 39–40, 61
"You'll Love the Way We Fly" (Jakiela), 105–106

Zinser, William, 65